Please return/renew this item by the last date shown.

To renew this item, call **0845 3459177** (automated)
or visit **www.librarieswest.org.uk**

Borrower number and PIN required.

Libraries**West**

1 9 5003488 8

TEARS ON MY PILLOW

Ray O'Donoghue

Book Guild Publishing
Sussex, England

First published in Great Britain in 2007 by
The Book Guild Ltd
Pavilion View
19 New Road
Brighton, BN1 1UF

Typesetting in Times by
IML Typographers, Birkenhead, Merseyside

Printed in Great Britain by
Athenaeum Press Ltd, Gateshead

A catalogue record for this book is available from
The British Library.

ISBN 978 1 84624 114 7

For Sandra

Contents

Introduction

It was February 1976 and drizzling with cold rain, the kind of day that Ireland is well known for. In Ireland they often refer to it as being 'soft rain'. I stood in the middle of a quiet and bleak country lane about half a mile from a little town called Glin in the South of Ireland. There wasn't another soul around, as most sensible people were indoors. Glin Town has a very wide main street, which almost runs down into the river Shannon, with some pubs and houses on either side, which looked as if time had stood still. As I drove up through the street, I remember trying to pick out the house where I and many of the other boys in the Glin band went to for some private violin tuition, which also gave us a short break from the boredom of the school for a few hours each week. As I approached the top of the street just before bearing left I saw Mr Tarrant's old blacksmith shop on the right hand side. Mr Tarrant used to come and teach us Irish dancing a few times a week. I still remembered him very well. He was short and stocky and very well built, as blacksmiths tend to be, but he was amazingly light on his feet and seemed to fly in the air as he showed us some fancy footwork. I was on a sort of pilgrimage of discovery from England to where I had emigrated 20 years previously. The purpose of my pilgrimage was to see an Industrial School, an orphanage-cum-borstal or approved school, called St Joseph's, where I had been incarcerated from June 1951 to June 1956. I often wondered if 'approved' meant that it was approved by some official or other as being a fit place to look after boys like myself who needed to be taken into care for one reason or another. The school was no longer in use and it stood in the distance, in the middle of some elevated fields, and was barely visible through the drizzling rain and it looked like some unused empty prison.

It was a big grey building with some slates missing from the roof, which was letting the rain through. It looked bleak and desolate as it stood, isolated in the middle of the countryside, towering like some long forgotten monument to all the thousands of boys and Christian Brothers who had passed through its by now decaying structures over the last 50 or so years. Anyone passing now would hardly give it a second glance because it was set back off the road on private land, but to me it had been my old school and my second home.

St Joseph's school, Glin, had been my home and home to all of the other boys. It had been my home for five very long and mostly unhappy years. When I had been sent there, in June 1951, against my will, I had hated the place and everything it stood for. No one had asked me if I was happy leaving Limerick to live with total strangers in a strange new home, especially a home for bad boys. I did not realise that I had been bad, although I did not go to school and I was in the habit of robbing, whenever I had to, but then nearly everyone in Limerick seemed to be a thief in those days.

I was not even eleven years old and I had not realised the enormity of what was happening to me. To me it was an adventure and I felt that I would not be there long anyway. I knew that my mother would soon rescue me when she discovered what had happened to me and take me over to England to live with her. When I lived in Limerick, I had never travelled more than a couple of miles away from home, except out to Corbally or up to the far end of O'Connell Street, except of course when my mother had taken me to Dublin, but at least I had always been with my family. Now I was 32 miles from home, with no one but my companion Andrew from Limerick who was my only friend in a hostile environment. At least having Andrew helped me to cope a little easier with the strange surroundings. After all he was a little bit older than I was and seemed more confident, so we would be okay.

Everyone who was sent to Glin hated it while they were there, yet here I was standing in the rain almost 25 years after I had first set my eye on the place, gazing in awe and feeling choked with emotion at my old school. All my past memories and the experiences were flashing through my mind. I felt in a trance and just kept gazing into the cold, misty rain and feeling privileged in some ways that I had attended the school, survived and made many new friends. I felt some sadness too that the school was now silent, closed for ever more and no longer would it be a haven and a place of safety for young unwanted boys and uncontrollable delinquents, like I used to be. It had been so full of life, with 200 boys and now it was silent.

The school looked like a once great ship, now deserted and abandoned to the elements, left to rot and decay. It all seemed unnatural and so quiet.

No more would the surrounding countryside be disturbed by the noise of 200 unruly boys. Maybe that's progress, not needing such large institutions any more and not having to send boys far away from their families and all that was important to them. I had just travelled from Limerick where a lot of people had told me that nearly all such institutions in Ireland were now closed, although delinquency was as bad or worse than ever it used to be. I walked up the narrow drive to the school to have a closer look and to indulge myself in a little nostalgia. I felt hypnotised and just could not leave without having a closer look at the place. After all it had been my home for a very large part of my life and surely no one would object to my looking around. The white iron gate with the cross on it, indicating that it was a religious order was unlocked, much to my relief. The palm trees, which had lined the drive were no longer there, giving a much clearer view of the school now. The little cottage at the top right side of the drive was still there but obviously neglected.

I looked through the window, half expecting I suppose to see big Jim Cushing, the caretaker, who used to live there with his family. Jim used to work on the farm in the school and did odd jobs around the place, like reporting any boys wandering off down the drive, with a view of not returning again! His front door and window faced down towards the drive, an ideal position to spot unauthorised trips towards the town. I often wondered why he never had a machine-gun mounted on the roof of the bungalow and shot any of the boys who tried to run away, just like in the prisoner of war films that I used to watch in the Thomond cinema in Limerick. Most of us boys were in awe of Jim and feared him and were very wary because he was, after all, employed by the school and no doubt his loyalties must have been to the Brothers who ran the school and paid him. We always felt that if we stepped out of line and Jim knew about it then we assumed he would tell. He was a fearsome looking man with big shoulders and huge big hands, like all farmers seem to have. I would not like to have crossed swords with him. A little further on up the drive the statue of St Joseph, after whom the school was named, still stood with outstretched hands, offering a welcome to all who came through the gates, though I wonder if anyone had told him that the school was no longer in use and that he could now put down his weary outstretched hands!

You could not go through the school without noticing the statue of St Joseph as he leaves a deep groove in your memory, despite the now peeling white paint on his face. It is one of the first noticeable things that you see on entering the school and the last as you leave. The goalpost is still standing a couple of yards behind the statue of St Joseph on the school playing-fields, which explains the reason for the iron frame at the back of St Joseph's head. It was to offer protection to prevent his head being knocked off by a flying football over the years. As I wandered towards the front entrance I noticed three goats in the football field, looking at me with a quizzical look, which made me feel like I was a trespasser, which I suppose I was. I made my way towards the old dining hall, half expecting the doors to be bolted, and was surprised to find they were not. All the large dining tables were gone and so were the old pew type seats that we used to sit on while having our meagre meals nearly 25 years ago. The hall was empty and quiet now and the silence made me feel sad. It was so different to the days when it used to be filled with 200 noisy boys, all talking and eating at the same time, though if my memory serves me right, we did more talking than eating. The more we talked the longer the food lasted. The concrete floor was cold and damp and the plain walls were desecrated with obscene drawings, probably done by the workmen or local boys. If the Brothers could see this place now, I thought. Brother Cullen, now dead, used to sit on his high chair at the top of the hall watching and making sure that no one stepped out of line during meal times. No one would dare to write on the walls if he was still around! He was mainly in charge of the dining-room during most of the meals. I can still see him now taking his snuff and blowing his nose on his handkerchief, which was the size of a tablecloth. Brother Cullen played an important part in my life and was probably one of the most well known Brothers who ever passed through the school in its long history. He was like the commander-in-chief. Because of him I learned to appreciate music more than I might have done if I had not been in Glin.

He left an impression on anyone who ever met him, that's for sure, and must have made an enormous contribution to the life of the school. I remember him being a hard, unsmiling man, although he did soften occasionally, very occasionally, mind you! I had enormous respect for him and you can't talk about Glin without mentioning Brother Cullen, because although he was small in stature he was a giant of a man with enormous power and authority. I stood in the dining hall reluctant to leave, trying to conjure up in my mind the sounds and images of 20 years ago. It was not hard to do.

I went out the side door and across the yard towards the dormitory where I slept for five years. It was a three storey building and my old dormitory, St Kevin's, was at the top. On the ground floor on my right was the music room where Brother Cullen taught music. I was one of Brother Cullen's violin protégés for about three years, but I was no virtuoso and always struggled to read the music and usually day-dreamed while practising until I would be brought back to earth by Brother Cullen's knuckles on the back of my head. 'What are you doing, O'Donoghue, concentrate will you.' That usually focused my mind very quickly back to the *Blue Danube*, which I was trying to master, but never could, although his knuckles brought a tear to my eye, it never did improve my playing of the *Blue Danube*. It was criminal what I did to the *Blue Danube*, because it is one of the most beautiful pieces of music that has been written, and although try as I may, I never could make it sound pleasing to the ear. It is still one of my favourite pieces of music and whenever I hear it, I realise how badly I played it.

I then walked up the stony steps with the iron hand rails towards the top floor dormitory and suddenly my mind was transported back to 11 June 1951 on a late summer's evening when I first walked up these stairs with my mate Andrew and escorted by Brother Murphy. I remembered seeing pairs of black polished boots on each of the steps all the way up to the top to St Kevin's and thinking how funny it was at the time. The brass plaque of St Kevin's was still over the door, which I removed with great difficulty to keep as a souvenir, as I felt that I was as entitled to have it as anyone else. I remembered all the lonely nights crying for my mother under the sheets, because I did not want anyone to see me crying and thinking I was a sissy, although I often heard some of the other boys crying.

I then went over to the classrooms, which were now littered with paper and dust everywhere, and felt the draught from many of the broken window panes. I sat for a while at an old desk and cried and listened for the sounds of all my old pals, but I never heard them, only the sound of the wind coming through the broken windows. Except for the dirtyness of the room, it looked as if everyone had just left in a hurry, but never came back again. I took the old wooden blackboard duster, which was still laying on a table as it had been left, and stuck it in my pocket. I also took some ink-wells from the desk and some old and faded hand-made cards depicting the stations of the cross, which used to be stuck all round the walls of the classroom. I remembered how we used them to do the stations of the cross. I think that Brother Dobbins, who was very artistic used to make them. I stuck them under my shirt in an old piece of newspaper, just in case someone might see me on the way out and report me for stealing. Old habits die hard! I still have those mementos and I'm glad I took them, for at least they are safe and in good hands. I would not like to have seen them destroyed, as they mean a lot to me.

I drove back to Limerick through the dreary rain to get the plane back to England, my pilgrimage complete. Some years later when I visited Glin again everything was gone, flattened to the ground with some houses built on the football field, which I somehow resented. The only sign of a school having been there was the front facade of the administration block and the Brothers' sleeping headquarters. It was still standing with the Christian Brothers insignia on it. It was the first building that I and my friend had been taken into on our arrival in June 1951.

St Joseph's school, Glin, had been home to me and to hundreds of boys over the years and I did not like to see its history being erased. The physical history of Glin might be destroyed but its memories will live on forever in my mind, both good and bad. It should have been kept for posterity. I promised myself that one day I would try and write a book on Glin and my life. I felt that people should know what it was like being there and its effect, good and bad, on me and how I came to be there. It would be another 30 years before I would eventually complete my story.

1. My Early Life

I was born in Southern Ireland in one of Ireland's biggest towns in a place called Limerick. It was 12 June 1940, and although I did not realise it at the time, it was a very uncertain and perilous time to be born. The Second World War was in progress. 'The whole bloody world's on fire' to quote one comment of the day. In fact during the time I was conceived and born, the Battle of Britain was in progress, France was being invaded and was about to surrender to the Germans. Dunkirk was happening. Mussolini took Italy into the war and Churchill was making his historic speech. Japan advanced into China and Leon Trotsky was assassinated in his own home. There was an aerial blockade of Britain for an expected invasion, which thankfully never came.

Auschwitz was officially opened, and to cap it all Bethlehem, the birth place of Christ, had a blackout for the first time in history, which I could easily identify with, because every night there was a blackout in my house. The electricity had long been cut off because my father could not afford to pay the electric bills. So we had candle-lit meals every night, which sounds romantic today, but not so when you are a child. The shadows that candles throw in a cold, damp and dark house can be scary to a young boy, which did not help my already nervous state of mind. The dark would always hold certain terrors for me.

There was nothing much happening in Limerick at the time to make me aware of the ravages of war, except for the food shortages, although as most families had very little, I was too young to connect my social situation to the war. I was aware of the name of Adolf Hitler but John Wayne and Errol Flynn had more significance to me.

John Wayne was much more real and important to me than Adolf, because going to the movies was the love of my life, and my reason for living. I could imagine being in Apache country fighting the Indians or in the jungle swinging through the trees with Johnny Weismuller as Tarzan. I could be the tough guy like James Cagney or Humphrey Bogart and pull my shirt collar up and pretend that I had a gun in my pocket. Errol Flynn was also a great inspiration and hero and I admired how he could wield a sword in those swashbuckling films and fight off a crowd of villains all at the same time. The good thing was that he rarely got hurt and the heroes in those days never died. They always seemed invincible. I wanted very much to be like them, the good guy, and be heroic; to be strong and look after the underdog and of course be loved by everyone. It was great escapism and my imagination took me into different adventures a few times a week, and all from the safety of my seat, if only for a short time. Going to the movies then was just as important as eating.

I have always unashamedly loved everything American and maybe it was John Wayne's influence and all those great American movies I had seen and loved all my life that cemented my great love.

My sister Phyllis is five years older than I am, and although we never spent much time together after I was eight, we have a bond because of our unique and disturbing memories and images that only we experienced. My sister's memories vary slightly from mine and I seem to remember events that she does not, despite being five years younger than her. Many of my memories have haunted and affected me all my adult life and probably my sister too. I have dealt with mine by talking about them, but she finds it easier to try and forget.

I realise that my childhood was far from normal, but as a child it seemed just like anyone else's, happy and carefree. As a young boy it was hard to tell what went on in other people's houses. Kids especially did not discuss family matters amongst other kids and anyway we were too busy with our lives to think too deeply, and most of us did not have the capacity to do otherwise.

2. Limerick City

I know very little about the circumstances of my birth, due to both my parents dying prematurely, so I have never been able to ask the questions that I would like to ask. What kind of a child was I? Was I good or bad? Was I troublesome, was I wanted? I do not even know how or where my parents met, but what I do know is that they were not a happy couple as I would come to realise later on.

My parents' marriage seemed strange and maybe ill-conceived. Friends who knew my mother very well told me that they believe she came from gypsy stock and possibly from the Galway area and that she was abandoned in Limerick at the City Home Hospital as a baby and was brought up in the hospital as an orphan. She was then placed in a number of different orphanages, which were generally run by the Catholic nuns in what may have been, at the time, a workhouse type of environment. Her name McDonagh is a fairly common name in the Galway area, where a large number of gypsies and travellers come from.

What the emotional effect of being in care for most of her young life had on her I will never know, although some of her behaviour later in her life gives a strong indication that she was affected quite badly. It is now very well documented by child psychologists and professionals alike that separation from parents, especially up to the age of five, can have disastrous effects on an individual's behaviour for the rest of its life. Even animals who are separated too early display abnormal and antisocial behaviour later in life, and my mother was no different. My own life would later mirror my mother's in many ways.

I remember my mother once introduced me to a fat gypsy woman in a black shawl when I was only a few years old. She said she was her mother, my grandmother. I may have met her more than once, though I can't be sure, so in effect I never really knew my grandparents from my mother's or my father's side. In Limerick in the forties you could often see women wearing black shawls. Black-shawled women scared me for some unknown reason, maybe it's because they reminded me of funerals and death.

My mother, it seems, grew up in one or more of these institutions, until maybe around 14 years of age, and was then sent to work in the hospital environment, where she remained until probably around 16 years of age. I

3

was informed, later on in my life, by her friends, that an arranged marriage was what probably occurred between her and my father straight from the hospital.

My mother spent some time at the Good Shepherd convent in Limerick City as a baby and probably stayed there until she was at least 14 years of age or moved to some other institution as she became older. Whether she ever had contact again with her parents I do not know, but I do know that she never spoke much about them, so it is quite likely that she lost contact. She must have felt abandoned and unloved and unwanted and her life as a child must have been very empty.

She was only 16 and my father was around 20 years older, i.e. 36 when they married. My father was very rough, uncouth and uneducated and could not even sign his own name, although at that period this was not that unusual.

I have been reliably informed by our neighbours, the Moores, who lived opposite us in Columcille Street and who were very supportive of my mother and regularly offered her short term shelter and comfort, that my mother ran away on her wedding night. She was obviously very confused, frightened and probably very innocent. As she had been educated by nuns, her sex education was, it is fair to assume, non-existent. Around 1934, sex education was probably non-existent anywhere, especially in Catholic Ireland, and especially with nuns for teachers. My own sex education was so bad, that up until the age of 18, I believed you had to have sex every day for a year before you could have a baby.

Although my parents' marriage started off badly, it was to get a lot worse over the next few years. If they were ever happy together, I doubt it very much. My sister Phyllis was born within a year of my parents' marriage, so at least my father knew something about sex. Why my father started physically abusing my mother I do not know. All I do know is that he was a physically very violent man with a fierce temper, which he displayed frequently to each of us at times, but mostly to my mother.

Why or when my mother started drinking heavily I do not know either. It's possible she may have left home from time to time before I was born, because of the abuse which my father regularly inflicted on her, which may explain why there was a five year gap before I was born, although she did say that she miscarried several pairs of twins either before or after I was born. My parents were not compatible as a married couple and they seemed to have nothing in common. My mother was very innocent, possibly because of her convent upbringing, and consequently she was better educated than my father, although probably not streetwise, and

4

unaware of the ways of the flesh in 1935. The fact that she ran away on her wedding night is some indication of her inadequacies or innocence, or maybe it was a combination of my father's lack of charm or just ignorance. I will never know the answers.

My mother was a very kind woman who would give her last penny away even if she needed it herself, and seemed to go out of her way to seek out down and outs and comfort them and bring them home for shelter, although that was something that I became aware of many years later when we lived in Brighton in England.

She was a very quiet and gentle woman and hardly ever said a cross word to me or my sister. She only ever hit me once and then I deserved it. It was when I played truant and I was hiding in the graveyard, which was at the end of my cousin's garden, and it was in the middle of winter. I was sitting under a tree in the pouring rain waiting for school to finish so I could go home and pretend I had just come home from school. My cousin Josie, whom I idolised, found me in the graveyard sopping wet and brought me home, and when my mother saw me she smacked me across the back of my legs with a thin branch of a tree. I cried a lot and begged my mother not to hit me, and I told her, 'I'm sorry, I won't do it any more, mama, I promise, don't hit me any more. I'm sorry, I'm sorry, please don't hit me, I'll go to school.'

I was about seven or eight at the time, and I was heartbroken because my mother, whom I loved, trusted and relied on so much for love and attention and who never spoke a cross word to me in my life, had done the unthinkable and hit me. No doubt I deserved it, but I did not realise it at the time, and I was briefly devastated.

My feelings were hurt more than anything else. My mother was crying more than I was. No doubt, love hurts. She had been very worried about me sitting in the rain and maybe getting ill. A week later an ambulance came to my home and I was taken to hospital where I spent a week suffering from a bad case of pneumonia. It was my first Christmas spent in hospital and my first time away from home.

I lived at 135 St Munchin's Street, St Mary's Park, when I was born, and we moved to number 102 a few years later, before I was about seven years old. At the time, we called St Mary's Park, the Island of Saints and Scholars, but people outside referred to it as the Island of Rogues and Robbers, which looking back now seems a more appropriate name, as we were devious, mischievous and thieving bastards, no doubt about it, and I should know!

The estate I lived and grew up on until my departure in June 1951 was very scenic, with lots of space, fields and a river. We were in fact living on an island, King John's Island with one small street leading out. Although the river was very pretty, it meant the houses were always damp and very cold as they were built virtually on a river. I could see the river bank and the river from the back of my house, which was less than a hundred metres away.

We swam in the river, which we called the 'Newfound'. I don't think anyone of my tender age had a swimsuit in those days, so we always swam in the nude. In fact I don't even remember having a towel. We used to roll in the mud by the river bank, jump in the river and then run up and down the bank to dry ourselves and flash to the little girls at the same time. They were innocent and briefly happy days.

The river was very treacherous and many young children drowned while I lived there during my eleven years. On one occasion someone called O'Donoghue drowned, and as there were many families with a similar name, I know my mother was frantic, wondering if it was either me or my sister Phyllis who had drowned. We always hope that tragic events will happen to others, but tragedy will always visit each of us at some time in our life.

There was one drowning in about 1951 which I found devastating, because the boy who drowned was my friend, Joe Moore, the son of my mother's best friend. Mrs Moore was the very woman who was such a comfort to my mother and to my sister and me, whenever my father was violent. It was where we always went for refuge in our hour of need. I don't think Joe's mother ever recovered from the tragedy of losing her son, who was only eleven years old at the time, despite having many more children and living for another 30 years.

I was so fond of her and made sure I always sent a card at Christmas time and I always tried to visit her whenever I visited Limerick. I only wished I had asked her more questions at the time because she probably knew more about my mother than anyone else alive. Mrs Moore did more for me and the rest of our family than she could ever realise.

I was nearly drowned in exactly the same spot as Joe had been a few month's earlier. I attempted to walk out into the river and was about to disappear down a deep hole that suddenly appeared between the flat rocks, when I shouted for help. I was pulled to safety at the last minute by a girl, the sister of Andrew Fitz, my pal, and a guy who was to be closely linked to my future in no small way later on as I grew up. I don't know if she realised that she saved my life. I had felt as if I was about to drown, but maybe God had other plans for me and felt that I had some useful purpose in life, but now I was grateful.

We had a huge open rubbish tip within yards of the houses, which took rubbish and filth from miles around and you could see huge dirty rats scurrying around every day rummaging for food. They were horrible, with long hairless tails and hunched backs and they terrified me, and I hated them. To this day I can't stand rats, they make my skin creep.

My friends and I used to scavenge for food amongst the rubbish. My favourite was looking for tomatoes that were only partly damaged. A guy named Connie Donoghue owned a huge warehouse, which sold wholesale fruit, and it was next to the rubbish dump. We used to relieve him of old tomatoes before he dumped them and sometimes a few good ones too, especially when he was not looking! As far as I remember no one ever died of any serious illness from eating such disposed food with rats crawling all over it, but I do remember that I had many serious stomach aches as a kid, but nothing too serious. My mother suffered greatly from stomach upsets all of her adult life, so maybe she scavenged from the same rubbish dump, as I had done. We were doing what people from Third World countries are now doing.

In our first house we had gas lamps, which were not very bright and they cast eerie shadows and strange shapes around the walls when they were turned on. The odd lighting and the shapes that they created did not help me to get to sleep easily, which may have accounted for all the nightmares I had and still have after all these years.

I don't remember an awful lot about living in our first house, probably because I was too young and I do not recall my parents fighting or arguing either at that time. It was only when we moved to a house further up the street at 102 that I became aware of the disharmony between my parents, or maybe it was because I became more alert and just was older, or extra sensitive. When your parents are arguing and fighting most of the time, it is hard not to notice the difference.

All the houses were the same, two up and two down with a small garden out front and a bigger one out the back. The floors were cold bare concrete. Cooking was done on a black range cooker, which was generally kept hot with sawdust, which was available free of charge from the city docks for those willing to go and collect it. It was then carried home in canvas sacks wheeled in wooden boxcars. Very early in the mornings, especially in the winter, you could see and hear the women of the houses walking and pushing their home-made wooden boxcars all the way to the docks, a round trip of maybe three miles or more. I remember looking out our front bedroom window, rubbing the ice off of the inside of the window and seeing all these women making their way to the docks. The rattle of the wheels of the carts on the concrete road would always wake me up. The sound seemed to carry a long way in the early morning. It was a very hard existence. My mother also had to do the same journey. There was no other choice. The women would return home some hours later with the boxcars full up with three or four big bags of sawdust, which they would put in the range to cook the meals throughout the day.

Life was very hard, but everyone seemed to be in the same boat. I suppose we were lucky in some ways, as my father, Christy, always had a steady job working for the Corporation or the City Council. He was a dustman and earned around £5 a week, between 1940 and 1950. The wages were barely sufficient to keep a family of four as we always seemed to be struggling for money, and always hungry. We only had the clothes that we lived in.

The hunger is what I remember vividly. It never seemed to leave you, although at Christmas we always seemed to have a goose for dinner. A pig's head was a great treat and delicacy especially on Sundays. I remember we occasionally even had a cow's head. I remember the great big eyes staring at me, as I was about to eat it. The eyes and the tongue were especially tasty. Another treat when there was enough money in the house was pig's head and tail with the ribs attached with potatoes and cabbage. Bacon, cabbage and potatoes was and still remains one of the favourite meals of Irish people.

The pawn shop was used a lot during the war and the most famous of them all was Paashey Brown's up in Irish Town. My mother unbeknownst to my father used to pawn his Sunday suit for a pound or two to make ends meet and retrieve it before the weekend so that my father would not notice it was gone. As he only wore it at the weekends, he never noticed it was gone until one time when my mother could not afford to get it out. I remember she was frantic trying to borrow the money, which she was unable to do. My father was a fiercely proud man and would have nothing to do with pawn shops, as they were only for the destitute and un-employed. He went berserk when he found what my mother had done, bringing disgrace on the family by pawning personal items. He beat her badly and wanted to know what she had done with the housekeeping money. I don't think she ever pawned his suit again.

Up to about four or five I was not aware of the uneasy relationship between my mother and father and maybe it was fairly normal, I don't know.

In 1943, in the good old USA, the antibiotic Streptomycin was discovered, and just a day after my third birthday, in a place called Bath in

Somerset, England, a baby girl was born, called Sandra, who I was later to marry. God works in mysterious ways.

I can't exactly remember the first time I saw my father physically abuse my mother, but it left a terrible impression on me then, and still does to this day. On one occasion my mother had been out dancing and drinking without my father and I doubt if he ever socialised as my mother did. My mother seemed to go dancing or whatever she did on her own, without my father's company at least. He was a very quiet and introverted man who rarely mixed with other people and when she returned around midnight she was quite loud, singing and probably drunk. She had gone upstairs to bed and the next thing my sister and I were aware of, was my father shouting very loudly and beating and punching my mother for what seemed a very long time.

We both heard her high-pitched, terrible screaming, begging my father, 'Christy, please don't hit me, please don't hit me any more.' This pleading went on for ages, although it fell on deaf ears. My father continued to punch and kick her. He had been quite a good boxer and must have hurt my mother really badly. My mother was a very small and delicate woman. I was disgusted by my father's behaviour even then and it seemed very wrong to me, although I was a mere child. His behaviour was a lesson that I would learn from. I would never in my life ever hit a woman because, to me, it was a crime of the worst type.

My sister and I had our arms around each other downstairs sitting on the bed screaming in terror and feeling our mother's pain. Thoughts were going through my head, 'Oh God why doesn't he leave her alone? Leave her alone, wait till I get bigger and I'll kill you. I wish that I had a fucking knife to stick it in you. I hate you, I hate you forever, you bastard. She's my mother and you're hurting her. Someday I'll kill you, and I hope you go to hell. Why doesn't he stop? He's going to kill her, she can't stand much more. Why can't someone help her, I'm only five, what can I do?' My feelings of inadequacy, helplessness and anger were profound and were swirling through my mind.

This abuse and violent drama, was a scene that was to be repeated over and over again, until my mother eventually left home and took my sister and me with her. What brutal physical abuse and mental traumas my mother suffered I'll never know or indeed what effect it had on her, but it would stay with me for ever. The damage it did to my mother I could only guess at years later.

She had spent most of her young life in care and she deserved a better life than she was having being married to my father. More than likely she

9

had been abused in some way while in the care of the nuns, who had a reputation for sadistic behaviour. Oh God, what a cruel and sadistic man he was. His behaviour and terrible treatment of my mother would haunt me all my life and I suppose in many ways it would play a big part in forming my own character and personality, especially in how I treated women. I made sure I would be the complete opposite of him, in every way that I could. Nothing about my father inspired me in any way.

Despite our harsh family life at times, life in Limerick had its fair share of excitement. For devilment, when it was dark, my pals and I used to go around the back streets and tie a long string to the door knockers, walk around the corner and pull the string, which would knock on the door. The lady of the house, usually an old widow, because we knew she would not catch us, would come out to answer the door and be perplexed as to who or where the person was who was knocking at the door. She'd go back indoors and then we would pull the string again and she'd come out again looking all around and she would now suspect what was going on. 'May the curse of Jasus be on ye, ye little bastards, I know ye'r from the Island field so I do. I'll tell the guards on ye and have ye all arrested. Mother of God can't ye go home and lave an old woman in peace, ye dirty little blackguards. I'll kill the fecking lot of ye when I catch ye all.' We must have made their lives hell, but we didn't care. We just thought about our own immediate gratification. It was of course before TV was invented and we made our own amusements and entertainment. We knew nothing else.

Jimmy Welsh, who lived across the road from my cousins was one of my pals in those days. Tommy Tucker, or Thomas Cuddihy as was his proper name, was another pal. Tommy lived opposite. Jimmy was a lovely fella, kind, good natured and always seemed happy. His father was a huge, powerfully built man, and had been an officer in the British army. He walked very upright and proud but as I remember he did not seem to mix a lot and said very little. His wife always wore a black shawl, which even then seemed very old fashioned. Jimmy's sister Kishey (Kitty) was very old fashioned like her mother and was no Maureen O'Hara. She was often described as Maureen O'Hara gone wrong! That was an expression often suitably used to describe a woman with perhaps more personality than looks!

Jimmy had been kicked on the forehead by a horse and the imprint of a horse's hoof was branded on his forehead for the remainder of his life. I don't think the horse survived the impact! Jimmy was always regarded as being a bit soft in the head even though you could not meet a nicer guy. He once jumped out of his upstairs window using an umbrella as a parachute to float to the ground to break his fall, and guess what happened? It didn't work and Jimmy hit the ground like a ton of bricks, but just got up and walked away. After being kicked in the head by a horse, nothing could hurt that much, but it was another blow on his already vulnerable head. I think the ground sustained more damage than Jimmy. He was a real hard case but as soft as a kitten. I never remember him being in a fight. He would later spend a brief spell in Glin Industrial School during my time there. Tommy Tucker also spent a short time in Glin as did two of his brothers, Paddy and little Jimmy, who was very small in stature.

Years later, in 1996, I was watching a TV documentary on a drug addict named Christine Kitch whom I had nursed while she was being treated for her drug addiction problem in Tooting Bec Hospital. Christine had got her life together and she was now at Oxford University where she had gained a degree and written a book about her life, *Pavement for my Pillow*. I saw little Jimmy, who featured briefly on TV, in a drunken state, battered and bruised and under the influence. It made me feel very sad indeed. Jimmy was also a pal of mine and has since died.

My mother's name was Bridie, but she was nicknamed Birdie. Why? I don't know. Maybe it was because she was a very good singer, but other kids used to tease me about her name, which I used to hate and it made me very mad and got me into fights. My father also had a limp in his leg all his life, due I have been told to an accident at work when he was apparently dragged along the road by a horse. Kids used to tease me and take the piss out of me because of my father's bad leg, which I somehow felt ashamed about as if it was my fault. I often responded by lashing out. Kids want their parents to be perfect. Although his name was Christy, his nickname was Krikky.

Another devious prank we got up to was we used to go begging for bread from some old houses opposite the old playground near the convent on the way out of the Island Field. I'm sure they were old widow's houses, again very vulnerable old people, who could not chase you! Me and a pal would knock on the door and when the old woman came out we'd ask her, 'Have you got an old spare cush (slice) of bread, misses, we're starving and dying with the hunger.'

'Sure God love ye, come on in a minush,' she'd say, inviting us in. Although we wanted bread we also had more devious reasons for going into the house. We wanted to rob her! Yet she was trusting enough to invite us into her home and to give us sustenance. While the unsuspecting woman went into the back to get a slice of bread, we'd quickly look around for any money that was lying around, which was usually kept on the mantelpiece. We'd take everything that was there and run out the front door, before the woman returned, probably not realising for a while what was going on. I told you we were devious little bastards from the Island Field, and we deserve to be damned in hell, but I'm sure God will make allowances for our circumstance and life of deprivation and our very tender young ages, as we were barely seven or eight at the time. We needed a bit of excitement and a little extra food.

Another way we supplemented our meagre existence was stealing from Woolworths. Who could resist all those shelves stacked with all those sweets and toys when we had nothing? And all within easy reach of our grubby little hands! The temptation was too great for our weak little minds and our restless and energetic spirits, so we helped ourselves now and again.

Woolworths was on O'Connell Street, and the shelves were just below our chin height, which was very tempting and ideal for robbing. We would look for a while, fondling different items as if we were about to buy something, and as soon as the assistant moved away we'd grab something quickly and run for our lives, often chased by the attendant through the store shouting, 'Come back ye little feckers, I'll kill ye all and get the guards on ye, God blast ye all and may ye all go to hell. You're all a load of little whores so ye are.' Terrible language for a grown man to use on such innocent little children! Trying to send us to hell at such an early age did not seem very charitable for a grown man, who went to mass every Sunday and who seemed to be a pillar of society. Though I haven't gone to hell yet, there's still time.

There was a shop opposite the Grand Central Cinema, which is still there, and it sold sweets and cakes and fags etc. It had a little wood and glass cupboard extension display unit outside on the pavement, but still part of the shop. It contained mostly big bars of chocolate on different shelves and the doors were closed by a clasp, which could easily be lifted up and opened. We soon discovered that we could stand or lean against it with our backs so as not to look suspicious, put our hands behind our backs, push up the clasp with our fingers, slide our hand in behind and lift out a huge bar of Toblerone chocolate. We would then slide the bar of chocolate up the back of our dirty shirts or jumpers and move slowly away, and no one was the wiser. I certainly was never caught. We then went into the Savoy or the Central Cinema and we were in heaven eating our free chocolate, watching John Wayne ride across the prairie. That was the best chocolate I ever tasted. It was heaven sitting in the dark watching John Wayne and eating chocolate. Life could not have been better for those brief few hours.

Robbing from cars was another way of supplementing our meagre pocket money, although my mother always seemed to find enough money to enable me to go to the cinema three or four times a week. Going to the pictures was more important than eating at times, depending on what films were on. If a John Wayne or Roy Rogers film was on, I would make my mother's life hell until she got the money from somewhere. Westerns were the most popular films amongst us kids in Limerick, and whenever I did miss one I would be depressed for ages and would find it very hard to forgive my mother, but I always made sure to find out what happened to John Wayne by asking my pal, if big John killed many Indians or how many bad men he had killed.

The Thomond and the Tivoli were our local cinemas, the Thomond being the nearest. Although it cost about tuppence to get in, occasionally you could sneak in for nothing. You could get in by stooping down low so that the usherette did not see you, and especially if the man taking the tickets had gone into the cinema to show someone else to their seats. The male attendant was often open to a bribe. You could often slip him a penny instead of the usual tuppence, which he would pocket and he'd let you slip in. Even in those days, people could be bought for the right price. It was a great system, when you could afford the penny.

As young children we were only allowed into the first showing, which might be from 7 p.m. to 9 p.m., and then when we came out the courting couples would be queuing up to go into the next showing from 9 p.m. to 11p.m. In those days the cinemas were always closed on a Sunday.

The Thomond had wooden bench seats, which often moved around as kids came and went and the floor sloped quite a lot towards the screen. Sometimes while you watched the film, especially when you were barefoot, you would become aware of a wet sensation on your feet. Due no doubt to the sloping floor, you soon realised that someone behind you was pissing on the floor again, which happened quite regularly. Someone would shout back, 'Stop that you dirty hoor', but we thought it was funny anyway, because I did it myself as well. Like most children, you copy other children's behaviour quite a lot. Kids seemed to be constantly shouting or talking during the show and we always got excited if John Wayne shot an Indian or beat up a few baddies. We all identified with the hero of the movie, because they always lived. The good guy always won the day.

After the show we would hang around the fish and chip shop and beg chips off the grown-ups. We would pick chips up off the floor that had either been dropped or thrown away. Every chip bag that was thrown away would be picked up and examined to see if there was a chip that had been accidentally missed and eat it with relish. God there was nothing like fish and chips especially when you were hungry. We would also go inside the fish and chip shop and drink the vinegar straight from the bottle, and I'm still alive to tell the tale. After seeing a western movie, we would all gallop home whooping and whacking our arses as if we were on a horse. It seemed to get us home quicker anyway. I was as fast a runner as most of my pals and much faster than most, especially on the way home. We walked and ran everywhere.

The Tivoli Cinema was opposite Barringtons hospital and it was known as the flea house. It was a right dump, but it had lots of atmosphere and was my favourite cinema. The floor sloped down towards the screen at an incredible angle so that you had to look almost up towards the ceiling, which meant your head was bent back at an awkward angle and gave you a terrible pain in your neck by the time the film was over, but you only sat up near the screen if you could not afford the better seats at the back. Even then the cinema looked very old fashioned. It had old pointed lights all along both sides of the walls and they just gave off a great atmosphere, just like a sleazy bar in a Humphrey Bogart movie. Sometimes I used to take part of my supper along to the pictures to finish, so that I would not miss the start of the movie. Sometimes my mother brought my sandwiches of bread, butter and jam along to give me half way through the show. Seeing so many movies made me want to be famous one day and be on the big screen. It also started my life-long passion with American movies, especially westerns and war movies.

Playing dobbers (marbles) was a great pastime outside our houses in the Island Field, and we would play for hours in the gutter, because it was easier to see where the dobbers were rolling to, so as not to lose them. As we could not afford a hurling ball we would get an old tin can and continue to hit it to each other along the road for ages until eventually it became more compact and would travel further down the road as the game went on. It was probably better than any ball, because it never travelled too far, which meant you never had to chase it and it cost nothing.

The slaughterhouse was on our way to and from school and was a great source of interest. We had to pass it on our way to the convent, which was my first school. We would always stop and look through the cracks in the old wooden door, and hear all the cows mooing in terror. No doubt they guessed what was about to happen to them. We could actually see the cows being shot and dropping to the floor instantly. I can't remember feeling any compassion for the animals.

14

The sheep or cow would be cut up almost immediately, and we would see the steam and heat rising from their cut bellies, with the blood and guts flowing all over the floor. We thought it was exciting at the time, although I could not watch something like that now. The slaughtermen would always shoo us away if they saw us looking through the cracks in the door. We used to get the cow's bladder from the slaughterhouse, blow it up with our own breath and use it as a football. Nothing was wasted in those days.

I do not remember my first day at school, in the convent, but one of the more famous nuns was called sister Philomena, and as I recall she was a right battleaxe, who seemed to enjoy whacking us lovely, well behaved, little children. Sure God love us and weren't we lovely little creatures and little angels who were as innocent as the day was long.

The toilet in the school was opposite my class window, and during a visit there we had a pissing competition which I won! The first time that I won a sporting competition! I was competitive even as a seven-year-old. As kids do, we were trying to see who could piss the highest, which would normally be no big deal, except that on this occasion we were unfortunately doing it outside the entrance to the toilet and in full view of the nun who was teaching us! It was not a good idea. When we went back into our class after our wee break, the nun called me and my pal up and slapped us with her leather strap, to let us know she did not approve of our outrageous behaviour. I learnt a good lesson that day and that is: if you want to do something naughty, make sure that no one sees you!

Another favourite pastime was getting hold of an old bicycle wheel and having races all around the Island Field streets against each other. We would get a solid piece of wood and make the wheel go by running alongside it. We would make it go faster by pushing the stick against the wheel. The faster you ran the quicker the wheel went. I was quite a good little runner in those days and usually did quite well, and it cost nothing, kept you fit and gave you a good appetite, which looking back now, was probably not such a good idea as we could not always go home to a good meal. At least while I was playing it took my mind off food and any other problems.

Barrington Hospital was where we went for non-serious out-patient treatment. It was more for cuts and bruises and minor accidents, but we had other devious motives. A lot of the people going there went by bicycle. The women especially had to park their bicycles somewhere, and the main place they parked was outside Barringtons. We knew this and we would wait until the bikes were parked and as soon as the woman had gone inside we would borrow the bike and cycle all around the area, and when we had

15

enough we would park the bicycle some way from Barringtons. We would then run hell for leather, never knowing whether the owner ever found their bikes again. Later it became too risky as people started to get wise and became more vigilant.

On our way to the convent school we used to pass a Protestant school with big iron gates, which were always locked. We never passed without shouting obscenities. The usual one was, 'Proddy Waddy ring the bell, all the Proddys go to hell.'

I can honestly say I never saw anyone behind the gates and I don't know now why we hurled such abuse and such racist remarks but it seemed the thing to do. It now seems a cruel thing, because we were shouting abuse at other kids like ourselves. Maybe it was because they were better off than we were and were Protestants, because I can't see any other reason why we were abusive. I often wonder how those kids who went to that school felt.

As we were hard up in those days, like everyone else, we used to collect old jam jars and old lemonade bottles and bring them back to the local shops and get a halfpenny or a penny back on each item, depending on the size. We also used to go to the fields behind the Island Field houses and sift through the old fire ashes and pick out bits of coal or coke that we thought could be used again, and sell it back to the people for sixpence a bucket, which would help pay for the price of the pictures, and maybe a couple of sweets.

Something very sinister went on in the fields around the Island Field which I have never spoken about to anyone in Limerick before now and I don't know how many people alive today would remember it, but I certainly have never forgotten it. It was sexual abuse, which I knew at the time was wrong.

I was probably around seven or eight years old and an older boy who would have been around fifteen at the time was sexually assaulting young boys openly in broad daylight in the fields, in front of other boys. It had been a fairly regular occurrence. I witnessed it myself and I remember going home to tell my older sister, who can't remember me telling her now. She told me at the time to tell her if the guy ever tried to touch me. He never did try to touch me because I was pretty single-minded even then and I had a terrible temper on the odd occasion I lost it. My vague recollection is that that particular guy may have died very young and I certainly could never remember his name except I know he lived in the Island Field at the time. No doubt he must have had problems of his own and I sometimes wonder if those abused children ever told their parents

16

and wonder what type of mental scars they have been carrying around with them all these years.

Even though I was a very quiet and placid little boy and slow to anger, I did have a bad temper when aroused. I was being bullied by a boy who was thirteen around the time I would have been eight or nine. I got so mad at being bullied for nothing, I grabbed this boy by the throat and threatened to 'Fecking kill you if you don't leave me alone'. He did leave me alone and he was scared to death of my swift and violent reaction, and he did not retaliate. The reason I remember this incident so clearly is because the boy in question died some days later and I always wondered if I was partly to blame. The feeling has never left me despite realising now it had nothing to do with me.

Family feuds, due mostly to drink, were part of life in the Island Field when I was growing up in the late forties. They terrified me, because they were often bloody and violent affairs. I remember families fighting openly in the street, and broken bottles being smashed over heads and blood streaming down faces, with people shouting abuse at each other. It seemed to go on for ages, with adults and children crying and people looking for help from other families to assist them and to take sides. It was all very terrifying for a young kid like myself to witness. I'm sure even the adults must have been terrified. Sometimes it was fuelled by alcohol and other times by family feuds, which I did not understand at the time. It is hard to visualise now and I never did understand what it was all about.

3. A Wake

A wake is what happens in Ireland after someone has died, and it used to provide an opportunity to go into someone else's house, somebody's house that you would normally not go into. It was also an opportunity to have something extra to eat, free of charge. Food and drink would be laid on for the mourners, as they talked about the deceased, often making comments such as, 'Sure he was a lovely man, sure he was, wasn't he now?' and, 'Doesn't he look lovely, so he does.' And, 'Isn't he laid out lovely, Mary, lovely he looks.' And, 'Sure he never looked better now, sure he didn't? May God rest his soul and sure he'll go straight to heaven, so he will. Sure he never did no harm to no one, sure he didn't, did he?'

'Ju know, Mary, old Jimmy lying there, God rest his soul worked in the corporation all his life and never late for work, so he wasn't, and he never missed a day's work in his life. Never missed a day's work. Now isn't that a grand thing to be proud of? He never laid a hand on those children of his, so he didn't, and ju know, Mary, he never touched a drop of the drink, so he didn't. Sober all his life, so he was. Took the pledge, so he did, when he was only thirteen years old. Now wasn't that a grand thing to do, give himself to the Almighty. Never touched a drop all his life, atall, atall. Sure he's a saint already, so he is. If anyone deserves to go to heaven, sure it's himself, so it is, God bless him. If he's not in heaven this very minute, then there's no hope for any of us now, and that's a fact, so it is. Ah well now, sure there you are.'

The conversation would go on and the neighbours would get more charitable about the deceased, the more they drank. 'Do you want another ham sandwich now, Mary, do you, ti's a lovely bit of ham, so it is, isn't it? Goes well with a glass of the old Guinness, so it does.' Often the glass of Guinness would be held up to the light as if to admire its contents.

'Grand stuff, Mary, so it is. Jimmy was good with an old song too don't you know. He sang like an angel, so he did. Could have been another what's his name? You know the fella who sang all them high songs. Don't you remember his name atall, Mary?' Mary would have another long gurgle, trying to consume the last remaining drops of stout straight from the bottle, giving herself time to think, and then she'd follow it with a pinch of snuff, while the effects of the Guinness took hold.

'Was it Gigigili (Gigli) or Carioso (Caruso) or Marian Lanzeroto (Mario Lanza), something like that?' Mary would suggest.

'Sure ti's something like that. The name sounds familiar, so it does. A lovely singer so he was and, ju know, Mary, ju know that Jimmy was nearly as good as them Italys was, so he was. No singing training atall, atall, so he hadn't. Natural, so he was and gifted. Mind you he never knew the words, so he didn't. Just made them up as he went along, so he did. Wasn't that clever of him now? Ah well, sure he's now gone to a better place and singing up in heaven for the Man himself.

'Ju know, Mary, old Jimmy could have gone to Hollywood, so he could, and gone into the filums and become famous all over the world, so he could. Can you imagine that, Mary, a man from Limerick and the Island Field being in the filums and making all that money? Not for him though. He preferred to stay on in the old corporation, with a steady job and a steady old wage and the old pension after forty year. Sure now, wasn't he just as happy here in Limerick all the same? So he was, bringing the old wages home to Theresa every week.

'He never looked at another woman, ju know, for all the years he was married. He loved old Theresa and ju know, Mary, Jimmy was the spitting image of that great Hollywood filum star Clark Cable, the great lover, and I heard old Jimmy was a bit on the old romantic side when he was younger, so he was! Could have had any woman in Limerick, so he could. Sure wasn't I mad about him meself, so I was, but he only had the eye for Theresa.

'Resotted by her, so he was. Ju know they met at the Tivoli, watching *Gone With the Window*? Sitting next to one another so they were and the next thing they were engaged! Very cheeky, so he was, so Theresa told me. Ju know he put his hand on her knee, while she was watching the filum and he hardly knew her. Would you ever believe it! Mind you, he could have put his hand on my old knee any time, so he could. Sure there's nothing like a bit of the old romance and a bit of the old what you know! Especially in the dark, where even the priest couldn't see you. May God forgive me for my evil thoughts.

'Could you pass another slice of the old ham, Mary. Grand so it is. I haven't tasted as nice a piece since old Paddy across the street died a few years ago, God have mercy on his soul. Sure we'll be dead before too long, Mary.' Mary's eyes would be looking glazed and she would just give the odd nod now and again as the Guinness seemed to be having a sedative effect on her disposition. She would be having difficulty chewing the ham, which was not surprising, considering that she had only a few teeth left, all

20

of which were distributed unevenly around her mouth and especially one very discoloured one in the centre of her lower jaw, which jutted up like the Mountains of Mourne, but she persevered, chewing the ham, and was not about to be beaten by a tough piece of Matterson's ham. Matterson's Hams of Limerick were well known all over Ireland and probably consumed by every family in Ireland, at least on every Sunday for dinner.

Suddenly old Johnny Ryan from across the street, who's sitting next to the bed where the corpse was lying would burst into song with, 'Oh Danny Boy', but Mary would admonish him and tell him to 'Be quiet, hush now, sure the poor man is hardly dead.' Hardly dead! Surely an understatement! The corpse looks dead all right. He must be, because I've been observing him very closely and he hasn't moved a muscle in 20 minutes. I used to look very closely at the corpse's face just to make sure there was no movement whatsoever and look at the chest to see if there was any breathing. I used to think what would happen if the corpse suddenly started moving, what would the mourners do? I had not quite understood that when you're dead you're dead.

I also often wondered what did the dead person think, just lying there with his hands folded and a set of rosary beads placed carefully through his fingers, and people, strangers mostly, laughing and joking as if everything was normal! I also wondered what he needed rosary beads for, and what was he going to do with them? I never thought of asking anyone. I was only nine years old, so what did I know! Since growing up, I have always felt uneasy at the pleasantries at funerals. It always seems inappropriate.

Newcomers would be coming and going all the time to pay their last respects. Some would kneel down by the bed and say a few Hail Marys out loud, usually in what seemed like a great rush, as if to get out again as soon as possible or maybe by saying a few quick prayers they could then justify having a drink or a ham sandwich. They would often then confer with one of those already present. 'Terrible isn't it, Bridie? A lovely man like himself, lying there like he was after going to sleep. Sure he looks very happy now, doesn't he, so he does, God bless him. What's the old ham like now? Sure I think I'll try a slice just to be sociable. A grand man, so he was. Ju remember when he sang in St Mary's church that time?'

'Ah sure enough I do an all,' replied Bridie, holding on to the glass of Guinness as if it was the last drop in the world.

Suddenly a neighbour's dog dashes into the room and starts barking. 'Holy Jasus who let the fecking thing in,' asks Mary making the sign of the cross as if to pardon herself for taking the Lord's name in vain. 'Give him a piece of the old ham, that'll get him out.' Mary throws a piece of ham out into the front garden, while calling the dog to 'Come out you little fecker and leave the dead man rest in peace atall.' And the dog shoots out like a bolt of lightning for his prize piece of ham, which was more of a luxury for him than it was for the rest of the guests.

Personally I never could understand why everyone seemed so cheerful at such a terrible time! I never thought that the corpse looked better dead than alive, despite all the very wise adults saying so, but then I had not been drinking. I also wondered why old Johnny sang 'Danny Boy'. Was it to do with having too many free Guinnesses, which loosened his inhibitions. I never heard him sing before and I doubt if anyone else had.

Wakes had their good and bad points. First of all, it was good to get a bit of extra food for nothing, but often I would lie awake for nights afterwards, dreaming of the corpse. Seeing dead bodies never seemed to bother us as kids although I could not say that now, because as I've become older I've become more sensitive to a dead body and more aware of the ramifications and sadness that can be part of someone dying. One of the things that scared me was when a body had been washed, and the water was thrown out into the gutter. I could not bear to touch or have that water touch me. It seemed to be contaminated. Years later when my own mother died I found it very traumatic and frightening to stay in the same house as her, and I was 19 years old at the time. Somehow death altered my feelings and relationship with my mother.

Going to mass on Sunday always seemed a great effort, although one of my nicer memories of a sunny Sunday morning was hearing the church bells ringing out 'The Bells of Saint Mary's' all over Limerick, calling the faithful to come and worship the Lord and give thanks for all He gave us, even though we didn't think He gave us much at the time. I never remember my father going to mass, and on at least one occasion when my mother took me, we stood at the back and my mother started eating ham from a wrapper as if she was at home. My mother certainly was different, that's for sure.

We did not concentrate much on what was going on in the church. We used to sit upstairs at the back and look down on the other church goers and call other kids names in a low voice. St Munchin's church, with the famous Treaty Stone outside it, was our favourite church, but only because it was nearest to get to and not far for our little legs to carry us.

Even though the famous Treaty Stone was across the road from the church, the men generally would sit and stand by it and hear mass from there. They would be talking away as if in normal conversation, and if you were a passer-by you would not be aware that someone was attending mass. However, whenever the bell rang inside the church, the men at the Treaty Stone would go silent and pound their breast in acknowledgement and then carry on talking as usual. Their intentions were honourable I am sure and they were at least there in spirit.

To my shame I once stole money from a church. It was at St Augustines on O'Connell Street in Limerick. It was a very cold and wet day and I was starving hungry, and I went in with the premeditated idea of stealing money. There was an open box, just behind some low railings inside the church, where people put in money for lighting a candle. I put my grubby little hand in and stole from the Lord, but I figured He could afford it. It was only a couple of shillings and anyway the church is supposed to give to the poor, so it couldn't be too much of a sin could it? The priests always looked fat and healthy, so I'm sure they never even missed it.

Another prank that we got up to was we used to love putting lighted bits of paper through the letter-boxes for a laugh, to see if we could burn any letters that were inside, although we never hung around long enough to see what happened.

Gambling schools were constantly going on down Island Field. Men and young boys, including myself would toss halfpennies down the side of one or other of the semi-detached houses. There was one next door to my cousins, at the side of May Daly's house. A crowd of males would gather and take turns tossing the halfpennies into the air and lay a bet to see whether it landed either heads or tails. Individuals would bet on one side or the other landing face up. A lot of money could be at stake and men regularly gambled their wages and went home with nothing to feed their families for the coming week.

Vicious fights often broke out, especially if someone was losing a lot of money. As soon as the halfpennies hit the ground and someone guessed the result was unfavourable to them someone would push someone else into the crowd, disrupting the game and shout, 'Sulk', which was a sign to help yourself, and everyone grabbed what money they could, which had been placed on the ground.

Punches were thrown and people were kicked in the face as they bent down to pick money that may or may not have belonged to them. During a game, sometimes someone would shout, 'Police', and everyone would scatter in all directions, mostly down the back of May Daly's house into the nearby fields and into the graveyard just behind. The police would do occasional raids, but more likely than not it was a false alarm and excuse to break up the game so that people who were losing could pick up the money that was left on the ground.

We also used to play pitching halfpennies on the floor towards a stationary brick some yards away, and whoever got nearest the brick won all the money. Sounds simple enough, but it wasn't, as often there would be a number of people who claimed that their halfpenny was nearest, so the distance from the brick was measured by using fingers placed on the floor, either one, two or three, depending how far away the halfpenny was from the brick. Disputes broke out as to who was nearest. Again more fighting and kicking. It often got nasty and spiteful and I knew it was time for me to disappear home.

Through watching the gambling I became addicted myself and the grown-ups didn't care who played so long as you had money. I became as good as the next man or boy at tossing and pitching the coins and I won and lost as often as the next person, but like most gamblers I usually finished up losing more than I won, and that is where my problem started.

My father used to gamble, though not in his own locality because I never saw him. He gambled up the city backstreets and came home with a couple of bicycles on one occasion, which he had won while gambling. He also came home with a black eye on another occasion, probably because he had a fight while gambling. He advised me strongly never to gamble, and like most kids I ignored my father despite being terrified of him. I knew better and thought that I was going to win a lot of money, poor sucker me. Things got so bad with me that I started to steal from his trouser pockets on a regular basis, although not while he was wearing them, I wasn't that skillful or daring yet.

I would wait until he was washing his feet in another room in the basin, as there was no bath in those days. He would leave his trousers hanging over the chair and I would work very quickly going through his pockets. At first it was pennies, then a shilling and as I got really brave or stupid, I began to steal half a crown regularly.

On the last occasion I remember stealing from his pocket, he got wise and almost caught me. I had taken two half crowns, a lot of money then, and probably enough to feed our family for a day or two. It was also enough for him to notice. As he put on his trousers he put his hand in his pocket and said, 'Have you been stealing money from my pocket, you little bastard.' In my most cherubim voice I said, 'No dadda, I haven't.'

He was not convinced and started to put his hand down into my pocket, and but for some miracle did not feel the money. I was petrified and was waiting for a punch, which thankfully never came. 'I'll fecking kill you if I ever catch you at my pockets.'

He made his point and I also got the point and never stole from him again, but instead I moved on to my sister, Phyllis, who also stole from my father's pocket.

Phyllis, because she was five years older than me, did in many ways have a more difficult time than I. She was often given the blame for things that I did wrong and I wouldn't own up to, because I was too scared of the consequences.

My most vivid and cowardly act was when me and Phyllis went shopping at the back fields on the way to the shops. Being clumsy as I tended to be at times, I lost the half crown I was carrying, in the high grass, and it was the only money left in the house and our only source of a meal. We returned home and Phyllis, God bless her, told my mother that she had lost the money, while I kept quiet, being the coward that I was. It did not seem the right time to be honest!

My mother who was normally very quiet and rarely said a cross word, was furious and marched Phyllis down to where she had lost the money. She was pushing Phyllis from behind in the direction of where the money was lost, with me trailing sheepishly behind. She pushed Phyllis so hard that Phyllis fell over and sustained a severe cut to the inside of her wrist. My mother felt dreadful and I was feeling very sheepish and bad, though not bad enough to own up. Phyllis must have felt very scared.

My father made Phyllis leave school early, around eleven years old, to go to work to bring more money into the house, and as a result, her education suffered. She left school unable to read or write. (She taught herself in her twenties.)

Because she worked, she had more money than I had, and although she used to buy me the *Dandy* and the *Beano* comics weekly and gave me the price of the pictures now and again, it still was not enough for me. So I made more demands on her, which she could not meet. When she did not give me what I wanted I used to shout and scream until she weakened and gave me something to keep me quiet. I was good at throwing tantrums, behaviour that I would recognise in myself into my adult life.

On one occasion Phyllis had left a couple of shillings on the mantelpiece, which she was going to use for the dance. I grabbed it off the mantelpiece and ran out into the back garden with Phyllis in hot pursuit. 'Give me back that money, you little fecker, or I'll fecking kill you.' I was in no mood for compromising and continued running, knowing she wouldn't catch me, but suddenly I was brought to a full stop with a searing thud to the back of my head which virtually knocked me over.

I felt my head, which by now was bleeding quite badly. Phyllis, in desperation had picked up a pound pot of blackberry jam and had thrown it at me and hit me right on the back of the head, a bull's-eye. Of course I was in tears and Phyllis was feeling guilty. God, I was a horrible little bastard for a nine-year-old and I must have made her life a misery, although she rarely complained.

Phyllis, with my encouragement, used to sell cups of sugar to neighbours, so that we could have a bit of money to play card games in one of the local houses, for money. The main games were pontoon and forty-five. When I look back now I find it hard to believe that I did such grown-up illegal things when I was so young.

My father was a very proud man in many ways and always insisted we eat butter only. He wouldn't dream of having margarine in the house. Firstly because it tasted terrible and secondly because it was only for the really low class families, although I didn't think there was anyone who was lower class than we were, but there you go. A certain type of snobbery existed even in the Island Field. Some people will always see themselves as better than their neighbour, and my father was no exception, despite the fact that he could not read or write!

Phyllis and I decided that the next time we were asked to buy a pound of butter, which came off of a big slab in the shop, we would only buy a half pound and mix it with a half pound of margarine, and pocket the difference, because margarine was a lot cheaper. My father would never tell the difference, would he? We hoped that he wouldn't.

As we sat down to eat with a certain amount of anxiety, my father instantly recognised something was wrong and spat out the bread. 'Have you been buying margarine,' he said to Phyllis.

'No, dada,' she said innocently, 'the shop must have given us the wrong stuff.'

Whether he believed her or not I don't know, but he gave her an old fashioned look and said, 'If I ever catch you buying margarine again I'll break your fecking neck, ju hear me?' Yes, we heard him loud and clear and never tried that trick again, but at least Phyllis's quick thinking saved the moment. Well, who wants their neck broken at such an early age? My father had a wicked temper and was likely to carry out his threat although it didn't stop us from trying new tricks and disobeying him, despite the fear of a broken neck hanging over us.

Phyllis started going to dances, unbeknownst to my father, and against his wishes, as dancing was seen as evil and likely to lead to temptation and mortal sin. In other words some form of sexual activity might occur! All that dancing close together, and sure, didn't the priest always warn us on Sunday at mass about the evils and temptation of dancing so close together, and that you could have a baby? He certainly was right about the temptation as I discovered later in life. Wearing make-up was also frowned on, (especially for the boys!) but as I was too young for either of these activities, they didn't concern me that much. Most parents in those days had a similar attitude, especially to their daughters.

My father came home one dark evening and asked me where Phyllis was. I knew she had gone dancing up the city somewhere, but being a fairly good liar and not wanting my sister to get into trouble, I thought quickly and said, 'She's gone to the knitting club, she goes every Tuesday I think.'

'Do you know where it is?' he asked me.

'Of course I do,' I said cockily, expecting that would satisfy him. My father could not read or write but he sure was streetwise.

'Come on,' he said, 'I want to find her.' I doubted that he totally believed me, but at least I tried.

'Now I'm in trouble,' I thought. We headed towards the city in the dark, looking for a knitting club that did not exist, and me feeling very tired because it was way beyond my bedtime. I kept leading my father up and down different side streets, pretending at not being sure where the club was. 'Are you blackguarding me?' my father said.

'No, dada,' I said innocently, 'it's here somewhere, I've only been once in the daylight and I forget where it is.'

'If you're codding,' he said, 'I'll kick your fecking arse all the way home,' so I will.' We never did find the knitting club and Phyllis was off the hook for now.

My father was very unusual in lots of ways. Firstly he was a complete teetotaller, and non-smoker, and never wanted to mix with our neighbours very much, and he often told me not to bother talking to them either.

I believe he and his brothers and at least one sister, came from the six mile bridge area in Clare, about ten miles outside of Limerick. I did hear that one brother may have emigrated to Australia, and there was one wizened, wrinkled little old man whom I briefly met, named 'Pa-jo'. He did not seem to be all there and not quite right in the head. I later discovered that he was in the city asylum for those not right in the head. My father's other brother was named Jimmy, who was married to Doris McVoy. Doris was to play a very large part in my life later on. My father also had a sister named Mary Drew, who lived in one of the rooms in the big houses in Patrick Street. She seemed to have a lot more class than my father. Didn't everybody!

My father was extremely violent, and as he never drank, it's hard to understand or excuse what he did. I have been told by many different people that he was a very good boxer and very fast with his hands, and could beat men twice his size, and women too so it seems! He was quite short and stocky, maybe around five feet five or six. Now, here is the contradiction. He was well known as an unusually quiet man who kept himself to himself, and rarely went out, yet at home he was probably as violent as any man in Limerick. He physically abused my mother regularly, physically abused Phyllis at least once and myself many, many times. Not a good record for an ex-boxer who never touched alcohol? I now see him as a rather withdrawn man who was maybe shy or just lacked confidence, but that does not excuse his behaviour.

It's the beating of Phyllis I remember so vividly, as does she herself. I remember it was in the kitchen and my father was punching and shouting obscenities of the foulest type at her, and she was cowering in the corner behind the chair, terrified and crying. He then picked up the broom and broke the handle across her back with enormous force and brutality. How could a father do that to his own daughter and why would he want to?

I was screaming in terror, witnessing all this myself. And what was it all about? Neither Phyllis nor I can remember, but whatever she had done, she did not deserve this humiliation! Yet after all this Phyllis thinks he was not that bad. The mental and psychological scars that that beating inflicted on her should have been quite serious and long lasting but it says a lot for her strength of character that she seems well adjusted and has led a very happy life and been married to the same man since 1960, with two successful daughters who are both well educated barristers. (Phyllis has not returned to Ireland since she left in 1952.)

As I became older I often tried to understand my past and my parents' relationship with each other and why my father treated us in such a violent manner. Were we all that bad? Was I so bad, or was he just trying to guide me on the right path in the only way he knew how?

Maybe it is because I witnessed so much violence, and also being at the receiving end myself, that I detest violence, especially against women and children. I am also very aware that there are incredible similarities between my own behaviour and temper and my father's. I have had a number of occasions during my life when I lost my temper and control and I do not like myself for it.

I now see that my father was a very frustrated and very angry man. Perhaps my mother and her behaviour had caused him frustration, although that could not excuse his violent behaviour towards us. I realise that some bad behaviour can be misdirected. I do think there was probably some sexual frustration, on both of their parts, as they both seemed to have had many affairs. Both Phyllis and myself now believe that my father had an illegitimate baby who we think died at birth. She clearly remembers a baby being born and actually seeing it, and that it looked like my father. While I never saw a baby, I was aware of rumours that a baby had been born and had belonged to my father. The baby may have belonged to a woman lodger who my father had moved into our house during one of my mother's absences. Maybe she was more than a lodger, but I got on okay with her. Maybe he took her in to help bring me up and then had an affair with her.

What I do remember very clearly was a secret burial at midnight in a house just up from us, and beyond Columcille Street late one evening and that there was a dead baby in the house. I remember the baby was wrapped in white sheets, and lots of adults about, and they were talking about what to do with this baby. Whether it was my father's baby or not I do not know, but I do remember that they decided to take it in the dead of night up to the new burial ground to bury it secretly, and that was my last memory of the incident, but I never forgot and always wondered if the baby was my father's and if so, it meant I had a step-brother or sister whom I never knew.

4. My Father

I remember when I was about to make my first communion there was a terrible argument between my mother and father as to whether they should buy me a suit as most kids wore, or just a new jumper and trousers. My father wanted me to have a jumper and trousers, but my mother insisted that I should have a suit like everyone else. I also wanted a suit, because I wanted to be like everyone else. My mother and I had our way and I got my suit in the end. It is funny how even the poorest people have their pride, something that comes from within and others can't control. I would inherit a very strong sense of pride as I became older.

My father never missed a day's work and was always very conscientious, and he would be seen sitting on the wall by the river Shannon, outside the corporation yard at five o'clock in the morning, whatever the weather. He was basically a road sweeper, and occasionally worked on the corporation van, which was a step up from sweeping the road, and it had more status.

His last job before he died was a toilet attendant at the toilets down at the city docks. I used to bring his sandwiches down to him now and again. Even then I thought it was a terrible job and I was determined not to follow in his footsteps. I used to dream that maybe I could be a filum star, or maybe even a stuntman, and fall off the horses like John Wayne did, without getting hurt and just get up and walk away, very casual like.

Or maybe I could be a great fencer like Errol Flynn, because I would do a lot of fencing with a piece of stick with the other boys in the Island Field and I nearly always won, so I must have been good enough to get into the filums? I thought that I could always swing through the trees as good as Johnny Weissmuller in those Tarzan pictures, because I was always practising with a rope hanging from the trees along the Island bank. And sure, didn't I have my mother's good looks, thank God, so was bound to be famous one day, so what was the point of working for the corporation anyway, no point all, so I would just keep practising my fencing, running and swinging from the trees and when I got to England or America, I'd just tell them how good I was and what I could do and then I'd be up on the big screen at the Thomond and the Tivoli and I'd be famous and have loads of money. I'd be able to eat fish and chips and pig's toes all day long and be happy ever after. I'd be the first filum star from the Island Field and the

31

most famous man in Limerick (unfortunately Richard Harris beat me to it). A nine-year-old can dream, can't he!

My father's job did not seem very appealing to me. It was cold, damp and very lonely and no one to talk to all day long, just sitting there waiting for someone to come in and have a piss, God what an awful job, and it was definitely not in my future plans as a career. Not for me, I wanted to be famous and somebody. I would stick to my dreams of maybe being rich or famous one day. Either one would do me. At least my father's job kept us all in the basics and stopped us from starving to death. I went to school now and again in bare feet, but so did a lot of other kids, and maybe my father hated his job as well, but he knew he had to do it. What else could he do, what other choices were there? So maybe I should be more grateful, he was as good a provider as he could be, and maybe doing that boring job caused him to be frustrated, bitter, resentful and angry, and he took his frustration out on his family. He had no education and his choice of jobs was limited, especially more so during the forties. He was a very quiet man, except during his periods of violent behaviour.

5. My Mother

My mother seemed to have a completely different personality and outlook to my father. She was outgoing, loved singing and dancing, and like me she dreamed of meeting film stars of the day. She liked heartthrobs like John Loder, whom she had a picture of on her bedroom mantelpiece, and Ramon Novarro, whom I was named after. Oh yes, and she loved a drink, a lot of drink, but that was down the line a bit, although she was setting a destructive pattern that would shape her later life; what was to be a very short life indeed.

As one neighbour, who knew my mother years ago, said to me recently, 'Sure your mother loved the pint, but she harmed no one but herself, sure she didn't.'

I'm not so sure of that, as having lived amongst heavy drinkers and helped to treat alcoholics and drug addicts in my job as a psychiatric nurse for over 30 years, I know that everyone involved with a heavy drinker will be affected in some way or another, and they can cause a lot of pain and lasting damage. They leave a trail of destruction behind, that can last a lifetime and often destroy other people's lives as well as their own.

My mother seemed to have been drinking fairly heavily early on in her life and in her marriage. I often wonder whether it was as a result of my father's treatment of her or was it because she was unhappy being married to my father at such an early age. Or was she doomed from the start, having been abandoned by her parents as a baby and spending her whole life in institutions being cared for by nuns.

The nuns did not prepare children in their care for marriage, sex, children and a husband, and they seemed to show very little compassion and understanding to young girls in their care. My mother was virtually straight from school, with I imagine no experience of the opposite sex. Nuns could also be very cruel and sadistic. My father was almost twice my mother's age and totally the opposite to her in every way. She certainly was not prepared for marriage and when she ran away on the wedding night, her big mistake was in not staying away. But then neither my sister nor I would have been born.

My mother had been in and out of hospital on many occasions, certainly between the ages of 20 and 30 and I don't really know why, but as I've started writing, things at last seem to be falling into place. She obviously had

33

many other babies that died at birth, which could be an obvious explanation why she was in hospital so much. Also my father's regular physical abuse could have caused her serious injuries, requiring hospital admission. The most serious conclusion must be that she may have lost all those babies due to miscarriages caused by my father's constant beatings. These events will remain a mystery and I can only speculate as to what might have occurred.

What must have all that mental and physical trauma have done to her? It hardly bears thinking about. How she managed, it's hard to say, but of course she did not. She turned to Mrs Moore, her great friend and neighbour for help and she turned to drink. She also turned to other men for comfort and affection, which she did not seem to be getting from my father. Turning to other men may also have been another cause of conflict between my parents, but I will never be sure. I knew at least one of my mother's men friends in Limerick because I met him a number of times with my mother. He was in the Irish army, and I thought he was a lovely man who was always nice to me and gave me money and sweets, and best of all he did not hit me. I often wished that he was my father. I was aware that it was an illicit liaison and my mother knew I knew, but she trusted me and knew I would not tell my father. Somehow I understood why she was doing what she was doing and I approved. I have never judged my mother over her behaviour, as I seemed to understand her reasons, despite my very tender years.

My father was a very cruel man. Why else would any man beat his whole family so severely? And he could not even use the drink as an excuse. He once shaved my head absolutely bald when I was only or seven or eight years old for no reason that I can remember, except for sheer spite. I was almost traumatised and cried for days and sat on the stairs in our house, too ashamed and unable to face my friends for days. I was absolutely shocked and my mother was furious with my father. Shaving my head bald would leave a lasting effect on me. As an adult I have always been very vain, especially about my hair and I feel it may be due to my father's abuse of me that day.

My mother too, did some peculiar things that I cannot explain to this day. She would lie on the parental bed and I would lie beside her like children do, when my father had gone to work. She would lie absolutely still with her eyes closed, pretending to be dead! She would not move or open her eyes and not respond to cries of, 'Wake up, mama, you're not really dead are you? You're frightening me, please wake up, you can't die, I love you, mama, don't frighten me. Don't leave me with dada, if you die I want to die 'cause dad will kill me.'

34

After more pleading she would open her eyes and say, 'You know I won't leave you.' She did this many more times in the future and it always frightened me to death. Maybe she wanted to die, due to her unhappy life, or maybe she was preparing me for the future?

She was to die, ironically, at a tragically early age, but for now I was happy. My mother was here to love and nourish me and be my only protection from my cruel father. My mother often told me that she loved me and that was always comforting and reassuring.

On another occasion when I slept in my father's bed during one of my mother's absences, I had a little black and white kitten, which I had in the bed with me, playing with it. I loved cats and had a great love affair with most animals as a child. My father came into the bedroom and told me to put the cat outside the room, and then he left the room for something. In the meantime I thought I would hide the kitten under the bedclothes, hoping that my father would not notice, and then I could cuddle the kitten all night, and he could cuddle me and I would feel wanted.

My father came back into the room and asked me if I had put the cat outside. 'Yes, dada,' I said, pushing the cat down under the sheets as far as it would go. My father was barely into the bed when the kitten's head suddenly appeared from under the bedclothes, miaowing. My father went berserk and he grabbed the kitten and threw it on the floor with great force, then he hit me with another great force across the ear, which made me see stars and have recurring earache and discharges for a long time afterwards.

'You little fecker, I told you to put the fecking cat out of the bed didn't I? I'll fecking kill you if you don't do what I tell you again,' he said. 'Do you fecking hear me?' I heard him but I was too distressed to reply as I was in tears for a long time afterwards with my whole body shaking as you do when you're small and been hit by a very strong man. I was only about seven years old and although I had deserved some punishment, surely this was out of all proportion to what I had done.

'God, am I that bad, why does he hate me so much? I was only playing with a kitten, what's wrong with that? I am only small, there's no need to hit me that hard is there? You're my father, you're supposed to love me and not punch me in the ear, like you were hitting someone you hate, in the boxing ring.' These were the thoughts that went through my head then and all through my adult life. Over-sensitive? Yes I was and who could blame me? During my life, when I seemingly overreacted to some situation or other and was criticised by some individual, I wanted to tell them how I was abused by my father and to tell them about my other childhood traumas, but no I couldn't, instead I was made to feel ashamed by the way I was reacting. 'God, will no one ever understand or listen to me and help me with my pain and feelings of inadequacy and worthlessness?' I would always remain very sensitive throughout my life and often be criticised for it, as if I could alter it.

6. Life in Limerick

Life in Limerick, at least outside my home, was quite exciting and free for us young kids growing up, despite being hungry and going to school barefooted now and again. You could always ask one of the other kids to get you a cush (slice) of bread and jam, when their parents were out or you could go down the orchards in the Island Field and risk being beaten to death by the owner, just for a few crab apples. He couldn't eat all them apples himself anyway, sure he couldn't?

One day while I was playing truant and just coming away from the orchard, with a load of crab apples under my jumper, I saw my father coming towards me, and I was petrified. How did he know I was here?

'Have you been robbing the orchard again? I told you before what I would do if I caught you robbing orchards and mooching from school.'

'I wasn't robbing the orchard, dada, honest I wasn't,' making a desperate attempt to stop the apples from falling out from under my jumper. He grabbed me forcibly by the shoulders and pulled me along and sure enough all the apples fell from under my jumper. Another box on the ear, another thumping. That always seemed to be my father's first response – lash out.

'You little fecker, what am I going to do with you? You'll go to fecking Glin if you don't go to school, and you'll be away for a long time.' He never seemed capable of trying to reason with me and maybe he did not know how.

We often heard terrible tales about Glin, some probably exaggerated; how they would starve you and beat you up if you did not do as you were told, and you might never see your parents again. It sounded like a terrible place and somewhere neither I nor any of my friends wanted to end up. The thought of being sent there was frightening, but obviously not enough to stop me misbehaving and disobeying my father. Maybe I misbehaved to get attention, I don't know.

It was seen as a terrible disgrace on the family to have one of your sons sent down there; even people from the Island Field had their pride, especially my father. He warned me many times, 'You'll go to Glin over my dead body, so you will. You'll never go there while I'm alive.' How right and prophetic he was to be.

Going to school in bare feet was not too bad, but it was the sitting at the classroom all day long that was really hard especially in the winter, on cold wooden floors at St Mary's school, but I was not in bare feet very often like some of the poorer kids from even poorer families.

One very happy memory was when I was sleeping upstairs in the front room. When it was dark a group of young men would be up late standing under the street lamp and singing the popular tunes of the day in melodious harmony. The favourite ones were:

> Underneath the lamplight, by the barrack gate.
> Darling I remember the way you used to wait,
> And I remember tenderly, that I loved you
> And you loved me.
> Cause you're the lily of the moonlight,
> You're My Own Lily Marlene.

This was a song made famous by the Hollywood German actress, Marlene Dietrich.

Another song that was a parody of another famous song went like this:

> They say you're in the army,
> They say it's mighty fine,
> But you ask for Betty Grable
> And they give you Frankenstein.
> Momma, I want to go,
> Momma, I want to go,
> Momma, I want to go home.

Those lullabies used to send me to sleep in a happy frame of mind, and they remain very happy memories of that time for me.

Often when my mother went drinking during daytime hours she would take me with her to one of the local pubs in Mary Street up the town. She would be drinking a bottle of stout and I would be drinking a lemonade. I used to ask her to put some of her stout, especially the froth, into my lemonade, to see what it tasted like, making I suppose what is now known as a shandy. Although I did this regularly, I never liked the taste of alcohol. More likely it was because I was affected so personally by seeing what it did to my own family and seeing my mother behaving so badly as a result of being drunk.

I have been reminded so many times over the years, by English and Irish people, that I was not a 'proper Irishman' or, 'You're a funny

Irishman, you don't drink.' That's unfortunately how a lot of Irishmen have been perceived and judged over the years; how much they could drink before they fell into the gutter. I hated what alcohol did to people and I can't see or understand the great passion for the stuff. Personally I'd prefer a piece of cake and a cup of tea, but I often felt out of place and an outcast just because I did not drink, but I learned to live with the stigma.

Opposite my house at number 102, there was an old white-haired lady named Mary Jane Kelly. She was the local gossip and knew everyone's business and seemed to hate all children and was always telling us off or complaining about something or other. We always tried to avoid her. One night, when my cousin Thomas was asleep in our front downstairs room, to keep me company while father was working a late shift through the night, there was an accident with a candle. We did not have electricity due to the fact that it had been cut off for non-payment of bills. We were in the same bed and the end of the bed was against the fireplace shelf, which had a lighted candle resting on it. We used to keep the candle alight all night as we were afraid of the dark.

I was suddenly aware of Thomas shouting at me, telling me the bed was on fire, due to the candle falling on it. I looked at it in a hazy sleep and fell back to sleep again, only to be woken up by loud banging on the door, shouting at us to get up, the room was alight. It was the nosy parker, old Mary Jane Kelly, God bless her. Because she used to stay leaning over her front gate until after midnight, she luckily saw the light, so to speak, and probably saved our lives. I saw her in a different light from then on.

My sister and I used to visit different houses to play cards for money in the evenings, especially while my father was working a late shift, and after the games we would sit around the fire and the adults would tell horror stories, nearly always about the banshee, a female folklore ghost that seems to be relevant to Ireland only, and had a habit of turning up and being observed and heard the night before someone was about to die. At the time I wholeheartedly believed in the stories I was told. When you're seven years old everything seems true, no matter how far-fetched.

One story I remember vividly was about the 'Headless Coach', another fairy story. The headless coach was apparently seen one night after midnight, coming up the top of Columcille Street, just opposite our house. It had four black horses, with two drivers sitting on top with long black whips, but the drivers had no heads. The coach then pulled up outside the house on the corner of the hill, and stopped.

As the story was being told to us we were by now shaking with fear, at least I was, but still anxious to know what happened next. The person

39

telling the story said, 'You must not let the coachmen see you looking out of the window, otherwise they would take you instead. If you want to look, you must peep discretely from behind the curtains, so as not to be seen.' I did as I was told.

The story then continued. The men on the coach got off, opened the back, which was a hearse, and pulled out a coffin. The coffin was placed in the front garden and a shadow that was on the wall of the house was lifted up and placed in the coffin. Then the coffin was put into the coach again, and the men got up and rode off down the street, with the sound of the horses' hooves clattering against the hard concrete road, echoing in the dark, still night. The next morning, sure enough, someone had died. The point of the story being that the coachmen had come for the person's soul before they died. It was very difficult leaving that house and going back home through dark streets, late at night to a dark and lonely house with no lights. I was only around eight years of age and no doubt was affected by such horrible horror stories, and I would remain wary of the dark all my life.

Another tale I was told was never to look into the mirror after midnight, otherwise you would see the devil. Unfortunately for me you could not get to the toilet without passing the mirror in the scullery area. I became a nervous wreck trying to get to the toilet after midnight, without looking in the mirror. I believed this tale so much that I was well into my twenties before I would look into the mirror, and then with great trepidation and anxiety. It was a horrendous tale, which caused me many nightmares.

For many years before I left Limerick we had no toilet door as it was used for firewood, and all the back downstairs toilet windows had long ago, been knocked out by other children.

I enjoyed my school time at St Mary's and do not have any real bad memories of my time there. Academically I was as good as the next boy. When I started to mooch from school, things quickly went down hill and I lost interest, which I now think was because of my unsettled home life and my mother not being around. I also got in with older boys and started going off the rails and doing things that I normally did not do. My mother seemed to be leaving home for longer and longer periods, and whenever she would come back home, it was like Christmas every time. I can't explain the excitement that I felt each time. Often she would come back from wherever she had been and try to see me or my sister without my father knowing. Her visits were only fleeting and then she was gone again. I pined for her and never knew if I would see her again. I never stopped loving or missing her, but I somehow understood why she did what she did. I had no way of contacting her and often fretted for her.

Our next door neighbour was named 'Peepy Dark', a nickname given, I think, because he was always peeping from behind closed curtains in his front room. A lot of peeping from behind curtains was going on then. Some people did not mix very well, but were interested in knowing what was going on around them. Peepy was a very old, little man who could not read or write. He used to come into my house so that my mother could read and write letters for him and tell him how much a cheque or such like was worth. Some of his relatives came in from the country to live with him, probably his daughter whose name was Hackett. They had some children, and after a short while they emigrated to England.

I was in England in 1953 for six weeks. My mother had taken me illegally to England while I had been on my annual holiday from Glin, and while we were in a cafe having something to eat, my mother, who was reading the paper, suddenly noticed an article about a murder. It was about a young girl who had disappeared from the bottom of her parents' garden and was later found buried underneath a church. She had been sexually assaulted and killed. It was a shock to see it was Hackett, our next door neighbour and probably the granddaughter of old Peepy.

In the winter we used to throw buckets of water down Columcille Street. The street was on a slope and it would freeze over so that we could skate down it. We had the first ski-slope in Limerick, and it was free and great fun, except when someone put salt on it just for devilment.

We also had a lot of trenches at the back of the houses down the fields, which were of varying width, and some were half full of water, and we would spend hours in the summer time jumping over them, according to our jumping ability. It kept us fit and out of mischief and always gave us a big appetite, which was not necessarily a good thing, in view of the shortage of food. These trenches had been used during the war for the soldiers to practise on. It was a carefree time in my life, even if it was only for a very short period.

In the 40s and 50s when I was a child, many families from the Island Field emigrated to England to get work and a better standard of living, which meant a lot of my pals left, never to be seen again. This was very sad because boyhood pals I grew up with were gone forever and their names and faces quickly faded into the past. Everyone's ambition was to go to England; it seemed like the land of milk and honey, and so it was, providing you were willing to work. At least there were more opportunities there for those brave enough to want to leave the cold and damp of Limerick. Most never returned and some not even for a holiday.

Girls, especially, who wanted to go to England, and particularly those who wanted to get married would say, 'I'm running away to England.' That was because in some cases their parents did not want them to go to England, so they ran away before anyone knew about it.

We used to have a laugh with the courting couples in our street. Late at night, after the pictures had finished, they would be leaning against the garden hedges around our locality, kissing and cuddling, which to us children was a terrible waste of time. We used to hide in the garden behind the hedges and listen to what they were saying. It certainly was better than going to bed early, and you often heard things you were not supposed to! Many illicit affairs took place late at night, and as children we often knew more than the adults about who was doing what to whom, but we never spilled the beans. To us it was just a laugh.

Another pastime was finding out which girls were wearing knickers. (What's changed?) Word was quickly spread as to who was and who was not wearing knickers, and then we would focus on a particular girl. Whenever she kneeled down we would try and look up her dress to see if we could see her 'Hairy Molly', which I did, at least once! It was exciting and a real challenge, but you had to be quick of course and grab the opportunity. I must have been reaching sexual maturity very early, as I still was only about nine or ten!

Although the Island Field always had a rough reputation, it was set in one of the nicest locations in Limerick City, surrounded by the river Shannon, with lovely fields and the even lovelier Clare hills in the distance. There was also a lovely path all the way around, following the river. What more could any young boy want?

Tinkers often came down to the Island Field and would mend pots and pans for a couple of shillings. No one could afford to throw things away. Recycling waste in the Island Field was happening long before the rest of the world caught up.

The tinkers used to bring donkeys with them, trailing behind. One time I found this donkey outside our house, and being fond of animals, brought it into our back garden through the front door, with the intention of keeping it, not realising it belonged to the tinkers. A few minutes later the tinkers came banging on the door demanding their ass back or they would 'cut your fecking throat'. Scared to death, I hid under the stairs and let my father do the explaining and the situation was diffused. Even at such an early age, someone was already threatening to cut my throat! I seemed to bring the worst out in some adults.

Looking back now it surprises me at the extreme consequences that grown-ups used to threaten children with. Phrases like, 'I'll knock your fecking block off', 'I'll break your fecking legs', 'I'll tear your head off' and 'I'll bury you alive, you little bastard'. However, despite all these threats of going through life with only one leg, I still got up to mischief and frequently disobeyed adults' commands and the various threats towards me. They would have to catch me first and I knew that the adults could never outrun me! Someone described me as ' little flyer', because I was a faster runner than most of my friends. Running would play a vital part in my life much later, in a way that I could never have imagined.

I remember a photographer used to come around and take photos of families for payment, which had to be paid in advance of course. My mother arranged for him to take a picture of all of us in our front garden on a nice summer's day, sometime before 1948. The photographer would put the blanket over his head with one of those old-fashioned cameras and shoot away and promise to return with the photos in a few days. We never did get those pictures and it was the only one I remember ever being taken of our family as a group. So wherever that dirty bastard is I hope the curse of Jasus followed you forever and I hope your camera never worked again and that bad luck always followed you. I hope that all your photos were overexposed, you cheating bastard, I still haven't forgotten you, whoever you were. It is quite possible of course that he did not even have a film in his camera. Scams are not just a modern day experience.

On St Stephen's day we used to black up our faces and put funny clothes on, but as I wore funny clothes all the time, I did not have to worry about that part too much, and we would go around with a box begging for money, pretending we had a live wren in the box. We would go along to the posh houses along the strand with their long gardens and the even posher ones out on the Ennis Road (where Richard Harris, the actor, was born). It was hard work as the bastards didn't like giving their money away, especially to dirty beggars and robbers from the Island Field. 'Go away home to your mothers you little blackguards and have a wash behind your ears, and haven't ye anything better to do than to waste our time.' So much for good Catholics who were supposed to give to the poor. We would say under our breaths and to each other 'Sure they must be Protestants, and I hope they all go to hell and be dying for a drink forever and I won't give it to them, God blast them.' I often wonder if Richard Harris refused us poor little beggars, long before he became a film star of course.

My cousins lived at 10 St Munchin's Street near the shops. My father's brother, Jimmy, was married to Doris McAvoy who came from the

43

beautiful Killaloe area about 20 miles outside Limerick. Theirs was a very large family with a least eleven children, and at least one other that had died, and all living in a house that was no bigger than ours was, two up and two down. The end of their garden backed onto a graveyard, with just a high wall between. It was very scary looking out the back window late at night. I used to spend as much time there as I could and regularly slept there over night and I was always treated like one of the family. It was great being there, as they had two horses and lots of chickens, and Josie, my cousin also kept pigeons.

I could always be sure of an egg for breakfast, or given a good feed of back bones or pig's head for dinner. The horses were stabled down in the back of the garden in the sheds, which had their fair share of rats. The trouble was, there was only one way into the sheds and that was right through the house, which could be very tricky when you were sitting down for a meal. The piebald mare and foal would come through the front door, then through the kitchen door, then stop where we were eating, and then they had to do a sharp left turn through one door and then another sharp left and then right down into the garden. Thank God they were house trained and always well behaved!

The horses' dung was put in the garden, just outside the shed, and of course it naturally piled up over the years. It became quite deep; just how deep I did not realise until one time I did a John Wayne jump from the shed onto the garden and into the dung, hoping I would land and roll over like I saw the film stars doing from their horses and from trees. I landed all right but I sunk right up to my knees, steadfast as if in quicksand. I didn't know whether to laugh or cry. As there were no baths in those days I must have smelt like a skunk for ages after. I never did that jump again.

Most of the family worked for the corporation, which at least meant steady work and always some money coming into the house, but with such a large family Doris needed every penny she could get to feed them. Mickey, one of the sons, used to work at a butcher's shop and he would come home at lunchtime, usually with a load of free sausages, lovely fat sausages, which I would share if I just happened to be there.

Mickey could play the piano by ear, so it was a very musical house, with Thomas who had a powerful voice and sang all the latest Mario Lanza songs. Lanza was the great Hollywood tenor and film star of the 50s. The trouble was, Thomas never knew any of the words except for the odd one, and while he sang the right tune, you never knew what he was saying, but it didn't matter as none of us knew the words anyway.

Instead of singing, 'Be my love, for no one else could end this yearning', Thomas would sing something like, 'Be my ove fa noy you else is in dis lernin', but despite that he still sounded good and was admired all over the neighbourhood. He could not read or write. Jimmy, the father, and my father's brother, was another singer, but only when drunk. He would stagger in the door and do an Al Jolson song, and usually the same one, which was, 'Oh, how we danced on the night that we wed, we danced and we danced, cause the room had no bed.'

The oldest brother Jimmy was the best looking in the family and I think the first to emigrate to England before 1950. I remember the first time he came home around 1951 and he had a lovely looking girlfriend with him whom he later married. I was so impressed that I made up my mind that if I got married it would have to be to an English girl, which was a dream that would eventually come true.

We would listen to tales from older boys coming home from England telling us how sexy English girls were and that they were easier to get to bed than the Irish girls, and probably it was true, due to the Irish girls' religious upbringing. So I couldn't wait to get to England, but that would be a long way down the line. Come to think of it, I seem to have had naughty thoughts about girls long before I was supposed to, but then I was probably backward in other ways.

Josie, one of my cousins, with whom I got on especially well, kept breeding racing pigeons, and he would spend a lot of time showing me the newborn pigeons and explaining what to look for and what made a good racing pigeon. He was, I think, very shy and I always admired his muscles, which he liked to flex. One of his favourite expressions was, 'I've got a concrete heart', meaning very strong.

Paddy, another brother, was in the RAF in England during the war, and was a very good professional boxer and I believe fought the great British Freddie Mills, who was the world lightweight champion at one time. Paddy returned to Limerick shortly after the war and joined the corporation, where he remained until he died, aged about 56, in the late seventies. He was also a member of St Mary's brass band, which he tried to encourage me to join later in the sixties when I returned to Limerick for a holiday, but by then I was only interested in rock and roll, and brass band music did not appeal to me. It was old-fashioned and not very cool.

Paddy, himself, had been in Glin Industrial School long before I had, where he learned music. He also took on a patriarch role in the family, making sure everyone left for work on time, and I remember he would be calling Mickey for a long time each morning to get up for work. Paddy had a very bad stammer, which I suppose could have been caused by his

45

boxing career. Every penny coming into the house was vital so it was important that no one missed a day's work with the possible risk of losing their job. Paddy had to go through this procedure almost daily, constantly cajoling Mickey to get up.

Bridie, the oldest sister, had nine children and used to give me and Thomas great meals and let us listen to her Mario Lanza records and she would always insist that we had something to eat, which I never disagreed with. She was great and one of the most generous people I knew, despite having such a large family. I never saw her angry or in a bad temper and more importantly she always seemed to have spare food.

Doris was the mother and the head and organiser of the family, and she used to like a pint but rarely went out of the house. She used to give me a bottle and ask me to go up to Halpins Pub and get them to fill it up and bring it home, without Jimmy, her husband, seeing it. 'Keep it under your coat, Raymond, and don't let Jimmy see it, ju hear me now, and leave it under the bed upstairs and don't tell no one now. You know what Jimmy is like, if he sees it he'll want it,' she would tell me.

I did what I was told, but Jimmy often suspected where I'd been and would ask me, 'Did you get Doris any drink, Raymond?' I always replied 'no', which made me feel bad, because Jimmy's tongue was hanging out for a drop of Guinness, but then so was Doris's.

Mealtimes at my cousins' were like a relay type of affair, due to the small kitchen. Paddy and Josie would eat first, together, as they were the eldest, and then two or three of the younger ones would eat until everyone had finished. Sometimes the tablecloth had to be changed several times during the mealtimes. When I say tablecloth, it was long sheets of clean quality paper that were brought home free from the corporation, and may have been used as building plans, which would have been thrown away anyway. As least it was quite inventive and more than we had in our house, and another case of recycling waste.

How Doris kept such a large family fed every day for years without complaining is beyond me. It seems amazing now looking back. At one time Doris had a fish and chip shop installed in their kitchen, selling fish and chips to the locals. If they ever made any money I'll never know, but I know I got loads of free chips.

They had a piano in the house downstairs at one time, which Mickey used to play. During the middle of the night on one occasion when everyone was asleep there was the sound of a piano being played downstairs. Thomas was convinced there was a ghost in the house or maybe the banshee, and that it was a sign that someone was about to die.

Terrified, he got down under the blankets, too scared to shout out until eventually he got up enough courage to go downstairs to face the music, so to speak. He quickly put the light on and the piano keys were moving up and down, a real scary moment. This went on for a few more minutes, until Thomas bravely lifted up the back of the piano to reveal the cat who was walking up and down, and trying to get out. What a relief!

Doris used to love her pinch of snuff, and she also played the accordion, or mallogen, as we used to call it. She was a very quietly spoken woman who rarely got annoyed, despite having a very hard life. Holidays were not heard of then, although there was the odd day out in the country or at the seaside town of Ballybunnion in County Limerick, but that was on a very special occasion. She was a very hard-working mother, and to my mind was as good as any mother could be. Her life would, however, eventually take its toll and she would die in her early fifties. A great woman who did so much for me and never complained about her life.

I used to love sleeping in my cousin's house because of the large family and the atmosphere of singing, and they also had a radio, which was a novelty, as not that many families had radios or record players at that time. I used to love switching it on and looking for different radio stations. Some of the pop songs of the day were: 'Buttons and Bows', a big hit made famous by Bob Hope from one of his movies *Son of Paleface* and 'My Truly, Truly Fair', a big Guy Mitchell hit record. Oh, how simple pleasures made us happy.

We used to keep the regulatory enamel piss pot under the bed (and I don't mean my father), but my cousins, because of the larger family, went one better and kept a bucket on the landing on top of the stairs, which was used by a lot of people in a night, especially after a heavy night of drinking. Most families lived in the same way. Two or four to a bed was not uncommon, and when I slept in the back room, I would wake up in the middle of the night to the sound of rain, only to see Thomas balancing on top of the window ledge, holding on with one hand and pissing out the window onto the backyard, because the bucket was full up and no one seemed to want to empty it. I know I became quite expert myself at this practice, provided Paddy was not around, as he did not approve of such gymnastic manoeuvres and disgusting behaviour. Having lived in England, Paddy had moved up the social scale.

I started thieving now and again like most other kids did then, and one of the favourite shops was a little shop around the corner from the Treaty Tavern, just across from St Munchin's Chapel. It sold groceries and sweets and small items of clothing. As the owner was in the back of the shop, we would wait until a customer had been in and the owner had gone into the back room after he had served the customer and we would run in, grab the nearest box, hoping it would be food. Once I grabbed a box and ran over the bridge to the Island and when I opened, it to my horror, all it contained was a load of new handkerchiefs, so I threw it over the bridge into the river Shannon and watched it float away into the night. We must have stolen the man's weekly profits that day and all for nothing.

By now I was becoming a bit of a gang leader and I often instigated robberies and small heists. We once scrambled in over a very high wooden gate at the bakery near the Thomond cinema in Mary's Street, and stuffed ourselves with fresh cakes that had been baked only a few hours earlier. I remember holding a huge slab of what was going to be used for making Swiss rolls and trying to get through the whole lot in one sitting. God, it was lovely and fresh, too fresh! Getting back over the gate was not quite as easy, as we were very full up and I know I was feeling very sick and wished I'd never seen and eaten all that cake. The 'big bakery break-in' was soon known all round the Island Field the next day, spread mostly by myself, of course.

Guard White was a white-haired policeman, who we were all terrified of. He came to the Island Field and took me on the crossbar of his bicycle up to the barracks to question me about the robbery, and warned me that I would go to Glin if I carried on blackguarding and robbing, but by now I was on a slippery slope to a life of crime and there would be no going back, at least not voluntarily. Guard White's dire warning went unheeded, but maybe by then circumstances were already beyond my control, and unbeknown to me, my future was already mapped out in a way that I could never have foreseen. Can we ever foresee?

I do remember a woman from the Island Field was murdered over in England around the late forties. She had been a prostitute. News spread very quickly in those times and everyone knew everything about everyone else's business. Neighbours would often pop in to borrow a cup of tea or sugar till next week, and the local shop always gave food on tick because it was the only way families could manage. Most people used Pashey Brown's, the pawn shop up in Irish Town to help make ends meet. To my recollection, although everyone was poor, people seemed just as happy then as they are now. Children were protected from the real worries and hardships that our parents had to endure and just got on with their simple lives.

Excursions used to be arranged out into the country in the summer for groups of children and adults on the back of a big float, pulled by a horse.

We would each pay a couple of coppers for the privilege. I hated missing an excursion. Each person would bring something to cook, like sausages, if you were lucky enough to have them, on an open-air stove, often by a river.

Like most mothers, my mother used to have outdoor cooking in the summer on an old tin bin, with holes in it and filled with sawdust for the fire. The smell of bacon all over the Island would be lovely. My mother often cooked old nettles picked from the garden, which I ate quite heartily and which seemed to do me no harm. At least I was getting my greens and they were free.

It is probably fair to say that when I was growing up in the Island Field almost every family had someone who emigrated to England, and I know in some instances whole families left and never returned again, although there were some people who just did not like England and returned and never went back there again. My cousins, Josie and the youngest, Barney, never could settle there, and Paddy never returned again after he came back to Limerick after the war, so England wasn't everyone's cup of tea. The pace of life in Limerick was slow and peaceful, for most of the time. No one ever seemed to be in a hurry.

A very dear friend of my mother's, Mrs Ryan, who lived opposite my cousins, had a child that had died accidentally, and the funeral was being arranged from the house. For some reason I was not allowed to go, but instead I was locked in the house on my own until they all came home again. I was hysterical and begged and screamed not to be locked in and to let me go with them but my mother would not let me go. I never knew why. I was very frightened and cried for hours and I could not get out. The incident left me feeling my mother did not love me after all. I was devastated and badly affected. I was only around seven years old.

I once was in Barringtons Hospital for a week as result of falling off our veranda, while trying to get out of our upstairs window. I fell quite hard on the concrete backyard and damaged my knee. Phyllis, my sister, somehow found it all very funny and could not stop laughing, but put me on the back of my father's bike and pushed me all the way up to Barringtons, where I remained for a week.

At least I had a room with a view and I could see the Tivoli cinema opposite. I got very jealous watching all the kids going in every night to watch some John Wayne western. It was the longest week of the year, but at least I was well fed for the week. I can still remember it all so clearly. When I eventually stepped out of the bed after a week I fell over and thought I was paralysed. I couldn't walk, but an old man in the next bed reassured me I would be all right in a couple of days.

This was another time when I didn't have my mother's love to make me feel better, because it was an occasion when she was gone from home and no one knew where she was or how to contact her. As a child a mother's love and reassurance is so important to help you cope with life, especially when things go wrong. My mother's absences were becoming much more frequent, as a result of my father's abuse of her, but maybe they were never really in love anyway and maybe she got comfort and love elsewhere.

There was an incident when Phyllis and I were in the kitchen one night. We only had candlelight then. I was asleep on the range with blankets under me because it was lovely and warm and I could just fit on top. Phyllis woke me up with her screams and pointed to the back window. There was a man outside wearing a hat trying to look in and we both screamed as loud as we could, and we were absolutely terrified. Phyllis now thinks it was a boyfriend of my mother's, trying to look in for my mother.

Because of having no electricity for a while, I was often unable to undo the laces on my boots in the dark and I would sometimes go to bed with one boot on, which would not be a problem except I was sleeping in the same bed as Phyllis, but she never complained. She took on the role of a surrogate mother I suppose. She was always good to me, although I did not always show my appreciation.

Boils were a common occurrence, probably because of the poor diet back then. My mother's treatment was to put a poultice on the boil, which was made of very hot mashed bread and sugar, and it seemed to work.

I also remember eating hard candle grease, although not too often. I also remember shopping very late at night, trying to buy a loaf of bread everywhere, often without success, as all the shops had sold out. Times were indeed hard.

7. The End of Family Life

The final disintegration of our family came dramatically and in a most horrendous fashion on a very cold winter's night, when there was a heavy fall of snow on the ground. It was around midnight, about 1948. My father had gone to bed, but Phyllis and I were still up sitting at the table by candlelight, waiting for my mother to come home. She was on the town doing what, I do not know, but my father had left instructions to call him when she came home.

We were waiting in dreaded fear, knowing what was coming. We were very cold and frightened and felt powerless to prevent what we knew was going to be another beating for our mother. I can't even remember if my mother was drunk or not that night, but my recollection was that she was not, as she seemed very quiet when she came home, hoping probably that she could go upstairs to bed and not be seen by my father. She may have been out with another man or maybe just to a dance. What happened that night will haunt and stay with me for ever, because it is etched in my mind and I will never forget it until the day I die.

My mother came in quietly, probably trying not to awaken my father, and we told her what we were told to do. We had to waken my father and tell him that she was home. Why she never left then I don't know, but she did not. Perhaps she had nowhere to go or did not want to abandon us. She went upstairs and put on her night-dress, which was a very flimsy thing with just tiny lace straps over the shoulders. We reluctantly called my father, because we were too scared not to.

He bounded out of the front room bed and immediately started up the stairs where my mother was. Immediately we heard her screaming not to be hit as my father was ranting and raving and calling her 'fucking this and fucking that', and that he was going to kill her. He certainly killed his marriage forever or what was left of it that night and he also broke my mother's spirit. It was to be the final nail in the coffin. He also broke my heart that night and no doubt Phyllis's, and destroyed our home forever and left me hating him even more than before. I loved my mother as much as any child could love their mother and I would never lose my hatred for my father for the rest of my life. What I witnessed that night is very painful to recall and those events would haunt me for the rest of my life.

After the beating, my father dragged my mother down the stairs, covered in blood and looking like a limp, broken doll. She was crying like a baby and she sounded very distressed and she was begging my father, 'Please, Christy, don't hit me any more, I can't stand it, you're killing me. Please don't hit me any more.' Her pleas for help fell on deaf ears as he dragged her to the front door, which he opened and then he dragged her into the dark of the night onto the snow-covered garden with the freezing cold temperatures, bleeding and bruised and wearing only the flimsiest of clothing. He told her not to come back in again and locked the front door, and then told us, 'Don't open that fucking door to your mother, do ye hear me?' We cuddled each other but we never replied, because we were crying so much and too shocked to speak, but we both knew instinctively what we had to do. We decided we would wait for an hour or more until we thought my father was asleep and then let my mother in. It was like an eternity.

Phyllis and I drank tea and cuddled each other as the clock ticked by, wondering if my father was asleep, yet we had to be sure, because if he heard us opening the door he might start all over again on all of us, and my mother could not stand any more punishment, she would surely die. How my father could return to sleep after inflicting such punishment on my mother, his wife, I'll never know. I will never know what his thoughts were or why he gave her such a severe beating.

When we thought it was safe to do so, we went into the front garden to let my mother in. She was lying there, on the freezing cold grass, hardly moving as if she was either dead or asleep. She was helpless and alone and seemingly unable to move, and almost frozen to death. She had no one to help her for an hour or more and with no one coming to her aid. It's impossible to imagine her loneliness and pain. My sister and I felt her pain very much.

God, what a shocking image, even a cat would not deserve such punishment. The degradation that she must have felt, not knowing if she was going to survive the cold winter's night, and we could not give her comfort for at least another hour. 'Will she die before we bring her in? Surely she'll die in the cold, even Jesus and Mary had a stable to sleep in, and hay to keep her warm. She can't die, she's my mother, and she's only small. Oh God, help her.' God rarely comes to your aid when you need Him most. My mind was tortured and going around in circles. A family is supposed to be a happy place to be and why is all this happening to us? Haven't we got enough problems to cope with, without my father doing these horrible things to my mother?

We both lifted my mother's almost frozen body up and helped walk and drag her back into the warm house. She was unable to speak and nothing much was said. She looked like a living corpse, and she was still crying, but more of a whimper, just like a little puppy that has been abused. She tried to speak but she was unable to, due to the terrible cold. I wanted to go in and stab my father to death there and then while he was still asleep, but my mother needed me, she needed both of us, because there was no one else. We were her only lifeline, her only comfort. Her two children were all that stood between her and possible death and her only source of comfort, little though it was.

God, how she must have needed us that night, and I like to think we were a great comfort to her, and I'm glad we were there for her and on her side. It would always be a small source of comfort to me over the years that both my sister and I were able to give my mother some help, when she needed it most. We covered her frail and frozen shoulders with an old jumper and gave her something hot to drink and caressed and comforted her as much as we could. We tried to ease her terrible pain in the only way we could. I was only about eight years old and Phyllis only about thirteen. Is this what family life is about?

While our trauma was going on in 102 St Munchin's Street and most families were fast asleep in their beds, I often wondered over the years how many other families in the Island Field were in a similar situation – none I hoped. When some life eventually returned to my mother's body, she decided that we were all going to leave that night and go to Dublin the next day and stay with her sister for a while. We didn't argue because we knew it was the last straw and something drastic had to be done. It was the end of our family life one way or another.

We gathered some small possessions, basically the clothes we were wearing and left the house with the snow still falling in the dark of the night, with a few street lights to guide us on our weary way. We stayed in Limerick railway station for the remainder of the night until we left for Dublin the next day on the first available train. We must have been a pathetic sight, all three of us walking the mile up to the station in the middle of the night with heavy snow falling. In some ways we must have looked like the Holy Family in Bethlehem 2,000 years previously looking for somewhere to stay the night, but at least they had a donkey for transport and they did find somewhere to sleep eventually. We had neither!

That terrible night, in 1948, was the last night we were all together as a family and it was probably the worst experience of my life and I was still only eight.

8. Out of the Frying Pan

I don't remember much about the long train journey to Dublin, which was over a hundred miles away, but it was going to be a new start, no more beatings for my mother, or for me or my sister, and it seemed to offer great new possibilities for all of us. I remember thinking, 'If I never see my father or Limerick again it won't be too soon.' God how wrong was I to be! The situation in Dublin would be as similar as the situation we had just left in Limerick, but for now I was not to know that and everything seemed different and fresh and most of all we had hope.

The street was called Mount Street, a narrow street with some kind of a commercial building at the far end, with large, wooden gates to keep people out. My mother's sister turned out to be a worse drunkard than my mother, if that was possible, and her husband, a huge red-headed, balding man, who worked for the post office, had a terrible drinking problem, and hated my mother and all of us. He also had a vile temper and quite likely did not like us being a new part of his family.

I was sent to the local school, which was called Westland Row School, and I settled in there without too many problems. My worst problem was being picked on and laughed at because I was from Limerick, and I had a funny accent. Me with a funny accent? I thought that was funny because I couldn't understand a word the local boys were saying, but I gradually got used to this peculiar Dublin accent, which I had never encountered before. I eventually settled down, at least for a while.

The nice thing about the school was that you could buy a lovely halfpenny hot dinner at lunchtime, providing you had a halfpenny, which I did not always have, but at least we usually got a free half pint of milk and I think a piece of Swiss roll during the day, which for me was sheer luxury.

I remember coming home from school one day and being stopped by a load of other boys who lived quite near me. They stood in my pathway and refused to let me by, and despite my pleas to let me go home, they still refused. I was getting annoyed by now and my father's temper came out in me. I reached into my school satchel, which was over my shoulder, and I pulled out my old-fashioned pen with the long handle and the old style long nib and I stuck it into the leader's right arm as hard as I could. He gave out a great sigh of pain, which was a signal for me to hightail it as fast as my little skinny eight-year-old legs would carry me, away from the screams from the bastard who had dared to stop me going where I wanted to go. I could never tolerate being bullied and usually reacted physically to my adversary. I did not look behind to see if I was being chased, but I was running for my life and the old adrenaline was working overtime and no one would have caught me that day. It was nice to be able to run away from people who wished to do me harm. In those days I ran everywhere and it always seemed natural to me.

Sooner or later I expected a pay back, but anyway the bully should have known better than to mess with someone from the Island Field. We were not called 'rogues and robbers' for nothing, even if I was only skin and bone. Dublin kids may have been tough, but so were we from Limerick. My running ability soon took me away from the scene and I did not stop until I got home, and I remained indoors for a couple of days, because I heard there was a contract out on me, and I did not want to die just yet! But perhaps the bully had learned a lesson and, who knows, might have thought twice in the future. He never bothered me again. The incident blew over and maybe the guy thought I was too dangerous to mess around with, but there was another bully who lived in the same street as I did, who I decided to play a game on one day. I sent him a little present, just for a laugh, through someone else of course. I never told my messenger what was in the parcel. It was all neatly wrapped up, but the bully was not too pleased when he opened it up. The little present I carefully wrapped up was a load of old fish heads, and he was out to get me, for taking the piss out of him and making him look stupid. I had to spend another few days indoors until the incident blew over. I obviously was living dangerously, but I often took risks, despite being a stranger in a new town, so to speak. At least the bully slept with the fish that night!

The only real beating I remember having, came, I hate to say, from a girl, who was probably around 13 and much bigger than I was. During an argument she grabbed me by my golden locks, and while my head was down, she proceeded to bash me several times on top of the head with a rock of some kind, leaving me battered, bruised, bleeding and with very low esteem. Imagine being beaten up by a girl! How degrading was that? But I reckon she was nuts anyway, she had to be to behave like that.

I remember we used to dance to a song in groups in the street. The song was 'Lambeth Walk', a very popular English song around that time. Trams were in use in Dublin at that time and I well remember grown-ups lying in the streets protesting and possibly being on strike.

I soon became very aware of the conflict between my mother and her sister's husband, and I'm sure alcohol played a big part, as I remember the

56

husband seemed to be drunk every night, and was always shouting and arguing with my mother, who was also drinking heavily. No doubt he must have naturally resented having to tolerate three other people in the house and it can't have been easy for him, especially as I had to sleep in their bedroom at one point, which was not a pleasant experience for me.

I would be asleep on the floor and they would come in late and drunk, with a lot of screaming and shouting and a lot of verbal abuse and threats to my mother going on and telling her to 'Fuck off back to Limerick with your fucking kids, before I fucking kill you.' They would come into their bedroom with the lights off, jump on the bed and I was aware of lots of grunting and groaning and pushing and shoving and it was not the furniture they were rearranging. I tried to cover my ears to block out what was happening and I found it all very frightening, especially as I was only eight years old.

One night there was an almighty row between my mother and the husband and he told my mother to leave and to take me with her. Phyllis was not here at this time and may have left for England or was perhaps working somewhere else in Dublin. It was in the middle of the night, winter and very cold. We trundled out into the night not knowing where we were going, and marched all around the streets looking for somewhere to lay our heads. I was beginning to realise just how Joseph and Mary must have felt with no room anywhere for us to stay and no money or friends. Everywhere was closed, and we finished up trying to sleep in a telephone box for a few hours, sheltering from the cold winter's night. We stayed there trying to rest as best we could, but it was proving very difficult and impossible to stretch even my little legs, as I spent most of the time on my haunches. We eventually left the safety of the phone box and moved off into the night and tramped the streets again and we finally spent the remainder of the night sitting and lying on a stone staircase at a block of flats, twisting and turning all night, trying to sleep, with great difficulty. I remember being very tired and cold but most of all very, very hungry.

The next morning my mother returned to her sister's flat when she knew that the husband would have left for work, and left me there and went to England and promised to send for me soon, but she never did and I remained there for nearly another year, with no choice in the matter, and not being able to contact either of my parents. I really felt abandoned and forgotten, with virtual strangers who I knew did not like me.

My aunt had a son, Dermott, who had been in 'Artane' Industrial School in Dublin, which was famous at the time all over the world for its famous brass band. He had just been released because he was 16 and he was coming home to live in his mother's house where I was living. We did not get on and he seemed to resent me quite a lot and made my life very difficult. He always seemed to be telling me off, hitting me and complaining about something or other about me, and I had no one to take my side or to complain to.

He was especially unpleasant to me during mealtimes and was constantly criticising my eating habits. I once sneezed during a meal and did not put my hand up to my mouth (not a good idea), and he hit me very forcibly across the head, knocking me off the chair, and then shouted a long tirade of the foulest abuse at me. 'You dirty little fucker, sneezing your snotty nose over my dinner, I can't eat it now. Is that what you are all like in Limerick, sneezing over other people's dinner?' I wanted to say 'Yes', but he was in no mood for clever answers. I certainly deserved to be reprimanded, but not knocked off the chair, and besides, I was not aware that I was supposed to put my hand up to my mouth when I sneezed. I never saw anyone else in Limerick doing that, it was only what posh people did, wasn't it? No doubt he had learned all these new modern ideas and manners in 'Artane'.

'I bet the Christian Brothers made him do that,' I thought to myself. 'You must always put your hand up to your mouth, Dermott, it's polite and it's what polite people do,' I imagined, 'because if you don't do what the Brothers tell you to do they'll beat the shit out of you until you do what you're told.' Oh, God, I had so much to learn but would I live long enough?

Dermott was a nasty piece of work, and used to grill me about sexual matters and kept asking me if I had ever seen a girl's privates, and how many times, and what did it look like and did I enjoy it. Did I ever see my sister's privates and how often? He would beat me until I told him what he wanted to hear. Eventually I would make up stories just to stop getting hit. No doubt it was a form of sexual abuse. I hated him. I now realise that he may well have been sexually abused himself while in Artane.

I started mooching and being difficult and my relatives decided they'd had enough and decided to send me to 'Artane'. It was the most famous or infamous school for wayward boys and delinquents in the whole of Ireland. Me going to Artane, for what? I was not a criminal and I know that my father, for all his faults, would not let me be sent there. He said that I would only go to one of these places 'over my dead body', and he was hopefully still alive, so I thought. I had not heard from him for nearly a year and I did not think that he knew where I was living.

As the days ticked by waiting for the day when I was going to appear in

58

court and be sent down, I was feeling desperate and doomed. The night before my court appearance, I was out playing in the dark street and enjoying what I assumed to be my last days of freedom, as I realised boys who were sent to Artane would be there until they were 16. Imagine that, I would be there for the next eight years and I would surely be an old man of 16 when I came out again! God what a sentence, and how could I survive it? I remember seeing a James Cagney movie when he was sent to prison for life. He nearly went mad and then he eventually broke out. That's what I would do if I went down. I'd organise a mass breakout. I remember how James Cagney did it. Watching all of those movies would not be a waste of time after all!

Then it seemed like a miracle happened. A couple of my friends told me that my father had been around to where I was staying, looking for me. I didn't believe them, how could he? He did not know where I was. I dashed into my aunt's to ask her if it was true and she confirmed that it was, but I still had my doubts until I eventually appeared in court early the next morning and saw my father and my aunt Doris who had come to Dublin with him.

It was one of the highlights of my life. My father had come to the rescue and saved me from hell at the last minute. I could have kissed him, but didn't, because the memory of him beating my mother violently the year before was still very clear in my mind, but I was happy nevertheless. Being rescued by him at the last minute was the lesser of two evils. After the court hearing I was set free, because I had a responsible adult to look after me. Well, if the judge thought that my father was a responsible adult, who was I to argue! We all had a meal in a Dublin restaurant for my first time ever and then we returned to Limerick on the long train journey. I was very excited and I could not wait to see all my old pals again from St Mary's Park and get back to my old school and freedom! But I had changed.

In later years Artane would become notorious for its abuse of boys in their care, but during this period, around 1948/9, it had a reputation for being one of the best boys' brass bands in the world with no hint of any scandal behind closed doors, and it made me realise what a narrow escape I had. I never again saw my mother's sister or her horrible husband or her bad-tempered son, which suited me fine.

9. Back Home Again

It was great being back home in Limerick again, back to where I knew everyone, knew the area, and it was where all my friends were and I was somebody here. I never wanted to leave Limerick again. However, there was one problem that I had brought back with me and that I had not been aware of while living in Dublin. I had acquired a very strong Dublin accent, which was not appreciated in St Mary's Park. 'Sure it's nearly as bad as having an English accent', I was told. I had a bad time for a while being called a 'Dublin Jackeen' and I had the piss taken out of me until I finally lost my posh accent. Of course I was not aware of how differently I spoke. I went back to St Mary's School again but somehow I found it very difficult to settle, and I started mooching more than ever.

Phyllis had returned to Limerick from England due to my mother's frequent bouts of illness, which necessitated her going into hospital and leaving Phyllis alone. My mother had been working in a boy's private Catholic boarding school called Prior Park in Bath, which was in Somerset, England. The job was a live-in post as a cook, and no doubt due to her illness she lost her job and had to leave, and so did Phyllis.

My future wife, Sandra, incidentally, was born in Bath in 1943, so she was about five or six years old when my mother and Phyllis worked and lived there, and it was the closest she ever came to meeting my mother. Now, all these years later this seems an incredible coincidence. Prior Park school is still there and it is still a very exclusive school.

I became disenchanted with school for some reason and I started missing days, thinking no one knew about it, but I had not been as clever as I thought I had! I would go off to school every day and hang around stealing and getting into mischief and then go home at the end of school time as usual. No one had been the wiser, or so I thought.

On this particular day my friend in crime, Andrew Fitz, had brought me home on the back of his bicycle and was waiting outside the door for me to come back out to play cops and robbers again. Well, in our case, we played the robbers for real. I was just going to go in and pretend that I was just home from school and then go back out again – at least that was the plan! I came in as usual and as soon as I walked in the door, Phyllis said to me, 'Dada knows you have not been going to school, and wants to see you as soon as you come in.' I was very nervous and felt frozen to

61

the spot because I guessed what was coming and it wasn't a box of chocolates!

My father was in bed asleep, following his night-shift down at the docks. I asked Phyllis not to wake him up, because, after all, he needed his sleep, didn't he? Due to working all night! But it was no use, the game was up, and I was for the high jump. There was no way out, not this time. I was about to face the music and it wasn't my type of music. I was nervous as hell.

'You dirty little shagger,' my father said, 'haven't I warned you about not going to school? Didn't I tell you what would happen to you? You'll go to Glin and be put away for a long time. Come here till I fucking kill you', he screamed and lunged at me, but I ducked and dived around the kitchen table with Phyllis in the background looking on.

I didn't fancy the thought of being killed just yet, so I circled around the small table, trying to keep out of his reach, and all the time screaming my head off with fright at the prospect of dying at any minute and never seeing my mother again. I'd fake going one way to fool him for a while, and we played cat and mouse, with him screaming blue murder about what he was going to do to me when he caught me. My plan was to dash out the front door, out to freedom, but I realised, as I quickly tried the door, that Phyllis had locked it! At that point my father grabbed me, pulled me against the wall and told me, 'I'm going to fucking strangle you, you little fucker.' He grabbed me by the throat with both hands and lifted me about a foot off the floor. My past short life was already flashing before me – was this the end?

I was about to be strangled to death and being told at the same time that I was a little fucker, not a pleasant way for a ten-year-old to go. I struggled like mad and somehow got away from the grip of the strangler, and again I ran around the table several times with the hope of getting out the front door this time. Because my dad had a bad leg, and being an old man of 48, he could not move as fast as I could. As he chased me around the table shouting abuse and obscenities, I made a final dash for the door and this time I managed to unlock the door and dash out to where my friend Andrew had been waiting with his bike. I jumped on the back of his saddle and he peddled as fast as he could, never looking back until we got to Arthur's Quay nearly a mile away up in the city, where I jumped into one of the small rowing boats and hid under the canvas sheet for hours, hoping my father hadn't followed me on his bike. Every time I heard some noise above me I thought it was my father, but he never came for me, and maybe he'd had enough and did not have any more energy left to cope with my tantrums and wayward ways. I would soon realise why he did not chase me that afternoon.

I had noticed in recent months that he would have to stop to get his breath every few yards and I did not know or understand why. What I did not know then was that his shortness of breath was due to his heart problems. He would be dead in less than a year of heart failure, at the early age of 49. The strangling incident, or why I had not been going to school, was not mentioned again, which suited me fine.

We had a little brown and white terrier dog at one time named Pongo, and like most kids I was mad about animals, and I used to love going for walks with my father along the strand by the river. I used to feel really proud and happy when my father let me hold the lead and walk beside him with Pongo trailing alongside of me. It was nice to be trusted, by Pongo and my father. Leading a dog, I felt, was a responsible job and it made me feel good.

I came home from school one summer's day and discovered Pongo lying all wet and motionless across the front door porch. He was dead! I was heartbroken and tried to wake him up. How could he die just like that? He wasn't sick? I asked my mother but she did not know what had happened, but if she did she wasn't saying. I later heard rumours that my father had thrown Pongo over the bridge into the river to drown him, as was often done in those days with pups and kittens tied in a canvas bag. It was cruel but it was the way it was. My father never said anything about the subject and I believed the rumours and still do. It's heartbreaking now to think a little dog came all the way home to die, back home to those he trusted, but who had let him down and killed him and for what? I'll never know the answers but I have a nice feeling that perhaps he came home to see me for the last time.

My mooching from school became more frequent and brazen, and I remember going to all sorts of places just to kill the time, hiding down by the river, in fear that someone would see me and tell my father. I started robbing more frequently and taking more chances. The conclusion that I eventually came to was that it was less complicated to go to school instead of mooching and then going home at the end of the day, pretending that I was at school, but always worried that I might get found out. I lived in constant fear. I used to like school at one time and never found it too hard and cannot now explain why I stopped going. I always felt miserable and found the day dragging so slowly, and I was always worried about being found out sooner or later. I also missed my friends and hated the isolation and loneliness each day by myself. I hated myself for mooching, but like all bad habits, I was unable to change my bad behaviour, at least voluntarily. Perhaps my unhappy home life and the absence of my mother made me unsettled.

I had been stealing from cars more and more and would take anything that was available, but I never broke into a car, and only stole when the opportunity presented itself, like a window being left open or the door being unlocked. I stole a camera one time, which belonged to an American couple, and I was found out somehow. I was brought to the police station to face them.

They were very friendly to me and treated me like a friend and not a robber from the Island Field who had just stolen their camera from their car. It was quite humbling and sobering and although I don't remember exactly what was said, they told me they were not cross with me and if ever I came to America they would love to see me again and wanted to keep in touch with me if possible. How nice and how American, no wonder I have liked everything American ever since. Their kind gesture impressed me, even at such an early age. The thought of me ever going to America was beyond my wildest dreams. What chance did I have? Unless, of course, I became a filum star one day and called in at the address they left me, which I promptly threw away once out of the police station. God bless them for that kind gesture, which I have never forgotten, but I never stole from another car again. Their sympathetic approach made an impact on me. Even at such an early age I seemed capable of learning from my mistakes, but of course as an unruly and wayward child there were always new mistakes to make along life's difficult path, no matter how good my intentions were!

Time was running out for me, but time was really running out for my father very quickly. It was a sunny March afternoon, crisp but not too cold. I remember my father in the kitchen, sitting in one of the only two chairs we had in the house. We did have a round tree trunk, which was about a foot high, that I used to sit on. His head was hanging low and he did not look well. He did not look up and acknowledge me in any way, as if he did not even see me. He started talking to imaginary people in the corner, and now I realise that he was obviously hallucinating. My aunt Doris was there and so was Phyllis. Doris told me that my father was not well and that they were waiting for the ambulance to come. My father was taken to the City Home hospital, while Phyllis and I stayed at home. I certainly did not realise the seriousness of his situation.

The next morning as I was walking towards the shops in the Island Field with one of my friends, I heard another friend say to another, 'Christy

Donoghue died last night.' The boy that I was with said to me, 'That's your father, Raymond, isn't it?' he said looking at me. 'It can't be my father,' I said , 'sure he only went into hospital last night and people don't die in a night, sure they don't, he can't be dead can he? My aunt would tell me, sure she would.'

I definitely did not believe it. I said to my friend, 'Imagine that, telling someone their father had died when he was only a little bit sick. I've a good mind to fecking hit you, so I have.' I went down to my aunt Doris where I was staying overnight, and told her what I had just heard and asked her was it true.

'Yes, Raymond, he died in the middle of the night,' and that's all she said. There was no need to say any more.

My mother was away and now my father was dead and I was only three months from my eleventh birthday, but I did not feel any great emotional loss or sadness and neither did my sister. All that concerned me was, 'Who is going to look after and feed me now?'

My mother could not be contacted at that time in England, so the funeral was arranged at the New Burial Ground in Limerick. I remember a fairly large crowd being in the funeral parlour with the open coffin, and my father lying there with his hands folded across his chest, looking very peaceful, but how else could he look! I still did not feel any real emotion or sorrow and no tears flowed from my eyes. My uncle Jimmy, my father's brother, went to the coffin and shook my father by the hair and I heard him calling my father's name, 'Christy' and he was crying.

At the graveside, the coffin was lowered down into the deep black hole, and as the coffin reached the bottom, my aunt Doris walked over to the graveside and threw a very small packet wrapped in white linen onto the coffin and then stepped back without saying anything. I later learned that the packet was my father's dentures and that was the end of my father's short life, but the beginning of a very turbulent time ahead for me.

My sister recently talked to me regarding the funeral and how she felt at the time. 'I didn't cry or feel sad, remember? I had a raging toothache at the time.' At least Jimmy, my father's brother, cried for my father. I would never feel sad about my father's early death because of what he did to my mother, neither would I miss him.

Much later, while writing and recounting my father's funeral, I cried for the first time in connection with his death, so maybe for me it was a healing process that I have bottled up and carried with me all my life. When I picture my father now in the kitchen looking lonely and frightened it makes me very sad to think about him. Did I cause him to be like that?

Did I break his spirit and send him to an early grave? He once said to me, 'You'll break my heart, so you will', and he had now died of a heart problem. I now recall very vividly that my father used to talk to himself quite a lot, and wonder if perhaps he may have had some minor mental or some physical problems in his brain?

A few years ago I sent to Limerick for my father's death certificate, and when I saw the cause of death I was shocked! The cause of death was heart failure, as a result of having syphilis. As a psychiatric nurse, when I first became a student, there were some patients who had become mentally ill through contracting a brain disease and they were referred to as GPIs (General Paralysis of the Insane), which occurred because they had contracted syphilis, which if left untreated affected the brain and often led to people getting the above mental illness. Most in those days finished up in long stay psychiatric hospitals, and as far I can recall, it was untreatable once it had taken hold. My father may have been in the early stages, but died of heart failure before developing more serious mental health problems. It was sad to learn.

After my father's funeral, I rode back home to the Island Field, sitting on top of the hearse with the driver, which was pulled by four tall, black, shiny horses with lovely shiny black leather tack and long white plumes protruding from their heads. I felt like John Wayne in my favourite film *Stagecoach*. I wanted all my friends to see me, and wondered if I should be crying or not, so I tried to look sad, but I had no feelings of sadness or great loss at my father's passing.

I moved in with my aunt and she looked after me for now, but I was getting into more trouble with Andrew Fitz, and not going to school. I had no sense of direction, and going to school no longer interested me. One day Andrew's mother, who was exceptionally tall, was at Doris's front door and wanted to see me. She did not look too happy and she came into the kitchen and rushed in screaming and shouting at me and pinned me against the wall.

She grabbed me by the neck and said, 'I'm going to fecking strangle you, you little fecker, you. You're leading my little Andrew astray, so you are, and I want you to stay away from him, so I do, do you hear me, do you? I don't want him to go to Glin, so I don't, and don't come around to our house any more to play with him.'

As I was half choking to death and felt my life ebbing fast, I meekly said, 'Yes, Mrs Fitz.' As my life was in mortal danger I was not going to argue with such a big, strong woman who seemed intent on doing me serious bodily harm. Her lovely little Andrew was nearly two years older than me and here I was being accused of leading him astray and almost getting killed again, by strangulation!

I never understood why so many people wanted to strangle me. Was it just a Limerick trait or what? I was barely eleven years old and already I had been the victim of two strangulation attempts, once by my father and once by a woman who must be surely drunk or something worse, but at least I was still alive although badly shaken. Three of my nine lives had already been used up before I was eleven, which did not bode well for my longevity.

Andrew and I still continued to pal around together despite his mother's dire warning to me, but the law was closing in fast. I was now really getting out of control and becoming too hot even for Doris to handle. I wanted to be the most famous crook in Limerick even at such an early stage. Hollywood would have to wait until I got older, taller, stronger and hopefully better looking!

One day there was a knock at the front door and Doris went to answer it and I heard her call out, 'Raymond, there's someone here to see you.' I hoped it wasn't Andrew's mother again. I did not think that I might survive another strangulation attempt, but worse, it was the guards. Reluctantly I went to the front door, as I didn't feel there was time to run out through the back garden.

There were two big guards outside the door and they politely asked me to come to the police station, I was being arrested so it seemed. But why did they need two big men to arrest me? It was very flattering because they must have perceived me as being dangerous and hard to handle. They walked me to the waiting black police car at the entrance to the house and one opened the door for me to get in, which of course I had no intention of doing if possible. I had seen too many situations in the gangster movies that once you were taken for a ride you may not get out alive again. I knew once inside that was the end. As my brain was ticking, a small crowd had gathered out on the pavement and I overheard the next door neighbour Mary Mannix saying out loud, 'Sure God love him, they're taking him away, so they are.' At the last moment just as the policeman politely held the car door open, and as I was about to step into the back of the car, I quickly sprinted to the left, catching the guards by surprise and I ran up to the shops, down the side, which was semi-detached and over the graveyard wall, which was around six foot tall, into the graveyard and away to freedom, at least for now. I knew the area very well and I had a certain advantage over the police, but no doubt they knew that there was no hiding place for a top criminal like myself.

It was not long before I had to appear in court, along with my accomplice Andrew, and the judge asked my aunt Doris and Jimmy if they were willing to look after me any more and they answered, 'No', a decision that was later to cause a lot of disharmony and bitterness between my mother and Doris, unjustified I now realise. Even though at the time I was a bit annoyed at Doris, I soon realised she had no choice. I was going away to Glin Industrial School after all, despite my father's dire warnings, something I had always dreaded, but somehow I did not feel too concerned as I sincerely believed my mother would have me out when she became aware of what had happened to me and where I was. At least my father's prediction had come true that I would only go to Glin school over his dead body.

Unbeknownst to me, my mother had been in hospital in England, being treated for stomach problems during the time my father had died and I had been sent away to Glin. I was described by the judge as being out of control and I had no grown-ups to take me under their care, which was not surprising considering all the emotional upheaval and financial responsibility and constraints that it would entail.

My mother later told me of the terrible shock that she felt when she was eventually contacted by telegram regarding my father's death and my incarceration in Glin. The telegram to her read, 'Come home. Christy is dead. Raymond in Glin.' Not the best of news to receive while recovering from a major operation, but there it was, stark and true. My mother had been living in Brighton in England at this time.

Meantime after our court appearance, Andrew Fitz and I were taken to Mary's Street barrack police station to await our transport to come from Glin to take us back there. We waited there a few hours and the police who had probably dealt with this situation many times before, from the Island Field and other parts of Limerick, fed us and gave us some jam sandwiches to take with us on our long journey of 32 miles to Glin.

I still did not appreciate or understand the enormity of what was happening, and Andrew and I laughed and joked while waiting patiently for our transport. At least we would go on a nice long journey in a posh car, but with no return ticket! I even had the audacity to steal a fountain pen from the shelf in the police station, while they were out of the room, no wonder I was being sent away. What a nerve!

The Christian Brother who eventually came to take us to Glin was quite old, and he was wearing thick glasses and he had very sparse white hair, with some long bits combed from the side of his ear right to the other side of his head. His hair seemed to be fixed with glue by the looks of it, as it remained motionless, despite the rest of his body moving.

68

He never smiled and he said with great authority, 'Hello, boys, I'm Brother Cullen, come with me.' Brother Cullen! His name spread terror immediately from deep inside my frail body. His name was already familiar all around Limerick from boys who had been to Glin school. Even I had heard tails of what a cruel bastard he was, from boys who had come from Glin on holiday. He would fecking kill you with his big leather strap, if you didn't do as you were told, and if you answered him back he would beat the shit out of you with his fists.

Whether these stories were true or not I did not know. But at this time I believed them. 'Oh brother, now I'm in trouble.' God, I was suddenly beginning to realise that this was serious and the smile and carefree attitude suddenly left me. This surely was the end of my life. I was leaving Limerick, maybe forever, and I might never be free again. I no longer had parents, so who would ever miss me if I died there or was murdered? These were thoughts that went through my fertile childish mind. We often heard tales that some boys went there and were never seen again! It was June 1951, just a few days before my eleventh birthday, and I was going on a journey that would alter my life forever.

10. Glin School

We were guided into the back of Brother Cullen's big black car, but this time there was no way for me to escape into nearby fields, because there was a guard on either side of me and Andrew as they ushered us in and banged the door closed behind us. It was like being thrown into a cell. Was this going to be our last journey into oblivion? We drove the long journey along the coast road, through Foynes town with the river Shannon on our right, and passing little one street towns and places along the way that I never knew existed. Brother Cullen rarely spoke except to point out some of the names of some small town or other. I would later learn that he was a man of few words. A stare and a scowl was how he would let you know what he meant. He would rarely need to use violence, although I did see him lose his cool once or twice. He had an expressive face and, even at my tender age, I soon learned about body language, at least Brother Cullen's! I wondered to myself if he had ever murdered any Limerick boys who had been sent to Glin? I was not prepared to ask him, but he seemed capable of it.

It was almost dark when we arrived at Glin. We were led into the administration block and then we went up to the dormitory, where I would remain for the duration. All the inmates were in bed and the place was in darkness except for the light on the top of the stairs. There was an eerie silence and not a sound or whisper could be heard in the still of the night. The light on the stairs lit up the stone staircase. I noticed the words 'St Kevin's' on a brass plate outside the door. St. Kevin's dormitory was on the top floor, where I would spend the remainder of my incarceration.

As we walked up the stairs, led by Brother Cullen, I noticed there was a pair of black hobnail boots on each step, which for some reason I thought was very funny and I started to laugh to myself and nudged Andrew at the same time. How strange, as I'd never seen anything like that before. You couldn't leave your boots like that in the Island Field because someone would rob them in a minute, so they would, and I thought everyone here was a robber. So there must be some kind of honour amongst thieves!

There were three rows of beds in the dormitory, with a row by each wall and one down the centre. There were around 30 beds in each dormitory. I was allocated a bed against the wall where I would remain. The fellow in the middle row of beds started to talk to me and I discovered he was from

Limerick, Ballinacurra Weston. His name was Eamonn Fitz, and he was to remain one of my best friends during my time there.

Eamonn was always telling jokes and always kept me and everyone else amused. He was around two years older than I was and he was a real hard case, and best of all we became good pals. He had a younger brother, Gerard, who often got into fights, but he was okay and he later boxed for the school and did all right. Eamonn could look after himself and no one bothered him, nor me, because he was my pal, so it was a good start in some ways, to have my very own minder on the first day. Eamonn will never know how much easier he made my time in Glin, and how much he meant to me. I admired and looked up to him with great respect.

I met Eamonn a few times in the nineties in Limerick and had some brief conversations with him. I told him that I still had enormous respect for him and genuinely felt I owed him a great deal of gratitude, and his reply was, 'What ju want me to do, kiss you?' And he was still telling jokes: 'Did you hear about the two blokes who stole a calendar and the judge gave them six months each.' I thought that it was funny that Eamonn still made me laugh over 40 years since I first met him in Glin. In fact he had far more effect on my personality than even I realised, because I have spent all my life telling jokes and trying to make others laugh, but I could never be as good as Eamonn.

A psychologist I once worked with told me, after I told her some jokes, that I must have suffered a lot as a child. I asked her why she thought that. She told me people who have suffered a lot in their childhood often use humour to hide their pain and suffering. I half-heartedly disagreed with her but knew she was right. I had been found out and my cover was blown. I was exposed, despite telling jokes. No doubt my friend Eamonn was probably telling jokes for the same reason, to cover up some unresolved pain and hurt, as we all probably were.

Many of the 200 other boys in Glin often laughed and joked at that time. We were all away from home in a strange place and worst of all we were away from our mothers' caring caresses and love, as had been the hundreds of boys who had gone through there in the last 30 or 40 years. We rarely talked about our feelings and our terrible sadness. It was difficult at our age to express our true feelings and we were all in the same situation anyway, so there was no point complaining.

Glin had in fact originally been a poorhouse for the local people back in 1860 or somewhere around that period and had nuns and girls in it, but it was taken over by the Christian Brothers around 1926. It was then turned into an Industrial School until it was eventually closed in 1967. God what a sad thought all us boys suffering, for all those years, keeping it bottled up inside with no one to talk to and no one really knowing how much we were hurting except ourselves. There was no doubt that for most of us in Glin life would never be the same, and we would all be scarred by our experiences there. I realise that Eamonn certainly did ease my pain and probably a lot of the other kids while we were in Glin. He was good at making kids laugh.

Recent (1998) scientific research has proven that a lack of fun in children can have serious social consequences as they grow into adults, and that laughter and play are crucial to the development of the brain. Eamonn Fitz knew this long before these scientists, way back in 1950.

I had a very restless night with all sorts of things going through my mind, but I still did not realise the enormity of the situation that I was now in. The next morning I awoke early and got up to go to the lavatory with my bare arse showing and I heard Eamonn say to me, 'Raymond, you can't do that here.'

'Do what?' I asked.

'You can't run around with your arse hanging out, the brothers will kill you, so they will.'

I soon learned that although I could run around the Island Field riverbank and flash to the girls as naked as the day I was born, this was Glin and such sexual behaviour would not be tolerated. I would be causing temptation to the other boys, wouldn't I? Would I really? God I hardly knew what the word temptation meant and how could I be causing temptation to other boys? What did that mean? It's only girls who get tempted by boys isn't it? In many ways the age of my innocence was over and sexual connotations came into play, although I still did not fully understand what all the fuss was about. One day I could run around naked in Limerick and the next day I could not.

We had to get up around 7 a.m., to go to the lavabo' (or the sink, as we called it in Limerick), wash in cold water, whatever the weather, and then be inspected by the Christian Brother, who would be standing at the exit, just to make sure we had washed. You would stick out your hands for him to look at and turn them upside down several times until the brother was satisfied and then he would inspect behind your ears, and let you out if he was satisfied. He would regularly make boys go back if he was not satisfied. It was my first taste of strict discipline and camp life and I did not like it. What else was around the corner? I was soon to find out.

Now the really big shock came, instead of going to breakfast we were marched to the chapel to hear mass. 'Can you believe it, mass in the middle of the week! Jasus, sure no one goes to mass in the middle of the week, sure they don't, this is terrible.' What I soon realised was that we would have to go to mass every morning from now on unless the local priest was sick, which was very rare. The priest was always available for mass despite all our prayers for him to drop dead, or to get pneumonia or something worse.

On the odd occasion when the priest was unavailable, the church bell would ring, which we could hear in the dormitory, indicating the mass was cancelled. The 'hurrahs' would resound all around the dormitory and in all the dormitories in the school for what seemed like an eternity. When the church bell rang it was as if someone had said, 'The war is over boys.' What a relief, no mass today, another half an hour in bed, how wonderful.

It is difficult to convey the real sense of relief and excitement that we all felt at not having to go to another boring mass, especially when it meant that we had to get up earlier and wait a bit longer for our meagre breakfast, especially on a very cold winter's morning. I never did understand why we needed so much mass and prayers, especially as we were all innocent boys anyway and most of us would not have committed a mortal sin at such tender years.

An even bigger shock was awaiting when Eamonn told me that we also had the rosary every evening, which lasted over half an hour, and that was rarely cancelled because it was one of the brothers who took charge of it, and there were eleven brothers in the school! 'Jasus, they're trying to make me into a saint, so they are, and I have only been here half a day! God, I don't need to be this holy, no one needs to be this holy. I'm going to go mad with all this praying, I don't want to be a Holy Joe.' When we had religious education in Limerick, we were always being told that all children were innocent and were like saints already and that God loved us all, so if that was the case why did we need mass and rosary every day?

After the first morning's mass, we marched in an orderly fashion to the large dining hall that looked like something out of Oliver Twist, except worse. It had about 24 large wooden tables with long movable benches, and there were about 12 boys to each table, with a chair at the head of the table where the monitor or boy in charge sat. He was in charge of organising his table and had a bit more choice of the food, as he helped serve it before we were allowed into the hall.

I sat down and Brother Cullen, who was sitting like a king on a very tall throne in the centre of the top of the hall, overseeing his kingdom, suddenly shouted at me at the top of his voice, 'Get up will you. Wait until I tell you to sit down.' He seemed to be asking and telling me at the same time. I wondered what I had done wrong now? I soon learned. I also realised that I was the only boy who had sat down, the others no doubt had already been indoctrinated and house-trained to the brothers' satisfaction, and were awaiting instructions regarding the next move.

There were more prayers, grace before meals? I felt that I was on the way to becoming a saint, so I was. 'All this praying, sure it can't be good for me, sure it can't' I thought to myself. I then heard Brother Cullen say, 'For what we are about to receive, amen,' which, looking at the plate, was not a lot, but maybe this was only the first course! I hoped so, but I was wrong! Breakfast was what was on the plate, two very thin slices of bread and a small piece of margarine, which would hardly cover half a slice. As I took the piece of margarine with my knife, I heard an older boy with a rough country accent shout at me, 'Put that fucking back, that's for four of us.' I wasn't about to argue because the guy looked like a huge ugly gorilla, but not as pretty. He looked as if he could break my frail little body in half. He was much older than me and twice as big, and already looked like a grown man. He terrified me with his menacing appearance and I knew that his intentions were not necessarily loving towards me. There was a pecking order, according to age and size, and I was very small and barely eleven, so I would have to adapt and use my Limerick City intelligence and streetwise experience to somehow get by for now.

I soon realised that not everyone in Glin was from Limerick City, although most were from the surrounding areas outside of Limerick. There were boys from all around the county of Limerick, from places I never even heard of like Kilrush, Ennis, Ballylongford, Nenagh, real country people I'd never met before. They were boys I had nothing in common with, real wild fellows with red faces and unruly hair that would have looked better on a goat. They also had big hands and snotty noses, and they would belt you for nothing, and you couldn't understand what they were saying half the time. They did not seem to like city boys and saw us as softies, which we were compared to them, but I soon realised that Limerick boys stuck together and we felt superior to our country colleagues and that we could always get one over on them. Brains would always beat brawn in the end, at least that is what I told myself.

When I came to drink my tea I spat it out because I thought it had poison in it! I realised there was no sugar in it. How could anyone drink tea without sugar, it's going to poison me! I didn't drink it, nor did I eat the bread, instead I had some of the jam sandwiches the guards had given me in Limerick, so I ate a couple of them. You rarely got more than one cup of tea at any meal, and there was no menu to choose from. You ate what was given to you or you starved, and even if you did eat what was given to you, you still starved!

One country boy asked me how old I was and when I told him nearly eleven, he said, "You have five years to do then, you'll be here till you're sixteen.'

'No I won't,' I said cockily, 'my mother will be taking me out in a couple of weeks when she comes home from England, sure she will.'

'Oh yeah, they all say that,' he said, wiping his snotty nose on the end of a rough jacket sleeve.

'Of course she will,' I said, 'just wait and see.'

This guy was an ejut and was beginning to annoy me and starting to put doubts in my head. He seemed to get pleasure in telling me that I would have to serve my time just like everyone, but I thought differently. 'But what if he's right? God, I couldn't stay here for another five years could I, could I?' I put the idea out of my head, it was too horrifying to even think about. I know my mother, she loves me and wouldn't leave me here, she'll come and take me back to England and then I can get into filums and become a filum star and meet John Wayne and all the other famous filum stars and be famous all over Ireland, and everyone will look up to me. What do these country bumpkins know anyway! I bet they don't even know who John Wayne is. All they know about is milking cows and digging ditches. I'll show them and then they will realise how important I am.

Brother Cullen told us to stand up when breakfast was over, and would you believe it? More prayers. Grace before meals and now grace after meals, but I'd hardly eaten anything!

'This is getting too much and the sooner I get home back to Limerick the better. All this praying can't be good for me, it's enough to turn me into a Protestant, so it is.' But I kept these thoughts to myself for now. I had not been here a day and already I was getting some serious foreboding about my future.

'What if my mother does not come for me? I can't stay here for another five years. I would surely go mad!' I quickly put those horrible thoughts out of my mind. My mother would not let me down. If she says she will take me home, she will. The only trouble was that I did not even know if she knew where I was. I was just guessing to myself that she would never leave me in this God forsaken place in the middle of nowhere, and she would come as soon as she found out. She was the only one who could rescue me now and I just had to hope and trust in her. My confidence in leaving was still high, although I was already feeling out of place. For the first time in my life I felt like a prisoner. My freedom had been taken away.

We had a couple of hours before Andrew Fitzgerald and I were taken up to the classroom to be assessed to see how bright we were. A giant of a teacher, with short, grey, wiry hair, which was in a severe crew cut, named Brother Murphy, said hello to us. If his severe haircut was meant to intimidate us, it was effective, but he put me at ease by his apparent friendly manner and his big smile – that's what I remember most about him, his big, wide smile. My first impressions were right as I later discovered he was a friendly brother, but you couldn't mess with him and I don't remember anyone ever backchatting him. He seemed to be built like Tarzan with a big barrel chest and square shoulders. He was kind but firm and well liked by all the boys.

He asked us a few simple arithmetic sums, and he asked Andrew what 2×8 were. Without hesitating, Andrew replied, 'Aisheen (18)'.

Brother Murphy then said, 'Eighteen what?' (He spoke posher than Andrew.)

Andrew said again, 'Aisheen.'

Brother Murphy said, 'Eighteen, sir.'

Ah, I quickly realised that he wanted to be called 'sir', no doubt to assert his dominance and to let us know just who was boss, as if we needed reminding!

He then asked Andrew another mathematical sum. 'What are two elevens, Andrew?'

Quick as a flash Andrew said, 'Twenty-aish (28), sir.' Andrew was getting the hang of addressing Brother Murphy as he wished to be addressed, even though his sums were not good, but at least he got the 'sir' right. One out of two wasn't bad at such an early hour. Andrew was always smiling and happy and maybe it is what I liked about him. Nothing seemed to faze him and I looked up to him.

Brother Murphy then asked me some sums and although I had done better than Andrew, I heard him say to one of the other boys, 'Take them both down to the first class.'

I was flabbergasted. I was in fourth class in Limerick and although I had missed a lot of schooling since my father died three months earlier, surely I shouldn't be going to first class, that's a baby's class, and I felt humiliated. I could imagine Andrew going there, because he had got all his answers wrong, so why was I going to the same place? I was bemused and I felt dejected.

As we were led into the first class I thought that we were in the wrong room, because I saw all these big boys, and they all looked around 14 or 15, and they were all much bigger than I was. I soon learned that they were all a lot older than me, and obviously a bit dumb, so I thought, and I proved to be right. 'Probably all country bums and farmers,' I thought to myself.

I don't recall a lot about my first few days at school, but I remember we had a break around 11.30 in the morning for a cup of sugarless cocoa and a small currant bun, and we had dinner around one o'clock. Dinner, now that was a misuse of the word and would never have passed the Trade Descriptions Act if there had been one in 1951. There were potatoes, which were fairly black, and some gristly looking meat with a little bit of lean hanging on it. It was basically an attempt at making some kind of a stew, and that was the type of dinner we would have most days. We sat down to meals feeling hungry, but it was rare to leave the table feeling full up.

During the dinner break we played in the large exposed playground, which had one big high wall. Part of this high wall had a large section of fine mesh wire, through which we could look out and see the river Shannon in the distance, and on a cold day, which seemed to be most days, the strong wind would blow through and freeze you to death. In the winter the cold was hardly bearable, so we always ran around and kept moving. There was little else to do.

On my first day, as I gazed towards the river Shannon through the mesh wire and out into what seemed like an alien landscape, I pined for Limerick, my mother and my boyhood friends and I wondered if I would ever leave this place alive. Negative thoughts went through my mind and my confidence was slowly ebbing away. I had not been here even 24 hours! Already it seemed like the longest day of my life, but I kept my thoughts to myself.

The cold wind from the Shannon must have been affecting my brain already, as I took out the remainder of my stale jam sandwiches and threw them over the wall. I was immediately reprimanded by a country yokel, asking me why I had thrown the sandwiches away. 'Because they are stale,' I said.

'You won't be saying that in a few days' time,' he told me.

Although he put nagging doubts in my mind I ignored him, but he would prove to be right, because a couple of days later I'd be starving like everyone else, with a hunger that was constant. 'I won't be here in a few days,' I thought to myself. I went to the lavatory in the playground, and when I came out, one of the Christian Brothers was waiting for me, looking very serious.

'Where have you been?' he asked me.

Inwardly I thought, 'What a stupid fecking question, where does he think I've been? Woolworths, shopping, sir,' I felt like saying, but I somehow knew that he would not appreciate my Limerick humour and maybe he would not appreciate any humour! I soon became an expert at reading body language and facial expressions, especially from the brothers who had a bad reputation for not taking any backchat. I had to learn quickly or go under.

'To the toilet,' I answered.

'To the what?' he said.

'God, he's fecking deaf as well as fecking stupid,' I thought. 'To the toilet, sir.' At least he didn't ask me what I had been doing!

'Do you know you must get permission before you go to the lavatory?'

'No, sir,' I replied.

'We'll let you off this time,' he told me.

'Jasus, now you have to get permission before you go for a fecking piss, so you have. He must be fecking mad, sure he must, and what does he mean? "We'll let you off this time?"' I soon learned that if you did not ask permission to go to the bog, you might get a serious hiding. This was all getting too much for me and I had not even been here a full day yet. Time was also dragging and I hoped that my mother would come for me in a few days. I knew that I could not last long in this shit hole. I was already cold, hungry, fed up and longing to go home. It was already becoming the longest and most miserable day of my short life. Maybe her letters have gone astray or maybe no one has told her where I am. We had rosary that evening in the chapel within the school, which was not much fun, and then we had a lousy supper, which was identical to the breakfast, only worse. It generally consisted of two very thin, ropey slices of bread, and I'm sure bits of rope were used to add flavour and fill us up, which it never did.

A couple of weeks passed and still no news from my mother, and I was beginning to think that maybe I might have to stay here until I was 16. The thought was more than I could bear. I had my eleventh birthday within a couple of weeks of being there, but it went unnoticed as most of my birthdays would. Every boy's birthday went unnoticed. No birthday cakes or special treats for us. No one to sing or to wish us a happy birthday. It was as if nobody cared and I do not suppose that anyone did. For most of us, our birthdays were just another day that came and went. For the rest of my life birthdays would never really matter, at least not to me. For the first couple of weeks there, we occasionally had porridge, but that stopped, thank goodness. It was vile and I had been told that quite often 'creepy-crawley' things could be seen moving about as you ate it. The thought of it made me shiver.

Climbing into bed was a hazardous affair and took great skill, which took some time to perfect. We were each given what was called a wrap, which was a cut down woolly sheet type of thing, which was meant to protect our modesty as we got into bed, while you slowly took off your trousers, just like being on the beach. Mind you, occasionally I would dispense with the wrap and take my chances, and became quite nifty at jumping into bed without even exposing a bare knee. I just could not bother with all the nonsense of wrapping a wrap around me, unless of course a brother was present, as it seemed to bother them more than it did us boys. I never knew or understood what all the fuss was about, especially in a dormitory full of very young, innocent boys.

I remember on my first night there Eamonn told me about our morning keep fit routine just before we went into school. There was a real old brother called Brother Kelly, who was in his late sixties or maybe in his seventies, who took the keep fit classes out in the open playground. 'Exercise to me is no problem,' I told Eamonn.

'He's a cruel bastard, if you don't touch your toes, he'll beat you on the arse with a thick black thorn stick,' he replied.

'Jasus, sure I can't touch my knees, not to mind my fecking toes, he'll kill me then, so he will.' That was all that I needed to hear just before I went to sleep, but sleep didn't come easy. I was feeling homesick already and I wanted my mother like any eleven-year-old would, and I tried to put any doubts out of my mind that I would soon be going home.

Every morning on the playground there would be an inspection and God help you if you were not wearing the right shoes or socks. After the inspection was over we had to participate in physical jerks in the open air with the infamous Brother Kelly, a man feared by everyone. Two hundred boys could be seen in the large playground doing all sorts of stretching and jumping up and down. It must have resembled a POW camp in one of those war movies.

When it came to touching our toes, you could hear the odd scream of some unfortunate boy who, because he was unable to touch his toes without bending his knees, was given a slap on the arse with a piece of stick by Brother Kelly. As far as I remember, the stick did not induce any extra flexibility from the boy concerned. I tried like mad to touch my toes without success. It was a contortion that I had never attempted before, and what was the point of it anyway? There was never a great need for these kind of gymnastics in Limerick. Running fast and being able to fight were far more important.

As Brother Kelly moved along the rows of boys, my heart quickened. I did not relish the thought of being whipped on the arse by a stranger, just because I was unable to touch my toes. 'What kind of a sadist is this man?' I wondered to myself. As he got nearer me, he suddenly blew his whistle and shouted, 'Dismissed.' What a relief! I was saved from a possible thrashing at the last minute. I did develop my own technique of appearing as if I was touching my toes, but luckily for me these morning exercise routines stopped a few weeks after I got there, either because Brother Kelly died or was moved or maybe he just retired. It was my first piece of good luck and most of us boys sighed with relief. As Eamonn later said, 'At least that's one bastard gone, ten more to go!' Eamonn had a way with words.

One of my cousins was at Glin when I was there, and some of the Dalys from next door were also there, as were a few others, so I at least had some point of contact and did not feel totally isolated. Older boys, around 14, who had already finished their schooling had a choice of either working in the tailor's shop, the cobbler's shop, or on the farm, which were all on the school premises. I was advised not to volunteer to work on the farm. None of the Limerick boys volunteered for the farm, firstly because it was too hard for us city boys, but most of all because Brother McGrath, who was in charge, was a right nasty bastard who would beat the shit out of you for no reason at all, so he would. He looked a bit like Himmler, the top ranking Nazi in the Second World War. He was a small, scraggy looking man, and wore Himmler-style spectacles to hide his small pig-like eyes. He had a small mouth with thin lips and I never saw him smile. However, we all had to do some time on the farm in the summer. The farm, which was run by the brothers was quite big and it had its own herd of Friesian cows, its own plough horses, pigs and some chickens and while not self-sufficient, it supplied a certain amount of its own food for the school, although I do not remember getting any of the home-produced food. The bread came from Limerick and the stuff with bits of rope and twine in it came from a fairly local bakery in Rathkeale. When I later went into psychiatric nursing, I met someone called Tony Quinn, who came from Rathkeale, and would you believe it, he used to help deliver the bread to Glin all those years previously. I forgot to ask him what the bread was made from, but it was probably a secret recipe, which hopefully died with the owner!

At the end of school hours we would all go for an hour or so to one of the above occupations. I chose the tailor's department, only because I had heard that the tailor in charge was a local layman and everyone seemed to like him. The guy who was in charge of the cobbler's department was also a layman, but he was a cruel bastard and loved hitting boys across the head for no reason at all. He had balding ginger hair and the worst country accent that I ever heard. He might as well have been Russian, because I could not understand a word that he said, and he always seemed to be in a bad mood, as if he did not like his job or the delinquents that were under his care. There seemed to be more bastards in Glin school than in the whole of Limerick.

In contrast, the guy in charge of the tailor's department was a real nice gentle man and he rarely hit anyone. Better still, he would often share some of his sandwiches with us, which was a bonus. Most of the boys' clothes that we wore were made in the tailor's shop as were the brothers' cassocks. Before I left I could virtually make a whole suit under supervision, and later in life those tailoring skills helped me become fairly famous. One of the nice things about the tailor's department was that it looked out into open fields where we could observe all types of birds, especially plovers. I regularly day-dreamed, looking out of the window, wishing that I was somewhere else, which would be a recurring theme throughout my life.

All the brothers used to keep an 18 inch long, half-inch thick, 2 inch wide, black leather strap down inside their deep cassock pocket, which they always seemed to have in their possession, ready to belt someone with. This was no doubt to show their authority and to keep us bad boys under their control. It certainly worked, for most of the time. I suppose it was cheaper than keeping a gun, and shooting us with bullets, and it cost nothing to use and never wore out. A very clever invention, I now realise. I often wondered why the brothers needed to carry such an instrument of torture with them all the time.

11. The Great Escape

There was no wall to keep us in and it was easy enough to run away if you chose to. Sometimes you would wake up in the morning and someone would shout excitedly, that someone had escaped during the night. Some boys would manage to stay away for a few days, but were always caught and brought back by the guards sooner or later. For running away the standard punishment was a beating and your head shaved to the bone, which marked out the escapee and shamed him for all to see, and as a warning to others. A shaven head was seen as worse punishment than the beating. It was a humiliating experience to see. Boys would cry for days afterwards because of how they felt, yet to us other boys they were like heroes. They had tried to defy authority despite the risk involved and it was always a great talking point for days afterwards.

I had been there a only a few days when I became sick and finished up in the infirmary sick bay for a few days. It was either the flu or a touch of pneumonia. A memory that still stays with me is that while lying sick in bed I heard the voice of some other boy who was on the upstairs sick bay, singing, 'If I were a blackbird, I'd whistle and sing', a song made famous by the great Irish tenor Josef Locke around that time. It was a beautiful clear voice and in perfect tune. I listened attentively while he sang the whole song. His voice resonated around the normally quiet building. He sounded just like I thought an angel might sound. I never did discover who he was, because I hardly knew any of the other boys just yet.

While I was in bed feeling weak and sorry for myself and with plenty of time to think, I suddenly felt the urge to go home back to Limerick. In other words I wanted to escape. I'd had enough and I wanted to break out, and I never gave much thought to the consequences, because I knew that I would not get caught. There was very little supervision in the infirmary, so one day, full of confidence, I slipped quietly away, out through the ground floor window, wearing only pyjamas and no shoes. I was not very discreet or wearing any disguise, like they did in those Hollywood war movies. I looked just like a prisoner in my uniform of striped pyjamas and I would have been easy to spot by the locals. I did not go down through Glin town, but instead I headed over a small country wall near the end of the school drive and cut across country and down onto the Foyne's Road which ran along by the river Shannon. It was a straight and easy road to follow into

Limerick. The only trouble was that it was 32 miles to Limerick City and although I was a fast little runner I never gave the distance much thought. Every time I saw a car coming I would dive into the fields because I feared that every car that came along would be looking for me.

I had gone nearly a couple of miles, and I was feeling very tired and very hungry, and still feeling a bit sick and weak due to being ill, when it suddenly dawned on me that I had another 30 miles to go before I reached Limerick. 'Jasus,' I thought, 'I'll never get there and what's the point? Who am I going to? No one wants me, and besides, it's nearly tea time back at the school and if I get back quickly maybe no one will have missed me!'

I doubt if my eleven-year-old legs would have made it into Limerick, in fact I know they wouldn't, but at least I had to try, so I decided to return to the school and hope that I had not been missed. When I reached the school drive, the bread man was walking up the school drive at the same time and advised me to walk on the opposite side of his cart and sneak back into the infirmary unnoticed, which I hastily did and got back into my bed through the still open window. I couldn't believe my luck, I had escaped from Glin and no one knew! I felt great.

Shortly after I was back in bed one of the older brothers came and asked me how I was feeling. 'Very well, sir,' I said politely and with my innocent smile. 'And did you enjoy your little trip?' he said with his sweet, innocent smile. I could feel myself getting bright red, but I couldn't talk with fear. He just walked away and that was the end of it. I was lucky and got off lightly. Maybe it was because I was new and on the sick list or maybe because that particular brother was kind, as some were. I learned a lesson and never ran away again. I made my mind up there and then that from now on it was in my best interest to co-operate and do as I was told. It was a wise decision for an eleven-year-old, because I felt that it would make my life in Glin a lot easier for the few weeks until my mother came to take me home, which it did.

12. Life at Glin

Boys at Glin who had parents or relatives could go home for a month's holiday, every July, if they were willing to have them home. Some kids never ever had a holiday away from Glin for one reason or another, and I dread to think how they were affected as a result, and some kids were in there from as young as five years old. This meant that some boys were there for ten or eleven years without a holiday!

I never understood the logic of having eleven Christian Brothers looking after 200 boys with no female input. Some brothers were only 18 years old and had very little, if no training in child care or understanding of child psychology. It really baffled me and I was only eleven years old, but it was 1951 and I suppose that some of the brothers at least did their best. After all, it could not have been very easy looking after other people's problem children and cast-offs, for that's what a lot of us were. Rejected by our families, and given to someone else to correct and rehabilitate, and to take responsibility for. How could they possibly know how to handle such very young and very disturbed children at that? It must have been a depressing job and I now often wonder how they felt and how difficult they found it. Some coped better than others.

It is also not very surprising that years later most children in care, myself included, would suffer badly from low self-esteem. We already knew or felt that our families did not approve or value us, otherwise why would we be sent away? The brothers did not seem to trust or like us or indeed spend any individual time with us, and it always seemed that they were against us and conspired to make our lives as difficult as possible, by not giving us enough food and always making us unhappy. They also seemed very quick to give out severe punishment for what seemed trivial reasons. Neither could the brothers show us love or compassion. It was a sterile environment and not a family. There was no one to turn to if you were sick or hurt or to console and cuddle you. Many of the brothers seemed unable to show any real warmth or emotion towards us, at least not openly or that we were aware of. The brothers were certainly very quick at handing out punishment, but they were not all monsters by any means. Generally I got on quite well with most of them, but I also had a few unpleasant experiences, like most boys did, but that was a long way down the line.

We had the occasional film show, mostly on saint's days and Holy days, although very few days would feel holy to me. The film show was stopped many times to change reels, but that didn't matter, because it was like being at the Thomond cinema. Of course there was no pissing on the floor here, like in the Thomond. No, sir, and neither was there throwing apple cores at the screen. If we were ever too noisy during the film show, Brother Cullen would threaten us with the words, 'I'll stop the show boys, now if you all don't keep quiet, do you all hear?' 'Yes, Brother Cullen,' we would say meekly while giggling to each other, because we wanted to know if John Wayne survived being shot by the Indian attack on screen. Yes, Brother Cullen knew where to hurt us all right. I never remember seeing Brother Cullen smile, cry or show any emotion, except scowl a lot.

It was coming up to July 1951, and holiday time for those lucky kids who could go home, and there was great excitement and anticipation in the air, although not from me. I was still here, over a month by now, and I still had not heard from my mother yet. I was getting very worried and what was even more worrying was being told by the other boys that because I had been here only about a month, I would not be allowed to go home even if my mother wanted me to. I wondered out loud, 'I have to go home, I can't stay here while all my friends go home to Limerick. I'll go fecking mad. My mother won't let me down.'

Boys who were going on holiday were told as soon as they were invited home by their parents, and each boy was usually given a new set of clothes the night before. On the day before the holiday I still had not heard from my mother and I was feeling very rejected and at the lowest point in my life, and if I had known how to commit suicide I may well have done it. 'How could my mother leave me here, it's not fair, I trusted her and now she's let me down again.'

I cried a lot that day and as I was in the dormitory that evening, getting ready to go to bed, a boy came and told me, 'Brother Cullen, wants to see you, Raymond.' I felt like saying to him to go and tell Brother Cullen to 'feck off and leave me alone. I don't want to see anyone.' Reluctantly I went to see Brother Cullen with my head hanging low and trying to hold back the tears of disappointment I was feeling, because I would not be going home tomorrow. 'I bet he's going to tell me off or something, because that's all they ever do,' I thought as I made my way down to Brother Cullen's office. Never a man to beat around the bush, he said bluntly, 'Cheer up, Raymond, I want you to go to the tailor's shop right now and get some new clothes, you're going home tomorrow. Your mother's home from England and she phoned. She's in Limerick and she wants to take you home.'

I could have kissed Brother Cullen, ugly as he was, but I resisted the temptation. He made me very happy, to say the least. That moment of good news would rank as one of the high points of my life and a moment that I would never forget. My mother had come to my rescue and maybe she would take me home forever. Needless to say none of us boys slept much that night. We talked all night about our excitement at going home in the morning.

As the bus pulled away from Glin the next morning on the way to Limerick we waved to the boys left behind and we did not give a lot of thought to how they felt. I had nearly been left behind and realised how lucky I was. The boys must have felt sad at not going to see their mother, brothers and sisters, but I never gave them much thought at the time. How could I? I was only eleven years old and I was so excited I could not think of anyone else's misfortune.

As we approached Limerick it is hard to describe the excitement and sheer joy to be going back home. I could not wait to see my mother again. It had probably been a year or more since I last saw her and that is a long time when you are only eleven years old, and as fond of your mother as I was. The coach pulled into Limerick railway station where we would be met by our relatives, and we were all anxiously looking out of the window, with some kids spotting their mothers before the bus stopped. We all tried to get off the bus at the same time, only to be reminded by Brother Cullen to, 'Mind what you're doing boys, will you, and let's have some order.'

Boys ran excitedly to their mothers and hugged and kissed them, but I couldn't see my mother yet. Where was she? More anxious moments went by and still no sign of my mother. 'What if she does not come, will I have to go back to Glin again?' I wondered to myself. My anxiety was mounting and tears were about to fall. I had been there nearly an hour and all the other boys had gone home. I was about to despair, when I heard my mother's voice in the distance coming from the Railway Tavern pub across the road, and she was drunk! It was often the case with my mother that I would hear her before I saw her, but nevertheless, God was I glad to see her, but a bit disappointed that she was drunk, and I hated it. I felt ashamed and let down.

After hugs, kisses and tears she led me over to the Railway Tavern, which was not where I wanted to go. I just wanted to go home and not to a pub where everyone seemed to be drunk. We spent a couple of hours there, my mother getting more drunk, and more tearful and nostalgic about the past, which was upsetting for me and not what I wanted or expected. My excitement at being home in Limerick was fading fast. Glin suddenly did not seem so bad after all. I began to resent my mother and her drunken behaviour and felt that the bond between us was probably broken for ever because of her continuous and prolonged absences away from me. Her behaviour was very upsetting for me, and I felt that she was like a stranger to me and no longer the loving mother that I missed and longed for so much. It was not a nice feeling, but that's the way I felt, seeing my mother drunk and acting so stupid. I felt so unhappy and badly let down. I could not understand why she needed to get drunk. I was only eleven and I was unable to comprehend the need for alcohol. I did not realise then that my mother was probably already an alcoholic and she was just 32 years old.

My mother, who was by now stone drunk, eventually took me to my aunt Doris, because that's where I would be staying for the holiday. I wanted to run away, but where to? My mother also promised me that she could take me out of Glin, but not just yet. She told me that I would have to return to Glin after the holiday and if I still did not like it I was to tell her by letter, when she returned to England. I told her I couldn't say that in a letter because all our letters were censored before they were posted, so I came up with a code, which would let her know I was not happy and then she should take me out.

The code was that I would ask her, 'How is Spot?', the dog, and she would know what I meant. Most of my letters over the years to her contained some reference to Spot, the fictitious dog. Brother Cullen, who usually read all of our letters before they were posted must have thought I was obsessed with Spot, because he often asked me how my dog was? I was only grateful that Spot lived so long. On arrival at Doris's house my mother was truly pissed and in a very bad mood, because she could never hold her drink and was always abusive when she had too much.

She abused Doris at the front door. Doris was a very quiet woman, and I personally never saw her drunk although she liked a drink, but in moderation, a word that my mother never understood when it came to alcohol. She accused Doris of sending me away to Glin. Doris took it all with great dignity and invited my mother in to the house and she told her, 'Not to be making a holy show of yourself in the street, and in front of Raymond.' My mother's drunken behaviour was persistent and embarrassing, and it was a regular occurrence during the holiday. It was very unfair to Doris, who, after all, was letting me stay in her home for the four weeks. I was very unhappy whenever my mother turned up at Doris's house, and I could not wait to go back to Glin, despite all its hardships, just to be away from the drinking and the constant arguments and embarrassment due to my mother's drunkenness and outrageous behaviour. Oh, how I hated the drinking, and it would get worse as the years went by, driving me at times to despair. I developed an aversion to alcohol at an early age that would never leave me, and in many ways would make me seem at odds with everyone else around me.

During the holiday, my mother regularly turned up at the house after midnight, drunk and disorderly, shouting abuse and obscenities for everyone to hear. Paddy, one of Doris's sons usually dealt with the situation, and got quite cross and went out to the street when he found that talking to my mother from the upstairs window did not work. 'Why don't you piss off home for yourself and fecking leave us alone to go to fecking sleep. We have to get up in the fecking morning, so we have.' My mother was not put off that easily and continued with a tirade of abuse, and her language was not as polite as Paddy's.

'I want my fucking son, and I'm coming to get him. Raymond, come out to your mother, I don't want you in there with those fucking McAvoys.' (She often referred to Doris's maiden name when she was being abusive.) God, I was feeling very embarrassed and ashamed and I would not go out because I knew it would only prolong the situation and the noisy argument, which was by now waking up the nearby neighbours. I just wished she would go away. She was not behaving like a mother should.

Paddy came out again, now with his patience running thin, and who could blame him? 'Look, Birdie, Raymond is all right, so go on fecking home will you, for God's sake. Go on home to your fecking bed now, ju hear me?'

My mother would eventually go, after what seemed like hours. It was a nightmare, and I often wondered why I did not have a normal mother, like Doris. I also got the feeling that I might have to spend the next five years in Glin. I certainly did not want to be with my mother. I was too young to ask why she drank so much, but it would be many years before I could gain some understanding of why she drank. Even though I did not like my mother's behaviour, I always loved her very deeply, and I know that she idolised me, but she was unable to show it in a normal way.

After my month's holiday in Limerick I returned to Glin and settled down. There was hay to be collected, which I had never done before. Collecting hay could be exciting at times as we were out in the fresh air and we had some carefree fun, but the trouble was that all this open air activity gave you a terrible appetite, and we never got any extra food to compensate for all this extra work. Although the work may have been therapeutic, it seemed as if we were doing men's work for nothing and we had no choice in the matter.

We occasionally had to weed the furrows on the farm in the fields, often for days at a time, and oh how I hated it. Jasus, they were at least a mile long and very wide, and seemed to go on and on for ever and ever. My back was constantly aching and many a time I thought I would die on the spot, if not from the pain and overwork, then surely from starvation or thirst. It was the middle of summer, around August. You had to half sit on the dirty furrows and move the cheeks of your arse from one side to another, otherwise everything would go to sleep and you might never be able to move again for the rest of your life. I did not want to finish up being a cripple at such an early age!

Once, one of the boys caught a field mouse and brought it back to St Kevin's dormitory, with a lot of encouragement from me, and then let it go. Some time later there were a load of mice running around; it had been pregnant and soon there were a lot of other little feckers running all round St Kevin's. The brother got fairly mad and somehow found out the boy who did it and gave him a severe beating with the leather, about 12 slaps on the hands. I was a witness to it like all the other boys were, and I was sweating in case I would be implicated in the dastardly deed. Jasus, I couldn't stand a beating like that, because I was much smaller than my friend.

The brother then asked who the other boy was who was involved. At first I kept quiet, hoping there might be someone else besides me involved. As no one else owned up I did something very stupid and I owned up. God, all this praying is turning me into a fecking saint already, and I've been here only a couple of months. But there was a method to my madness. It occurred to me very quickly that maybe the brother already knew who the other culprit was and maybe he was just waiting to see if the boy in question would own up. My hunch paid off. The brother did know it was me and commended me for my honesty, but nevertheless still gave me four slaps of the leather, and although it hurt it was not as bad as getting 12, so I was learning fast; honesty could pay off, so long as you were not honest too often!

What made me laugh a lot and still does to this day is that there were some boys who were absolutely terrified of the leather and would pull away their hand at the last minute, and it did not please the brothers one little bit, especially when they hit their own leg!

There was one particular boy who would always do it, no matter what threats were made to him. He would hold his hand out, and as the leather came down he would pull it away at the last minute. In frustration, the teacher would threaten him with all sorts of things and start all over again, but on each occasion the boy would hold his hand closer to his body to avoid getting hit. I do remember many a brother hitting his own leg due to the boy pulling away at the last minute. Now that was funny!

By now the brother would be furious, and the rest of us in the class would be desperately trying not to let the brother see us laughing. God, it was funny to watch, and often the boy in question was so terrified that he'd already had enough punishment. But in frustration the brother would swing the boy around and hit him as hard as he could on the arse several times, but even that was not easy for the brother to do. The boy would now start running around in circles, trying to get away from the brother, all the while screaming at the top of his voice, 'Please, sir, don't hit me any more, I'll be good from now on and I won't do it any more, honest, sir, I won't, so I won't.' The brother by now would be in a fit of rage and was not about to let the boy off scot-free, and be made to look stupid in front of the whole class. His efforts to land a few blows on the boy's arse would continue until he scored a hit that would satisfy the brother and, I suppose, give him a feeling of superiority.

These little situations helped to make life a little more bearable, and I suppose it might compare, in some small way, to men being prisoners of war, because we were in prison, and in constant battle with the brothers, trying to outwit them whenever we could. We had a brother named D from the north of Ireland who had a good sense of humour, but only if he was telling the jokes! He was quite a good-looking man despite wearing spectacles and he kept reminding and telling us how the American actor Alan Ladd looked like him, Well I suppose they both had the same colour hair, but I don't recall Alan Ladd ever wearing glasses!

Once he was showing us how to write a letter up on the blackboard and started by writing, 'Dear so and so', which we all thought was hilarious. Brother D was not amused. As we were all laughing in unison, a brave or stupid boy shouted out, 'Knock knock, who's there? A baldy man with a head of hair!' This joke made us all laugh even more. Our laughing muscles were now warmed up and we were in the mood for a good laugh, which had originated with brother D's initial comment on the blackboard. By now the brother's sense of humour had deserted him and he was not amused, so he wasn't. Jasus he went mad and pulled out the boy from his seat and gave him a terrible hiding, which seemed totally out of order. It brought our moment of happiness to an abrupt end. Suddenly there was a

91

deathly silence in the classroom. The brother's reaction seemed totally out of place and his behaviour was very extreme.

There was another boy in my class who had the most appalling stammer and he could hardly put two words together. It was a terrible affliction. Well this same brother had a bizarre idea of how to cure the boy's stammer, and if it had worked he would have made a fortune marketing the cure. He would get the nervous boy up in front of the class, to make him practise this new technique, which was enough to make an already nervous boy even more nervous.

The brother would clear some space, and give the poor fella a skipping rope. He would ask the boy a question, but tell him to answer it only after he started skipping, and not before. 'What are four elevens, John? Now away you go.'

After a couple of attempts John would start skipping and try to answer the question. 'Fo, Fo, Fo, Fo, Four ti, ti, ti, times el, el, el, el, eleven, is fo, fo, fo, fo. I do, do, do, do, do, do, do, don't know, si, si, sir.' I think having to concentrate on the skipping didn't help the boy's arithmetic very much. This would go on for quite a while, and needless to say the boy never answered the question, at least not while skipping anyway. It now seems like a humiliating experience, although it did not stop the rest of us from laughing behind our hands. Boys can be cruel and we often got pleasure at watching some other boy being humiliated.

There was another experience which was funny, and it was during one winter, with the snow on the ground. We started throwing snowballs like boys do and one hit one of the older white-haired brothers on the head. Not a terrible thing to do normally, except the boy, Jimmy Welsh, from the Island Field, who threw the snowball, had put a potato inside it to make it travel further, and it hit the brother right on the back of the head, which did not please the brother one little bit. So it was the strap for Jimmy and maybe deservedly on that occasion.

During our playtime, especially if it was wet, the brothers would open up the main hall to let us sit in it for shelter. The brother who had been hit on the head with the snowball, used to organise little quizzes, and ask questions like, 'Who was the President of the United States?' Either myself or one of the other Limerick boys would immediately shout out, 'John Wayne, sir', knowing full well, of course, that it was not the right answer, and it usually got a big laugh from a captive audience. Because that particular brother was not very familiar with film stars we were just having a laugh at his expense, to cheer us up on a dreary day.

The brother, being none the wiser, would commend us on our efforts, and ask us to try again. On another occasion I shouted, 'Is it James Cagney, sir?'

'No, Raymond, try again.'

As the boys were in with the joke and in fits of laughter by now, I struck home quick as a flash, 'Then it must be Alan Ladd, sir, isn't it?' As many of us were from Limerick , the brother probably assumed that we were a little bit on the slow side and that we were doing our best.

Mealtimes could be a laugh now and again, especially the supper around five o'clock, which would be the last food of the day. (No cups of hot cocoa or a kiss goodnight for us at bedtime.) Brother Cullen, who seemed to have his finger in everything, was generally in charge of the dining hall and he sat in what could only be described as a huge wooden throne in the centre of the floor, at the top of the hall. The huge chair had two or three steps on it, and he would go up, turn around and sit down, facing us all. We dared not sit down until we were told and until he was ready. Sometimes he seemed to keep us waiting for ages and he would wait until we were orderly and quiet. Holy Jasus, we'd be starving and dying to get at the two lousy slices of horrible bread, and you could feel the tension amongst the boys. Sometimes one boy would sit down, in anticipation of the command to do so, only to be told, 'Get up, will you, Hogan, and wait until I tell you to sit down.'

Despite the dire warnings from Brother Cullen, some boys would have eaten their two slices of bread before we actually sat down, as it only took a few quick bites and it was gone in a flash. We were always ravenous and never got enough of anything. Occasionally there would be some spare slices of bread, which would be put in a large wooden tray and placed on a long table next to Brother Cullen, but just outside his field of vision, or so we thought! When everyone had finished eating, he would call out, 'Monitors', which was a signal for those in charge of each able to go up and get another slice of bread, but this had to be done in a very orderly fashion, meaning no kicking of the table accidentally as you got up, which was not an easy thing to do when you were starving hungry and not knowing just how many slices of bread were left in the tray, because it varied every time. The monitors tended to be more organised than the rest of us riff-raff, and generally proceeded in an orderly manner, although I did eventually become a monitor myself before I left Glin.

The boys would have to go up towards the brother to his right, go round him, and turn left where the tray was and take one slice, then return to their seats. Generally this would go okay especially if the brother was not paying attention to what was going on behind him. Naturally all the rest of

93

us would be transfixed, ready to be called up in case there was some bread left. You had to be fast, because it was first come first served.

As the monitors went around the table, frequently one boy would decide, at the last minute, to pretend to walk away, but then put his hand back in and take another slice, all the time keeping his eye on the brother. I saw one boy do this three times without being caught. We would look on and admire the nerve of the boy, while Brother Cullen was apparently unaware of the barefaced robbery going on behind him. Often, though, the brother would see what was going on and as the boy was walking to his table, would shout out, 'Put all that bread back will you, Murphy.' The boy got nothing, except claps on the back from his fellow boys. Brother Cullen would then shout out, 'Number seven', or whatever number table, and there would be a great noise and kicking of tables, all desperate to get one of the remaining slices of bread. 'Back will you, and let's have some order,' he would shout, and invite another table up instead. This could go on for ages, due to the lack of discipline and desperation. It was sad to be part of it. It did bring some light-hearted relief, although it did not disguise the fact that we still left the table as hungry as when we first sat down.

We never had a meal, meagre though it always was, without first saying the compulsory prayer. What I remember most were the words, 'For what we are about to receive!' Even the good Lord must have thought these words funny and if He had a sense of humour, which I somehow doubted, I could imagine Him chuckling to Himself up in the great beyond. For what we were about to receive would not have fed an anorexic mouse on a diet, but nevertheless we still had to go through the charade.

Some boys were too hungry to wait for the prayer to end, and often the meal was gone before the prayer ended. I am sure that the Lord would have understood our temptation and automatic reaction to gobbling down our helping of food. I remember in the Bible where Jesus went for 40 days and nights without food, but he was not a growing boy and it was voluntary on His part!

The monitors and their sub-monitors would go in at dinner time to serve the food about 15 minutes before the rest of the boys. I know when I was monitor this was a good time as you got perks. That is, you would give yourself a bigger helping and often stick a few potatoes into your pocket. Mind you, some boys got a little greedy and piled up their own plates so much that the brother would notice and either give it to the boy next to him or take it away all together. Discipline was very strict, and boys very rarely backchatted the brothers, as the consequences could result in a severe punching and the leather, although I myself did backchat on a couple of

94

occasions when I was nearly 16. I remember one boy, during the hay-making time, got a severe beating with a blackthorn stick. He was beaten so badly that the boy was black and blue and the stick had actually broken.

During mealtimes, any letters that had come for us would be given out. Brother Cullen would call out your name if you had a letter and you would go up to collect it. The letters would always be opened and censored if the brother thought it necessary. I was very fortunate and probably received more letters, money and parcels than most of the boys. My mother sent me stuff almost monthly from England, and the parcels would be mostly full of sweets. She would send me money as well. If it was a letter only, I would eagerly look on the front of the envelope to see what number was written on it, as the brother would write the amount of money you had been sent in big letters on the outside. My mother regularly sent me either one or two pounds without fail, which was a lot of money in 1951–56. The money could then be spent in the sweet shop at certain times.

The excitement and the difference those parcels made to me is almost impossible to describe and I don't know if I ever told my mother what they meant to me. It made an unbearable situation just about bearable. I do know there were a lot of boys there who never got anything from anyone, during all their years there, and it is horrendous to even think about it. They must have felt so forgotten, so bitter and so very lonely. How my mother, despite her chaotic lifestyle managed to keep in touch with me, is amazing. My love for her was always great and unconditional, which made her absence that much harder to bear. I pined for her every day and I sometimes wondered if I would ever see her again. I became quite popular because of my parcels, as I would share some of my sweets with my best pals.

13. Christmas Time at Glin

Christmas time was especially hard, although the brothers made a special effort for us. Thinking back, it certainly can't have been very easy for them either, being away from their families and having to look after a load of very ungrateful delinquents. I often wondered what they really thought about the situation. For me, Christmas at Glin was the best day of the year and a memory I cherish, and I can't say that about any other Christmas in Limerick. I have very little recollection of anything memorable happening to me during Christmas in the Island Field with my family, except for one Christmas when I was in the City Home hospital being treated for pneumonia, for a week. I remember my mother bringing me a leg of chicken, some toys and a little cowboy outfit that looked like leopard skin, with a little gun holster and a silver 45 gun, and a cowboy hat. I loved it and couldn't wait to put it on, and I strolled around the ward, ready to face the 'injuns'. The nurses, of course, made a big fuss of me, as I was so cute!

Christmas at Glin was very exciting, firstly as we were allowed to choose something to the value of ten shillings, which was a lot of money in those days, and quite generous. Secondly, we had what was called a scoff, meaning we got loads of sweets, cakes and biscuits, lemonade and plenty to drink. I know that I nearly always chose a mouth organ, because my mother had taught me to play some years before, and I would be asked to play a few tunes in front of all the other boys. I suppose it was a way of getting some attention, and even at an early age, I seemed to like to show off.

We would also have extra film shows at Christmas time and there was nothing like a good film to make you forget your troubles and for a while forget you were in Glin. Westerns were always my favourite, as they were for most of the boys in those days, and you could really lose yourself for a couple of hours. Pure escapism, and it was very uplifting and helped to make us happy and to forget where we were.

Good old Brother Cullen was in charge of choosing and showing the films, and I soon found myself, along with a couple of other Limerick boys, acting as consultants, and we were often asked to choose some films, because Brother Cullen knew that, as we came from Limerick, with all its cinemas, we were quite knowledgeable. It certainly made me feel a little more important and gave me a little extra status, and I did not mind doing a bit of grovelling if it made life easier and meant I could see the films I liked. It helped me to build up a lot of knowledge and interest in movies at a very early age, which continued for the rest of my life.

During my time at Glin I had a fairly good relationship with most of the brothers and I tended to avoid those who had a bad reputation. Brother Gill was one of my favourites and probably the youngest. He was only 18 when he first came to Glin, almost a child himself, in many ways, and hardly equipped to cope with disadvantaged boys, such as we were, but he managed to cope and seemed to have a genuine caring attitude.

He was very tall, around six feet, and very athletic, with short red hair, and he wore glasses. He was a great runner and was great at hurling and football, and would join in the games with us down the fields. He was a great role model and someone I wanted to be like. Later in my life, around 21, when I became passionate about running, I often wondered if I would have beaten him? Oh well, we'll never know now. At the time none of the boys could match him, but then we were only half his age.

One thing Glin did for me was to give me a great passion for sport and keeping fit, which I have done all my life, and in a strange way, I owe my whole lifestyle and virtually all I have achieved, even down to my wife and two children, to my passion for sport and running in particular. But that's jumping ahead of myself and would be almost 20 years down the line.

There was one very kind act that Brother Gill did for me, which I will always remember. Glin school used to put on shows for the local town people and the surrounding areas, and quite a lot of people used to come along. We put on plays and concerts, where we sang, did Irish dancing and played music with our little band of fiddles and other light instruments. During the interval we would sell raffle tickets.

I was one of the ticket sellers on one occasion, a trustee, so to speak, and I collected quite a bit of money and decided to keep a little for myself, a sort of percentage, as any normal Limerick City boy would do. I handed the money over to Brother Gill, who was the organiser, and that was that, because there was no way he could know who collected what, and he would not know if money was short or not.

The next day, however, I got a twinge of conscience and decided to give the money back to another teacher, as Brother Gill was not around. Being surrounded by all these holy brothers and hearing mass and rosary every day was playing havoc with my inner self and making me start to go straight. I knew that if I carried on getting twinges of conscience, I might finish up as a saint! St Raymond had a nice ring to it! The brother thanked me and didn't belt me, and said he would tell Brother Gill.

I had a day of anxiety, wondering what Brother Gill would say or do, and then another boy, late in the afternoon, told me that Brother Gill wanted to see me up in his room. 'This is it,' I thought, 'Judgement Day is here.' I knocked on his office door and he told me to come in. With sweaty hands I eventually turned the doorknob, and saw Brother Gill sitting in the corner of his room by the window, with just about enough light coming in to see him. 'Jasus,' I thought, 'What's he going to do to me, strangle me in the dark, so that there are no witnesses. I'm a gonner for sure.' He beckoned me over and told me there was something for me on the table, which was all wrapped up in brown paper. I reckoned a guillotine or something was going to chop my hand off or something worse as I reached for the bag, but no, it was a box of chocolates. 'Maybe it's a trick or something,' I wondered to myself.

'Do you know what they are for?' he said in a quiet voice.

'No, sir,' I said.

'They are for being honest,' he said.

'Thank you, sir,' I answered and picked up the chocolates and walked sheepishly out, in total astonishment and with enormous relief. I had learned another valuable lesson, which was that honesty might well be the best policy, if used cautiously, intelligently and sparingly, of course. I also learned not to make a habit of it. At least it worked this time. Brother Gill's attitude towards me would certainly influence my life in later years. Although I liked Brother Gill, it was partly for self-preservation, because although he was on the whole kind, he seemed like a brother not to backchat or to get on the wrong side of. He had what I could only describe as a reluctant smile. Maybe the brothers did not always show their true selves or maybe they did not know how?

14. Adapting and Making Friends

One of the weekly routines that we all hated was the compulsory Sunday walk. Jasus, we all hated it. It was almost worse than trying to learn the Gaelic language, which was another pet hate. I never could learn, and wondered why we were always wasting so much time trying to get the hang of it. It might just as well have been Dutch. None of us boys had any interest in learning it. Maybe it was the way it was taught or the environment was not right, or maybe I just was not bright enough to take it in.

Anyway, back to the Sunday walk, which started off about ten in the morning, and you were only excused if you were fortunate enough to have died during the night, but even I could not fake that. It was surprising how many kids suddenly developed stomach aches on a Sunday morning, or a bad toothache. I was once excused due to a genuine ankle sprain, which was worth the pain that I had to endure.

These walks nearly always turned left out of the school gate and meandered down through Glin town, which still looks the same today as it did that first Sunday morning in 1951. We walked along the coast road towards Tarbert town, never going quite that far, but we walked an awful long way, probably around five or six miles in all. Six miles may not seem a long way but when you are only eleven, with skinny legs and starving hungry, you can see why we hated it so much. Because the walks were compulsory made them all the more frustrating. However, I do not remember anyone ever dying on the enforced march, but many of us felt as though we might.

We marched two or three abreast, 200 of us going through the town, kept in order by one or two brothers. I don't think anyone ever ran away from these walks. We would usually stop for a rest and to empty our bladders before going back, absolutely shattered and even hungrier than ever, and not even a decent meal to look forward to. I now had some understanding of what some of these prisoners of war felt on their marches. Nevertheless we laughed and joked our way through the walk to pass the time. During some of our pit stops we would go into deserted old houses to steal anything that might be worth stealing. I constantly asked myself why my mother had not taken me out of this prison-like institution, but my hopes were fading.

101

One day while we were all playing in the playground, I saw two new boys who had just come to Glin, standing by the hall wall, looking lost on their own. I went up to speak to them and found out that their names were John and Jimmy, two brothers from Tipperary. I immediately became friends, and our friendship continued long after our departure from Glin. John was nearly a year older than me, while Jimmy was a year or so younger. Our friendship continued in England and we all eventually worked for the same Tarmacking firm William F. Rees, for a few years. We also lived together in Brighton for a while, following our departure from Glin. John and Jimmy were orphans, but at least they had each other. I would later learn that in some Industrial Schools some boys who were sent there at different times did not even know that their own sibling was in the same school! Another boy had told me that he was never told when his mother had died!

We all joined the boxing club in the school, but I was there purely for the training and trips to other towns with the boxing team when tournaments took place. As part of the boxing team we got some extra provisions. Because I was still hoping to get into the movies one day, I had to protect my good looks, just in case the lucky break came and I was called to stand in for Alan Ladd! I had to dream, didn't I? John and his brother proved to be very good boxers, and John fought for the All Ireland schoolboy championships, probably around the six stone mark, up in Dublin, and only lost out in the final. I was more disappointed than he was, as I thought no one would beat him.

John's brother Jimmy was almost as good in my opinion, though Jimmy always said that John was the better. They were also very good hurlers. Coming from Tipperary I suppose they had a lot to live up to. Glin, around 1951–56, had a very good boxing team and competed against other counties. We were respected a lot, as we had quite a few other boys also competing for the All Ireland championships, including my old pal Andrew Fitz. There was no doubt about it, Jimmy and John helped put Glin on the boxing map and it was a great boost for the school and our morale, because we saw them as our heroes and we looked up to them a lot. They were both extremely modest and rarely spoke about their boxing prowess in later years. John and Jimmy's cousin was also in Glin and he was an incredibly gifted athlete, probably one of the best all rounders in the school, and the best looking, though to be fair my own looks hadn't quite developed yet!

The boxing club, if I remember, was started by our own Alan Ladd look-alike, Brother D, who had great enthusiasm and gave us a lot of encouragement. But as he was not very athletic, it was the more athletic Brother Gill who used to take us out running, which could be hazardous at times. We used to run around the hilly country lanes in the Glin area, in the pitch dark, often backwards! Luckily there were very few cars around then, although a herd of cows would sometimes block our pathway. This was useful training and it was great practice for running away from an opponent who was about to do you damage!

At one time Brother Gill introduced voluntary cross-country racing over the back of the farm, and although they were enjoyed very much by the boys, they had to be stopped due to the fact that some boys just kept on running and forgot to come back to the start, at least not until a few days later! And then they were assisted by the police!

Brother D was very artistic and was great at drawing. He taught some of us how to draw, unfortunately I was not one of them, as I could hardly draw a straight line. I had to wait nearly another 40 years before my artistic talents came to the fore. People used to come to put on shows for us, and once we had a show, called 'Yankee Doodle Dandy', which was also the title of one of James Cagney's most famous films. What I remember most was that there was a very young girl singer in the show called Ruby Murray, who only a few years later was topping the charts in England, her most famous hit being, 'Softly, Softly'. At one time she would have about four records in the top ten at the same time, which I doubt has ever been equalled, but back at Glin she was an unknown.

After school hours we would spend a couple of hours at our trade of choice. In the tailor's shop there was a fairly large raised wooden platform where we would all sit, as tailors do, in a sort of lotus position, with one leg crossed over the other to facilitate using a needle and thread, without stooping down too much. The whole area was strewn with old clothes belonging to the boys, and we would repair them as best we could. All school clothes, except the boots, belonged to a pool of clothes, so there were no personalised clothes for anyone, just like a prison or an mental institution.

Attached to the tailor's shop was a place where we would make and stuff mattresses. There used to be lots of fights between the boys, with guys falling all over the torn clothes during the fight, especially when the tailor had gone out for a while. I can't remember what the fights were about, but I remember Paddy O'Donoghue, who lived next door to my cousins in the Island Field, being involved in a terrific punch up one day. It was a vicious fight, which Paddy won. Paddy was also in the boxing team and was good at fighting. He was almost fearless; he was not afraid of anyone, regardless of their size, and he had a fairly quick temper, but he was also very artistic and good at drawing and painting. Country boys rarely got the better of the Limerick boys, because although they may have been physically stronger, the Limerick City boys were more cunning and usually quick with their fists, no doubt partly due to watching all those movies.

Paddy's brother Willie was also a very good boxer. Another brother, Jamsey, who was also in Glin, was a terrific hurler and someone I admired an awful lot. Three from the same family in Glin, and all because they would not go to school! While writing this section I was able to contact Jamsey, now living near the Elephant and Castle, in London. He told me he used to pretend to go to school, but instead hid up a tree outside the house and waited for his father to go to work, then came back into the house and went back to bed again. Jamsey said he hated going to St Mary's school in Limerick, the same school I went to. There were about nine or ten in their family, and he told me that he thinks his mother, who was called May, had about 22 children but a lot of them died. Jamsey's impression of Glin was that, 'It didn't do me or any of my brothers any harm.'

Jamsey also spoke very highly of Brother Gill and said that on the day he was leaving Glin, while he was walking down the avenue away from the school, Brother Gill called after him and gave him a hurley and told him, 'You can use this when you play for Limerick.' Now that was a nice gesture and goes to show how good a hurler Jamsey really was and the faith that Brother Gill had in him. Jamsey told me that one of the jobs he got when he left school was working for the nuns in Kilkenny in Ireland, looking after very young orphans, helping to wash and dress them, but he left because the nuns were very cruel to the little boys. It made me wonder how my own mother might have been treated while in care.

Working in the tailor's shop was enjoyable, because it was nice and warm in the winter, sitting on all those old clothes, and we always had a bit of a laugh. The tailor, a local man, was a very nice bloke, and hardly ever hit anyone, and seemed more normal. I'll never forget something he said: 'You can always tell the biggest idiot in a group of people; he's the one who talks the most.' If it's true, then I must be more stupid than I realise!

Daily life in Glin was very boring for most of the time, and one day seemed the same as the next. Time seemed to drag terribly, except when we had an event on, like a film show or a boxing outing. Winters were very hard and very cold, as the wind seemed to be always blowing up towards us from the Shannon, because we were very exposed on a hill. We only

104

had short trousers, at least I did in my early years there, and a shirt, jumper and a little short coat. We were never allowed to wear any more than that, no matter how cold it got, so we had to keep moving and run around as much as we could to keep warm. We were not allowed to go into the hall for shelter, no matter how cold it was until the brother in charge decided it was cold enough and opened the hall for us. It was okay for the brothers because they had long trousers and a long black habit to wear, and they always had the best of food to eat. I often wonder what their conscience felt like as they sat down for their tasty, plentiful meals, knowing all the boys in their care were continually hungry.

There was an effort to improve the food after I had been there for a couple of years, and they employed chefs from the local area, who gave us a little more sugar in our tea. One boy who wanted to ingratiate himself with the brothers, complained to a brother that there was too much sugar in the tea! Can you believe it! Needless to say, that boy was nearly assassinated later on by a crowd of us Limerick boys, so he was. He never complained again, that's for sure. We nicknamed him 'The Squealer' after a gangster movie we had seen.

Summers were the most enjoyable because we would be playing down the field, either football or hurling, and sometimes the brothers would organise games between us, which would be very competitive. I remember my old pal Andrew shouted at one of the boys to, 'Pass me the fucking ball', which the brother heard. 'Now,' I thought, 'Andrew is going to get a hiding.' The brother in charge called to Andrew and beckoned with his finger to come to him, while the game was temporarily stopped. 'What did you say?' he said to Andrew. Sheepishly Andrew said, 'I said "pass the football will you".' I don't think the brother believed Andrew because he slapped him around the face. We all got a great laugh out of Andrew, swearing in front of the brother, and wondered what all the fuss was about, as Limerick boys, especially from the Island Field, swore all the time. It was never done in a malicious or nasty way, it was just part of the daily vocabulary and culture and was often used in normal conversation without the user even being aware of it.

One of the brothers organised a game of hide and seek, except he got one of the boys who was seeking the others to wear a blindfold to make it a little bit more difficult. We all ran off to hide, but unfortunately the boy wearing the blindfold walked into the pebble-dashed wall around the field perimeter and sustained some nasty bruises, which we all thought was hilarious. The game was called to an immediate halt and never played again with a blindfold on.

15. Lonely Nights

For the first year or so we did not have any radio in the dormitory, but that came later. Nights were the hardest to bear and it was the time I would start thinking of home as I lay there, often unable to sleep. The first few nights were not too bad because it all seemed just like a holiday that I knew would end as soon as my mother came to take me back to England. But I remember getting very lonely one night and I started to cry under the bedclothes, hoping that no one else would hear me because I did not want anyone to think I was a sissy. I was missing home and wondering why my mother was not taking me home when I heard Eamonn's reassuring voice in the darkness saying, 'Are you lonesome tonight, Raymond?' Eamonn was always reassuring, and he made me feel better, talking to me for a while. He seemed to have taken me under his wing and was in many ways my Guardian Angel, like a big protective brother to me. I liked and admired him a lot, and being from Limerick, we had a lot in common. I often wondered who listened to Eamonn's problems? He certainly had a very caring nature towards me.

The lights were put out by the watchman around nine or ten and there was supposed to be no talking after that, at least not officially, but we laughed and giggled in the dark as little boys do. We had to be careful because sometimes the night watchman would sneak in to try and catch us talking and give you a right hiding if he caught you.

He was a big man, (isn't every man big when you're only eleven?) with a very straight posture, and he always wore a Humphrey Bogart-type raincoat with the collar standing up. He also had a stiff leg, which may have been artificial, which accounted for the stiff walk. He was also very strong because he would occasionally demonstrate to us when we saw him during the day. He could lift a square 56 lb weight, which had a hook on the top, with his little finger, which seemed impossible when you were only a puny eleven-year-old. No one ever backchatted him. This amazing feat of strength fascinated me for years after and I was determined to see if I could do it myself one day, and I did, once I got into physical fitness and weight training later on in my twenties, so maybe he was not that strong after all!

Before I had gone to Glin I had been suffering badly from nightmares, no doubt as a result of my disturbed family environment, and probably due to the horror stories we were told in the Island Field about the banshee. The nightmares consisted of being crushed from above by a huge stone and not being able to breathe. I would wake up in a sweat and panic, and in the dark room I would wonder if the banshee was coming for me. I would hide under the clothes as best I could, because I felt a little safer there, waiting for something terrible to pull the bed clothes off and take me away. Having no lights in our house was no help because in the darkness everything was more frightening. These nightmares would remain with me all my life.

At Glin I had nightmares most nights, but I had no mother to put her arms around me to reassure me and tell me I would be all right. There must have been a lot of boys in St Kevin's with similar problems, and how could the brothers know how bad we felt? Men are men and do not have the same sensitivities that women have. Oh, God, how nice it would have been to have had a woman in our midst to show us some compassion and warmth, and to cuddle us and show us that they cared.

How could we expect the brothers to show this kind of emotion and affection? After all, they were dealing with a load of strangers who they guessed resented them for taking their freedom away. It was certainly a very abnormal situation and if some of the brothers did get attached to some of the boys it's to be expected. There were two women working in the school, in the brothers' headquarters and in the kitchen, but they had very little to do with us.

Maybe the brothers' repressed sexual feelings and frustrations came out as aggression towards us, or maybe it came out in other ways. I know one brother in particular used to come to the back of the class where I was sitting and sit on the seat beside me. He would ask me how I was doing and put his hand on my knee, then his hand would rub the inside of my thigh, until gradually his elbow would be practically resting on my little privates. This would go on for minutes and would make me feel very uncomfortable as he talked to me about my school work, and while I wanted to pull away, I didn't have the courage to. This happened on many occasions and I didn't like it and I knew it was wrong, but he never went any further. This was the nearest I ever came to any sexual impropriety and it was only from one particular brother. Nothing untoward ever happened from any other brother at any other time. I certainly did not hate him because he had a lot of good qualities, but it was not a very nice experience. Who could I complain to anyway? Distressing as it was for me, I certainly had witnessed more abnormal sexual behaviour in Limerick down in the fields and in Dublin from my cousin, which for me had been much more distressing.

I really do not know how much sexual abuse went on in Glin during the period I was there. I only heard whispers and innuendoes, but nothing concrete. It is possible boys would not disclose it anyway; boys generally disclosed most things to one another, but sexual abuse would be more difficult to talk about. However, from a personal point of view, I found the seemingly casual beatings much more disturbing, more difficult to understand, and more difficult to forgive or forget. Sexual abuse could be seen as a sign of affection for a boy, but some brothers were downright cruel. Again, from a personal point of view, I had two experiences in my later years at Glin, which left a nasty taste in my mouth.

One was when I took a short cut through the kitchen in the hope of stealing a little bit of food. There was a lovely smell of meat in the air, and all the boned meat was just out of the large pots and sitting on the wooden table with no one in sight. Who could resist that? I was with my two friends and we all started taking bits of meat off the bones like a pack of starving lions, with me as the instigator. Suddenly a brother named 'N', and one of the most hated brothers, came in to the kitchen and shouted, 'Get out and put that meat back!'

We dropped the meat, and my two friends dashed for the door, whereas I walked out a little more slowly and casually. That was my mistake because it seemed to irritate 'The long stream of piss of a brother', as we later nicknamed him. He rushed towards me from the side and threw a punch at me, which due to my lack of boxing skills, I was unable to avoid. He caught me right on the nose and caused me great pain and a bloody nose. I had not expected such a severe reaction and I ran out into the yard not knowing whether he might throw more punches at me.

I was hurt and mad as fucking hell, so I was. When I was out of reach I turned round and shouted a flurry of swear words that even surprised me, as I had never before that point backchatted a brother. My pride was hurt and I did not think I deserved to be punched by a grown man and I didn't like it. I shouted out at the top of my voice, 'You long stream of fucking piss, I wish I could fucking kill you, and you are a nasty bastard and I'll fucking kill you one day when I see you in Limerick.' I wasn't finished with my tirade of abuse just yet and I searched the garden for rocks to hurl at the bastard, which I did, one after the other, while my friends advised me to come away.

That brother's unfair treatment of me left a lasting impression, because I have found on a number of occasions throughout my adult life, that while I have a great tolerance and dislike of violence, I can tolerate an awful lot of bullshit from people, there comes a point when I find it difficult to control my temper and often lose control, and do not think of the consequences. A mirror of my father's behaviour and temper, no doubt, and I did not like it.

That particular 'long stream of piss' of a brother was about the most consistent and obnoxious son of a bitch to my mind. He had a tendency to pay more attention to boys when they were changing in the shower room area, so he seemed to have a sexual hang-up as well as a violent streak, which is not that surprising, knowing what I do now about sexual abuse of young boys.

One of the dormitory routines was to polish the wooden floor every morning and I hated it, as I thought it was already well polished and was just another way to break our already broken spirits. We had to get down on our hands and knees, about three abreast, with a piece of old blanket as a rag to polish the floor. With both hands on the rag we would polish the floor from side to side and the three boys would have to swing in harmony, unfortunately without the music, and we would gradually move backwards to the end of the dormitory. Suddenly I felt the leather strap across my arse, which was unexpected, and it stung, and as a natural reaction, and without thinking, I shouted at that brother, who also had an abusive streak. 'That fucking hurt, you know.' I expected another blow but instead he said, 'Oh, don't be a baby, Raymond, I hardly touched you.' 'Well,' I said, 'it hurt and how would you like it?' He never responded but at least he never hit me on the arse again.

I did have another incident with that particular brother. He had come to Glin a couple of years after I had been there, and one afternoon I had gone to the toilet in the playground, and as I and some of my friends came out, he asked us collectively why we had not got permission from him. He gave two of the boys ahead of me a slap on each hand with the dreaded black strap. He then asked me to hold out my hand and I refused. I pulled away and reminded him that we did not need permission at that time of the afternoon and that he had no right to slap us. By now a crowd of boys was milling around, wondering what was going to happen next. Brother Fucking Nasty, which was a name I later gave him, made a grab for me and I pulled away again. I pulled out a small kitchen knife, which I had been carrying around in my inside my pocket, and I told him, 'I'll fucking stab you if you come near me, you're not going to slap me for nothing,' and I ran off around the back of the toilets, cheered on by the crowd of boys now gathered outside the toilet.

I eventually went back to the dormitory later that night ,wondering what was going to happen to me, but nothing did, because by now 'Brother

110

Nasty' was probably in bed reading his Holy Bible and looking for guidance as to the best way to punish me. The next morning I saw 'Brother Nasty', but he never mentioned the previous night's incident, but told me to move to a different and much shorter bed, as a punishment no doubt. Although the bed was uncomfortable, at least it was better than the old black strap, but it was another example of just how vindictive some of the brothers could be. At the time of this incident, around 1956, I had only a couple of months before I would leave St Joseph's for ever.

I was doing quite good at school and I'd moved to the second grade. I had been there only a month or so when the teacher told me he was moving me to the third grade, because I was finding second grade too easy. It was good for my morale to skip forward nearly a year, so unexpectedly. In the fourth grade I had another lucky break and came in touch with 'Glider', a nickname for Brother Flynn, because of the way he seemed to glide over the ground when he walked. He also suggested that I be put into the band, where I finished up playing the violin. (I use the word 'play' very very loosely.) When I eventually moved to the fifth grade, I had been there less than a month before he moved me to the sixth grade, again missing almost a year, and although I found it a struggle, I managed to get my leaving certificate just before I was 15, which was another boost to my generally low morale. Again I felt a great sense of pride and it also justified Brother Flynn's faith in my academic ability. He was another brother who played a very important part in my life while I was at St Joseph's school in Glin. I liked him a lot and he always treated me with respect and kindness, and more importantly, he saw some potential in me and he acted on it.

For a number of years after I left Glin, I corresponded with Brother Flynn and I still have a letter in my possession indicating that he gave me an extra push to help me to complete my leaving certificate.

In later years, after I had left Glin, two different Christian Brothers wrote to me, telling me that they always thought that I had something special and that my personality was very different from most of the boys. While I was very flattered, I personally had not been aware of being very special. I just did the best that I could, and although I held my own academically, I was far from being the top of the class. Nevertheless I was always very conscientious and happy to please and get on with people. I had an easy going nature and was quiet and shy, most of the time.

My own best qualities at school were spelling, writing, composition and arithmetic. I was amongst the best in spelling and I found writing compositions fairly natural compared to many other boys.

Prayers were a different matter, some of which I didn't say properly because I would say them parrot fashion, never having seen them written down. One was 'Remember to keep the sabbath holy,' whereas I was saying, 'Remember to keep the donkey holy.' Oh well, I liked donkeys and I thought that we should be kind to donkeys anyway.

We had prayers on several occasions during the school time, so all in all we had an awful lot of Bible bashing. Added to all that praying, we would have the occasional 'retreat'. Now that was hard, that was! Basically we had to go almost the whole day without speaking, and praying as often as we could during the allotted time. Jasus, it was very hard and we were told that to speak without permission during that period would be a mortal sin. We did our best, but inevitably we would be giggling and whispering long before the day was over. I often wondered why we bothered to pray. Surely being starved to death day in and day out was enough sacrifice and punishment for our little lost souls? But obviously the brothers thought otherwise. All that praying and sacrifice must have been having some bad effect on me, because at one time I seriously thought and prayed to be a priest. Luckily that feeling soon went away when I left Glin and went to live in Brighton in England. Seeing all the half-naked women lying on the beach made me realise that being a priest was probably not such a good idea after all!

The downside of too much religion for me was, I suppose, that I had, and still have, a tendency to have a guilt complex about enjoying the simplest of pleasures, and not just sexual. I remember that we had a brother who seemed to be a mind reader. He could somehow tell you if you had, 'Been interfering with yourself'. His cloaked expression, in other words, meant masturbating, which was a word I would not have understood anyway. This brother amazed me because how could he know what we did under the bedclothes, in private and on our own? I never could work out how he did it. Perhaps he was some kind of superman and could see through walls. Or perhaps he was just remembering what he had done at a similar age! It was all very confusing for me anyway.

Then one day all was revealed as I heard him say to one boy, who shall be nameless, 'You have been interfering with yourself again, haven't you, I can tell by your eyes, so I can, and you'll go straight to hell and stay there forever.' Ah, now, that's how he could tell. Personally I never could tell, no matter how often I looked into someone's eyes, but then I did not have these special powers of seeing through walls and into other boys' minds. I often wonder what effect these, more often than not, false allegations, had on these already guilt-ridden boys later in life.

112

I had been writing regular letters to my mother asking how Spot the dog was, in other words to: 'Get me out of here.' My mother would write back, 'Spot is missing you and hopes you will see him very soon!' These coded letters went on for years and I only wish I had kept them.

When we eventually got radio in the dormitory, it made our nights a bit more bearable and sad in many ways. At the close of the show, one of Walt Disney's most famous songs used to come on: 'When you wish upon a star, makes no difference where you are'. That tune always made me really sad, because none of my dreams ever seemed to come true and my mother seemed to have forgotten me, despite our regular communications. But things were about to change, and for the better.

16. Brighton 1953 – Holiday of a Lifetime

The summer of 1953 was a holiday with a difference!

Brother Cullen had dropped us at Limerick station by bus, and my mother was late as usual and pissed out of her mind as usual. She was telling the whole of Limerick in the loudest possible voice how wonderful her little Raymond was and if anyone harmed a hair of my lovely head she would 'cut the legs from right under them', so she would. This violent threat always seemed a bit extreme to me, but then I was not a doting mother, and I was not drunk. Again, I was totally embarrassed and wanted to run away, but as I had nowhere to run to I had to listen to all the verbal abuse being heaped on these innocent passers-by. Seeing my mother drunk always spoiled our reunions and took the edge off my excitement at seeing her again. No child likes to see a parent drunk and abusive, and as a 13-year-old I felt nothing but shame and hurt.

'We're going to England tomorrow,' she said in a slurred voice. 'I'm taking you away from that fucking place forever, so I am.' While it was a surprise, I was not going to argue with her because I had been writing lots of coded letters telling her how unhappy I was, and so it was that we found ourselves on the long journey by train and boat to the famous seaside town of Brighton in the south of England.

Officially, of course, my mother was not supposed to take me out of the country, but I was game and ready for an adventure if she was, and no one would know until I failed to turn up for collection in a month's time! I was just gone 13 and about to undertake the journey of a lifetime, and what a journey it turned out to be, full of drama, terror, stress and anxiety, at least for me. My mother, as usual, was oblivious to how I was feeling. For me it would be 'Terror on the Limerick Express', and a journey that I would never forget.

My mother had had a few drinks at the Railway Tavern opposite the railway station in Limerick before we left, but she was not too drunk, at least not yet anyway, but as the journey proceeded she got more and more pissed and more nostalgic and melancholy. She talked about how she missed my father and how she missed me and my sister Phyllis. The constant tearfulness and confusion was beginning to make me feel very unhappy, but that was not to be the worst part of the journey.

The train would stop at different stations on the way to the boat and sure enough my mother would dash into the bar, wherever there was one, and have a quick drink. Most of the drinks she had were downed very quickly, but during many of the stops I would be hanging out of the train window wondering if she was going to get back on the train in time, and if she didn't, what would I do? Would I get off at the next stop or keep on going to England, or what should I do? The stress was unbearable for me all through the 100 mile journey, and I was full of anxiety. During one stop, the train whistle sounded and steam billowed into the sky and all around the station. It just started to move when my mother suddenly appeared from behind a group of people and somehow, to her credit, managed to get on the train before it departed. When she saw I was upset she comforted me as best she could, but her drinking did not stop.

At another station along the way my mother was by now dangerously drunk and had stopped off for yet another drink. I couldn't believe it! She didn't seem to realise what effect her behaviour was having on me and just carried on like a woman possessed. The inevitable happened. She did not get on when the train took off and I was now in a state of panic. I looked around the station as the train pulled out, but I could not see her anywhere. I wondered if I should get off and at least be with her, or stay on and see what happened, but the train was picking up so much speed by now that I had little choice but to stay on the train.

By now my heart was pounding with terror, wondering what was going to happen. I was in a terrible state of tension, so I decided to walk along the corridor and see if I could find the strange man with whom my mother had been chatting on and off throughout the journey, maybe he could help me somehow. After I had walked along a couple of corridors, to my amazement, I saw my mother talking, as cool as you like, to this man, totally unaware of my predicament. When I told her what I thought had happened she reassured me, saying, 'You know I'd never leave you alone.' She could have fooled me! I was so excited that I forgot all my fears and annoyances for the moment because my mother had come up trumps again and I could forgive her anything. But my anxieties and fears would stay with me forever. I don't think that my mother ever realised what effect her drinking was having on me then or at any time. Most alcoholics are not aware of the effect that their drinking has on other close members of their families, and my mother was no different.

We eventually got on the boat at Dublin in the middle of the night, and many hours later we arrived at Paddington station, having crossed the Irish sea in uncomfortable conditions. I know that I nearly froze to death. Paddington railway station seemed so vast, with platforms everywhere, and I was beginning to feel very excited, if a little tired, and I couldn't wait to get to Brighton by the sea. I had never been to the seaside before, except near the river Shannon.

Brighton was a beautiful place in July 1953, so much more affluent and cleaner looking than Limerick. I loved it straight away. It was sunny and warm with lots of open spaces and very posh buildings. Our flat was in Brunswick Square, which was officially on the Hove boundary, a very posh area with a green just outside where kids used to play. The flat was also less than a minute from the sea and there were at least seven or eight cinemas all within walking distance of where I lived. What more could a young boy of 13 need! We lived in a cellar flat and my mother had a partner named Jock with whom she had already been living for a few years, and I found out he was the one who had been helping my mother to send all those parcels to me over the years. He was a really nice, gentle and kind man who treated me and my mother very well for years and was to play a major part in my life later on when I started employment. I always thought that he looked a bit like James Mason, the British film star, and better still, he was a foreman on a tarmacking firm in London, which he travelled up to and back each day. I felt so happy, probably the happiest that I had ever been, and life, it seemed, was going to be great from now. I was no longer in that horrible Glin school, away from all those nasty brothers and I had my freedom again.

I remember my mother gave me a letter to post on one occasion, and after posting it, I came back and asked why the English didn't know how to spell the word 'letter'. When she asked me what I meant I told her, 'Well it says "Litter" on the box.' My mother laughed, which for her was a very rare thing. I had put the letter in the litter bin by mistake, thinking that it was a letter-box, partly due to the fact that I had never seen a litter bin in Limerick, and I certainly did not know what the word 'litter' meant anyway. My mother retrieved the letter, and I had added a new word to my vocabulary. I also saw my first ever condom in the road and I thought it was a balloon! Oh how innocent I was then.

The West Pier was quite close by and I used to love going on both the Palace and West Piers, listening to the orchestras and admiring proper violin players, because they didn't seem to make the screeching cat-like sounds that I made when I played in Glin. I was on holiday and blissfully happy and probably never going back to Glin. It was a nice life for a while. The piers in Brighton were amongst the best in the country around 1953.

We had a next door neighbour, a man who used to sell his home-made pies to the neighbours, and naturally my mother bought some several times during the weeks I lived there. They were very tasty indeed and I loved rabbit anyway. They were delicious, and nothing like the food that we had to eat at Glin. However, we were a little shocked later to hear that the pie-maker was arrested for killing cats and turning them into pies! But by then it was too late.

What started getting me down was, firstly, I had no friends and of course no one could understand a word I was saying because very few Limerick people lived in Brighton then. Nearly all Irish people seemed to go to the Acton area in London and certainly none of the shop assistants where my mother sent me were from the Island Field.

I was painfully shy anyway and I did not have an awful lot of confidence. I hated going to the shops because the girls used to laugh at my accent and used to keep asking me to repeat what I had just said, which made me become flustered and annoyed, because I felt they were taking the piss out of me. Looking back now, I realise that it must have seemed like I was from another planet, and those young shop assistants really did not know what I was saying. I mumbled a lot and spoke much too fast and I did not speak clearly, due, no doubt, to my lack of confidence. Strangely enough, I never had that problem in Limerick!

The other major problem, which made me very unhappy and unsettled while living with my mother, was that she and Jock drank every day, the difference being that Jock had a drink and was quiet and went to bed and then went to work the next morning, whereas my mother got paralytically drunk every day and wanted to fight everyone and sing old Irish rebel songs at the top of her voice late at night in the middle of Western Road. Her favourite song was 'Kevin Barry', an old Irish rebel song. She never stopped talking about the 'Black and Tans', who she said were 'dirty bastards', accusing them of all sorts of atrocities. The Black and Tans were people sent to Ireland back in the twenties to quell any type of Irish resistance to British rule and apparently carried out some atrocities on the Irish people. The Tans were mostly prisoners from English jails who volunteered to go to Ireland for a specific purpose, in exchange for their freedom. What the people of Brighton thought about the Black and Tans I'll never know! And what they thought of my mother's behaviour can only be guessed at. My mother was beginning to get on my nerves and I was beginning to wish I was back at Glin. I found myself crying into my pillow at night and missing my friends and the structured routine and security of Glin. I told my mother that I wanted to go back home to Glin and take the consequences of running away to England. I also lived in fear in case the English police came knocking on the door any minute to take me away and maybe give me some terrible punishment for escaping from Limerick without telling anyone.

So, after about six weeks living in Brighton, and constant nagging, my mother arranged for me to go back to Glin on my own, which was a daunting prospect for a boy of 13. She came with me up to Paddington station to put me on the boat train up to Fishguard in Wales, but she was drunk again and very tearful.

She gave the train guard a tip and asked him to look after me on the long night trip and she asked him to make sure I got on the boat at the other end. I had a berth on the boat train so that I could sleep, and when I woke up it was around midnight at the harbour. It was cold, dark and windy on the lonely platform. It was very quiet and I realised that almost everyone else had got off the train. I started to panic, in case I didn't get on the boat in time, but I did, and when I landed at Dunlaoire harbour in Dublin in the early hours of the next morning I was met by Brother Cullen. He greeted me warmly and asked me if I had had a good holiday. He did not seem angry as I had expected him to be and we drove back to Glin after he had bought me a meal in Dublin. I felt I had made the right decision, at least for the moment!

17. Back at Glin

I soon settled back into the routine of school life at St Joseph's, and concentrated on my school work. I was certainly holding my own as far as academic work was concerned, but I suppose what was wearing most of us down at Glin, was that we could not go home at the end of a hard day at school to our families and relax in our own way and get some comfort from our mothers if things did not go okay. The brothers could do anything they liked to us and we could not complain to anyone.

They could starve or beat us, which some of them often did, and be over zealous with all that religion, and we had to accept it. We could not write to our families and complain because we knew that our letters would be censored. Glin itself would have been bearable if it had been a local, rather than a residential, school, because I think, on the whole, many of the brothers did the best they could under the circumstances.

What Glin provided was discipline, which most of us needed, and a structured environment where we had to learn a certain amount whether we liked it or not. There was no way out until you were 16, although some boys did manage to get out a couple of years early for various reasons, usually due to connections or some improvement, perhaps in their family circumstances. We envied those boys. As far as we were concerned we might as well be prisoners. There were no bars to hold us in, but most of us had nowhere to escape to anyway. We felt like we were rejects, branded and unwanted, social misfits, and many of us would carry that label for the rest of our lives. During the writing of this book, one Glin boy told me: 'My wife does not know I have been in Glin, I never told her. I am too ashamed.' How sad! Was it that bad, were we that bad? It is as though we were hardened criminals! All of us were victims of our different circumstance and none of us had volunteered to go there.

In my own later years I was able to talk about my time at Glin and tried to see the positive side as best I could. I was already burdened by too many hang-ups from my home life, and I could not afford to feel guilty about being at Glin. Christ, I was only a child, and hardly aware of what was right or wrong. I never hurt anyone in the physical sense. I take responsibility for any childish pranks and wrongs I did, but maybe if I had a normal upbringing I would not have had the need to misbehave. Like most boys who came into Glin, I lacked security and a stable background and understanding in my own family. That was why we had to be taken into care. I think most people today now realise that we were not criminals and that we should not be ashamed of our past, or feel guilty about it, but some still do, and feel stigmatised, and it's sad. My last school report in Limerick, in late 1950, was an excellent report. It said that I was always well behaved and had a 100 per cent attendance rate, so maybe the fact that my mother was no longer around affected my behaviour and caused me to stray.

Most of the boys, if not all of them, who were sent to Glin, felt that they should not have been sent there, which is probably true. In my own case I was certainly out of control and would not have stopped my antisocial behaviour, which would have escalated into more serious crimes had I not been sent to Glin when I was. At the time, my only ambition was to steal as much as I could, and I was taking more risks and becoming more and more daring the more I got away with it. A lot of boys I know were sent to Glin purely because their parents had died and their relatives were unwilling to take responsibility for them. They have a justified reason to be bitter and resentful, and who can blame them? But they may well have had to pay a high price for harbouring all this resentment for the last 50 years, in some ways remaining a prisoner of their past and a 'Glin Boy' forever, instead of letting go and trying to get on with their lives. Many were unable to talk to anyone about being in care, lest they be seen as outcasts, thereby denying people most close to them the chance of listening and trying to help or understand them. I know that I was affected very badly by my own past and my time at Glin, but hardly a day went by when I did not talk to my wife Sandra about my past, which was always very therapeutic for me. I at least knew that she was able to understand my peculiarities and make allowances for some of my, at times, odd behaviour. It was a great release to know that someone close to you is willing to listen to you in a non-judgemental way.

Now and again a group of us would go to the records office, where there was a register of all our dates of birth. We would ask the brother in charge to double check, just in case there might have been a mistake with our dates of birth and we could get out early, but it was just a dream, a futile grasping at straws.

It was beginning to dawn on me that if I stayed until I was 16 I would be here for another three years, having already served two. The prospect was frightening and too horrible to contemplate. 'God almighty, why did I want to come back here again away from the lovely seaside town of Brighton.' My head was in turmoil at times thinking how I could survive and remain sane. Three years out of anyone's life is a lot, but when you're are only 13, it seems even longer.

I started writing to my mother again, asking about Spot the dog, but somehow I felt it was a hopeless cause and I was wasting my time. I would have to resign myself to being here for the duration and do my time and make the best of it, but time was going so very, very slowly. I, like most of the boys, would count each day to the day of our release. It was like watching a kettle boil and it didn't help, except it gave us something to hope for and to focus on, even though it was way down the line but you just had to have something to look forward to.

A lot of the boys who left, especially the country boys, were given jobs with farmers around the county of Limerick area at about 10 shillings a week, which is equivalent to about 50 pence today. They also had some meals and accommodation. Some of the boys came back to Glin within a few weeks, unable to cope with the hardship and the exploitation by the farmers. We heard tales from the boys on their return of overwork and starvation and not being paid. No doubt a lot of boys became institutionalised, due to being in Glin for too long, and were not properly prepared for the outside world. Some returned to the security of Glin, because for some, it was the only home they had known for the last few years. One person told me that he had been hired to a local farmer when he had left Glin, and during his stay there, he had to eat his meals all alone and in a separate building.

During my work as a psychiatric nurse I would see a lot of patients who became institutionalised over a few years and became very dependent on the hospital and the hospital regime, so it is not surprising that the boys became too reliant on the school set up. During the fifties very little was known about the long term effects of institutionalisation and how to prevent it, so it would be a little unfair to apportion too much blame to the brothers and the system during that period, the knowledge just was not there. A lot of boys also joined the army when they left, and in many ways they just swapped one institution for another. Many of the boys were probably institutionalised and needed a structured and disciplined environment and someone to tell them what to do and how to behave. Surprisingly, not that many boys ran away from Glin, despite the open gate.

It was around 1954 that I was recommended for the band, and so it was that I found myself on the fiddle in the care of Brother Cullen, who seemed to have his hand in everything; head of the 'Glin mafia'!

Although I had a good ear for music I was not a natural musician and I did not have a lot of natural ability, certainly not with the violin, but I did not know that at the beginning. I was also inclined to be lazy and relied more on my ear than reading music, a bad mistake. I also preferred sport, so there was constant conflict, especially as the sports field was just outside the music window and I could see the other boys playing football and wished I was out there, especially in the summer, instead of trying to play the *Blue Danube* or Minuet in G Minor.

I'm sure there must have been times when Brother Cullen also wished I was out playing football instead of assaulting his ears with my appalling playing. I was terrible, and for years I envied the professionals who made such lovely music with the violin. It made a heavenly sound when played as it should be, but trying to learn the violin at the age of 14 is about ten years too late, and my heart was never really in it, although I had no choice but to keep playing. Many times during practice I would be day-dreaming while playing the violin. Instead of reading and following the music, I was looking out the window at the other boys playing football, when I would suddenly be brought back to earth and feel a large bunch of knuckles across the back of my head, which certainly took my mind off the football and refocused my mind on the music. It was Brother Cullen: 'Pay attention will you, O'Donoghue, do you hear me now?'

'Yes, sir,' I would reply with tears in my eyes and a pain on the back of my head, which I was unable to rub because I had to keep one hand on the bow and hold the violin with the other while I tried to keep up with the music. I was always day-dreaming and always wished that I was some-where else doing something different. It was an attitude of mind that would remain with me all of my life.

We used to go to an old, senile, half-deaf music teacher down in Glin for extra tuition, and we used to drive him mad and take the piss out of him something rotten. We were also taught Irish dancing by a blacksmith who lived in Glin, a short, balding, stocky man who was very lively on his feet. I enjoyed trying to learn that, but as I was on the fiddle I had to stop and play for the other boys. I became fairly competent at playing jigs and hornpipes in a group. With all the noise of the dancers on the floor no one noticed the odd bum note or two, so long as you kept time. Yes, we were doing 'River Dance' long before Michael Flatley did it, but purely accidentally, and we always apologised for it afterwards, so we did. I was also in the choir and I enjoyed singing in church and especially during Christmas mass.

I also practised the piano for a while, which I felt a little more competent at, but somehow I was not cut out to be the next Liberace. Sport was my passion and it always took first place in my priorities then as it was to later in my adult life. One of the most popular singers of the day was Josef Locke. We often heard him on the radio and sang along to many of his world famous songs: 'Hear my Song' (eventually made into a film of the same name); 'The Soldier's Dream'; 'Good Bye'; 'If I were a Blackbird' and many more. I idolised him and would remember many of his songs all my life. Josef Locke helped make my life that bit more bearable.

I think I was fairly good at Gaelic football and enjoyed the running up and down the pitch, though I found myself outplayed at hurling. We also had a handball alley, which I was reasonably good at. We used to play the local teams at football, which helped get us out of the school for a while, and we used to go swimming in the river Shannon down at the pier just outside Glin.

We had a certain bond as boys who shared a certain way of life together and we felt a great affinity towards each other. I sometimes feel very privileged to have lived with such a group and shared all the unique experiences and heartaches and the odd few laughs we still managed to have together while in care.

Sometimes I look back at my time in care and wonder if it was all a bad dream as I rarely come in contact with any Glin boys, but then I meet someone like Jamsey, who reminds me about people and events I have forgotten, and I realise I certainly was not dreaming and I feel very good that I have at least survived. Many would not be as lucky.

I have heard of boys from Limerick who were determined to punch a certain brother if they ever saw him in Limerick, and would feel very bitter about the whole experience all of their lives. I also know quite a few who have had serious drink problems.

Jamsey recently told me a story about his brother Paddy, which was the way I had remembered his character and his quick temper. Paddy used to use a pub around the Elephant and Castle area and regularly went in there after work to watch the news around six o'clock. One day he went in as usual, but *Coronation Street* was on instead of the news, so naturally Paddy asked the barman if he and his mates could watch the news as usual, but the barman said no, that he was watching *Coronation Street*. This annoyed Paddy, so he took a bottle of beer off the counter and threw it straight through the TV and said, 'You'll be watching fuck all from now on, you bastard,' and then hastily departed. The next day Jamsey was in the same pub and the landlord told Jamsey what his brother Paddy had done. Jamsey said to the landlord innocently, 'My brother wouldn't do anything like that, guvnor, he's very quiet, you must be mixing him up with someone else.' I laughed out loud to myself when Jamsey related this story to me because it was just like the Paddy I had known at school, very quiet but quick to respond in a physical way if someone ever annoyed him. The whole family were nice.

My mother continued writing and sending me money and clothes from England and for me that was an absolute life saver. I continued to do well at school and I did my Leaving Certificate around 1954. I then I worked full time in the tailor's shop within the school, which was certainly better than going to school. It was a nice relaxed atmosphere, and most of us boys who worked there got on well together. In the tailor's shop we were under the control of the tailor who treated everyone fairly, and it was good to be out of the way of the brothers for a while, which meant there was less chance of getting a hiding. I enjoyed those couple of years away from school, and life at Glin was more bearable, but still painfully tedious. I could not wait to be 16 and leave. My old pal Eamonn from Limerick had gone because he was older than me. Whenever a pal left it made life that bit more difficult and it meant adjusting to different people and wishing it was you who was going home instead. Oh how we envied anyone who left. Sometimes I thought that maybe I would never get out and that I might be kept in forever just for spite. These feelings of insecurity would remain with me for the rest of my life.

It was around 1951 that my friend Joe Moore, who lived across the street in the Island Field, cycled all the way from Limerick, which was 32 miles each way, to see me and some other boys from the Island Field. It was a great surprise and great to see an old pal from Limerick, but sadly I never saw him again because he was drowned shortly after in the Island Field river trying to save two little girls. The girls were saved. I have never forgotten Joe who was only a little older than I was at the time and I know that his death naturally affected his mother very badly. A few years ago I discovered that my cousin Josie was actually involved in trying to rescue Joe at the time and what was even worse was that the girls were just fooling around, pretending that they were in trouble and had not been in any danger at all. How tragic!

In the summer we had potato picking on the farm, which was heartbreaking and back-breaking work, especially when you're hungry and can't build your strength up. We had to walk behind a horse and some implement attached to the horse, which would rake the ground and throw out the potatoes some distance away. We would be picking these bloody potatoes up from all over the place and putting them in a pile and it seemed never ending. My back was killing me at the end of each day and I hated it. One thing I did learn from working on a farm was that I never wanted to be a farmer. The idea of being a filum star was much more appealing, much easier and more lucrative; that was the life I wanted to pursue. I couldn't wait to leave and go back to England and then maybe Hollywood! I always had big dreams of being famous one day somehow. I always was a dreamer.

One thing is certain, some of the brothers did not appreciate my Mario Lanza impersonations. I remember that whenever I was in the toilet I would sing, probably because the acoustics always seemed better in the hollow of a toilet cubicle. 'Be my love for no one else could end this yearning,' I would sing out loud. I now realise of course that this was not an ideal song to sing amongst a lot of boys in a public toilet, but I was an innocent little boy and did not know any different, and besides, I had to practise my vocal skills somewhere! 'Stop that noise, O'Donoghue,' would stop me in mid sentence, just as I was about to hit the high notes. It was the miserable Brother 'N' who I had nicknamed 'The stream of piss'. His 'Stop!' command was not very encouraging to a young artistic boy who was hoping to make it in the music world one day. 'Why don't you go and fuck yourself,' I would whisper quietly to myself. 'I bet you've never heard of Mario Lanza anyway!'

As if my thoughts were being read, his lanky head would look over the top of the toilet door and he would mutter the immortal words, 'Hurry up, O'Donoghue, what are you doing in there?' Which seemed to be a very stupid question considering where I was! Even in the bog you had no privacy, there was always a brother prowling around wondering what you were up to, and you never knew when a brother's head would look in over the top of the door. It was a case of Big Brother. There was no chance of interfering with yourself with all those prying eyes about. It was as if the brothers wanted to invade every aspect of our daily routine.

We changed our clothes once a week, and more often than not we changed out in the playground unless it was raining. God help you if you avoided changing some of your clothing. This was something I frequently did. This was due to the quality of the clothing. If you were lucky enough to have had a new pair of socks from the week before, you wanted to keep them for as long as you could rather than change them for a very old pair that had been darned about a hundred times and often very badly, which resulted in great lumps of wool sitting under your heel, causing you great discomfort every time you put your foot to the ground.

Wearing a tie was compulsory, despite the fact that most of the shirts had no collars. I always hated wearing ties after that, and it was something that got me into trouble as an adult in the nursing profession later on in my life. One day I decided not to wear my tie, hoping I would not be noticed amongst the crowd of other tie-wearers, but sure enough I was noticed.

'Where is your tie, Raymond?' I was asked very politely by a brother.

'In my pocket, sir,' I said meekly.

'Why aren't you wearing it, Raymond?' the brother said.

'I haven't got a collar, sir,' I said, fumbling in my pocket, looking for a tie that I did not have.

'Well now we are going to have to make you a special collar then, aren't we, Raymond?' he said sarcastically and then told me to hold out my hand and he gave me four straps of the leather on the hands. But it was worth it because I felt good at showing a little bit of defiance and getting the attention of all the boys for a couple of seconds. Sometimes it seemed as if the brothers were determined to show that they were in charge. I knew that they might control my body, but my mind was my own and it always would be.

This defiant attitude would stay with me all my life and would cause me a lot of conflict in various job situations and single me out as a trouble maker, and many people would accuse me of trying to be different. I am different, but I did not have to try and it came very naturally. I did not want to apologise for it. I could be very stubborn and have had great difficulty with figures of authority all my life since leaving Glin. I have often found myself going against the flow of the general thinking of groups I have been involved with in my job as a psychiatric nurse. More than once I have been the only dissenting voice and found it hard to stick with my thinking and my very strong point of view. I have been told more than once, 'Why are you always trying to change the world?' And 'You can't beat the system.' Maybe not, but at least it has made me feel better for trying. I think that my defiant attitude was acquired as a result of being controlled for so long by the brothers, or maybe it was already there.

One of my many peculiarities or hang-ups as a result of my time at Glin, was to do with food. We only got treats or sweets at Glin on special occasions or if you were lucky enough to have a little money from your relatives. As a result, food has always been my passion. Wherever I go I have to make sure I have access to food without having to wait too long, and I tend to panic if I realise that I can't eat when I want to. I just can't go into a cake shop and buy one or two cakes, I have to buy at least half a dozen and I will regularly come out with a large bag of cakes instead of what I went in for. Whenever my wife Sandra bought a joint of meat for

Sunday dinner I would query whether it was big enough, because I hated the thought of running out of food. She was always right, but I continued to ask the same question most Sundays and she patiently told me, 'Yes, Raymond, there's enough there.'

We had at least one boy, to my knowledge, at Glin, who died during my time there, and I think it was due to some sort of sleeping sickness. He kept falling asleep during playing sessions and we would find him asleep in the middle of the hay-making. It was quite sad.

The dentist used to do a yearly check up, and most of us tried to avoid seeing him if we could by hiding in the toilet or somewhere else, but it did not work. I know on one occasion I had a really black tooth in the back of my mouth and I did not want it taken out so I stuck a piece of white paper into the hole and somehow got away with it. Perhaps the old dentist was aware of my terror and did not report the offending tooth to the brothers, for which I was very grateful.

There was one boy in particular who was always claiming to have swallowed something or other, often a needle, and he would be taken to Croom Hospital some miles away where he would spend a few days getting special treatment and proper food for a few days. Whether they ever found a needle or not I don't recall, but they had to take him seriously every time as a precaution. I envied him but I didn't have the courage to do anything similar myself. It was something that he did regularly. I think that they call it Munchausen Syndrome, which is a way of getting attention, and who could blame him! We were all desperate for individual attention, which was sadly lacking at Glin.

Most of the Glin photos in this book were taken by one of the older brothers, Brother Arthur. He was a fairly quiet man who always had a smile on his face and, even better still, he rarely hit anyone. He would take photos of the band, the boxing team and other events, and even of individuals so long as you paid him for each one, and he developed and printed them himself. Maybe the seeds of my own later interest in photography were sown by my old Christian Brother friend, with the smiling face! I remember that he was a nice man and I never saw him lose his temper. He also seemed much older than all the other brothers.

While I was in Brother 'D's class I remember having to read out a poem, which was basically about a donkey who was 'long and lanky and not much use'! I hated reading it out because I always felt it referred to me personally and caused me great distress and embarrassment. I felt I was made to read it out as a sort of punishment, though I suppose it wasn't done for that reason. The first seeds of paranoia were already being sown!

Nevertheless it made me feel bad because around 15 to 16 I became aware of my very puny build, and I wished I could be like the world famous body-builder Charles Atlas, who promised you a perfect body in seven days. He was an early inspiration, at least when it came to looking after my body, but a perfect body in seven days was a little imaginative and highly unlikely, but we tried at least.

Sex was not talked about much at Glin and there certainly was not much sexual stimulation or activity that was noticeable. Sex was not a word that I was familiar with anyway. I do remember one chap who was a bit on the effeminate side and he seemed to stand out a mile because he behaved in a way that was not like other boys. He was, in fact, the same boy who used to swallow the needles. He had a funny walk and tended to have girlish ways and mannerisms. On one occasion he stood in the playground with his trousers undone and his 'pride and joy' hanging out. It may well have been an accident, of course, and his trousers could have been lacking buttons, but it seemed odd at the time, and it did not seem to bother him. Maybe it was another attention seeking ploy.

My own sexual feelings were nothing to write home about, and how could I anyway due to the censorship imposed on our letters? But I do remember having an orgasm for the first time while lying on the grass and trying to have sex with the grass beneath my loins. At least it worked, but Oh, the guilt afterwards. I was afraid I might die before I got to confession and go to hell for ever more. I soon realised that the fear of hell goes once the old sex hormones start telling you to interfere with yourself. The trouble about going to mass every day was that you could not have an impure thought in peace, because you were always being reminded about the terrible consequences. God, it was terribly unfair on a young man with sexual urges, although I coped as best I could under the circumstances. But it was a constant battle, with the Lord winning one day and the Devil winning the next! But at least it was an equal battle!

I have since wondered if there were ever inspections of places like Glin by the local authority to monitor if boys were being treated properly, or was it assumed because the brothers were Irish and a religious organisation that they were beyond reproach? Or was the Christian Brothers organisation so powerful that they had a free hand to do as they pleased? After all, the courts and the local authority who sent us to Glin should have been aware that all our letters were censored, which put us in a very vulnerable position. We could not complain to anyone, so we never had anyone representing our interests or to listen to our complaints. It was not a healthy situation, looking back now, and it would be nice to know what the official situation was back in the fifties and before. Perhaps it was a case of 'Hear no evil, see no evil.'

1956, the year I was officially due to leave, was getting closer, and although time seemed to be dragging more than usual, due to the fact that I was virtually counting each day, there was a new work opportunity created for about six of us boys, which lasted for my last three months at Glin. It helped make those last months a lot more pleasant.

Lord Glin, who owned Glin Castle, which was a few miles across the fields from the school and which is still there today, had a forest nearby, and we used to go there each morning after breakfast. We would walk over the top of the fields where our farm was, and walk about a mile to help the head keeper cut the trees and stack and move the wood. We were out most of the day, and whichever brother came with us, would bring along plenty of food and cook it in the open air over a home-made stove. We had sweet tea and it tasted heavenly, and we even had sausages from time to time. God, it was like being in heaven!

I had a lot more freedom in my last three months, and sometimes the brothers would leave us there in the care of the forest keeper. Life was sweet and it was a wonderful feeling of wild exuberance. I felt like a newborn lamb, jumping for sheer joy, and for a short time I could forget I was at Glin. Strangely enough, the brothers who came with us seemed to have a different attitude as well, and seemed more relaxed. It was as if they were freed from the institutional and oppressive atmosphere that existed at Glin and that exists in any institution. In many ways the brothers were in a similar position to us. They could not just leave, because they had to look after us.

My last memory of working in the forest was having a cup of wonderful sweet tea and sitting on a hill with the warm June sun shining on my face as I gazed up at the azure blue sky, and looked out towards the river Shannon. As I watched the ships in the distance going up and down the river with Brother Gill and some of the boys, I felt very good but also a little sad. I was leaving tomorrow, and this was the last time I would ever see this view again and all of the friends that I had come to know and like. I had served my five years and had survived, and now it was nearly over. It had been the longest, slowest and the most painful five years of my life, and I felt I could face anything that life would throw at me from now on, except of course being locked up again, and that was unlikely to happen to me in the future. I had learned a very painful but valuable lesson, which I was not likely to forget in a hurry. I was a changed man or boy. I somehow felt very calm and at peace, ready to face the world. I also felt a certain pride and some feelings of gratitude to the brothers. I did not hate them, and never have done, although there were a couple who I would have strangled if I had been capable of doing so.

I had come to St Joseph's School at Glin in June 1951, a scrawny eleven-year-old, cocky and uneducated, a snotty-nosed boy whose only ambition was to be the biggest thief in Limerick. Although I was still on the thin side, I was at least feeling much stronger and I had acquired a lot of knowledge and confidence. The change in me was dramatic and whether it was for the better, only time would tell.

The downside was that I had missed out on a normal family life for five years, which I could never make up. I had not been exposed to normal family situations and a caring learning environment, and the only role models I had were the brothers, but that was the way it was and there was no going back. I had to look to the future. The brothers' job was done to the best of their ability and now it was up to me to put into practice what I had learned.

The day I left Glin I went up to the classrooms to say goodbye to my various friends and to Brother Flynn especially. He put his arms around me, gave me a friendly cuddle and wished me good luck. He told me that he would miss me and he reminded me to 'Always make sure that you go to mass every Sunday, Raymond, and say your prayers every night to the Blessed Virgin and you'll be all right.' Mass was the last thing I was thinking about. I had had enough of religion for the last five long years and it would be a great relief to wake up in Limerick the next morning and not have to get up at 6.30 to go to mass. However, when I did say goodbye to Brother Flynn, I thought that I noticed the hint of a tear in the corner of his eye. Strangely enough I also felt a little tearful. Brother Flynn was one of those brothers who had always treated me well, and no doubt he had formed a bond with me, and probably with many of the boys. I suppose we were a bit like their families, their children maybe. They had got to know us and no doubt felt some pride and sadness when we left to face the big world. I had liked Brother Flynn a lot and could not fault him in any way. In a different setting our relationship with many of the brothers might have been different. I had a terrible feeling of anticlimax. I had been looking forward to this moment for the last five years and now it was here, it did not seem quite so exciting.

Brother Cullen took me to Limerick where I would live with my aunt for the next few weeks, not really knowing what was going to happen to me. I got my first ever job, working down in the dockyards in Limerick in a woodyard. My job was catching and stacking planks of wood as they

132

came off a conveyor belt which I soon became bored with, a habit that would afflict me all through my working life. Luckily, my mother came to the rescue and sent some money for my fare to travel by boat over to England and back to Brighton again, where she was still living. Although I was very excited at the prospect, I had many reservations. My memory of when I was last there in 1953 was still quite fresh in my mind, but my mother insisted that I come to live with her. It was a decision that would change my life beyond my wildest dreams – eventually! I remember very clearly leaving Limerick railway station for the last time on my voyage of discovery. Many of my cousins came to see me off and they were quite sad. I had a little brown suitcase with one change of clothing, my travel ticket and about one pound in my pocket, but I did have a lot of hopes and dreams, which I hoped would come true in England before too long.

18. Brighton, Sex and Rock 'n' Roll

Brighton in July 1956 must have been the best place in the world to live, especially for a 16-year-old from Limerick. It had absolutely everything, the sea was just yards away, lovely shops and lanes and as many cinemas as Limerick, and the boys did not piss on the floor like they did at the Thomond, but then you can't have everything! I lived with my mother and her partner Jock at number 37a York Road, down in another cellar. Our flat was less than a couple of minutes from the seaside, with the nearest cinema only a minute away. God, it was like heaven. Life seemed very good for now and I felt very lucky. In 1956 nearly all the cinemas opened at about eleven o'clock in the morning, which meant I could go into one show and stay to see the same film again if I wished without paying again, because the show was continuous throughout the day. It was great and I loved it. For months after I arrived in Brighton I would come out of one cinema and go into another one and then into another and often saw about three different shows in a day. The beauty was that the films were changed about twice a week in all the cinemas, which gave a never ending variety of films to go and see. I suppose I was making up for all the films that I had missed while I had been locked away at Glin. I felt like a child in a chocolate factory and indulged myself to the limit. I just couldn't get enough of the movies. It was a great period for me and I did not have a care in the world. I was not working at this time, so my mother and Jock were subsidising my trips to the cinema. I just loved the movies and it was a period of great film making all over the world, but of course American films were my favourite.

As a matter of interest, the great British middle distance and 1980 Olympic 800 metres gold medallist Steve Ovett, whom I meet in 1983, was born in Brighton in 1956, the same year that I came to live in Brighton.

Brighton also had a couple of ice-rinks and a couple of theatres and a cinema where you could see naughty French films. When I say naughty, I mean some bare breasts, which for a young Catholic boy was very exciting and stimulating in 1956. The Hippodrome was also a great place for live entertainment and I regularly went to see the fantastic variety shows. I saw many of the pop stars of the day, including Frankie Vaughan, Dickie Valentine and of course my idol of the day Tommy Steele who was just starting out then.

135

Ruby Murray, the Irish pop singer, who had about three songs in the top ten at the time, also appeared at the Hippodrome. Yes, she was the girl who had entertained us at Glin some years before. I loved the live entertainment shows and I often went to the Hippodrome. I also spent lots of time and money on the piers, which were in the peak of condition in those days. I loved listening to the orchestras and I was amazed at the violin players and the sweet music that these old guys could produce. I often asked myself, 'Why couldn't I play like that?' But then these were professional musicians.

One day while I was on one of the piers, I suddenly heard this incredible sound coming from a large colourful box with flashing lights. It was a juke-box, which I had never seen before, and the song was 'Don't be Cruel', by a new American singer called Elvis Presley. Elvis Presley! What a strange name, I thought, but what an awe-inspiring sound. This was and still is, to me, the most fantastic rock 'n' roll sound that I have ever heard, and I could not stop playing and listening to it over and over again. I was hooked on this new sound, which people were calling rock 'n' roll. It was a great time to be a teenager and living in Brighton at the start of the great rock 'n' roll era. Life was sweet and as perfect as it could be.

One of my favourite haunts in Brighton was the ice-rink on West Street. It drove my young growing body wild with desire, which by now had an over abundance of sex hormones, and I was filled with lust and desire, watching all the young pretty girls. The ice-rink also played all the latest hit records while the young teenage girls skated around and around with next to nothing on. Those short dresses were incredibly sexy and I have to say that I was compelled to interfere with myself on more than one occasion because of my uncontrollable sexual desire. God, the guilt was terrible every time, but my desire usually overcame my fear of hell. It was good not to have a Christian Brother staring into your eyes every morning and telling you, 'You have been interfering with yourself again, Raymond, haven't you?' Well he would have been right if he had been at the ice-rink with me, but at least I could now tell him to go fuck himself. It was my body to interfere with if that's what I wanted to do! The sense of freedom was great and I was a happy teenager.

I was extremely shy and found it almost impossible to chat up girls, and whenever I did, I don't think they understood a word I was saying, which made my predicament even more embarrassing. Everything was new to me, but my new found sexual freedom was very exciting, although frustrating at times.

However, I was about to have a new experience that was quite enlightening and very strange, and nothing that I had ever been prepared

136

for. I found myself being chatted up by blokes, usually much older men, which at first I found very flattering! I eventually discovered that Brighton was a well-known haunt for gay activity, and even today it is recognized as the gay capital of Europe! I would not have recognized a gay bloke in a million years in those days and certainly would not have known what their intentions were. I know that there had been one funny guy at Glin, but that was all I knew and I would not have known what they got up to. God, I hardly knew where babies came from and I was 16! Sometimes I would be lying on the beach and an older man would sit down fairly near me and he would start talking to me. He would tell me how good-looking I was and what a great body I had, and then he would ask me if I had ever thought of doing modelling. I certainly had not thought of modelling and I did not think that I had a good body, never mind a great one, but I was naturally flattered that someone admired me. Maybe I would make it into the filums one day after all. The guy must have thought I had just come over on the boat, and of course he was right! But I wasn't that easily led and declined his offer to go to his flat for a coffee, as I was becoming a little suspicious of this behaviour and the way that he looked at me, up and down as if I was a horse he was about to buy. I would tell him that my mother expected me home for tea and leave hurriedly.

On one occasion when I eventually started singing in a pub, I was approached by an older distinguished-looking gentleman who told me that I was a good singer and would I go to this exclusive club and try a few songs with the resident piano player. He told me that he was in the music business, so off I went thinking that this might be my big break at last. I might, after all, get famous much quicker than I expected. It was only a small club and there were only about two other guys there besides us. I nervously sang 'Singing the Blues', and the guy who had invited me in to the club applauded loudly and told me how good I was, which was just what I wanted to hear.

He started to sit a little too close to me with his knee touching mine and I was beginning to get the feeling that perhaps being a singer was not that important after all. I felt uncomfortable and hot under my James Dean white T-shirt and so I made an excuse and left quickly. I was beginning to cop on as they say in Limerick, or wise up. Perhaps it was not my singing that he was interested in after all, but I was to remain very naive for a few more years yet. Looking back now I realise I must have seemed a bit odd, often sitting in a pub on my own, drinking a glass of lemonade with a sweet, innocent smile on my face. What a plonker I must have looked, certainly not the macho image that I thought I was projecting. It would have made my life a lot simpler if I had been an alcoholic or at least a beer drinker. I still had no friends, male or female, and I found it very difficult trying to get to know guys my own age. For one thing I did not drink so I found it that much more difficult to socialise and relax. My dancing skills were non-existent due mostly to my self-consciousness and my shyness, so I found it very hard, if not impossible, to chat up the opposite sex. I felt like a fish out of water.

One incident in particular highlighted my awkwardness with girls. I used to wander around Brighton fairly late at night in the summer due to the excitement of being in such a lovely place, and as I passed a row of houses near where I lived, an attractive blonde woman, probably in her thirties, was standing outside in her dressing-gown. As I walked by she asked me if I had change for the electric meter. I found some change and gave it to her and then she asked me if I would put it in for her, because she was afraid of the dark. (She wasn't the only one!)

She led me down to the cellar, in through her bedroom and into another room, where the meter was, and she gave me the money to put into the meter, which I did. When the lights came on again I was alone with this attractive woman, even if she was much older than me. I nervously made small talk and said I must be going and left. I did not think too much about the situation and the opportunity that was there before me. Somehow, as soon as I had left, it began to dawn on me that I had slipped up badly and what the woman was really after was my young and excited body! 'What a prick,' I thought, 'I've fucked up an opportunity of a lifetime.' So I wandered back in the hope she might be looking for more change for the meter, but no such luck. She must have gone to bed a slightly frustrated woman, though not as frustrated as I was. For the next couple of weeks I went up and down the same street, armed with plenty of change, hoping I would see the meter lady, but I never did see her again, and the memory of my missed opportunity has lingered in my mind ever since. So, if there is an 80-year-old lady still living in Brighton, wondering who the stupid Irishman was in 1956 who did not rise to the occasion, it was me! 'Sorry, madam, we both lost out that night and I am sure that you could have taught me an awful lot! But I have not forgotten you, whatever your name was.'

I did, however, learn from that experience, but in a different situation and with a woman who was even older than my mother. She was a piss artist friend of my mother and one afternoon she came to the flat looking for my mother, who was not in. The friend was just about sober and asked if there was any drink in the house. As it happened there were two bottles of Guinness in the bedroom, so I brought her in and plied her with the Guinness, with the thought of jumping on her and screwing her. I got her on the bed, which she was quite willing to do, and as I hovered over her she said to me while she gazed down between her legs, 'You must be hard up to want to shag that!' Not the most romantic of words on such a historic occasion! She was not a pretty sight and I was hard up, and I felt like it was my birthday so I didn't care too much. The whole effort didn't take a couple of seconds, but it ranks as the lowest point in my sexual experience and I felt terrible for a long time after that. Even confession and all the praying wouldn't take the bad feeling and guilt away. But looking back all these years later, two bottles of Guinness wasn't a bad price even in 1956, and I had to practise on some unfortunate woman! The woman swore me to secrecy, not to tell my mother, which was fine by me.

My mother wasn't a great help when it came to my love life. When I eventually got around to bringing the odd girl home, my mother, who seemed to be constantly inebriated, would immediately start telling them what a good boy I was and that I went to mass every morning and, 'He loves his mother, don't you know.' Not the best way to try and seduce or influence a young Church of England girl. Needless to say I was not that successful while my mother was around, but who would be?

I had a great opportunity one night when a friend of mine and his girlfriend had been round to listen to a few records and to show me a new tape recorder. It played music without records. What would they think of next? The mind boggles. His girlfriend was an ice-skater and had beautiful round thighs, as I was to discover later on in the night! She was dark-haired, very sexy, and an awful lot younger than the friend of my mother from my previous sexual experience. I wondered what she was doing with this guy who was not a lot to look at and who did not seem particularly interested in her. He was certainly not as interested in her as I was and I was lusting after her and wished I could somehow let her know without the guy knowing. After all, he was only a casual friend, and I did not feel any loyalty to him.

The guy must have been reading my mind, because at around 10.30 he said he had to leave and would I mind taking his girlfriend home. I saw my opportunity and said I was glad to help a friend. He immediately left, and neither I nor the girl was in any hurry to leave. After all, the night was still young and I knew this was going to be the chance of a lifetime. I would not slip up this time. I moved in for the kill; I used my Limerick charm and there was no resistance. She obviously could not resist the temptation to grapple with my young, vibrant and eager body.

We jumped on the sofa and as I lifted up her skirt I noticed that she was wearing the tiniest pair of white panties that I had ever seen, which seemed to exaggerate the size of her ice-skating thighs. She slipped off her panties with the help of my shaking hands. By now my heart was pounding and I couldn't contain my excitement, and that's exactly what happened. I left my sex hormones on the sofa! Jasus, what a waste, what a dick head! I couldn't believe it, it was over and it hadn't even started! This couldn't be happening to me, but it was, and I couldn't do anything about it. I felt humiliated. What a cock-up!

Very little was said and I felt about as bad as I could, and the girl was not about to hang around for my second coming, so to speak. One disappointment was enough for her in one night and she was not prepared to wait for me to get into second gear again. So I took her home with a heavy heart, with me trying to make small talk, and that was the last I ever saw of her, but my experience that night dented my confidence and left its scars on me, at least temporarily. I was only 17 and hopefully I would improve. It often occurred to me that I let the Irish nation down in that dark room in Waterloo Street, Brighton, in 1957. Would that young girl think that all Irishmen were so sexually inadequate and not the greatest lovers after all? I would have to keep trying until I proved myself.

If that was the low point on my way to sexual maturity, the exact opposite happened when I was about 18, and it could be described as some sort of a high point or a record of sheer lust. It was with a girl who had agreed to stay the night in our new flat, at number 50 Waterloo Street. The flat was over a kosher butcher's shop. That night I managed to have my wicked way five times! And that was long before the sex drug Viagra was on the scene. It certainly was not a record that I ever attempted again or was proud of, and it is the first time that I have recounted it. Mind you, I didn't manage to go to work the next day and I was in a haze for a little while after. I suppose I had to take it while it was there, because I also remember very vividly going without for nearly a year, so as usual my life seemed full of ups and downs, so to speak. To be honest the quality of my sexual performances was certainly nothing to write home about. I did not have a clue what I was doing and I certainly knew nothing about girls having periods or what the significance of them was. I was pig ignorant and certainly a total sexist, because all I ever thought of was my own self-gratification and what sex did for me. I doubt if I ever gave value for money in those days, and I don't believe I really knew how. My sexual experiences were not as frequent as they should have been.

19. Work

Work was one of the few four letter words that I did not use too often, but sooner or later I had to start work. One of my first jobs was working at Liptons which was a a well-known grocery store on Western Road in Brighton. I was put working down in the cellar, out of harm's way, which suited me down to the ground, because I was surrounded by all types of food. The manager up in the shop would shout down and tell me when he wanted something or other, whether it was a huge tin of ham or a tin of corned beef, which I would open and send upstairs on a chute.

One of my other jobs was to make the tea. A task that was to cause me great anxiety. Jasus, I never made tea in my life, and I started to panic because I did not want to let those nice English people know just how stupid I was. I had never made tea before! I eventually found the kettle, boiled the water and then emptied the whole quarter pound packet of loose tea into the kettle. How was I to know that I was supposed to use a tea pot and a spoon to measure the tea? The manager and the other staff drank some of the tea and spat it out straight away, and as I was still standing next to him with bated breath, he asked me had I ever made tea before? I had to admit that I hadn't and I was expecting the sack, but he just laughed and told me how to make it in the future. 'These English people are not as bad I was led to believe back in Limerick!' I remember thinking.

As I had a great appetite and I was not used to being in the middle of a mountain of food, I could not resist helping myself to the odd bit of food on the premises. I never took food away and only ate it because I was hungry. I was aware that it was wrong. First, it was a few biscuits, and then I would open a 7 lb tin of peaches, and when I was really hungry, I started to open huge tins of ham. Jasus, it was lovely, so it was, and it was more than I could bear to be surrounded by so much food and not touch it. It was like expecting a drug addict to be surrounded by drugs and expecting him to just ignore them. The spirit was willing, but my flesh was always my weakest link.

Things got a bit tricky after a while, because I soon had half-eaten tins concealed all over the place and I could not keep them in the fridge for obvious reasons. I was nearly caught eating a few times, especially when I had a large mouthful of food and the manager shouted down and asked me a question. Another part of my job was going out on deliveries in the van in the afternoon, and that's when I fell foul of the manager.

The driver suffered badly from asthma and he could hardly turn the key to start the engine in the van. Even getting into the van caused him great distress, so I finished up doing all the lifting, and the worst thing was that I was getting home about 7.30 on a summer's evening instead of about six o'clock. I was not very happy, so naturally I told the manager. I said that I didn't mind doing my share of the lifting, but I objected to getting home late every night and could I please have extra money or I was leaving. I was not very diplomatic and perhaps did not use the right approach. The manager was blunt and to the point and he basically said in very precise language, 'Goodbye!' In other words I was given the sack on the spot. It was to be my first run-in with management and it would not be my last over the years. I felt that I had to stand up for my rights and I paid the price, but I was not complaining. My mother, who had got me the job, was a little disappointed because she had known the manager personally. My old rebel instincts and attitudes were beginning to be established. I didn't want to be pushed around any more, following my five years at Glin. I didn't have to tolerate things that I did not like either, and I frequently made quick, silly mistakes and bad decisions because of my often misplaced pride, anger, immaturity and bad judgement.

Job number two was working in a very high-class tailor's shop called Cobleys, in Hove, as an apprentice tailor. It was only about a mile away and I learned a lot to supplement the skills I had already learned in the Glin tailoring department. So my time at Glin was proving to be of some use after all. I got on very well with the staff there and especially the guy in charge who was a real nice fellow and a great film fan, just like me. We had a lot in common, and every morning we would talk about the movies we had seen the night before and would recommend the best ones to go and see. I remember him telling me that the new John Wayne western *The Searchers* was one of the best movies that he had ever seen, so I went to see it that night and agreed with him completely. We also made suits for some famous people who lived in the Brighton area. One was the famous TV and film personality Fred Emney, who was a very large man, weighing probably over 20 stone.

I liked the job and I improved my tailoring skills considerably, but I hated working indoors in the lovely hot summers in Brighton, hovering over a hot iron. I would day-dream and wonder what it was like sitting out on the beach watching all the half-naked girls, so after nearly a year there, I left and stayed out of work for most of the summer. It was heaven!

I then got a job in a local engineering factory and I was told how lucky I was to have got a job there. I was there for a whole day! Basically I was

142

left on my own and ignored by everybody. I was left playing with screws and bolts with no direction from anyone and I hated it so I didn't go back the next day. 'A waste of a fucking day,' I remember thinking. I was beginning to realise that I became bored quite easily unless I found the job stimulating and challenging, at least that was my excuse and perhaps my own interpretation.

I also helped build Gatwick airport during my search for the perfect job and I worked for a couple of months during the hot summer. When I say build, I was helping to put the cables under the runway for the landing lights, but again I found it boring after a few days and I only stuck it because I was out in the open air, getting a free tan. During this period I suffered appallingly from acne all across my back, my shoulders and my face, which did not exactly help my confidence with the opposite sex. It caused me great embarrassment and annoyance, but while I worked at Gatwick, exposing my body to the sun all day, I found that all my acne disappeared after a few days and I felt normal again, until it all came back at the end of the summer. Acne plagued me from about 16 to 20. It affected my self-esteem badly, which was already very low.

One of the problems with working at Gatwick airport was that we had to bus it there and back every day, which was a lot of travelling for a young and virile teenager, and I found it tiresome and boring. During our tea breaks we often had to walk the whole length of the runway to get to the canteen, which could take up to ten minutes or more, and then back again. When we got there we often had to get in a very long queue and wait our turn before being served. We were expected to do all this in less than 30 minutes, which was not possible. I often took a few liberties and took an extra 15 minutes or more and blamed it on the long queues, but the foreman did not always believe me.

I soon became bored working at Gatwick airport and left after a few months, which was a slight improvement. This was a pattern that was to haunt me for most of my life; I had very little tolerance and a very low boredom threshold. I was very unsettled and I found it difficult to do the same things for very long unless I was happy there. Sometimes I would not give myself enough time to get used to a new job and I often paid the price by being unemployed for various periods in my life. My lack of discipline, for whatever reason, caused me a lot of heartache, but I never felt it was because I was lazy. Despite my often cavalier attitude to work, I have only drawn unemployment benefit for about three months while living in England, and that was during the severe winter of 1963.

My next job was working with the local council repairing roads and doing odd jobs. I stuck with it for about a year, which was an improvement on my previous work record. Labouring also helped build my quite skinny physique. I also joined a local body-building club, which was through an alley just opposite our flat , where a lot of the local body-builders trained. I was by far the puniest guy there, but all the guys were mostly English and they were very nice to me. I learned a lot about keeping fit and how to lift weights, and it would remain part of my life for ever more.

I was also realising very early on in my life that English people were very nice, and I never have seen anything during my life living in England that has altered that opinion. Any previous prejudices I had, proved to be unfounded. Although English people seemed a bit aloof and reserved at times, I have realised that they were on the whole genuine. I have also never criticised England as a country. How could I? England has given me a lot of opportunities and I owe it everything I have.

At first I accepted labouring as a way of life and just got on with it. I did not think I could possibly do anything else for a living and neither did I have anyone to advise me as to other possible careers. But deep down I always felt a longing to break away from this menial work and I often felt embarrassed at working on the streets, because I always believed that passers-by were looking at me and judging me. A touch of paranoia again! I remember standing in a shop doorway during a heavy downpour while labouring and thinking to myself, 'I don't want to do fucking labouring all my life, if only I could be a singer or something,' but of course I was only day-dreaming again. I did not really believe I could get out of the rut I saw myself getting into. I had a lot of pride and sometimes I felt that simple labouring was beneath me. I worked with a lot of really nice Irish guys, but all they seemed to do with their money was get pissed every night, and they all appeared to be content with their lot. That was not for me; I had ambition and I was going to be different somehow. I did not want to be a labourer like my father all my life, always covered in dirt and grime and never getting anywhere, never having any money.

At times I was very resentful of my situation, angry with the world and angry with myself for not being able to improve my situation. As I look back now, I am glad that I was angry and restless and always looking for the rainbow that was over the hill somewhere, otherwise I would have remained a labourer all my life. I also would not have met my wife Sandra if I had remained a labourer. Having said all that, I would not have missed my labouring experiences for anything in the world, because all the guys I worked with were genuine and they were straight and did not beat about the bush or talk behind your back. If you did not pull your weight they soon told you and called a spade 'a fucking spade'. I learned so much and realised that no experience in life is wasted in the long run.

The trouble was, the more jobs I left, the lower my self-confidence and my self-esteem. In some ways it was a vicious circle and it would be a long way down the line before I would achieve any kind of stability in the work situation. And even when I eventually did, I never could lose that restlessness and that longing to be famous, to achieve something really big. Whether it was just wishful thinking or a genuine belief in myself I did not know, but I always believed I would do something that would get me recognized someday. It would be years, however, before I would come to realise that whatever I did or achieved in life would never satisfy me, because basically, deep down, I would always feel inadequate, which stemmed from my childhood. Maybe I was inadequate!

I eventually left my job on the council and got a job working at Shoreham Shipping, a few miles along the coast from Brighton, bagging coal in some form or another all day long. It was really very hard work and it helped at least to make me physically much stronger. We worked underneath these huge great coal skips, which had a small chute and an opening that could be controlled by a handle, which in turn led into weighing scales. There were at least half a dozen of these skips, which had different grades of coal, and the lorries would back onto the platform, which was level with the end of the lorry. The lorry driver would indicate which of the grades of coal he wanted. He would have lots of bags and the idea was that he would help you fill up the bags as quickly as possible so that he could get back on the road as quickly as he could, deliver his coal and then come back again for another load.

After a while, I became very experienced at lifting up the handle of the scales to allow just enough coal to come out to make a hundredweight with one lift. Sometimes, of course, a great lump of coal would get stuck under the opening and then you were fucked, because you would neither be able to open nor close the opening and coal would come gushing out all over the place.

Time was money to the lorry drivers and to us, because the quicker you got him away, the bigger tip he would give you, and it also meant the more drivers you eventually got out, the more tips you would get in a day, so you had a great incentive to work hard. Sometimes I would make about £1 in tips a day, which was not bad considering that I was getting about £10 a week. Of course there were a few mean bastards who didn't give tips, and you soon got to know them. You never got caught more than once, and you soon learned to work to rule, so to speak, so that the driver would be in the

145

coal yard a lot longer, which meant he would lose money. We usually had them by the balls and they had to play ball, so to speak, eventually. At least I had some control over somebody else for a change.

Of course, all of the lorry drivers were on the fiddle, and this is the clever way it was done. All the lorries had to be weighed on huge weighing scales as they came and left the yard, and they were watched over by a guy in the room next to the scales. Whatever weight they had on was recorded and not just the number of bags. The trick was to have every bag a little bit underweight so that instead of having maybe the official 30 bags, weighing one hundredweight each bag, there might be 35 bags, each weighing a little less, so the driver would have those extra five bags to sell privately and would pocket the difference and no one was the wiser. The weight of the lorry was still recorded as having a certain amount of weight. The company was not losing out, but the housewife was, because they would never know the difference when the coal was eventually tipped down their cellars at their homes. We loaders were, of course, willing participants in the underhand scheme, because we would always keep the bags a little bit under weight. It was a very clever scheme and I am not sure if anyone was ever found out.

At the end of each day's work I would look like a black and white minstrel, or a black cotton picker from the American deep South. Showers were provided, which we had at the end of the day. There was a workman's cafe opposite where I would have rock cakes for breakfast, dinner and tea-break while listening to Britain's newest rock 'n' roll singer, singing his first big hit 'Move It'. It was, of course, Cliff Richard, who was around the same age as me. Oh how I longed to be a rock 'n' roll singer and have all the girls screaming for my body, which I would have gladly given away, free of charge!

Although the work was extremely hard, it suited me for a while, and I stayed there for about six months or so and felt a lot stronger when I left due to all that lifting. I wanted to try something different, but I did not know what. If only someone could have given me some guidance and put me in the right direction, but maybe I was too headstrong, and I would not have listened anyway. Sometimes I left jobs without any planning or good reason, and I rarely thought of the consequences.

20. My Mother's Drinking Problems

My mother's drinking did not bother me too much for the first year or so when I moved to Brighton, but I soon became aware that she was coming home later and later each night and becoming noisier and noisier, and it started to get me down. It was the screaming and the abuse and the knocking over of tables and furniture, and more often than not she was not on her own. Her partner Jock was either in bed after a few drinks or he was away on a job, and when he was around he was under the influence himself, so it didn't bother him very much.

My job as a labourer often meant that we got most of our work up around the London area. At first I would do my best to ignore my mother's noisy behaviour, and I tried to sleep, but most nights it was impossible. Eventually I would come down and ask her nicely to be quiet and remind her that I had to be up for work at around six to get the train up to London the next morning. I would plead with her to go to bed or at least to be quiet. My request usually fell on deaf ears, and often it made her even more noisy and she would then tell me to, 'Fuck off up to bed and leave me alone,' and didn't I know that she had cancer and did not have long to live! I usually paid no attention to her ramblings about cancer because she often came out with strange ideas and I never knew what was true and what wasn't. I would tell her it was all right for her and that she could lie in bed in the morning, but I needed my sleep.

My comments usually made her even worse and often she would get hold of the table, which had cups or plates on it, and she would up end it all over the floor. God it was a nightmare and it seemed there was nothing I could do; it was a regular routine, night after night. I have honestly never known a woman who behaved so badly and so often as my mother used to. Knowing what I know now, I realise that my mother was beyond doubt an alcoholic, and possibly beyond redemption at that point. When I was in Brighton in 1953 she had bad bouts of drinking, and as far back as I could remember she always seemed to have had a drinking problem. I often wondered if that was why my father was so violent towards her, or did she drink because of my father? These were questions that I would never get an answer to. My mother was certainly bringing the worst out in me. I felt as though I could strangle her, just to get a little peace and regular sleep. Glin school now seemed, at times, like a haven. At least I could get regular sleep there, not that I ever wished to go back. I had moved on.

I never remember my mother working during my years in Brighton. Where she got her money from I do not know and did not ask, but I had my own ideas and suspicions. She always seemed to have enough money for drink. She regularly brought men home even though Jock was with her, and it was usually at night and often when she was drinking. Her routine at this time was that she would get up around midday and go out, and I usually would not see her again until after midnight, drunk. I regularly had heated arguments with the men she brought home, who were also drunk and singing loudly and being very noisy and abusive. Again I would try to be as tolerant as possible for as long as I could, but eventually I would go downstairs and threaten to 'Kill the fucking lot of you if you don't fuck off home, 'cause you're all driving me absolutely fucking stone mad and I'll knife the fucking lot of you, and I don't give a shit what happens to me', and I meant it. They usually left very quickly because they realised I was mad as hell and near to breaking point and I could be relied on to carry out my threat. I certainly had inherited my father's temper and I could stand an awful lot of abuse before I lost control.

All this constant stress with no outlet was taking its toll on me and I wanted to leave, but I still felt a lot of loyalty to my mother and I could not bring myself to go. My sister Phyllis, whom I was in contact with now and again, advised me not to leave, but to stay with my mother because she needed me. When I was in bed I could not sleep properly because I was waiting in anticipation for her to come home, and what was going to happen when she did come in. I wondered would she come in at all and would she fall down and hurt herself as she had done many times in the past or fall under a car?

These thoughts would go through my mind every night, which did not help me to sleep. I was a teenager and I was worried to death about my mother, rather than it being the other way around. My teenage years were far from being normal. One night I woke about 2 a.m. and she was not in, so I started to get worried and could not get back to sleep. Suddenly there was a knock on the door. It was the police, but still no sign of my mother, so I feared that something serious had happened to her. What could it be? My heart was pounding, because although I hated my mother's behaviour, I certainly never stopped loving or caring about her, and I could not bear the thought that something bad may have happened to her.

'Does Bridie O'Donoghue live here?' the policeman asked.

'Yes,' I replied through sleepy eyes, and I was now becoming very anxious, wondering what I was going to hear next!

'Well I'm sorry to have to tell you that she has been in an accident and

148

that she is in hospital, but that she is okay,' said the policeman. I burst out crying when the policemen told me that my mother had been hit over the head with a bottle during a drunken argument and needed stitches. To know that the only person that you cared about in the whole world had been hit with a bottle was very hard for me to bear. I could feel her pain and wished it had been me, just like she used to defend me from my father when he was mad at me. My mother had been beaten up in her life many times before by my father, so why again? Of course, it was all to do with the drink as I was later to read in the *Brighton Evening Argus*. She had got into an argument with another woman and the woman had smashed a bottle over her head. The incident horrified me.

This incident had no effect whatsoever on my mother's drinking habits and she continued as if nothing had happened. My mother's bad habits were as regular as clockwork. After a night's drinking she would stay in bed until around midday and come then come down the stairs half-dressed and usually in a bad mood. She would then get dressed and go straight out without eating, probably to the pub, and that would often be the last I would see of her until she came home pissed out of her mind, usually around midnight. It was so sad. I was helpless and I did not know what I could do. I was hardly 18 and completely frustrated and very ill-equipped to cope with an alcoholic mother.

One day when she had come in during the daytime, and not too drunk for a change, she went straight to bed and then she woke up in the evening when it was dark and said she was going out again. I locked the front door with the key and said that I was not going to let her out tonight. I told her to try and stop drinking for one night at least. She tried to grab the key off me and I was determined not to give it to her, so she dashed out to the back and tried to get over the fence into the next door neighbour's garden. When I saw her trying to get over the fence I gave in and gave her the key to the front door and off she went. I cried again at my failure and she returned later that night still drunk and still very abusive. Some nights she never came home at all and that was even more worrying.

One of my worst experiences of living in England, around 1957, was when I had to appear in court at Lewes, just outside Brighton, to give evidence against two of my mother's Polish alcoholic male friends whom I had caught robbing our gas meter. The two guys in question were both drunk and I'm not sure if they were totally aware of what they were doing. They laughed when I asked them what they were doing and stopped trying to break into our electric meter. I did not want to make a fuss, but I made the mistake of telling my mother when she came home from the pub, drunk and out of her mind again. She could be very abusive when she had had a few drinks. She decided to go around to their house and confront them, in the middle of the night! I pleaded with her that no real damage had been done and that the guys were sorry and were drunk anyway, but it made no difference. The drink no doubt had affected her thinking, and as usual, made her behave in an irrational way. She had made her mind up. I did not go with her, but waited anxiously at home, waiting to see what the consequences would be.

Sure enough, there was a big scene and the police were called and the outcome was that I had to appear in court shortly afterwards to give evidence against the two Polish guys, whom I knew quite well and liked. I did not want to go to court, but had no choice. The idea of standing up in court in front of a group of people terrified me and I just wanted to run away. The last time I had been in court was in 1951 when I was sent away to Glin Industrial School, but I was only ten years old then and did not take it all too seriously, but the thought of appearing in court terrified me. I was a very immature 17-year-old.

The judge, of course, was English and although I was not on trial, it felt like it. I was asked to give my name, which I did, and then I was asked to speak up, as the old judge could not hear what I had said. Was it my fault that he was half deaf? I spoke as loud as I dared in a trembling voice and I felt like a condemned man as I stood in the dock shaking with fear and gripping the sides of the witness box to steady myself. I fiddled with my tie to ease my shattered nerves but it did not help.

The judge had heard me this time, but he could not understand what I had said. By now I was getting very worked up and wished I was back in Limerick where everyone understood everyone and no one ever said to me, 'Would you mind repeating that again, Mr O'Donoghue?' I have always been a very shy person but at 17 I was as shy as you could be with no confidence and now living in a very strange country where everyone spoke with posh accents. The judge, I was beginning to think, had it in for Irish people and was just trying to humiliate me, and he was succeeding! I eventually got the old judge to understand my name and then he put more questions to me.

I answered the questions as best I could, and again I was asked to either slow down, speak up or to stop mumbling. Jasus, I was starting to get really flustered and wondered if it was me who was on trial, and it was true after all that the English did not like the Irish. I was starting to feel very paranoid, but I made an effort to slow down, speak up, and did the best I could not to mumble. But it was a real effort to maintain for very long. It seemed an unnatural way for a Limerick man to speak. I felt like I was auditioning for a part in Shakespeare and not doing very well at that. Marlon Brando was making a fortune mumbling in all of his movies around this period and no one could understand what *I* was mumbling about. It all seemed so unfair.

The learned judge stopped me in the middle of my evidence and smiled at me. 'Ah, he's warming to my Irish charm after all,' I thought, but I was wrong! 'You have a lovely Irish accent, Mr O'Donoghue,' the judge said, but then he delivered the death blow, 'But I did not understand a word that you said.' To cut a long story short, needless to say the meter robbers got off, no doubt partly due to my inadmissible and misunderstood evidence. It was my first and last experience of the English criminal system and a blatant miscarriage of justice, but I was glad, because the meter robbers were friends and I did not want to see them going to jail. So for me it was a happy ending of sorts. It was my second appearance in a court and I hoped that it would be my last.

My mother came home one day, sober! and said to me, 'Guess who I have here to see you?' It was John, my old friend from Glin, whom I had not seen for a few years. He had left Glin in 1955. I could not believe it, and it was a great and pleasant surprise. I still had not made any friends in England. We renewed our friendship and he stayed with us and we hung around together and worked on a few different jobs together, including helping to build Gatwick airport. John left for London a year or so later due to lack of work in Brighton, but we had a lot in common, mostly girls!

Often, and usually late at night, I remember walking down Western Road after coming out of a cinema and I could hear the sound of a woman's voice singing in the distance amidst the noise of the passing traffic, and hoping it was not my mother. Some hope! I soon realised it was her when I heard the refrain of the old Irish rebel song 'Kevin Barry', which she always sang when she was pissed. I always tried to avoid her, because I felt ashamed and sad to see her displaying herself in a drunken state in public. I never heard or saw any other woman in Brighton behaving in this way. It certainly was nothing to be proud of and I wanted to run away. I tried very hard not to let her see me, but on the odd occasion when she did see me she would shout across the road to me. 'Raymond, Raymond, come to me, you're the light of my fucking life, so you are. He's my baby, you know!' she would say to herself or to anyone else in earshot, which was usually not many as most people tried to avoid her. 'Oh fucking hell, she's seen me,' I would think aloud and I would run

151

away as fast as my legs could carry me. My mother had a beautiful singing voice and I only wish I could have recorded it somehow.

She was a very intelligent woman and I often wonder what she might have achieved if she had been given some normality in her life. All of her life seemed to have been controlled by her addiction to alcohol; and it seemed like one big piss-up.

From around the middle of 1957 my mother complained about stomach pains and seemed to have had very little interest in food; I rarely saw her eating a meal of any substance. I know now that a lot of alcoholics do not eat properly and she never seemed to eat much anyway. Alcohol was a substitute food, like it is for most heavy drinkers. She was a small woman and was quite slight in build.

My mother started to have treatment in the local hospital for a few months in late 1958, but she did not pursue it because she said it was too painful. She told me it was radium treatment and it was for cancer of the stomach. (I recently discovered that this was cancer of the womb, but maybe it had spread to her stomach as well.) At first I did not really believe her for some reason. I suppose I did not want to believe it. A few weeks later while she was slightly intoxicated and I was annoyed at her for being drunk, she told me that she had less than a year to live and that is why she was going to continue to get drunk. I told her not to be silly, that these things can be cured and maybe the doctors were wrong.

In the meantime Jock, my mother's partner, got me a job with the tarmacking firm he was working for, but unfortunately I had to travel up and down to different parts of London every day and sometimes on Saturday as well for half a day. I had to leave my house at about 5.50 a.m. to catch a bus up to Brighton station about a mile away so that I could get on the 6.20 a.m. train to London Bridge, to take advantage of the cheap workman's fare. I would miss the bus regularly and have to run the mile to the station, which was all uphill. Not so easy when you have just got out of bed! About four of us from Brighton worked for the same firm, so we all travelled up together. One of the old boys was called Owen. He was a real character and did something to make me laugh every day, unintentionally of course. We would have to share the compartments with office people who were working up in the City and who naturally were mostly dressed in pinstripe suits and bowler hats. We were not fussy and did not mind who we shared with, though I think they did! We were usually dressed in our black donkey jackets and wore either wellingtons or leather boots. Sometimes a bowler-hatted toff would close the window while reading *The Times*, and Owen, who was sitting opposite would be reading the

Daily Mirror. Owen would look over the top of the paper, frown over the top of his glasses, and immediately open the window again. The toff would lower his *Times* and close the window again, usually without saying a word. While the toff was probably studying the stocks and shares, Owen, who was trying to study the horse races for the day, would bang his newspaper down in an aggressive manner, stand up and open the window and say loudly, 'Leave the fucking window alone will you, you fucking bastard,' and then sit down and continue reading his paper. The window usually remained open for the rest of the journey. I enjoyed the interaction between the different classes of people and I sniggered quietly to myself. It usually set me up for the day and put me in a good mood. I often wondered what these posh people thought of us workmen sharing the same carriage.

Many of my labouring mates would go to the pub at dinner time or before, depending on what time the pubs opened. My old friend Owen from Brighton would be dying for a pint after about 10 a.m. and could be very irritable until he got that first drink. Sometimes he would nip off to the pub and tell me to tell the foreman that he was gone to the shop for a paper, but of course the foreman got wise and went to the nearest pub and reprimanded Owen and would tell him to 'Get your fucking arse out here, there's a load of Tarmac to lay.' Owen would down his pint and out he'd come with a great big beaming smile on his face, happy as Larry, and he'd work twice as fast. I often thought, 'Jasus, this Guinness works wonders, he went into the pub miserable and came out five minutes later with a smile on his face, what a change!' It always intrigued me just how affective a pint of Guinness could be.

One of Owen's tricks was to leave his shovel standing outside one pub, but then go into another one, just to confuse the foreman. This would give Owen more time to drink in peace, and while the foreman was looking in one pub, Owen would dash out and be back on the job before the ganger knew where he had been.

There was also a lot of humour on the job, which helped to make the very hard and dirty work that more bearable. I also worked with two English guys called Alfie and Billy, and their dad was one of the head foremen. Alfie and Billy were extremely good looking guys (just like me), and they would be constantly chatting up the girls as they raked the Tarmac amongst the busy traffic in the middle of King's Cross High Street or some other well-known London street. They were full of confidence and certainly had the charm and the looks to back it up. I was amazed at their cheek. I tried to take a leaf out of their book, and although I never could match their chat-up skills, it was another great learning experience and I came to realise that while your chat-up lines will not always work, you had more chance than not trying at all.

One story I was told was that one of the guys knew this particular girl who had a strange habit of suddenly whistling 'Colonel Bogey', which was the well-known theme tune from the big hit war movie of the time, *The Bridge on the River Kwai*. I realise, of course, that girls whistle from time to time, but not usually in the middle of having sex! Her whistling had, I believe, a very deflating effect on the individual, so I was told.

My tarmacking days were a great experience and I remember most of the guys with enormous affection, and they would always have a special place in my heart. They contributed an awful lot to forming my character and helped me to keep my feet on the ground and an equal balance to my life.

I finished up being a spokesman one day for a group of new labourers and it was agreed that I would ask the head foreman to either give us all a rise or we would walk off the job straight away. Not a good idea to go straight in with a threat and an ultimatum! The foreman's reply was just to say 'Goodbye', and then he walked away without saying another word and that was it. When I reported back to the other guys they all backed down and did not want to know, which left me without a job. I had to eat humble pie and ask for my job back, which I got, but again I learned a valuable lesson and that was to do what I felt strongly about, because I realised that I could not always rely on other people to back me up. It was a humiliating experience, but it also made me realise that labouring was not what I wanted to do all my life. I felt that I was more ambitious and more outspoken than a lot of guys that I was working with and it was eventually to make me fall out with some of the foremen. I started to become more and more disenchanted and restless, and wanted to do something different, but what?

In the evenings in Brighton I used to visit the pubs where they had a piano player or a small band and I would get up and sing one of the latest pop songs. My first ever public performance was in a pub on the sea front opposite East Street. The song was 'Singing the Blues', one of the big hit records of the day by Guy Mitchell and Tommy Steele. I was terrified to let go of the microphone. Although I have always loved singing and have been told all my life that I had a good singing voice, I was not sure that I had the confidence or the real ambition to pursue my dream, but at least I had the cheek to try. I would often try different things and I preferred to fail than not try at all.

154

Brighton beach between 1956 and 1959 was often full of live music and groups just playing for fun, because it seemed that everyone wanted to be a rock 'n' roll singer, including me. There was a great sense of optimism, fun and ambition in the air, especially amongst young people like myself. It was a magical period and I was very lucky to hear all the great and original songs and rock stars of the day. Elvis, Buddy Holly, Eddie Cochran, Gene Vincent, Fats Domino (a great favourite), Guy Mitchell and of course Tommy Steele. Plus all the other British artists like Lonnie Donegan who were all jumping on the bandwagon just about then. Skiffle groups were all the rage as well and I used to love going on the sea front to listen to some great guitarists. Some of the guitar playing was awesome and I just loved to listen to real live music, and it was free!

It was, I believed, a great period to be alive and a teenager. I was very fortunate and thought that it would never end. Some hope! I was one of the thousands of teenagers who queued around the block to see the greatest movie of its time, *Rock Around the Clock*, but I have to point out that I was not one of the teenagers who smashed up the seats. We did not do things like that in Limerick, we robbed them and took them home and maybe we pissed on the floor from time to time, but we didn't smash them up.

The Dome in Brighton also used to have big stars playing there and my greatest regret was not going to see my favourite all time singer, the great American tenor Mario Lanza, who appeared there in 1959. It was a missed opportunity and I never got the chance again. He was to die a few months later at the young age of 39, and I was very upset to know that a voice like that was silenced forever. Listening to him singing would always give me goose-pimples. Very few singers would ever give me that feeling. I first heard him singing at Glin in the movie *The Great Caruso*.

21. 1959 – My Mother Dies

1959 was certainly not a good year for me or for my mother. Not only did my favourite singer die but so did my closest and favourite person, the one I loved and cared about more than anyone in the whole world. In the summer of 1959 my mother had gone into the Royal Sussex Hospital for more radium treatment but I think only stayed a few days and discharged herself. She couldn't stand the painful treatment. During this period I was travelling up and down to Brighton almost six days a week and was finding it very difficult to cope. I was leaving home about 5.50 a.m. each day and if I was lucky I might get home before 6.30 p.m. although sometimes it could be 7.30. The work and travelling was not the real problem, it was my mother. She was still drinking excessively and coming in very late and preventing me from getting a good night's sleep.

I had very little social life during this period, except maybe at the weekends, because as soon as I had my tea it was virtually time to go to bed and get ready for the morning again. I never did much socialising anyway because I was basically a very shy person, and dancing did not come naturally to me and neither did I drink. So going to the cinema was one of my few real pleasures except whenever I met a girl, which was rare for me. Sex, drugs and rock 'n' roll seemed to pass me by somehow.

What I found very depressing was that during the winter months when I came home, the house would be empty and in darkness, with no fire on and no dinner ready for me to eat, so I had to light the coal fire and cook myself something to eat, which took up more of my time. There was no sign of my mother anywhere and most times I would not see her until late at night. Somehow she would still manage to stay awake for hours, mostly in a foul mood, and it seemed never ending. I really wanted to pack my bags and leave, but somehow I felt trapped and obligated to my mother. Our roles seemed to have been reversed during this period. Instead of my mother worrying about me and what I was getting up to, it was I who was constantly wondering what she was going to do next, and the stress and strain was really getting me down. I had no support and no one to turn to for advice. I just had to get on with the situation as best I could and learn as I went along, but things were to get worse, a lot worse before it all ended.

The last three months of my mother's life were hell for her and for me because she was in a lot of pain and that was despite the fact that she was

157

on morphine. It was oral morphine and only in a liquid form. It seemed to work okay to begin with, but as her body became tolerant to the drug, she had to keep increasing the dose until eventually she would just swig it out of the bottle without measuring it.

She had a friend who came to see her most days, and then my sister Phyllis came to stay with us and she was there for the last three months of my mother's life. From my own point of view, I was finding life very hard because I still had to go to work up in London every day and I was getting less and less sleep due to my mother's constant pain, which kept her awake every night in agony. Her screams of agony, especially at night, would remain with me all my life. She rarely slept, and it was horrible to see her deteriorate before my eyes.

She would be screaming out in the middle of the night, unable to get relief from the unrelenting pain. Her scream used to go right to the depths of my soul and I could not help her. In the middle of the night I tried to give her sips of Lucozade in the hope it might cure her or at least wet her parched mouth, but she had difficulty even drinking that. She had no energy and just wanted to die, and be away from the terrible pain that she was obviously experiencing, but I kept telling her she would be all right and I tried to reassure her. I was not always as sympathetic as I should have been, due to my own immaturity, frustration and inadequacies, God, I felt useless, and I did not cope very well with the situation. By now, my mother was a shadow of her former self and was bed-ridden, and she found any movement painful. She never complained at any time and I often wonder what her thoughts were during the last few days. She never confided to me what her feelings were, no doubt she was trying to protect me from worrying too much. She was still concerned about my welfare. In a very weak voice she would remind me to look after myself and make sure that I ate properly. I lay awake often during the night crying into my pillow with no one to tell my troubles to. One thing that I did do was to play Gounod's 'Ave Maria' sung by Mario Lanza from the sitting-room downstairs at full volume in the hope that my mother might hear it and maybe get some inspiration or at least some temporary relief.

I went to work as usual and I was finding it difficult to concentrate and I never mentioned it to anyone at work. When I got home that night, my mother was dead. The sheets were pulled over her head and it was hard to imagine that there was a body underneath. She was emaciated as people often are when in the last stages of cancer. I pulled up the sheets to look at her, and her pain was gone, but so was my mother and my pain was about to begin. I was naturally upset but not as upset as I might have been,

158

because I had been expecting her to die for the last three months and it was in some way a relief, but I never knew that she was about to die when I left for work that morning. Somehow I had hoped for a miracle, but it never happened. Her whole life had been full of emotional and physical pain, and now it was over, and she was only 40 years of age, but she always looked much older.

I found it difficult to sleep in the house that night, and I suddenly felt scared and frightened of my mother's dead body, as if it would harm me. It was a strange feeling and not very nice. I stupidly went to work the next morning because I did not think that there was anything that I could do. One of the guys I was working with saw me crying and asked what was wrong. When I told him, he told the foreman who sent me home immediately. They were very sympathetic and understanding, despite their tough appearance.

On the train home to Brighton it suddenly dawned on me that my mother was dead and I'm sure I did not fully comprehend it for the first day or so. I had barely reconciled myself with her since I came back from Glin in 1956, and now she was gone again, but this time for good, and I was only 19. I was grateful that she had been in England for me, to help me settle and to put some roots down. She was buried a few days later in Hove cemetery. She had a great fear of being cremated. I would never stop missing my mother, whom I had barely known, but I always loved her dearly and have never thought badly of her. All in all I only had eleven years living with my mother, including the time in Brighton, but difficult as it had been living with her during the last three years, I would not have missed it for the world. I often think of the hard and tragic life that she led and it makes me sad. I have had a very comfortable life and a nice house, and wish I could have given her something back, some of the things she never had to make her life a little easier. She would never meet my future wife or know her grandchildren. That also makes me sad.

My mother died absolutely penniless, a pauper, but she was well known for her own generosity and her kind nature. She gave a lot more than she ever got back, but that is how she was. I'm not like that but wish that I was, and that is how I will always remember her. Generous and kind to the end. Her influence on me was very great, and although in many ways she was not a great mother, and was not always there for me, I could understand her reasons and I loved her none the less, despite her many failings. She was more a victim than I ever was. Both my father's and mother's early deaths would leave me with a legacy and a fear hanging over me all my life, and that was that I would probably die before I was 40.

My mother had written a little poem for me while I lived with her in Brighton and I never asked her if it was complete or not. It was obviously written while she was sober, but nevertheless I still find it moving. It reveals something about her own feelings and what she thought of me, my sister and who knows what else. There is no title but I have kept it all these years in her own handwriting. (The line in brackets is what she had crossed out.)

'As I sit here and wonder alone,
I am thinking of home
And the ones I love best.
Neath the moon and the stars,
And a million guitars.
I long to (lay my head on your breast)
have you in my arms.'

Bridie O'Donoghue, Brighton

22. Keep on Running – London, 1960

I continued travelling to and from London for about a year after my mother's death, until my tarmacking friends suggested I move to London and save myself all that travelling time and all the expense. I agreed and the Larter brothers who worked on the same job and who lived around the Mitcham area went looking for a flat for me in their own time while I travelled back to Brighton each day. It was a very kind gesture and the flat that they found for me was perfect, at number 40 Huron Road, which just happened to have Tooting Bec running track less than a half mile away and Tooting Bec common at the end of the street. Tooting Bec Psychiatric Hospital was also only a few minutes away. The flat was only a small room at £1.50 per week, but it did look out onto the landlady's back garden, which meant that I could at least see the sun and of course the land lady sunbathing now and again in her swimsuit, which was no extra charge!

My working mates knew that I was interested in keeping fit and they had made a special effort to get me a flat near the track, which was to alter my life for the better within a couple of years. My landlady and landlord were Polish and treated me with great kindness and were very understanding to me during 1963 when I was unemployed and owed them six weeks' rent. They never hassled me and trusted me to pay them eventually, which I did. Their name was Mankewicz. The landlady often gave me free soup during this period, when I had nothing, especially after I came back after a ten mile run in the snow and was unable to open the front door with my key due to my hands being frozen. They were the best and only landlords that I ever had. And I would remain there for about six years. My mother must have been looking down on me because her death was to change my life for the better in so many ways that I could never have predicted.

I soon found the running track and after a few weeks I met an odd character called Stan Allen who was in Herne Hill Harriers, one of the top local running clubs in south London. Stan is still around and is still an odd character (just ask his wife Joan!). But he is liked and respected by the many athletes that he has coached and the free time that he has given to the club over a very long period.

I immediately took to running and started training regularly. I was running every day, despite working very hard on the roads all over

London. The first race I ever ran in was the Herne Hill Harrier's club championship. It was a mile held at Tooting Bec track and I did about 5 minutes, 6 seconds, which, looking back now, was not bad, because I did it on mostly natural ability with hardly any training, but of course I was not happy. The reason being that I finished last, not an ideal position, but I knew that I could only improve, so I was determined to train harder and every day. Anything that I did I liked to do properly, especially if it was voluntary!

Running, for me, has been an absolute life saver in more ways than one and it was something that I took to straight away and I always gave it 100 per cent. As I have got older I have come to realise that life itself is like running and racing. You need stamina, strength and endurance, but most of all perseverance in the face of adversity and stumbling blocks.

There are usually more bad runs than good ones and in life there are often more disappointments than successes, but you can't have one without the other. But what can we do but get up and remotivate ourselves as best we can with no guarantee that everything will turn out okay. If being a distance runner has taught me anything, it is that it has given me a stronger will and has taught me not to give up easily in any aspect of my life, despite the many hills to climb and at times feelings utter despair and dejection. Like most runners or sportsmen, I have worked for years to achieve a particular goal, only to find it did not work out, but it never stopped me getting out training again the next day. I was always able to shrug off my many disappointments fairly quickly and rarely gave in to self-pity for very long. Running, for me, has been a great way to express my individuality and be judged simply on my own efforts, but sometimes in life things happen that can almost destroy and make you want to quit and that is when you have to dig deeper than you knew possible.

Over the years running has given me a lot of personal satisfaction, as well as many frustrating races and disappointments. It has fulfilled a need in me to be as physically fit as I could be. I would also make most of my friends while participating in running, and meet a great number of international athletes over the years.

I had learned a lot about keeping fit while I was in care in Ireland by being part of our boxing club and I always enjoyed the running and physical exercise and the extra few perks that went with it.

If I have a favourite race and performance of my own, and they are very rare, it would probably be the 1983 London Marathon when I ran 2 hours 45 minutes 47 seconds, as a 42-year-old. It was also a personal best after a ten year stagnation. I remember coming over Tower Bridge and feeling as if I was flying, with absolutely no aches or pains and feeling like an Olympic champion with all the thousands of people cheering. I averaged between 60 and 80 miles a week year in and year out, with the odd few weeks of over 100 miles, as I did not see how else I could improve.

Looking back now, I realise that running is a very selfish sport, and I regret that I spent so some much time away from my family, while pursuing my own blinkered goal, when I could probably have achieved what I did with a lot less effort. Would I do the same again? Probably, because it fulfilled a need in me, to achieve something personal and get a little recognition along the way for my own individual efforts. It was also good for my self-esteem.

The dedication and will-power to train hard regularly as a runner has I feel also helped me in everyday situations and made me very determined in all walks of life. From observing many of my running friends for close to 40 years, I have noticed many similarities between them. They have all applied themselves to regular hard training day in and day out, no matter what the weather was like. They have all been very determined with a very tough mental attitude and always gave of their best in every race. Most were able to pick themselves up after a bad run and put it behind them. Most of the runners who I am talking about had no special ability, and certainly no better than my own to start with.

Although my running abilities were very ordinary and I endured a lot of frustrations, I probably got as much pleasure and satisfaction as did the internationals, and I trained as hard for years on end. My attitude and enjoyment to keeping fit, went back to when I was in my teens and despite my serious emotional and health problems today, I somehow still manage to do some exercise on a daily basis. Once an athlete, always an athlete, even if only in the mind!

Back in 1960 there were very few runners who did manual work as heavy as I did, and it was not always easy going on a ten mile run after I had been tarmacking all day, but I loved the freedom of running and feeling extra fit. It was also a way of expressing my individuality and helping to improve my very low self-esteem. I was hooked and resented having to work so hard, which was interfering with my running. I was also much heavier built than the other runners. At one time I weighed 11.5 stone (of solid muscle, of course), but I eventually was racing at a regular 10.4 stone, which was more suited to distance running, achieved through hard training combined with weight sessions and, of course, my eight hour day tarmacking.

The foreman at work got very cross at the end of one very hard day's work when he saw me changing in the hut and he asked me what I was doing. 'I'm running home to Tooting,' I said.

'Running home to Tooting, that's nearly eight miles,' he said.

'It's only about seven and a half,' I replied in all innocence.

'How the fuck can you run seven and a half miles after a day's work?' he asked me, and now seemed to be getting annoyed at my cheek.

'You're obviously not working hard enough, I'll make sure you lay an extra ton of Tarmac tomorrow and that'll stop your fucking running.' But of course it didn't stop me running, nothing would, because it became a way of life.

I was bringing home about £11 per week in wages and eventually managed to save about £150 so I decided to go back to Limerick for a week's holiday, which was to be my first trip home since I had left in 1956. I stayed with my aunt Doris for the week and it was nice for a couple of days seeing all my own friends again. It was in the middle of a lovely hot summer, and one of my vivid memories of that week was hearing Elvis's big hit record of the time 'It's Now or Never' coming from radios in many of the houses whose doors were always open in St Mary's Park. It gave me a great feeling of friendliness and belonging.

'Hello, Raymen, how are you getting on then? How long are you home for? You got very big didn't you and how's your mother Birdie?' people in doorways would say to me as I passed by. They all still remembered me and of course my mother. Few people were aware that my mother had died. They had a way of making me feel special and important, and treated me with great respect. I felt glad to be alive and to be recognised and back home again.

I had enormous respect for the people in St Mary's Park, (now King John's Island) and I guess my heart will always belong there. It's a totally unique place, not posh or grand but unique, and the people are generous and genuine with no airs or graces. The memories of the people always amazed me. They are my people and I will always feel part of them. I was one of them and it was nice to be grown-up and feel a sense of freedom and equality.

I was reminded about an incident regarding my mother, who had left there in about 1950. One elderly lady told me, 'The guards were looking for Noel Hanley (a friend of mine), and he ran into your house, and your mother, God love her, hid Noel under the bed, and when the police came into your house she told the guards that Noel had run out the back into the garden, and he gosh (got) away, so he did. Holy Jasus, the police were mad, so they were. Aw, sure your mother was great so she was, she loved

164

an ould dance and an ould laugh, so she did. Harmless she was, wasn't she, Mary?' she said to her neighbour.

'Of course she was,' Mary replied, taking a pinch of snuff at the same time.

The same lady also reminded me that my mother loved to dance and how during a street party she would dance and lift her skirt up and pretend she was Carmen Miranda. 'Don't ever think bad of your mother, Raymen, she was a lovely kind woman and never did no harum to no one, so she didn't, she just liked to enjoy herself and have a good time,' the lady reminded me. These were my own sentiments regarding my mother. She had been well liked and known as a kind woman, which was the way I also saw her.

Limerick in 1960 was getting modern because my aunt Doris now had a gas cooker instead of the old black range, but somehow it did not look as homely. Doris would also be one of the first to get a TV back in the early 60s, but she was to die around 1965 before she reached the age of 60. A great woman to whom I will always be indebted.

Before the week's holiday was up I couldn't wait to go back to England. I started to panic and wondered what would I do if I could not go back to England again? I felt very insecure and had a feeling of not belonging, that Limerick was not my home any more, and I felt lost and out of place. I realised that maybe I was becoming anglicized, after all, most of my recent memories of Ireland were bad ones. It would be another five years before I would return again. I returned to England nearly a stone heavier due to all the bacon and cabbage that I had been eating and just lazing around. When I had come home a week earlier I was told how thin I looked, but now I was being told, 'Jasus, Raymen, you look healthy again!' I felt stodgy and unhealthy, which was not ideal for a would-be distance runner who one day might well be a prospective Olympic runner! Oh well, I had to keep dreaming to motivate myself. If I did not dream, how could my dreams come true? At least that was my theory anyway.

One Limerick or Irish characteristic that I had was being unable to pronounce my 'th's', and in an effort to change and be understood, I unfortunately started putting in 'th's' where they didn't even exist, and sounded a right idiot at times. I would say things like 'insteath' for 'instead' and 'eathing' instead of 'eating', and then I would feel so embarrassed and say, 'Oh fuck it,' instead of 'Sorry'.

Another Irish mannerism that I had was saying, 'You know,' after every other word. I was later pulled up about that when I became a student nurse. The tutor, Irish as it happened and who should have known better, pointed out to me one day, 'Mr O' Donoghue, you sound lovely, you know, but is it really necessary to keep saying "you know", all the time, because the patients won't know what you're saying, you know, they will think that you think that they are stupid you know.' He sounded just as bad as I did, and I would get hot under the collar, but I tried to take on board what he had told me. An Irish accent can be very nice, and is liked by a lot of people, but I preferred to be understood. I never made a conscious effort to lose my Irish accent, just to be understood. My Irish accent would always remain with me. Another thing that I remember about Limerick was the clocks changing. Months after the change; whenever you asked someone the time, they would ask you, 'Do you want the summer time or the winter time?' It could get very confusing after a while!

I got back to England and my tarmacking, and I was becoming more and more restless. Depending which foreman I was working with, I started having the odd day off during the week. I was becoming resentful about doing meaningless work and still being a labourer, with no chance of going up any ladders to a more meaningful job. I had an ambition to improve myself somehow, but felt that perhaps it was just another idle dream. I was becoming bored again and following my old familiar pattern. At least I had been in the same job for over six years by now, and with the same firm, but it was no longer challenging.

I used to go dancing two or three times a week to break the monotony of my boring job and to meet women. I danced at the 'Aran Moor', my local Irish dancehall in Balham, and it was only a few minutes from where I was living. During the week it was pretty dead, but during the weekends it was usually crowded. The best Irish show bands used to play there, especially during the Easter period. It was quite exciting because you never knew what the evening would bring.

During this period in my life, my mind was made up that I would never marry, not with all the choice of women at the Aran Moor, though there were rarely any there that I fancied. My mind was on sex and nothing else, but after a couple of years I was meeting the same women there all the time and I rarely ventured to other dancehalls outside of Tooting. And anyway I was getting seriously interested in running and competing in races, and found the late nights at the dancehall did not appeal to me that much. Parties and such like never appealed to me, and I was always a bit of a loner. I was also no Fred Astaire, and I had no great interest in dancing. I only went to meet the opposite sex. It was the only place to meet girls for me.

In the dancehalls in those days, the men stood on one side of the hall and the women in a large group on the other side, and when a new dance started, I had to walk right across the hall to the girl that I fancied, and ask her to dance. It was always nerve-racking, because if a girl refused me, I had to walk all the way across the floor again and would feel a right idiot. It was difficult to ask another girl straight way, just in case I was refused again. Sometimes I would go towards a girl, but change my mind at the last minute, due to some body language or other that put me off. I don't know how the girls felt about the situation.

It was just like a cattle market, picking and choosing and never quite knowing what response you were going to get, and I found it was degrading all round. Sometimes I wished that I could find one girl that I liked, and not have to go chasing and often being rebuffed. Whenever I did take a girl out and spent a few shillings on her there was no guarantee that there was anything in return! Oh, it could be very disappointing, and sexually very frustrating. Although I was only 23 and had the looks, I did not as yet have the personality to match, and I still remained extremely shy. I was often embarrassed by guys who kept telling me about all the girls that they had been out with and what they had done. I never knew whether it was true or not and I was not particularly interested because I felt that such romantic matters were very private. I liked to think that I treated women with respect, just like my hero John Wayne used to, and I never wanted to tell tales about any girls that I might have known. Big John had influenced me in a way that he would not have realised.

I once had a date with a black girl and I arranged to pick her up at Balham station after dark, because I did not want to be seen with a black girl in the daylight. I was worried in case my friends saw me, and I wondered what they might say! Attitudes were very different in the early 60s. The colour of someone's skin did not bother me if she was attractive, although I had never been out with a black girl, mostly because none went to the Aran Moor dancehall in those days. However, I need not have worried. The girl must have been thinking as I was, because she never turned up at all and left me standing at Balham station with egg on my face and a guilty conscience for being so racist and conceited, although that was not my intention. I also did not enjoy looking for different women all the time. I hoped that one day I might meet the right girl, someone a bit like me: fairly shy, a non-drinker and non-smoker; someone who was not a party-goer and probably liked animals.

Late in 1963 we had a very bad winter. The snow started and it remained on the ground for about three months, which was not ideal conditions for tarmacking. After weeks of inactivity I was one of the few who got the sack and I was told to come back in the summer. 'Like fuck I will,' I promised myself. I felt quite humiliated and I was not prepared to be treated like that again. Once bitten, twice shy. I had considered myself to be a good worker and as reliable as the next guy, but then I realised that I was not a piss artist and perhaps I did not fit in as well as the other guys. Or maybe I was a potential troublemaker and an agitator.

It was not a good time to be unemployed, because jobs were hard to come by due to the bad weather and I had no friends and no money saved up. It was a very hard winter for me and I had to draw unemployment benefit for the first and only time in my life. I found it very degrading, because I still had a lot of pride. I used to stay in bed until about midday because I could not afford to put money in the gas meter, and I also fell three months behind with my rent, although my landlady was very understanding. Things got so bad that I sold my collection of records and then I pawned my record player, but was unable to get it back again when I had the money, due to the fact that there was a time limit on it.

Lack of music was bad enough but lack of food was even worse, so, reluctantly my old thieving skills from my pre-Glin days had to be practised again. There was a small shop at the bottom of Huron Road, and I would go in to buy something quite small and would normally wear my long raincoat, to give me extra cover and room to manoeuvre things underneath. I did this on quite a few occasions and I always wore my running shoes, because if I was suspected and challenged I could bolt for the door and I felt confident that the lady behind the counter would never catch me, unless she sprinted for England!

Early in 1963 I had a stroke of good luck, and got talking to Tom Richards at Tooting Bec running track. Tom, who had been an Olympic silver medallist in the marathon at the 1948 Olympics, was also a charge nurse at the nearby Tooting Bec Psychiatric Hospital. Realising I was out of work, he told me that he could get me a job as a porter at the hospital and then I could run for the hospital in the forthcoming London Psychiatric Hospital cross-country championship, in March. True to his word, Tom got me a job a few days later and changed my life forever. He inadvertently gave me a huge lift up the ladder that I had been trying to climb for the last few years. It was to be the break of my life, and I paid him back by finishing second in the championships shortly afterwards.

23. Change of Career

I started my job as a porter at Tooting Bec Hospital and I found myself working on Tom Richard's ward, which was called H/3, and it was great! Tom was the charge nurse. I was working from 8.30 a.m. until about 4.30 p.m., five days a week and I could just walk across Tooting Common from my flat and be there in five minutes, which left me plenty of time to go running every day. It was a very important consideration for me, in fact, it was a priority!

For me it was absolute luxury working indoors and in a warm environment where I could have a cup of tea and a biscuit whenever I wanted, and usually a free dinner. The kitchen would nearly always send up more food than was needed, and sometimes patients would not want any dinner, so there was always loads of spare food left over. It was like heaven, and a complete contrast to the five years that I had spent at Glin school, starving hungry most days. There were just over 30 patients on the long-stay ward, patients who had been in the hospital for many years and who were mostly institutionalised. These patients were very dependent on the hospital and most were like children and would not have been able to survive out in the community on their own.

Tom Richards had a great rapport with the patients and they all seemed to like and trust him. They relied on him to care and manage them and the ward properly. Tom was certainly unconventional in giving out the medication during the day, and he knew by heart what medication each patient was on. There was no need for Tom to look at a medicine card for each patient, which is the proper and safe way to give medicine out. No, sir, Tom would carry a lot of different medications in the pockets of his long white nursing coat, and as each patient came for his medicine, Tom, in his very strong Welsh accent, would say, 'Hello, boyo, it's two whites, one blue and one yellow for you, and for you, Paddy, me boyo, your medicine has been changed by the doctor this morning and now, you're having two blues, two larger white ones and the yellow one has been stopped, don't you know.'

It was a totally unconventional and unsafe way to dispense medication, but it seemed to work okay, due to the fact that Tom had worked on the same ward for many years with the same patients. He knew them inside out, and, besides, if ever he did give a patient the wrong tablet, the patient would more often than not point out, 'It's the wrong tablet, Mr Richards,

169

I'm not on that blue one any more,' and Tom would make the appropriate adjustment and say, 'I'm glad you noticed that deliberate mistake, boyo, it means you're getting better, don't you know, I'll tell the doctor.' Many other nurses in those days seemed to have a very casual approach to giving out medication, and some gave extra tranquillizers to the violent patients, without the doctors knowledge, as they felt that the dose already prescribed was often too low. Most nursing staff knew far more about any particular patient than many of the doctors.

I soon realised that Tom had a very good sense of humour, but most importantly, he was like a father to them and knew each one as individuals. He also knew their different quirks and mannerisms and seemed to get the balance just right by treating them, as far as possible, in a very human way, which I would come to realise was not the same with every nurse. Tom was unconventional in many ways as a psychiatric nurse, and maybe it was this individuality that helped him to win an Olympic silver medal. Tom used to let me go running during my lunch break, and despite only being entitled to 30 minutes, he allowed me extra time so that I could do either a ten or a twenty mile run. He would cover for me during my unofficial extended lunch break and then he would provide me with a big dinner that he had put by for me. Of course he always advised me to, 'Go around the back of the hospital, boyo, so the managers don't see you.' Up to that point it was the cushiest job that I had ever had and the height of luxury.

In 1963 Tooting Bec Hospital had around a thousand patients and an enormous number of staff. It was like a miniature town. The hospital social club also put on dances, and if you could not meet a woman you fancied in this environment, then you would have to be very fussy indeed. At least three of my Irish friends met their future wives there, and they were all Greek women. The Greeks and the Irish seemed to hit it off quite well. The Irishmen also got on well with the English girls. Mind you, we got on with everyone due of course to our natural wit and charm!

I used to go dancing a few times a week. One time Tom gave me a new sports jacket and shoes to go dancing with as he knew that I did not have much money or clothes. I declined the shoes as they were too heavy to rock 'n' roll in at the dancehall and also two sizes too big. I was grateful and I proudly wore the check sports jacket to the local dancehall that night to see if I could impress the local Tooting girls. I thought that I looked like a mixture between a country farmer and Steve McQueen, but I sounded more like the former. I wasn't successful that night and realised that a new jacket on its own was not good enough to pull the girls. Knowing Tom's sense of humour, I have often wondered over the years if he had set me up to make me look like a plonker. I would not have put it past him.

The next day when I put my hand into the inside pocket of the jacket, I noticed some writing inside in very big black letters which read, 'PROPERTY OF TOOTING BEC HOSPITAL'. I was a little shocked and realised that the girls might have recognised the jacket as being from the local psychiatric hospital and thought that I was a patient! It certainly was not cool in 1963 to wear a tweed jacket made of very rough material and a few sizes too big, unless perhaps you were an Oxford graduate or a mad professor. The hospital clothing was definitely not made in Saville Row, and neither did it look like it! I returned the jacket to Tom with my gratitude and told him it did not fit properly. I was also worried about being caught wearing it as it was hospital property and I could have been had up for stealing. I later realised that Tom had a mischievous way about him, and maybe he gave me the free coat just for a laugh! I never knowingly wore hospital clothing again.

At times I used to irritate Tom by constantly asking him questions. 'What is an analeptic, Tom?' I would ask. 'The word is epileptic, don't you know, and sometimes patients get a sudden fit and become unconscious and fall on the floor.' 'Why are they epileptics Tom?' I had never heard of the word or the condition before. 'It's all to do with the brain, me boyo, and no one knows why they get it.' I thought I had better not push my luck anymore, though Tom was the most patient man.

One time a patient comes for his medication and Tom says, 'Here you are Morgan, your medication has been increased again.'

'Thank you, Mr Richards,' says Morgan politely with a nervous grin on his face and then walks away.

'You have to watch him, lad,' says Tom to me. 'Mad as a fucking fruitcake and a psychopath. Can't trust the bastard, and don't let that smile fool you.'

Psyclepath was another word I had never heard while I was a labourer.

'What's that, Tom?' I ask nervously.

'What's what?' asks Tom.

'A psyclepath.'

'It's a psychopath,' says Tom, 'and it's someone who is very dangerous and unpredictable.'

'Oh,' I say not wanting to sound too ignorant.

Another time an Asian patient, looking a little bleary-eyed comes for his medication and Tom gives him a pile that look like smarties. 'Why is he on more than Morgan?' I asked Tom.

171

'Everyone is on something different, don't you know, because they all have different conditions, and besides, he is a diabetic as well as being mad.'

'A Dia-a-what?' I ask timidly, realising that I was pushing my luck now.

'He's bloody diabetic and he might go into a coma if he does not take his medication, don't you see. If you want to know more boyo, you're going to have to study and ask the nurse tutors,' says Tom, now beginning to sound very irritated. 'I can't keep answering all these questions, don't you know, because I have to concentrate on giving the patients their medication.'

I took the hint and realised that I would never get the hang of this nursing business, as it sounded too complicated for my under-used, under-trained and possibly inadequate brain. Labouring was so simple in comparison. During my time with Tom on his ward, I would often annoy him with my constant questioning, but he at least pointed me in the right direction, even when he did not always know the answer. Tom was like many of the old brigade who probably never did nursing exams. They often got promotion because of their experience and longevity, and, besides, nurse training was constantly evolving. Nevertheless Tom and many like him ran the wards very efficiently and safely and cared very much about the patients in a very genuine way.

One patient suffered from something called 'Echolalia', a rare condition that I never saw again. What ever was said to this patient, he would repeat it exactly and would not be aware of what he was saying. 'Who's a silly bugger then,' Bill the Welsh charge nurse would say and the patient would reply, 'Who's a silly bugger then, who's a silly bugger then, who's a silly bugger then.' Unfortunately the patient would repeat this phrase over and over again until Bill would utter another silly phrase, though sometimes the patient would continue the first phrase and could not be sidetracked. It all helped to brighten the day's work. One student nurse on another ward where I was working would always try and read a book as he worked, which did have one strange outcome on at least one occasion. Most of the charge nurses on the geriatric wards were obsessed about having the wooden floor highly polished every morning, but on one occasion this student nurse had let some patients use the commode.

Although ideally the commode was supposed to be emptied every time a patient used it, this was not always the case due to pressure of work or just laziness or bad nursing practice. I know, because I did it myself. However, this student was wheeling a full commode from the top of the ward to the bottom to empty it, but was dragging it behind him with one hand while reading his book with the other and not really being aware of what was happening behind him. The commode was being tipped up as it was dragged on its back legs, and the contents were spilling out all over the lovely polished floor. I watched with great amusement, as I hated the idea of all this polishing, which I felt was unnecessary. Also it reminded me of my time at Glin, when I had to polish the floor on my hands and knees. 'You stupid fucking bastard, can't you see what you're fucking doing, you're fucking useless and I'm going to get you sent off this ward tomorrow.' It was the charge nurse who had just come out of the office and seen his lovely floor covered in shit from one end to the other. It was a sight to behold and it made my day: It almost caused the charge nurse, who was an unpleasant bastard anyway, to have a fit.

At around 3.30 p.m. each day another porter and I had to collect all the drugs from the pharmacy department. The drugs were in big brown leather boxes, which were locked, and we had to deliver them to all the different wards around the hospital, as quickly as we could, because as soon as we finished we could go home. The other porter was Tony Quinn, from Rathkeale in County Limerick. I later learned that as an eight-year-old he used to help deliver that terrible bread to us at Glin. It certainly was a small world!

Delivering those drugs was to turn out to be the biggest stroke of luck in my life as it happened. There were two pretty English girl student dispensers working in the pharmacy department and it was something that made the job of collecting the drugs more pleasant each day. However, I only fancied one of them, and I noticed her straight away. She was wearing a long white coat and slip-on flat navy shoes, and she was sitting on a table swinging and dangling her legs. Her coat was provocatively open almost to the knee!

She had the nicest, warmest and most welcoming smile that I had ever seen and best of all it was directed towards me! She had an instant appeal to me and she seemed to have great class about her. It was an overpowering feeling that I had never known before or since, and after a few days of chatting to her through the pharmacy open hatch, I found out what her name was. I asked her out and she said yes! Her name was Sandra. It may have been lust at *first* sight but the love interest would follow a few minutes later.

Sandra turned out to be more shy than I was, which I always found very appealing in a woman, and we hit it off straight away. She did not like alcohol and did not smoke and basically she had a similar attitude to life. I later discovered that her birthday was on the 13th of June, while mine was

173

on the 12th. She was three years younger than me and was coming up to her 21st birthday, while I was an immature 24. She also did not wear make-up, which I also liked and I found it refreshing, so what I saw was what I got. She always looked the same, very fresh and natural without make-up. She had a very warm and friendly personality and an innocent childlike quality about her that I could not resist. Sandra always seemed to be happy, with a very appealing smile. She had everything, and even better still she seemed to have a lovely figure under her long white coat. She was also the most attractive girl that I had ever seen and I soon realised that my plans to stay single all my life would have to be revised very quickly, but I was flexible and willing to change. Sandra had an amazing effect on me and all she did was smile at me! It was a smile that was so natural and appealing to me. Maybe it was fate?

Some days while I was out running in my lunch break around Tooting Bec Common I would bump into her and stop briefly to say a quick 'Hello', not a thing a serious runner does. She later told me that she used to go out at dinner time especially to see me because she knew that I used to train at lunchtimes. I soon realised it was not lust after all, I was madly in love and felt absolutely sure about it. This was the girl that I wanted to spend the rest of my life with and wanted to marry. My heart was on fire and, unbeknownst to me, Sandra was feeling exactly the same way. Very quickly I knew that she was the one for me, and very early on I realised that I could not bear the thought of losing her. We hit it off instantly and we were as compatible as any couple could be.

Sandra's boss advised her against colluding (a nice way of putting it!) with me and told her that I was not her type and was no good. How he came to these conclusions I will never know, but maybe he felt responsible for her welfare, being a young student and away from home. Luckily for me she ignored his advice. She had apparently asked another male pharmacy assistant to find out what my name was. Things did not go smoothly all the time between us and we came close to parting due to misunderstandings, mostly on my part. Many arguments that we had were due to my own immaturity and insensitivity. Sandra was about the easiest going person that ever lived. She had a lovely English accent, but not posh in any way, and I later found out that she came from a very good class of family. Her parents lived in Bath, which I had never heard of, and so she invited me down one weekend. I had never met any girl's parents before and I was nervous about it and rightly so, as it turned out!

I was certainly not made to feel welcome, and perhaps that was the deliberate intention. Both her parents hardly spoke to me for the whole weekend, and I felt really out of place and out of my class. I had very little confidence anyway and I felt twice as bad as a result of the way I was treated. I made my mind up not to go there again and began to wonder if I should stick to someone on my own level, i.e. working class, which Sandra's family certainly were not.

I later discovered that her dad was a company director and had his own furniture shop in Bath along with his brother, which did not make me feel any better. Sandra's parents were definitely not happy about their daughter going out with me. They asked her why she went out with me, knowing that I was a labourer, an Irishman and a Catholic, and they were the good bits about me! God, how low down could she go? It was a good job that her parents did not know that I was from the Island Field as well, otherwise they would have definitely suffered a stroke on the spot. To be fair, my prospects were not good and who could blame Sandra's parents for acting like they did, which now seems a reasonable response to me. But it didn't at the time, and I felt more inferior than ever.

In the summer of 1964 I returned to labouring and tarmacking as I missed working in the fresh air and the sun, but I soon became very disenchanted again before the summer was out, and luckily I got my old porter's job back at Tooting Bec Hospital, thanks to my old friend Tom. Whether it was partly the fact that I was going out with Sandra, who was training for a profession, or whether it was the fact that I was exposed to a situation where I had the opportunity to go in a different direction or not, I don't remember, but I decided to become a nursing assistant, working on the wards with psychiatric patients, rather than doing the cleaning and washing-up as I had been as a porter.

As a nursing assistant I did not need very much formal training, and the money was about the same as I was getting for doing portering, so it was worth trying to do something different for a change. However, after about three months, due to encouragement from Tom Richards and Sandra, I decided I would become a student nurse and try to become a qualified psychiatric nurse, although I had great doubts that I had the ability to study for anything worthwhile. The training was three years long and lots of studying to do, and I had great reservations about my academic ability and whether I had the patience to stick with it for three long years. I was willing to have a go, despite the high risk of failure, the only trouble being that every time I failed at something, my confidence and self-esteem would sink lower, but I preferred to risk failure than not try at all.

24. Back in Class Again

It was 1965 and it had been nearly eleven years since I had left school. During that time I had hardly lifted a book to read except to read the daily newspaper, usually the *Daily Mirror* and articles on film stars, which was not ideal preparation for use in psychiatry. I took to nursing and enjoyed the extra attention that all the student nurses are given by their employers and tutors. I felt a little bit special. The tutors we had around that period were extremely good and would do everything in their power to help you to pass your exams. Miss Budge was our head tutor and was respected by all the students and naturally knew her job.

She was good at her job, and without her help I may have given up trying to become a qualified nurse. She was always patient and encouraging, and certainly made me believe that I could get by okay. I bought all my own books rather than borrowing them from the School of Nursing. I tried to do a little bit of studying every day, as I found it difficult to study for long periods, possibly due to the fact that I had been out of the habit since I had left Glin in 1956. I also kept running every day because it was a great way to relax. I was very disciplined and would train whatever the weather was like. Tom Richards had advised me when I became a student, 'Listen, boyo, you'll have to cut the training down and concentrate on your studying, don't you know, otherwise you'll fail your exams and be back as a porter again.' But I didn't listen and felt that I could still manage training every day, so long as I did some studying each day.

I found the basics of anatomy and physiology very absorbing, and it was probably my favourite topic while I was a student. There was so much to learn, about all the different illnesses, both physical and mental, and all the hundreds of drugs and their side-effects. And there were all the different sections of the mental health act, which is all to do with the rights and wrongs and legalities of containing mentally ill patients in hospital. Some could come and go as they chose; these were classed as 'informal'. Others would be locked up against their will and classed as 'formal' patients. Even the informal patients could suddenly find that they might be denied the right to leave if they deteriorated while they were in hospital and were perceived as a danger to themselves or to members of the public. God, it was all so confusing and all too daunting at times. I often longed to be a porter or a labourer again, when life was simple and I did not have to fill my head with all this confusing knowledge. Sandra encouraged me to keep at it, though at times it all got too much for my brain, which was beginning to feel overworked. Everyone else in my class seemed to be finding it much easier than me. I seemed to be constantly lagging behind in all the tests and assessments, which we had periodically, and I often felt demoralised and dejected. I would study on my own and rarely join the study groups unless I had to. But I persisted and just quietly got on with my studying and hoped that what I was doing was enough.

My mother. This photo used to hang in our house in Limerick.

This picture of my father was copied from his passport, which read 'Bearer unable to write'. He died suddenly overnight from heart failure, which I later learned was caused by syphilis. I hated him for how he treated my mother and my attitude remains the same to this day.

My First Communion in 1947, looking very angelic – well, I was only 7!

102, St Munchin's St, St Mary's Park, Limerick. This is the house where I lived up to 1951 before I was put into care. My cousin Thomas is standing outside.

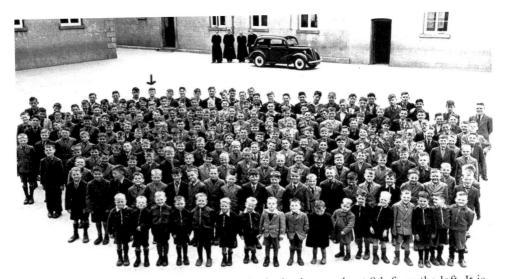

Glin Industrial School, around 1954. I am in the back row, about 9th from the left. It is amazing that many of the boys seem happy, though I look quite serious. I now find this photo very disturbing, looking at the very young children in the front row who must have been missing their mums.

Saint Joseph's Industrial School, Glin, County Limerick. I arrived there in June 1951, just before my 11th birthday, and left in June 1956.

Glin Industrial School band. I am second from left, and probably the least talented of the bunch!

The sleepy village of Glin. Us boys from St Joseph's School walked down this street most Sundays on our enforced 6-mile walk. I took this photo in 2001 and the street looks almost exactly as it did when I first walked down it in 1951.

50 Waterloo Street, Hove, where I lived with my mother and her partner Jock until she died in 1959, aged 40.

This is a very rare photograph of the Weaver family (Sandra's family). Sandra's dad, George, is in the back row, second from right, and her granny is on the far left of the middle row.

Our wedding day: March 27th, 1965 – the happiest day of our lives. I went for an 8-mile run in the morning and then had to run to St Anselm's Church at Tooting Bec because the taxi never came for me!

Our children: Cheryl minding Kevin, who was probably less than a year old. Kevin seems very happy and knew that he was in safe hands.

Kevin, aged 5. This is my favourite photo, which was taken by Sandra's dad, George Weaver, in their back garden in Bath. George was a great photographer and inspired me to be a better photographer.

Sandra on her 45th birthday. She gave me more happiness than anyone else ever could and ultimately the most sadness. I will never get over her loss.

Running in the Epsom half marathon in 1988. Running has given me a lot and helped save my life.

Sandra and me in our back garden in Worcester Park in 1988 on my new bike (and me in my secondhand leather trousers, well, imitation leather). Sandra was 45 and I was 48, going on 22.

Sandra on one of our holidays to Limerick with one of my cousin Bridie's horses. Sandra was a very competent horse rider, having learnt as a little girl.

A family portrait to celebrate Sandra's 50th birthday, with Kevin now 6ft 1in and Cheryl looking glamorous. Sandra and myself looking cool and casual as usual!

Sandra running along the beach in Ibiza in July 2002, our last holiday together. Less than a year later she was diagnosed with cancer and our world fell apart.

Sandra took this one of me in 1991. I always felt relaxed with her behind the camera. She had her dad's talent for taking photos, but not the interest.

Me with my old pal Steve Badgery in 2005. Steve is the runner I have admired more than any other. He ran 2 hours 15 minutes for his first ever marathon and only just missed Olympic selection.

25. On the Wards

I had to spend about three months on each ward, and if I did not like the ward it was hard to cope with. I was beginning to doubt the wisdom of my choice and wondered if I was really suited to this nursing business. Sandra reassured me again and again that I would make a good nurse because I was compassionate and had a good way with patients. It was true that I did like many aspects of the job, but my brain was becoming muddled and it seemed stretched to the limit at times. I also had a very strong tendency to identify too much with patients and wanted to make everyone better quickly and felt a sense of failure if I did not. It was an attitude that would always remain with me throughout my nursing career. I felt emotionally too close, and in later years realised that I was carrying too much of my own emotional baggage from my own unsettled childhood.

Whenever patients were locked up against their will for their own good and safety, it bothered me a lot and I somehow felt that it was wrong that I had to lock people up against their will. I have always found it difficult to shake off these feelings of emotional identification with the patients' problems, and I know now it can be unhealthy. I found it hard just to switch off my feelings and emotions and be just a professional nurse. We all like to think that we do not get emotionally involved, and perhaps as nurses we denied it to protect ourselves, but it is far healthier to at least recognize it and deal with it, rather than pretending to not be affected by our close involvement. I was once told by an Irish nursing officer, 'You'll make a good nurse one day when you knock off all those rough edges.' 'But I'll be like everyone else then won't I?' I replied in a defensive manner, but now, years later, looking back I realise that she was probably right. Whenever someone criticised me, I always became defensive and angry, rather than accepting what was said. Years later, when I did a year's counselling course, I found that if you accepted someone's critical remarks and agreed with them it instantly diffused that person's hostility towards you and caught them by surprise. However, I was into my fifties before I was mature enough to use this strategy, and even now it's not always easy to practise.

I had to do three months on night duty during my training and was not looking forward to it one little bit, because to me night time was for sleeping and being in bed with Sandra. Some nights there was very little to

179

do except have a quiet look around the ward and observe that everyone was still alive. That in itself could be difficult as you had to almost put your face against a sleeping patient, if you thought that they were breathing too slowly or sleeping too heavily, as most of them were due to the night medication that they were on. I would walk around with my torch and shine it against a patient's face which would often wake the patient up and he would jump up and scream in a frightened manner. This often scared the shit out of me and made my heart jump a mile, so I didn't do that too often and just hoped that all the patients in my charge would still be alive in the morning. No one ever died during my stint of night duty as it happened.

To pass the long ten hour shift, which I found very tedious, I would go into the kitchen on the ward, open the gas oven door, light the oven, put it on full blast and pull up a chair. I would put my feet as near to the oven as I could and either study or just write lots of poems and songs about all sorts of things, or just fall asleep and listen for the front door in case the nursing officer was coming. Most of the regular nursing officers were polite and would always tap on the outside of the locked ward door with the huge key to let you know that they were on the way in. I don't know when or where this practice started and if it was something that was only done at Tooting Bec, but it was very helpful and could prevent the nursing officer from witnessing some embarrassing situations that staff may be engaged in on the ward. I always used to carry one or two nursing books in my pocket so that what ever ward I was based on, I could do a few minutes studying if ever the opportunity arose.

I was led to believe that being on night duty was like an invitation to regular sex, which was freely available once you got to know the ropes. I had to take people's word on that as I was never molested or seduced during my three months, though I knew someone who had a whale of a time. His name was Ken, a Welshman who, on the few occasions that I did work with him, spent most of his time visiting different girls, either on other wards or in his car, which was parked in the hospital grounds. He often had girls, one at a time, of course, on the ward in the empty side room, while I covered for him. I did try to look through the keyhole, but was unable to see anything! Ken was, of course, single and free and a very lucky bastard. I envied him at times, but of course I was fairly newly married and not looking for spare crumpet. Besides, there were not many girls in the hospital that appealed to me as much as Sandra did.

One night a number of female staff were stopped by the police in Tooting somewhere in the middle of the night coming from a party and got into serious trouble with the management. They were officially on duty and had slipped out to a party. They said that one of their children had been ill and they went to check it out, all four of them! Another colleague who I worked with one night made a phone call to some female on another ward and told me excitedly, 'I'm going to meet her down by the social centre in about thirty minutes and she sounds very keen.' 'Do you know her very well?' I asked him. 'Never met her before but I heard that she's sex mad and will shag anyone.' He duly went to see the girl and on his return I asked did he shag her. 'I shagged her all right, but I had to do it standing up against the social centre door around the back where all the bushes are. I couldn't risk lying down because of all the nettles. If I went home with nettle rash on my arse I'd have to do some explaining to the wife wouldn't I now?' Very few words had been spoken apparently. He then told me that he could hardly see the girl's face in the dark and didn't think that he would recognize her if he saw her the next day! Discipline was lax in many ways in those days and we all took liberties, but it was the way things were, and as far as I know, patients were never deliberately neglected as a result of our misdemeanours.

During my student days I watched and observed how different trained staff dealt with patients and came to realise that it was important to have a good relationship with the patients in your care, but just as important to get on equally well with your colleagues, otherwise there could be a bad atmosphere, which would reflect on the patients in a negative way. I saw many nurses who were very controlling and very offhand with patients, and others like Tom Richards and Tommy Power who treated patients in a very ordinary and human way, and who seemed to genuinely like the patients. It was not just a job for them, but more like a labour of love, done in a very unobtrusive way. The patients too, most of whom had been in hospital for many long years, liked and respected nurses who were kind to them and treated them normally. I tried to observe and absorb the best elements of what I saw and hoped to be just like them when I was qualified and in a position of authority. If I was a patient I would have liked to be on H/3 being nursed by Tom Richards and Tommy Power.

I saw some bad practices as well, with staff often being impatient and sadistic towards patients who were not very bright or outspoken. One nurse used not to bother to peel the hard boiled eggs, knowing full well that some of the patients, who were disturbed or had some learning disability, would eat the shell as well.

I remember one patient on H/3 who would drink all the tea-leaves from the large teapot when it was empty, so you had to be very quick to prevent him doing it. He would swallow whole mouthfuls of tea-leaves and not bat an eyelid. On the whole I enjoyed being a student nurse and in ways it was to be the happiest part of my nursing career. I was carefree, with no real responsibilities, and my expectations were not very high. I assumed that if I ever qualified and became a charge nurse, then I could change a lot of things, but that turned out to be just another dream on my part. Changing the world and putting everything right was not going to be easy, but I was optimistic and focused and continued to dream. I did not understand the politics of hospital life until much later when I began to understand that everyone at whatever level was under some constraint or other, and that some people were more power hungry than others. I also began to see that the patients' needs did not always come first, and that staff's needs were just as important. Hospital life was good and I felt that I fitted in okay. I enjoyed being part of the hospital running team and with Tom Richards as organiser we did quite well in various events. A Swedish nurse named Goran Karlson came to work in the hospital and was also a runner so we trained and raced together on a regular basis and we had some great battles as athletes and were fairly evenly matched. He was a very easygoing guy, but eventually moved back to Sweden and I have not seen him for years. His name, when pronounced, sounded like urine, but I refrained from taking the piss!

Sometimes I felt that I would never understand the whole concept of mental illness. It could be so confusing and difficult to grasp. Even the doctors did not always seem too sure about what a patient was suffering from, because often a patient would be diagnosed by one doctor and later another doctor would diagnose something different. In the 1990s there was a very well-publicised case of a serial rapist who had been diagnosed a schizophrenic by about ten different psychiatrists, only to be proved wrong in the end. To avoid going to prison he had read everything about the illness and its signs and symptoms and had spoken to other patients and used his own observations to feign mental illness to avoid being sent to prison. Though he deceived the doctors for a long time he was eventually found not to be suffering from mental illness after all and was eventually sent to prison. I attended the case conference and was, like other nurses and doctors, flabbergasted at how this criminal had nearly deceived the doctors. It just goes to show that mental illness is not as easy to deal with as physical illness.

26. Marriage

My feelings and love for Sandra were getting steadier and stronger and I was really besotted with her. We became engaged after about nine months, which I later found out caused her parents a lot of heartache. I asked Sandra to marry me and she said 'Yes'. I was hooked. The only socialising that we did was to go dancing in the Aran Moor dancehall in Balham and we went for walks, and of course I had my running. Sandra cycled a lot as she had done since she was a child growing up in Bath where she used to cycle to and from school every day, despite suffering from asthma. She had beautiful legs, no doubt as a result of the cycling. She was also a very competent horse rider, which she had been doing since she was a very young girl.

Neither of us liked party-going. We had so much in common; it must have been fate that brought us together. I was not very compatible with many women or indeed with many people, but I was totally at ease with Sandra from the instant we met. She was so sweet, gentle and caring; I knew that I would like to spend the rest of my life with her. Luckily we seemed to feel exactly the same about each other.

Sandra was my ideal girl, a lovely shape, very attractive, and even the way she dressed appealed to me. She always wore casual clothes, like jeans, and only dressed up if we went to a dance or when she went to work. She never felt comfortable poshed-up, and could look sexy wearing wellington boots. I just adored her. She was also very modest and never thought very highly of herself. Sandra was also extremely intelligent but always played it down. Although I was more streetwise than she was, she was far more intelligent and she was very knowledgeable about so many things, so we were a good partnership in every way. I tended to be impatient, whereas she was always much calmer and more thoughtful, and she was usually right about so many things. I also found out, by accident, that she was very religious. One day I said, 'Good God'. She swung her handbag at me in a semi-playful way and told me not to swear! I did not use that term again, because I had great respect for her and never swore in front of her.

I had become a student nurse in 1965 and now I was also about to get married and the date was March 27th. Sandra's mother did not want to come to the wedding, and I think that she only came because Sandra's dad

183

said that he was coming along. Sandra's mum also came out in a rash when she heard that we were going to get married, a reaction that I have never had on any other woman before or since, as far as I know! Sandra was determined to marry me, no matter what her parents thought, and I felt very lucky and flattered. It was very hurtful not being accepted by her parents, and I never would be. I always longed to be part of a proper family, but it did not make any real difference to our relationship, although it would cause unnecessary friction over the years.

We were married at St Anslem's church on 27 March 1965, just next to Tooting Bec underground station, and I still managed a 12-mile run in the morning beforehand! It was a small wedding with only about 14 people present. These included my two Glin friends John and his brother Jim and John's wife, my sister and her family, and Sandra's relatives. We had our honeymoon in Tooting in our flat and we were blissfully happy. We managed to get a big one-room flat with a separate kitchen in the house that I was already living in, and the rent was about £2.50 a week.

Sandra's maiden name was Weaver, which I felt was a nicer name than O'Donoghue, and when we signed the wedding register afterwards, I felt a little inferior when Sandra's dad's occupation was put down as 'Director' while I had to put my father down as 'Refuse Collector'. At least it rhymed and it sounded better than 'Dustman', but only just! I have always been conscious of my lowly status and always wanted to break out of it. All my family connections have been labourers: my father, his father and his brothers. My mother's father was also a labourer. A lot of people from Ireland back then automatically drifted into labouring and never gave themselves the chance to try something more skilful or to try and develop their potential to the full. Most of us who came from Ireland in the fifties had no career guidance whatsoever, so we never knew what we might be capable of achieving, but I was always restless and somehow, deep down, felt that I might just be able to break the mould, or was it just another dream!

Getting married to Sandra was definitely the highlight of my life and it would never be bettered. Sandra looked incredible and happy, and I did not look too bad myself! She had a real stabilising effect on me and gave me security and a home life that I never really had. She was and always would be the only woman that I would ever love. She was kind and considerate, with the most loving personality, and an all-round beautiful person. She rarely lost her temper and was always level-headed, despite her own misgivings. She was also very organised and meticulous in everything that she did, no matter what it was. I learned so much from her.

She was always polite and tolerant and great company. How could I not fall in love with her? I soon realised that she was very easy to love and often wondered why I had attracted such an incredible person.

I had never met a more contented and well-adjusted person in my life, and I do not take the credit for that. Simple things seemed to make her happy and perhaps that's why she married me! She had no airs or graces whatsoever and she would prefer to cycle than to drive a posh car, not like me. Most of all she was my best friend and the only person that I felt I could trust and rely on. What also impressed me, even then, was her thoughts for other people. She had already registered as an eye donor in the event that something ever happened to her. I had never even heard of such a thing before, but to think that she had already thought of that before she was even 20 made me realise that she was indeed a very special person.

When I was a little hooligan in Limerick I used to call out names and abuse outside the Protestant school and wished that all Protestants would 'Go to hell!' and I now I had just married one. What a turn around! Sandra was staunch Church of England when I met her, though she had been educated by Catholic nuns in Bath from the age of six because her parents felt that she would get a better education and that the nuns would also be kinder to her, because she suffered from asthma. She did get a better education but admits that some of the nuns were not very understanding or kind towards her. One French nun in particular used to make her do extra errands deliberately, which would cause her even more stress.

The nuns obviously did manage to give Sandra a good education because in 1964 she had passed her 'Apothecary Hall' dispensing exam with flying colours and she was the only one in the country to pass with distinction that year, a great achievement that she modestly told me about, but never to anyone else. She also had a number of 'A' levels. As Sandra was a non-Catholic, her parents had to pay fees for her to be taught by the nuns. Sandra remembers coming home one day and asking her parents if she was a Catholic because she went to mass at school. Sandra had an innocence and childlike quality, and a certain naivety about her all her life that I found so appealing. I never saw another adult with such rare qualities.

I accepted Sandra's religious beliefs and made no attempt to persuade or to change her. I was quite happy to marry her, even though it was frowned on back in the sixties, but we were in love and our religious beliefs came second. Through her own search for something different she often asked me about the Catholic faith and decided that she wanted to become a Catholic. Although she was not a Catholic when we got married she later had instruction in the Catholic faith and became one sometime after. This probably did not please her parents very much, but Sandra had a mind of her own and always felt that the Catholic faith was somehow more relevant to her way of thinking.

Like most converts, Sandra was a more honest and dutiful Catholic than I ever was, although she never preached to others about it. In her case, I am not sure that religion made all that much difference, because she had a great sense of right and wrong, whatever her beliefs. When I first met her in 1963, she told me that she had loaned some school boys £2 for their fares home as they told her a hard-luck story and that they would repay the money to her in a few days' time. And she believed and trusted them! When I told her that she would not see the money again she got a bit cross at me for being so cynical. She never did get the money back but I would prefer her to be like that and trust everyone rather than becoming too cynical. We never tried to change each other, but just adapted to each other's ways and it worked perfectly for us. Sandra would retain the same attitude all her life and I loved her even more for it. In fact she had a lot of similar qualities to my own mother, without the alcohol! She seemed to able to adapt to any job and be contented and has never been materialistic in any way, but then she did have a very stable childhood, idyllic in a lot of ways.

She used to spend a lot of her childhood years in the company of her grandmother and her aunt Phil at Lacock village outside Bath. They had a farm and horses on which Sandra was taught to ride from an early age. She loved horses and was a very competent rider. When I think of the environment that I came from and all those miles between us, and our very different upbringing and lifestyles, it is an incredible coincidence that we ever met at all.

Sandra had tried to get into many different hospitals in the country to do her dispensing training and eventually settled in Tooting Bec. If my mother had not died when she did and my work mates had not got me a flat near Tooting Bec hospital, and I had not taken up running and met Tom Richards, I could not possibly have met Sandra in the way that I did. There were many coincidences, which enabled us to meet.

Having Sandra as a wife and best friend seemed to make up for all the negative and unpleasant things that had happened to me in my life. She cared so much about me that I could forget about everything bad. She made me feel that I was the most important person in the world and it was a great feeling. She gave me great strength, comfort and hope, and she was

186

optimistic about everything. No matter how bad things looked, she would always see good and always could reassure me in a way that no one else ever could. She seemed unable to see things in a negative way. I idolised and adored her and realised that my judgement in women proved to be right. I always liked being with happy people and I never could cope with moody people. Neither of us were moody.

Although I never really felt at ease with Sandra's parents, I did love going down to Bath for weekends and I loved the homely atmosphere and all the lovely cakes her mother used to make. Her home eventually became the substitute home that I never had and I loved Bath, so much so that we promised ourselves that we would retire there, because it was a most beautiful city. Sandra also had a younger brother Richard. Due to my own sensitivity I was affected by Sandra's parents' apparent lack of interest in me, but with hindsight I wish I had handled things different and tried to see things from their point of view. I was too wrapped up in my own feelings. I married way above my own social strata, but nevertheless 'Love would conquer all'. Sandra's dad George, was a great amateur photographer and his photos inspired me to try and be as good as he was.

In the summer of 1965 we went back to Limerick and visited Glin and met Brother Cullen again, but it was a disappointing reunion, because he seemed totally disinterested and had very little to say, not really that different from when I had known him, except that I noticed it more now. We also went to my cousin's wedding and it was Sandra's first experience of Irish drinking habits. She was very scared at the exuberance of some of the guests and she could not wait to leave. It was not a happy experience. I also realised that Sandra was not a great traveller and she had no great desire to see or to travel the world. She was always content for us to be at home together. Reading travelling books, or knitting jumpers for me, satisfied her.

Back in England I settled down to my three years of psychiatric nursing training, but have to admit that it was even harder than I had anticipated. I found it hard to get down to any serious studying due to lack of concentration and always dreaming of being a singer or an actor, so I devised my own way of coping with it. I studied for very short periods at a time, throughout the day, never much more than half an hour as a rule, and it seemed to work for me.

I found Anatomy and Physiology fascinating, because it was all new to me. While I was at Glin I was never given any information at all about the human body or indeed during my school days in Limerick. Perhaps the idea was, 'The less you know, the healthier you will be!' All the brothers ever told you about the body was 'not to interfere with yourself because you might go blind if you do and you will certainly go straight to hell'. Well, if any of the Christian Brothers are reading this, I can still see very well!

As a student nurse I learned a lot about human behaviour, and seeing patients with different types of mental illness was very interesting if not somewhat beyond me. I found coping with incontinent patients, and seeing patients dying, was more than I could bear, but it was part of being a nurse.

Tooting Bec Hospital was like a little town and was a great place to work in the sixties. There were all races of people working there. A lot of Irish and Welsh, West Indians, Greek and some from Hong Kong and some Asians. Many of the staff, including myself, met their husbands and wives there, and everyone knew who was doing what to whom. Even if it was not true! One group of staff took liberties and set up card games for money while on duty and regularly visited other wards to play and let the patients run the wards in some instances. One day a group of them were discovered and given the sack or demoted.

It has been said that people who enter the caring professions do so to either heal or to control, and I have seen both types. I realise that coming into nursing for me seemed purely coincidental. But I now realise that it was perhaps to heal myself in some way, and also to care for others, due to the lack of care from my own family and having been in care myself.

I got very upset whenever I saw a nurse being controlling towards helpless patients. I remember working on a long-stay ward for elderly and confused patients, some of whom were bedridden, and a nurse would put a drink of tea on the bed cradle, which was across the patient's bed, but often just out of reach of the patient. The nurse would return a few minutes later, and as the drink was still there, would remove it, seemingly unaware of why the drink had not been drunk.

One of my jobs as a student nurse was to remove any dentures from patients before we went off duty at night, to prevent a patient swallowing them when they slept, and that could be hilarious at times. Some old gentleman would be sitting up in bed and I would approach him and ask him as politely as possible if he could remove his teeth, knowing full well that he could not understand what I was saying anyway, but nevertheless it was good nursing practice to treat even the most confused patients as normally as possible.

I would try to put my hand inside the patient's mouth to remove the offending teeth only for the patient to snap his mouth closed at the last

188

minute as if he was trying to bite my fingers off while growling some obscenity at me, which would of course make me jump. At the same time the patient would be making growling sounds, just like an angry dog trying to warn me off, but I had a job to do and had to persist until I retrieved the offending dentures. This could go on for a few minutes before I would eventually manage to prise the patient's mouth open and then engage in a long struggle to remove the teeth, all the while watching his hands as he tried to belt me, because he did not want his teeth removed. It was a very undignified procedure for the patient and for me. Sometimes it would take two nurses to implement this teeth removal exercise, but it had to be done.

The teeth were then put in a little plastic box with the patient's name on it so that the right teeth would be put back in the right mouth in the morning. Quite a simple procedure you might think, but not so. For some reason, due to pressure of work or just carelessness, the teeth would in some cases not be labelled at all, which really caused a lot of confusion the next morning when we came back on duty to give out the teeth again. Bearing in mind that there might be about 30 patients on the ward, putting the teeth back in could be just as tricky as taking them out because the patient, who might have only just woken up, was even more confused than usual and was not in a very co-operative mood. As a result there was the usual struggle except in reverse!

After a few minutes and having eventually got the teeth back into the distressed patient's mouth, I often realised that the teeth were the wrong ones! The poor patient looked more like Burt Lancaster with an enormous smile, which somehow looked out of place, and the patient, who probably did not know the difference, could hardly close his mouth at all. After a long fit of laughter I would have to start the whole procedure again. Psychiatric nursing may have been hard and dangerous at times, but never boring, as no two days were ever the same.

One nursing procedure that I found barbaric and unpleasant to participate in was E.C.T. or Electro Convulsive Therapy. It consisted of putting the patient asleep and then administering a muscle relaxant and applying electrodes to both sides of the temple to administer an electric shock for a few seconds, which would produce a violent body reaction in the patient and produce an epileptic type fit. Meanwhile the patient would be held firmly by a couple of nursing staff to prevent any dislocations or broken bones. A rubber mouthpiece would also be placed between the patient's teeth to prevent him biting his tongue, but the patient would still occasionally bite his tongue or loosen a few teeth. E.C.T. was normally given for patients suffering from severe depression, and the results after a course of about six to eight could be startling. Often the patient's depression would clear. E.C.T. was usually only given if normal medication was not effective. However, it did not necessarily prevent the depression from returning again and sometimes it could affect the patient's memory, and it was used less frequently as the years went by.

E.C.T. was always distressing and we often had to forcibly drag a patient along to have electrodes placed onto his head. Most patients were aware of the procedure, so it would have been natural not to want to have it done, but usually the patient had no choice because they were often detained legally either as a danger to themselves or the public. Some patients just went along with it as if they were going to the dentist. On one occasion I had to help drag a man who was only a half grown midget, about the size of an eight-year-old. He was absolutely terrified and begged not to be hurt. I sometimes wondered if I was in the right job!

There certainly was a fair amount of humour on the wards, and I feel that a good nurse needs a good sense of humour, which could help you as an individual. If you are a happy nurse, it tends to filter down to the patients and to other staff. Nurses are in a very powerful and controlling position and it can be used for the benefit or to the detriment of the patients in their care, depending on their own personality and where they are coming from.

During my early training days there was a patient, now long dead, named Tommy Noble. Tommy was close to 80 years old in 1965 and he had been a professional boxer and had known the infamous American gangster Al Capone. Tommy was bedridden and had huge fists and cauliflower ears and an appropriate boxer's nose to match. He was continually being pestered by another patient who was stealing his fags because he knew that Tommy could do nothing about it due to his physical disability.

One day Tommy asked me to tell the thieving patient that he had some fags to give him and I duly obliged. I wondered why Tommy was suddenly being so kind, because he had already told me that he was very annoyed with the guy. The other patient warily came up to Tommy's bed and asked what he had for him. 'Here, in the bedside locker, come and get the fags because I can't reach them, just help yourself,' said Tommy. I thought, 'What a nice gesture!' The other patient reached into Tommy's locker and quick as lightning Tommy executed the best right-hander that I have ever seen from a man in bed. The punch landed on the patient's head and sent him flying across the floor. It was, I felt, poetic justice. 'That'll teach you, you thieving little bastard,' said Tommy.

Some patients used to try and get themselves admitted into Tooting Bec hospital for Christmas, long before there was such a shortage of beds. One patient, I remember, came in a few days before Christmas and he seemed in better mental condition than I was. The doctor, as usual, came to the ward to ask some regular and routine questions to see if the patient was disorientated.

'Who is the Queen of England?' the doctor asked.

'Queen Victoria,' replied the patient.

'And what year is it?' said the doctor again.

'1922, I think, doctor,' replied the patient.

'One more question,' said the doctor, 'Who is the present Prime Minister of England?'

Quick as a flash the patient replied, 'Is it Winston Churchill, doctor?' while looking very confused and anxious.

'Admit him,' said the doctor. 'He's obviously as nutty as a fruitcake.'

As soon as the doctor had left the bedside the charge nurse said to the patient, who was already a well-known regular to the nursing staff, 'You lying bastard, you know very well the right answers to all those questions, don't you?'

'Of course I do,' said the giggling patient, 'but if I told him the truth he would not admit me for Christmas, now would he?'

In some ways the nurses colluded with the patients' fantasies but the doctor would still probably have admitted him based on the answers that he had given. There was so much to learn about this psychiatric business and I often doubted that I would ever pass any exams, but Sandra, as usual, was encouraging and always supportive in my moments of doubt.

We had enjoyed living in our big bedroom-cum-living room flat, but in December 1965 we bought our first house at 45 Fishponds Road, just behind Tooting High Street for the enormous price of £5,200, which was a lot of money then. We only managed to pay the mortgage by letting a couple of rooms out to some of my student nurse friends. We had to buy all second-hand furniture, except for the new suite of furniture, wardrobe and chest of drawers that Sandra's dad gave us, which was really appreciated. My monthly wages were about £44 and Sandra was earning a little more because she was doing two jobs for a while. There has been nothing to compare to buying our first house together, and it was nice at last to have a home that we could at least call our own. It was paradise and we were madly in love and as happy as anyone in the world could have been.

I passed my first Intermediate exam in 1966, which was encouraging and a great boost to my morale. I felt a little more confident in my capabilities but I also realised that was the easy part of the exam, which everyone was expected to pass. However, I always tended to look on the positive side, even if it was only a small advance for now.

The admission wards were very unpredictable and you never knew what each new admission would bring. Sometimes the police would bring in a violent patient in handcuffs and just dump him on the ward and we would have to find out what the patient's problems were and what his reactions were going to be while we tried to assess what was wrong with him. It could be quite stressful until you had established a relationship with the patient, and you had to wait until the doctor had seen the patient to prescribe some medication regime. Other patients would come in confused, depressed or suicidal and others would tell you, 'There is nothing wrong with me, it's only my nerves.'

I never liked admission wards and I always preferred long-stay wards where you dealt with the same patients, often for years, and would have time to build up a good relationship with them. I found it more satisfying, less stressful and not so hard, but to get promotion it was always best to try and work on the admission wards where all the action was and where the doctors were coming and going all day long. It was a much more dynamic and high profile situation. There was also a lot more paperwork and administration, which was not my scene at all.

27. 1968 – Another Great Year

If I thought that 1964–5 were good years then 1968 must in some ways have been another highlight. First, I had passed my driving exam, with the sole help of my friend Danny Carey who would later be killed by a psychiatric patient, and I also got my first car. Danny was the nicest and most unassuming guy that I knew and always spoke quietly and was always cheerful. I got to know him very well while he taught me to drive because he spent about 30 hours or more of his own time accompanying me on my driving lessons, free of charge, and he would not even accept any reward as an appreciation for his time. He was a good teacher because I passed first time, and years later I eventually taught Sandra to drive without her ever going to a professional driving school, and she also passed on the first occasion.

Sadly Danny was knifed to death in 1974 by a psychiatric patient who he was helping to escort to another ward. What Danny and the other nurse who escorted the patient did not know was that the patient, a schizophrenic, had been known to possess a total of nine knives at one time and had a history of knife threats, which had not been recorded in his case notes. Such a patient these days would certainly not be treated as 'informal'. Any nursing staff who dealt with such a patient would be aware of the potential risk and take precautions.

Danny's death had a very bad effect not only on his wife, who was naturally devastated, but on the morale of the staff, who felt that their safety was being jeopardised by the management. The tragic irony of the whole situation was that Danny had volunteered to work overtime on that very day. Lack of communication between doctors and nurses, and staff shortages, were some of the factors highlighted as the cause of Danny's death, and recommendations were made to increase staffing levels and therapeutic care. It was also suggested that Tooting Bec Hospital was too large and it was inevitable that frequent communication breakdowns would occur as a result. There were recommendations that more cash be spent on such hospitals, especially Tooting Bec. What's changed 26 years later? None of these recommendations were of course any consolation to us nurses or indeed to Danny or his wife. Danny was only 52, and his violent and sudden death had been the second within a few years and cast a great cloud of darkness and unease across the whole of Tooting Bec, if not the whole nursing profession.

Another nurse, a girl called Liz Carlson, with whom I had worked closely, was also brutally killed in 1978 while coming off duty late one evening by a patient who had been fixated with her. He had planned to kill her over many months and finally did. He had waited for her on the stairs and stabbed her repeatedly with a huge knife. It must have been horrific for all those concerned and it had a terrible effect on the staff and morale of the hospital. The terror that Liz felt can only be imagined. She was only 34, and had a promising career ahead of her. I had worked closely with her in the Day Centre and knew her quite well. She was very popular within the hospital. I had just gone to Lauriston Cottage Running Club for a run when one of the runners told me that someone had been killed at Tooting Bec Hospital the previous night. Staff began to feel that their safety was not valued as highly as it should have been.

Some months later, after Liz Carlson's death, when the patient had been sent to the famous and notorious Broadmoor Hospital for the criminally insane, the text of the trial was gone through in the hospital library, and any staff who wished were invited to attend. As far as I can remember, this reading of the text lasted for about a week. It was hoped that we could learn something from the terrible tragedy and that it would help staff to move on by understanding what had occurred and why; and if possible that we could prevent it happening again. I attended on a couple of occasions to hear some of the events leading up to the murder and it seemed that a lot of warning signs had been ignored.

The particular patient who had murdered Liz had been attending the Day Centre for some time and he had been having one to one counselling with Liz, but unbeknownst to her or to other members of the medical team, the patient had started to become infatuated with Liz. The patient had also, on one occasion, taken his own case notes home, which was not allowed, and had physically assaulted the sister in charge of the Day Centre. None of these incidents, which were very serious, were reported to the medical team.

The sister later said that she did not want to get the patient into trouble! This again was unusual as such incidents would normally be seen to be dangerous and reported and investigated. Liz had also given the patient a lift in her car many times, which of course these days is discouraged for safety reasons. The patient had also described how he often sat opposite Liz, who wore short skirts, which in those days was the fashion, and he described how he became sexually excited during their counselling sessions, unbeknownst to Liz.

One to one counselling with patients was in its early days in 1978 and

194

perhaps the danger of a patient becoming emotionally involved with a nurse was not recognized, even though, as a student, it was something that you were made aware of. After consultation amongst the medical team, it was recognized that an unhealthy relationship was forming from the patient's point of view, and it was agreed that it was time to break off the one to one sessions. The patient did not want the counselling sessions to end as, no doubt, he was enjoying the individual attention of a pretty young nurse and he was angry and planned to get his revenge and to kill Liz for what he saw as a betrayal and rejection. Her fate was sealed from that point on. In fact, from the time that he had planned to kill Liz, a period of three months had gone by.

In the text of the trial, the patient had described how he had observed Liz from a distance, often in a car park within the hospital, with the intention of killing her, but had changed his mind on many occasions, as the circumstances were not right. He also described how he thought that Liz was in love with him due to the fact that she had spent so much time with him and gave him lifts home etc. Liz eventually did realise that the patient was forming an unhealthy relationship, and after discussion with the medical team, she ended the sessions.

The doctor who was first on the scene to deal with Liz was devastated by what he saw and was unable to do anything for Liz, who died soon after the attack. The Spanish doctor, whom I knew very well, used to work on the Drug Unit, and I remember that he was a changed man and had to take medication to help him cope with the trauma for months after. As one female nurse colleague said at the time, 'We are being killed off and no one seems to care.' That seemed to have been the general feeling at the time. We were all shocked and bitter.

When I first went to work at Tooting Bec as a porter in 1964 it was a lively and friendly place to work and I, like many of my colleagues, met their future wives there, but somehow, with the sudden and horrific deaths of two of our colleagues within a four year period in the seventies, the age of innocence was over and somehow part of Tooting Bec died. It is now closed like most of the large institutions, but those of us who worked there will never forget Liz Carlson and Danny Carey. They both paid a very high price for caring for the mentally ill, as did their relatives.

Since Danny Carey's death in 1974, management, it seemed, had taken little or no action to improve security or to improve staffing levels, which were considered just adequate by a later inquiry. I believe that relationships between management and staff never really recovered and it brought it home to us all just how dangerous our job could be at times. Psychiatric patients can be unpredictable and dangerous, and it is something that you always had to be aware of. Male patients, especially, often became infatuated with the female nurses who were administering care to them. Tooting Bec at this time had around 1,600 patients and it could be a violent place to work at times , as there were some very disturbed patients among them. 'Pro 2' was a locked ward with around 30 to 40 difficult patients, all locked together in the same ward. This was not an ideal number and not an ideal management strategy, but it was managed like that for convenience as much as anything else. Patients would be pacing up and down the ward like lions in a cage, often getting on each others' nerves. There were some occupational activities on the ward, though it was not always easy to get patients involved. These days you would rarely have more than ten patients on the same type of ward.

Working on 'Pro 2' always made me nervous, but as a student I had to work on all the different types of wards to gain experience. Danny Carey had worked on the ward when I was there and I often observed his attitude to some difficult patients and I learned a lot from him. The psychiatric patients in those days all seemed much bigger and more dangerous than they are today, and most were institutionalised. Fights could erupt at any time and a patient might make a sudden and unprovoked attack on either another patient or a nurse as a response to his delusions or hallucinations. Of course, as you became more experienced and knowledgeable, and got to know the patients better, you could often notice a change in their behaviour. It might be something as simple as a patient suddenly pacing up and down quicker than usual, or not responding when you spoke to them. Changes in body language was something you soon began to recognise and understand and act on to prevent a situation developing into something serious. You could often then pre-empt the violent behaviour by giving extra medication before an incident occurred.

Of course, some patients were just violent towards themselves, which might take the form of putting their hand through a pane of glass or cutting themselves, or often attempting suicide. When I was a porter in 'H/3' and we found one patient unconscious and almost dead from swallowing lots of Largactil tablets, which he had concealed, unknowingly to the nurses. Patients, like other people, could be devious and could outwit you quite easily when they wanted to. Early mornings, especially, were often the time depressed patients would attempt suicide, and they often succeeded. One patient who often said that he would commit suicide eventually threw himself in front of a number 49 bus just outside Tooting Bec Hospital gates, so threats of suicide always had to be taken seriously. Meal times

196

could also be anxious times, and we had to be extra vigilant due the utensils on the tables. Many days I just wanted to go back to the simplicity of labouring, where at least most of the Paddies' behaviour was predictable, although after a few pints at dinner time that could change pretty quickly.

I also passed my RMN exam on the first occasion to my great relief and surprise, which meant I was now a qualified psychiatric nurse and I was officially a staff nurse. I now had a profession and could officially leave my labouring days behind me. No more did I have to dig roads, and it was a great moment for me. I was the first in my family history to break the mould and get out of the gutter and show that my belief in myself all these years had been justified and that I was capable of being more than just a labourer. It was also a great credit to the Christian Brothers and Glin that I had come as far as I had. After all it was the education that they had forced on me that was now paying off and I had no qualms whatsoever in acknowledging that fact, although I had been quite bright in Limerick, before I was sent to Glin. No doubt my own very strong personality also played its part, as did Sandra for always encouraging and supporting me when I wanted to give up.

I thought that I knew a lot, but I soon realised that my real learning was about to start. Although I had a qualification, I had little or no experience, just knowledge from books, and I was dreading the thought of being left in charge of a ward on my own. The responsibility filled me with terror and I doubted my ability to do it safely. I just hoped that I would somehow bluff my way through. I spent a few months after qualifying on a new ward and did not enjoy it one little bit. It was an admission ward, where new patients came for treatment and assessment, and I found it nerve-racking. Patients often came in either very depressed or very disturbed and violent, and sometimes accompanied by the police. One patient who had committed a rape came in for assessment and was guarded by the police while he was there over a few days. Wherever he went the police followed closely, until on one occasion he was allowed into the toilet in his pyjamas, and as he had been longer than usual in there, the police knocked on the toilet and got no response. The guy had got out through the toilet window, which was on the ground floor and got clean away.

Another guy kept cutting his stomach open as a suicide gesture and kept having it sewn back up again. One day shortly after his stomach had been sewn up he came up to me and said, 'Can I show you some thing?' and proceeded to open his dressing-gown to reveal a great gaping slit going down his stomach, where he had undone the sutures from a previous cut,

197

which had not yet healed. He had perforated his bowel as well and the wound was anything from eight inches upwards. Blood and guts were protruding and I nearly fainted with the sight of it.

In 1968 Sandra and I had an even bigger thrill in store, because on 15 July our first child Cheryl was born. It was a great feeling to have our own child and maybe I could be nicer to her and give her a better life than I had had. She had jaundice when she was born but we naturally adored her. She always seemed to be smiling and happy as a baby, and all the photos I took of her prove the point. Her personality seemed very like Sandra's even at such an early age. We were a proper family now and I hoped I could do better than my parents did for me. Our life felt so much more fulfilled and it was great to have our very own little child to love and cherish. We vowed that we would have another child in a few years but felt it best to wait so that we could concentrate and establish our lives. I remember being present at Cheryl's birth and was glad that I had been there to witness her grand but delayed entry into the world, by about ten days. Cheryl weighed a healthy 7 lbs 13 oz, and strangely enough when our son Kevin was born three years later he was ten days early and weighed exactly the same. We both agreed that two children for us was about right.

28. The Drug Unit

A few months after I passed my exam I was restless and wanted something different to do. In the late 60s drug abuse was beginning to spread nationally, and Tooting Bec Hospital had quite a few drug addicts spread around different wards. The trouble was there was very little specialised knowledge available as to the best way to treat them, and the addicts who were having treatment were easily able to abuse the system as they were being nursed with ordinary psychiatric patients on ordinary admission wards. It was the late 60s with all the free love and flower power, aided and abetted by various illicit drugs, including cannabis, heroin and cocaine, uppers and downers, of which I personally knew very little. I got my kicks and highs from being in love with Sandra and my regular running training. I felt as if I was always on a high and I did not need drugs, stimulants or alcohol to add anything to enhance my life.

One of our jobs as nurses was observing drug addicts on an ordinary psychiatric ward who might be having a specific course of treatment and to report back to the doctor on the effect the treatment was having on him or her. Of course what we soon realised was that the addicts' visitors were often bringing extra illicit drugs on to the ward to give to their friends, which would give us a misleading and inaccurate guide as to the effect of the prescribed treatment. Addicts often said something, but meant something different, and most were either reluctant or unable to come off drugs.

In those days we did not search visitors for illegal drugs because often we were not aware of the devious ways and means that addicts would use to obtain an extra dose of heroin or whatever their choice might be. One of the admission wards that I worked on was on the ground floor, which made it very easy for friends to pass illegal drugs to their colleagues inside the ward, without the staff being any the wiser. I remember going into a toilet to check on one particular addict as he had been a long time and found him injecting heroin into his arm. I summoned staff to stop the patient. He was one frustrated addict and I have to admit to later feeling a certain amount of sympathy for him. Imagine that you are just about to have an orgasm with the girl of your dreams and you are forcibly stopped at the last minute, which is the way an addict would have described it, but we were there to do our job as best we knew how, and our views and aims were not usually the same as the patient's. He would have to have his orgasm at a later date.

The government and the hospital administration and medical team were becoming increasingly aware that due to the number of addicts there was need for a specialised unit to deal with the problem. So it was that the D.D.U. (Drug Dependency Unit) was set up as one of the first specialised units in the country, to deal specifically with some of the most hardened drug addicts in the London area. It was to be an admission ward and would be for mixed sex patients, and it would also be able to assess new addicts who claimed to have a habit. There was to be 26 beds, and the ward would be permanently locked, and would be on the top floor of the hospital block for better security and to prevent drugs being smuggled into the ward. At least that was the theory and the plan!

It was a known fact throughout Tooting Bec Hospital that very few nursing staff, and I was no exception, wanted to work with drug addicts in those days because of the very way that we viewed them. We felt that drug addiction was self-inflicted and most addicts did not really want to be helped and did not really want to come off drugs. They were devious liars and would cut each others' throats for drugs and they never got better anyway, so what was the point of trying to nurse or cure them? It was a terribly judgmental way to view addicts in 1968, when the D.D.U. was set up. It was a brand new unit with no expense spared, and the nursing officer in charge was going to be a friend called Joe with whom I had worked before. I had admired him a lot so I applied for the job of staff nurse and I got it, but I was advised by my friend and mentor Tom Richards not to work in the drug unit because I would never get promotion there and that, 'You can't cure them bastards anyway'. Both of Tom's comments proved to be very prophetic because the success rate as far a 'cures' were concerned was not very good. But the aim had not been to try and cure addicts, but more to try and stabilise, assess, and I suppose, educate them. Unfortunately I eventually had to leave to get a charge nurse job in another hospital, but promotion was not my immediate aim and that was a long way down the line anyway. In the meantime I had a lot of learning to do.

The D.D.U. was a new venture and I was glad to be on board. It was one of the first units in the country to treat drug addicts only, so it was an exciting job to be starting, and I was very happy to be there. We had about seven staff on each shift, nearly all qualified, which would be unheard of today. We also had a good alarm system, which in case of any difficult situation, could be activated and help summoned in seconds, which was a great source of comfort.

Working on the D.D.U. proved to be the most enjoyable period of my working life and I never again was to find the same enjoyment and satisfaction from any other nursing job. It was the pinnacle of my working life and it was to be a great learning experience for me in many ways. There were so many professional people working there, including nurses, social workers, art therapists and doctors. Dr Bewlew was the consultant psychiatrist and he was the top man and one of the foremost experts in the whole country on the treatment of drug addiction at the time. He was Irish and from a well-known family in Dublin. He was always very cheerful and pleasant, but he did not suffer fools gladly and you had to have the information he required when he came on the ward. He was of short stature and nearly always wore a 'dicky bow', instead of a tie. He was a very clever man, but more importantly, he was well-liked and respected by everyone. More importantly the addicts liked him because he would treat them fairly.

I have to confess that when I went to work there I was very inexperienced and felt very inadequate, but I managed to muddle by and just watched and learned from those more experienced nurses all around me. What I also liked was the very informal attitude that existed between doctors and staff, which I found very refreshing and it made the whole job that much more enjoyable.

All the nursing staff had volunteered to work on the D.D.U. and we were never moved to any other wards no matter how few patients we had on the ward, which meant we had all established a very good rapport with each other as time went on. We knew we could rely on each other in case of emergency, which would be many over the coming years.

Because the D.D.U. was new, we had doctors regularly coming from America on three to six month secondments to gain work experience and to observe the withdrawal treatment that we used and other aspects of the treatment on the D.D.U. In America at the time the treatment for drug addicts in care was complete cold turkey, which meant stopping all drugs immediately. Cold turkey could be very distressing and dangerous for the addict concerned, whereas on the D.D.U. it was a gradual withdrawal over weeks and sometimes months. This was more humane, though not necessarily any more successful, because more often than not, stopping the addiction was not the problem, but trying to keep the addicts from going back on again as soon as they left the unit.

We had regular staff meetings and staff and patient meetings, which at the time was quite new and turned out to be very informative and a good self-learning situation. I remember at one such heavy meeting some patients were looking for more sugar in their tea, when one male patient suddenly said, 'Excuse me, doctor, but can I say something. What I would really like is to be tied up by a woman in black leathers, suspenders and high heels and to be whipped, but not too hard.' It broke the ice and his comments brought fits of laughter all round. After the laughing stopped, there was a pause, and I said, 'Wouldn't we all, wouldn't we all.' No wonder I never did get promotion! Working and treating drug dependent patients proved to be a very frustrating and unrewarding experience at times, with very little progress being made towards their rehabilitation. It would be one step forward and two backwards. Addicts would come in for either assessment, detoxification or complete withdrawal. Some new addicts on the scene would be trying to become officially registered as addicts so that they could get a legal and regular prescription, because they were finding it impossible to maintain their habit on their own, due to the enormous cost of illegal street drugs.

Many addicts would often indulge in prostitution, steal or rip other people off. They would also steal prescriptions from doctors' surgeries. Even when they had a legal and regular prescription it did not prevent them from either selling some of their script or using it all up before the next one was due and then claiming that they had either lost their script or it was stolen. After a while we got to know all the tricks of the trade, but even so, I think that there was on the whole a fairly sympathetic approach shown to most of the addicts in our care whom we would come to know over the years on friendly and personal terms.

If ever there was a revolving door syndrome, it was in the D.D.U. For instance we would admit an addict who would be in a terrible physical state, emaciated, covered in ulcers from his or her own unsterile injection procedures. Addicts would regularly share needles and would use water from the toilet pan to dilute medication that was not meant to be injected in the first place, thereby causing an infection. The veins in their arms would collapse from over use so they would often inject into their groin and at times in their penis, which hardly bore thinking about! They would regularly develop huge abscesses on different parts of their bodies and would get hepatitis and some would often lose a limb through developing gangrene.

Many addicts also had a lot of accidents due to being stoned. One Irish guy fell asleep by his electric fire and got third degree burns on both of his legs. Another got out of the wrong side of a train and was killed. An awful lot died of overdoses, but why more never died in this way I never could understand because these overdosing episodes happened with great regularity and often with the same people.

We might spend three whole months going through a withdrawal programme with an addict, build him or her up physically, and send them out in a healthy state, only to have the same person return within a week or two in an appalling state. This happened many times over the years, with the same patients. I remember one patient who had been discharged. An hour later there was a phone call from the hospital gate-keeper to tell us there was one of our patients at the front gate stoned out of his mind. It was the guy we had just discharged! This type of behaviour would annoy us at first, but later on we became a little more tolerant, even though it was always frustrating, because we would often take it personally, which of course it was not, but the constant failure of the addicts to get better could at times wear you down and you would wonder if it was all worth while.

Because Tooting Bec hospital D.D.U. became well known as a drug haven, pushers and other addicts would either come to get drugs or to buy or to sell them, so drugs would often be freely available within the hospital grounds, which posed a constant problem and temptation for users who might be genuinely trying to kick the habit.

As a person who was almost obsessional about keeping fit and looking after my body I never ceased to be amazed at how the addicts survived their lifestyle for so long. Living rough, not eating or sleeping properly, getting serious illness and having accidents and regular overdoses seemed to be a part of their regular lifestyle. They seemed to have nine lives, if not more, but of course there were many who did come unstuck and died tragically young. It did affect us as nurses because we had invested a lot of time and effort, and in many cases, we had established very good therapeutic relationships with many of the addicts, and it was often like losing someone in the family.

We had come to know our clients in a very personal way over many years and we liked many of them and saw them readmitted on a number of occasions in a period of a year. We saw them at their lowest and during their blackest periods and we also saw them improve dramatically after a few months of treatment. Many of the addicts arrived as husband and wife or boyfriend and girlfriend, and were regularly treated as a pair at the same time. Some even had children at home, but still were unable to kick the habit. It was all very sad, as I and most of my nurse friends had a normal life. Sometimes we were just unable to connect with certain patients.

While most of the addicts naturally hated being locked up, they at least had a bed, regular food and most of all for them a regular script. I would say that without the D.D.U. many more young addicts would have died a lot sooner. No expense was spared in the unit and I think as far back as the

70s it was costing around £1 million a year to run, which tended to make those of us working there not very popular, because a lot of other nursing staff felt that we were throwing good money after bad and getting the best resources, which was true and understandable.

29. An Ordinary Day on the Unit

Although life could be harrowing on the unit, there were also many light-hearted moments that certainly made me laugh and made the job worth doing. No two days were ever alike and we usually had an incident of some sort or another. One of the male patients Brian, who was openly gay and half-caste, was about to have his blood taken by the doctor. As they nearly always said to reassure and calm the patient, the doctor exclaimed 'It's only a little prick and you've had it before.' To which Brian replied, in his usual camp way, 'Yes please, doctor, but haven't you got anything bigger?'

On Christmas Day when a nurse shouted, 'Anyone for more stuffing?' Brian was again first in line. Brian sadly died very young, probably around 25, of an overdose. He had been an extremely good-looking guy with a naturally good physique, but he bemoaned the small size of his chopper and it irritated him a lot. Brian was a very likeable person and he had a very nice personality, but he could also handle himself as I witnessed one day when he was in a fight with a much bigger patient. Many funny interactions took place in the course of a day's work and especially at the patient meetings, where doctors and all other staff and patients were expected to attend.

At around 7.50 a.m. the patients began to queue outside the clinic door to wait for their first fix of the day. Patients could be seen on occasions waiting outside the door at seven to be first in the queue, so desperate were they. Most would be dressed in their pyjamas still half asleep, while some of the girls would arrive in their see-through baby doll pyjamas, often leaving nothing to the imagination! But no one took much notice, except maybe me.

At 8.30 breakfast arrived and one of the female patients asked the nurse 'What's for breakfast then?' and the nurse replies, 'Sausages and spaghetti.' Jane the patient replied, 'I'm glad it's not fucking haddock again, I can't stand fish and the smell makes me sick.' Ah well, at least one satisfied customer!

Suddenly there was an almighty crash of plates and tins on the floor, accompanied by the screams of female voices. I rushed to the other end of the ward to see what was going on and saw two of the nurses struggling on the floor with a young Scottish male patient named David. The whole tray

205

of sausages and spaghetti and plates were all mixed up on the floor in one big pile. I thought to myself, 'There goes Jane's breakfast.'

David, it seemed, had turned the whole breakfast trolley upside down because the charge nurse told him that he could not have his fix at 8 a.m. The night nurses had told us that David was very agitated at 5.30 and was demanding his fix then, which was given, as it was felt that it was a special circumstance, and David had returned to bed. It was rare to go outside the regulated times for drug administration, but it was a procedure that the nurse had the authority to do. However, they would then have to justify their actions in the report and it could not be done too often, because it may be seen that the nurse had given in to a patient's demands and threats, which was not acceptable for obvious reasons. By eight David wanted another fix, because his 5.30 one was wearing off. Of course he could not have another one until midday and he did not like it and started throwing tantrums. When David had cooled off he left the unit for a few hours and turned up at the local outpatients' drug clinic and told the doctor that he had been beaten up by the nurses on the unit, which of course was not true and there were about 15 other patients to prove it. David, who was not normally aggressive, later returned to the unit and apologised for his behaviour. The LSD he had been taking lately had altered his behaviour and smoking cannabis did not help either, which accounted for his early morning 'trip'. All the other patients had lost interest in their breakfast and just sat around talking about David's trip.

At 9.45, Mick came looking for his breakfast and was too late as usual. 'No one fucking called me,' he pleaded. A nurse shouted at Mick. 'You shouldn't take so many barbiturates at night should you, you silly bastard.' Mick gave the nurse an old-fashioned look and stuck two fingers up as he walked away. He would not risk the consequences of doing it to his face. This was Mick's third morning in a row coming late for breakfast. I had a certain sympathy for Mick, because he was quite a nice guy, although he was unpopular with most of the other patients, due to the unpleasant rash all over his body, which he continually scratched during meal times, not the best way to make friends.

One of the female patients came to have the abscess on her hand re-dressed, which she got through injecting crushed barbiturates into it, and was complaining of the severe pain, which did not seem to be getting any better. 'What do you expect if you keep picking at it, and you should think about getting abscesses when you are fixing them barbiturates,' the female nurse shouted angrily. Not a very sympathetic approach, but sometimes it was necessary to be direct with patients. The patient's hand looked very sore and I could see the tendon showing through, which almost turned my stomach. It must have been very painful.

Dennis came along to have his foot dressed for an abscess in the same place, which he only recently had a skin graft on, as a result of injecting barbiturates, and I wondered to myself why patients never learned and continued to inflict so much pain on themselves, all because of their drug addiction. Barbiturates were not meant to be injected, but taken orally, but addicts needed a quick response and they also liked to mainline and get an instant reaction, despite the possible consequences.

The doctor tried to take blood from a newly admitted patient, but gave it up as a bad job and was unable to find a vein, due to the patient's veins being collapsed and too thrombosed. 'I'll try again in a few days' time,' the doctor told the patient. Thrombosed veins are an added problem for patients and doctors especially when emergency treatment is needed and the doctor is unable to find a vein quickly.

At 10 a.m. the chairs were put in a circle for the meeting, where doctors and everyone else were invited to attend. Patients came in dribs and drabs, and Doctor Bewley chaired the meeting.

'Anybody got any problems this morning,' he said in his quiet voice. No one responded to the question, as some patients were still chatting and coughing and moving noisily in their chairs. Sitting in the corner, stoned as usual, was Sandra, doing her best to look as normal as possible, but she was not doing a good job and everyone was soon aware of her predicament. No doubt she had taken some illicit barbiturates early that morning, which is what she liked to take.

'Any problems?' Doctor Bewley asked again, at which point Mallachy came through the door, late as usual. All eyes turned on him disapprovingly. As he looked for a chair to sit on, Sandra, accidentally knocked the heavy metal ashtray to the floor, making a hell of a racket and everyone looked at her and sighed, in quiet tones that could just about be heard.

'Shorry, doctor, shorry, doctor,' Sandra apologised in an obvious slurred reply, making even more noise as she attempted to right the ashtray. 'Fucking hell,' you could just about hear Sandra say under her breath, but it was heard and it caused a few more titters amongst us all. I loved these unrehearsed and unpredictable situations.

'What about the locked doors then,' Alan asked. 'When are you going to open the doors to the unit. It's about time isn't it? It gets everybody down and I'm sure it would be better for everyone, wouldn't it?'

'Well,' said Doctor Bewley, 'I'm not sure what is the best thing. We

207

tried to open the doors on one occasion and it was not very successful because everyone was continually stoned with illicit drugs most of the time.' Alan accepted the explanation.

'Why can't we have cornflakes every morning then?' Brian chipped in.

'Yeah man, why can't we have more cornflakes then?' a number of the other patients chipped in in agreement with signs of an open rebellion in the air. The question of cornflakes always came up at meetings.

'Cornflakes, that's all they think about, and why don't they do the washing up for a change?' said Carmen, the West Indian nurse. Carmen was a big woman close to six foot, with a build to match, and very few of the male or female patients argued with her, but despite her loudness she had a heart of gold and was well liked and respected by the patients.

Doctor Bewley, looked a little embarrassed by the question, unusual for a man who was used to lecturing all over the world. 'Well, it would be nice to have everything we wanted, but it's just not possible as we only have a certain amount of money and we have to do the best we can.' A long pause followed which was only broken by Sandra snoring who was now fast asleep, and everyone was now looking at her. Some patients laughed out loud at Sandra's snoring, but big-mouthed Mary laughed loudest of all. She was a bit of an exhibitionist and would do anything for attention. One nurse once told me in Mary's presence that she would do anything for a dare. 'I don't believe it' I said, surprised. In a flash Mary was stripped to the waist and started to take her dress off. 'I believe you, I believe you,' I said.

After the meeting was over, Sandra, who was unconscious by now was carried back to her bed by a couple of nurses and her blood pressure and other routine examinations were carried out to establish how deeply unconscious she was. She was not bad enough to be sent to the local casualty department and so was just observed for the rest of the day, but the whole meeting would have gone over her head.

Suddenly the ward was reverberating with an outburst of four letter words. It was Brian swearing for all his worth at the top of his voice at one of our new Indian doctors. It seemed that his request for more night sedation had been refused and he reacted in the only way that he knew how. No one payed much attention to Brian's outburst because everyone had heard it before.

After Brian's outburst, Bill emerged from the doctor's office with a big beaming smile, because he had had his methadone dose increased and that would keep him happy for a few weeks until he tried to get it increased again. There was a sound of broken glass and Mary emerged from the doctor's office. 'It's Mary again,' shouted one of the nurses.

'I wasn't stoned last night. I always get blamed for it, don't I?' Mary screams in the corridor. Mary had broken a window in the doctor's office, because he had refused to give her any leave for a week. Mary had been brought back to the unit last night, unconscious, by ambulance, which she could not remember and of course she thought that everyone was lying when they said she was stoned. Mary was one of the worst abusers of barbiturates. Mary could be very nice when straight, but when she is under the influence, she abused us all and we were called, 'Irish and black bastards' and she wanted to fight everyone and frequently broke windows, plates and anything that she could get her hands on. She could be a real Jekyll and Hyde, despite her tiny frame.

At midday the door bell rang and it was Mary, who had been out shopping, for the patients, but more likely for drugs. One of the female nurses let her in and Mary shouted at her, 'Aren't you going to search me then?'

'What's the point of searching you, I won't find anything, will I?' the nurse answered back.

'I haven't any drugs on me, honest I haven't,' Mary said to the nurse convincingly, but you couldn't trust Mary as far as drugs went. Even though Mary wasn't searched we kept an eye on her. Mary chatted for a few minutes with one of the female patients and then proceeded to the bathroom as a nurse kept an eye on her and waited for a few minutes before quickly opening the bathroom door where Mary was in the process of removing what later turned out to be barbiturate capsules wrapped in tissue paper from her vagina, her usual hiding place! She put up a fierce struggle as the nurse overpowered her and confiscated the barbs, much to Mary's annoyance.

Shortly afterwards, Mary was flat out in the chair, stoned and obviously having taken some of the barbs before coming into the unit. Mary used to speak posher than the Queen, though she came from the East End of London, but the posh accent usually dropped when she was stoned!

Mary had a broken nose as a result of a fall while stoned and the first time that I ever saw her was when she had been brought from another ward to the unit, stoned and being held up by two nurses with her feet dragging along the floor. She had been creating havoc on the other ward and had broken chairs and windows. She was wearing a dressing-gown, which was half open and half off. She was wearing one slipper and her pyjama bottoms were undone at the fly and you could see everything! From then on she was known as Ginger Brush on the unit. She was also wearing different coloured ankle socks, and to add to her clown-like appearance her face was thick with make-up and her eye make-up was running down her cheeks due to the crocodile tears she was shedding, as she normally did when stoned.

During dinner a female and male patient were arguing over something. John, the male patient, had been drinking tea and suddenly he spat all over Margaret who was caught unawares, and while she was drying herself, the male patient continued to eat. Margaret, quick as a flash, grabbed a plateful of spaghetti and poured it all over John's head and down the back of his neck. 'You bloody bastard, I'll fucking kill you, you dirty whore,' said John, trying to dislodge the spaghetti, not an easy thing to do!

Meanwhile Margaret ran as fast as she could down the ward with John in hot pursuit, waving a loaf of bread, which he eventually threw at her in frustration because he could not catch her due to having abscesses on his legs. We eventually intervened.

Alan, who was stoned, was attempting to eat his dinner and making a terrible mess, just like a young baby eating his first meal unaided. He accidentally dropped his plate on the floor, which resulted in a mixture of broken plate and food. He then proceeded to pick up the mixture and put it in his mouth as I passed by. I immediately emptied Alan's mouth of all the debris, and amazingly, he suffered no cuts or injuries. He was totally oblivious to any danger involved.

One of the other patients while under the influence of barbs, took out his penis at the table and showed it to all the others, because he thought he might have had a dose of the pox and was looking for confirmation. I don't know what his diagnoses was! He was the same patient who urinated into a cup in full view of all the others who were watching TV. He was very embarrassed the next day when I mentioned it to him. He didn't remember!

The front door bell rang in a continuous drone, as if someone's finger was stuck in the bell.

'Who the fucking hell is that?' I remarked as I went to the door. 'What's the great hurry?'

It was our Irish friend Brendan from Dublin, stoned as usual and being supported by two friends. Brendan was only discharged a couple of hours ago and for two weeks prior to his discharge he was begging to be discharged. And now he was back already, but this had happened many times with him and other addicts, who leave, get really stoned and come back in again before their bed has even had a chance to get cold! Somehow the unit had a certain family atmosphere, and although the patients complained a lot, they at least knew that they could get regular drugs, a clean bed and food.

210

Although it was annoying we got used to it. 'Hello Brendan, stoned again?' I said as I let him in the door.

'I'm not sch, sch, sch, schstoned, I'm only tired,' he said, which was the usual response from most of the addicts when they are stoned on the ward. Brendan's remarks raised a howl of laughter. He had been in and out of the unit more than most of the other addicts and was also one of the worst abusers of barbs and was normally covered in abscesses, and this time he was no different. He had a three inch open wound on his foot, and the tendon was clearly visible and was sickening to look at, all because he injected barbs under very dirty conditions and possibly using toilet water to water the powdered barbs down. These barbs of course were not meant to be taken intravenously, but the addicts used desperate measures to get a fix.

Brendan had long black hair and the clearest blue eyes you could ever see, but he was very anaemic and emaciated and had quite an immature personality according to the doctors. He would frequently break into tears, especially when under the influence of barbs. He did not seem to be able to tolerate many barbs or heroin and got stoned easily. Brendan was put to bed to sleep it off but at least he was never aggressive. Some years later Brendan fell asleep, stoned in front of his electric fire, and received some appalling burns to his leg. It was pitiful to see. We certainly shared their ups and downs and their pain and often wondered where it would all lead in the end. We often wondered how they survived for so long.

It was 5 p.m. and fix time again and as usual there was a queue outside the clinic room door, but we got the fixes ready as they were in the locked cupboard, and not according to who was first in the queue, which could cause bad feelings amongst the addicts who have been waiting outside the door longer than others. 'Mary,' shouted one of the nurses and Mary, who was down the other end of the dormitory, rushed up past the other addicts with a huge grin all over her face. 'Fucking bastard' shouted Sandra, who had been waiting for ages. 'You jumped the fucking queue and I've been waiting for bloody ages and you get your fix first, it's not fair.'

'Sorry, man, you can go first if you like,' said Mary, because she was aware of Sandra's temper.

'No one is first, and you're not supposed to queue outside the door,' said Tommy, the new charge nurse, trying to assert his authority. Tommy, the Irish nurse had a great attitude with the patients and was always kind and tolerant and would never tell a patient what to do, but would always ask quietly and politely and I understood why he got promotion over me, although I did not like it at the time. To the addicts on the unit, fix time was

211

all that mattered and most just killed time from one fix to the other, which for most was about four per day. It was their life blood and all that mattered in their lives. The patients, as a whole, were very suspicious of staff and spent most of the day trying to get one over on us and it was understandable, because we were in control while they were in our care, and they had to fit in with our system.

At 8 p.m. the door bell rang for the hundredth time and it was our old friend Pat who was being supported by two ambulance men, looking for admission again. Pat was only discharged about two weeks ago. We'd already had a phone call earlier in the day from the local casualty department where Pat had been admitted for an overdose of barbs for the umpteenth time, and the doctors had agreed to admit him to the unit again. He was filthy, unshaven and looked like a prison refugee from a war camp. We asked Pat if he had any drugs on him and he said, 'No' as he went through his own pockets and pulled out a piece of tissue paper and said, 'I have nothing, man.' We got suspicious as we knew that most of the addicts tended to hide drugs in tissue paper and suspected that Pat had something concealed.

'Can I have the tablets, Pat?' I said.

'Lishen, man, can I make a bargain with youse, let me keep the tablets and I'll shtay on the unit,' Pat muttered in slurred speech. Pat did not want to hand the tablets over and argued with us to let him keep them. 'Let's have the bloody tablets,' Tommy and I argued, as we grabbed Pat's hand just in case he decided to suddenly swallow them.

After a brief struggle and a flurry of four letter words from Patrick and us, we managed to confiscate the tablets, about 50 Ritalin, which Pat specialised in injecting. Ritalin was an amphetamine, and tended to make Pat high as they were stimulants. Pat eventually gave up the struggle and we invited him to have a nice hot bath, which he accepted willingly. We never admitted a patient without first having a bath, unless they were unconscious. When Pat took off his clothes there was the biggest abscess on his left buttock that I had ever seen; it looked as big as a teacup. Pat's hair was washed as it did not seem to have been washed since he was last here. All the while Pat was threatening to knock our fucking blocks off when he was better. He tended to be abusive when under the influence, but was generally okay and at that moment did not look as though he had the strength to knock the top off a soft boiled egg.

The rest of the day and night was quite uneventful, thank goodness. There could never be anywhere as stimulating, exciting and as frustrating to work in as the drug unit. It always kept you on your toes and every day brought some unknown event. I hate to think how many of the young addicts died while I worked there during those three years. We did hear of one of our former patients, a Canadian in his forties, who died when he stepped out of a train while it was still moving. He was stoned on barbiturates at the time. He was one of the nicest guys that I knew, and unusually, had reached the ripe old age of 45.

30. Addicts Are Human Too

During the three years that I worked in the unit, I never saw a patient cured of their addiction, but I saw a lot who led a healthier life and regained control over their lives and lived longer because they had been there. We never set out to cure addicts, only to stabilise them, and we tried to keep them alive as long as possible, and from that point of view I think we achieved our goal. Like most other nurses and people in society as a whole, I did not have a lot of time or respect for addicts, but as time went on I changed my mind, although I never did understand how they could inflict so much pain on themselves and their families. A lot of the addicts told me that they could not cope without drugs and I often asked the question, 'Well, how did you cope before you took them?' And the answer was, 'I couldn't cope.'

Addicts' conversation on the unit revolved around drugs, and instead of talking about their latest female conquest they would say things like, 'Man, my best fix was when I mixed heroin with methadone (Physeptone) and got a great hit.' Or they would talk about the amount of drugs they were on or that they used to be on, or the great trip that they had on LSD. They felt and knew that they were outcasts and saw themselves as rebels, and no doubt that in itself was quite appealing to them. In the three years that I worked on the unit, probably around two to three hundred addicts had passed through, most more than once, and some dozens of times.

'Layabouts.' 'The dregs of society.' 'They should be locked away', were all comments that were made, not only by society, but by many nurses and it is still an attitude that prevails today to some extent, rightly or wrongly. Most of our patients seemed as if their lives began from the moment that they got hooked on drugs. Not for them the thrill of recalling some happy childhood memories, because either they didn't remember or else they wanted to forget, or maybe they did not have any. Listening to the patients talking in 1971 often made me feel very sad.

There seemed so little time to do things and yet all they did was sit around bored, and just talk about drugs. All the junkies were somebody's children, and sometime, somewhere, some mothers wept for them. One addict told me, 'I'm just living for kicks and if I have to pay the price, that's too bad,' and that was most of their attitude to drugs. We once had two brothers on the unit and they were among the worst junkies that we ever saw and they also had another brother in some institution. It's hard to imagine just how much pain their mother must have gone through. One patient, aged 19, who was determined never to come off drugs, was visited by his parents, who told us, 'We are going to take Peter abroad on a holiday when he is cured.' I didn't have the heart to tell them what Peter's intentions were. He discharged himself the next day and went back on drugs again.

One of the saddest cases was of a woman doctor we had in for treatment in her early thirties. She turned out to be just as scheming as all the other patients. I don't know if she ever did get off drugs in the end. Doctors or nurses were not immune from mental illness either. We had at least one doctor from Tooting Bec who committed suicide and another who behaved very irrationally when she came to visit patients and once wrote on the front of a patient's case notes with a large black felt pen, 'BOLLOCKS'.

Our patients were loyal and often showed their human side, like on one of our female patient's birthdays. Her name was Izzy and she was celebrating her 21st birthday on the unit and none of us expected her to live for more than a couple more years, due to her frequent abuse of barbs. On the day of her birthday she received about a dozen cards from other addicts all over London, plus some cards from those on the unit. Izzy was really touched by the gesture, and so was I. As nurses, we tried to do something extra for the patients, and many of the staff would cook a special birthday cake for them.

Izzy was very sweet and had been a great friend of Gale Parsons (see Chapter 23). One of the nurses once remarked about Izzy, 'She has a smile that melts my heart,' and that from a nurse who was normally quite unemotional. One of Izzy's friends had died of an overdose some days before, and Izzy told me about the dream that she had about her the night before. 'I had a dream about Mary last night and I kept trying to touch her. I kept asking her, "What's it like being dead? You're not really dead are you?"' Despite having some of her fingers amputated through injecting barbiturates, she had been doing very well and had managed to stay out of the unit for a year.

One of the male patients was about to be discharged because of continually smuggling drugs into the unit and selling them. He had grown attached to one of the females on the unit but did not want to leave without her, but she could not leave for various reasons. Both of them were in tears as they said farewell. It was very touching and sad to witness. They never saw each other again because he died some days later when he got off a moving train while he was stoned. Another incident that showed the human side of the patients was when a wild bird flew in through the open window and could not find its way out again. One of the male patients caught it and handled it like a newborn baby, and when he was finished admiring it, he set it free again.

Addicts, too, could be very supportive whenever one of them attempted a cure. Alan was one such patient who was determined to attempt a cure, but he had changed his mind at the last minute. A meeting was called by Alan's doctor to talk about Alan's decision to go back on drugs, and if possible to try and change his mind. During the meeting the support that Alan got from the other patients was really moving and unexpected, and most of the other addicts said the same thing. 'You've come this far, Alan, don't give up now. Why not go to the Aftercare Centre and see what it's like? You have nothing to lose and everything to gain.' One other girl said. 'Fuck me, Alan, you've got this far, you can go back on drugs any time.' It was heart warming and moving to hear the other patients' pleas to Alan, but Alan had made his mind up to go back on drugs and that is the way it stayed. As nurses we felt quite bad, because of all the addicts who had passed through the unit, at last we thought that we would have our first cure on the unit, but Alan was not ready and we felt a great sense of loss and failure. As nurses we needed to see some success to boost our own, at times, flagging morale.

A non-nursing friend of mine once said to me, 'All those junkie bastards should be put away. They are no good to society.' I pointed out that people with mental illness years ago were treated like outcasts and were locked away just as he suggested junkies should be now, but we now realise that it was wrong to treat people with mental illness like that. This friend of mine had a daughter who was born deaf, and as a result was slow and behind in her school lessons. I informed him that if she had been born deaf a hundred years ago she also might have been locked away! He got the message.

31. Some More Amusing Incidents

When we first went to work on the unit, very few of the nursing staff swore, but after about six months everyone swore at the drop of a hat. There was one female sister who normally worked on the opposite shift from me who was stuck up and seemed to have an indifferent attitude to both staff and patients, but particularly towards the patients and they knew it!

One of the male addicts nicknamed her The Duchess, and she worked on my shift one morning. While we were having a cup of tea, Alan, the charge nurse, was sitting at one end of the table and The Duchess was at the other end. He had a habit of expressing himself in his Oxford accent (or was it Welsh?), in a very down-to-earth manner that we had come to accept and understand and took no notice of, but what about The Duchess, how would she react? Someone said something that Alan did not agree with and he blurted out, 'Balls'.

The Duchess stared at Alan with fire in her eyes and with obvious disapproval, but said nothing. Alan was not aware of The Duchess's disapproval as she never spoke, and Alan never raised his head. I nearly died laughing at the look on The Duchess's face, but no one realised what I was laughing at until I explained later on. The Duchess did thaw out before she left six months later. She did not fit in with the drug environment or its rough inhabitants, and she did not like the addicts either.

A very good friend of mine was Nancy, who was also Irish and had charm by the bucket load, although we did not always agree on many things. We were more friends than rivals and Nancy often accused me of trying to change the world, and she was right of course! To me it was normal to try and change the world. She was brilliant at her job and maybe I just felt inadequate in comparison. I envied Nancy especially, because of how professional and knowledgeable she always seemed to be. Nancy was a dedicated ward sister and remained on the unit for about 15 years and that took some staying power. She had the potential to go much higher but felt the D.D.U. was where she always wanted to work and was quite happy to remain a sister.

One of our male nurses on night duty swore blind that he saw a ghost, dressed in white, one night at about 2 a.m. standing on the fire-escape. No one believed him of course and said that he must have been drunk. I was the first person that he told about seeing the ghost and I remember that he was as white as a sheet as he told me, and that fact alone convinced me that he must have seen something, because he was a black nurse!

Another amusing incident was when one of our regular male addicts was brought back to the unit, stoned out of his mind, and did not know whether he was coming or going. He saw one of the female staff who was quite new to the unit and said to her in his thick Dublin accent, 'I think I've seen you before.' Then he paused for a few seconds and said, 'Fuck me, am I back here?' He thought in his drugged state that he had been in another hospital! A number of the addicts did manage to get out of windows, despite being three storeys up, and despite the windows being nailed down. A strip of wood used to nail down the window used to be removed, enabling the window to be swung inwards, allowing the patient to get through. They always chose a window that had a drainpipe near it, which was still about three feet away from the window. One girl was halfway down the drainpipe and fell and broke her ankle. The lure for freedom and a fix was strong and very overpowering indeed.

Romantic interludes took place, and the old saying that boys will be boys and girls will be girls was not always the case, because sometimes the girls wanted to be boys. The male dormitory was supposed to be out of bounds to the girls and vice versa. One day I found a man and woman in the same bed and told them, 'You know that you're not supposed to be in here.'

'We're not doing anything, we're only having a chat,' said the young girl.

'I don't mind you having a chat, but it looks very suspicious. John doesn't have any trousers on,' I said with a smirk, because I felt guilty breaking up an intellectual conversation! We often turned a blind eye where romance was involved, providing both parities were willing.

Mrs Murphy, our Irish domestic, had a great sense of humour and one day Alan, our charge nurse, saw her putting some old newspapers into the pig bin and asked her why she did that because the bin was for food only. As cool as you like Mrs Murphy replied, 'Oh that's for the pigs to wipe their arses,' and then she burst out laughing, and so did Alan who had been acting a little bit too officious. In fact he laughed so much that his teeth almost fell out!

Alan once dressed up as a bishop and came to bless the unit, so we led the patients to believe, and he walked around the unit giving his blessing and sprinkling holy water everywhere. An Irish charge nurse came with him and posed with the bishop for a photograph so that he could show it to the old folks back home and let them know how well he was doing in this pagan country!

Humour always played a big part on the unit, and in fact in all the other places that I worked during the next 25 years, but it was not always appreciated, at least by some staff. Patients always seemed to enjoy someone with a sense of humour, as mental illness is a very serious business as was drug addiction, and often there was not that much to laugh about. I was told by a senior nurse that I joked too much and that I should be a bit more serious! No doubt having my own sense of humour helped me cope with my job.

32. Gale is Dead

One young girl who had been on the unit on and off over the years had become well known nationally, as a result of a TV documentary made by the well-known broadcaster the late Desmond Wilcox, who was married to Esther Rantzen. Her name was Gale Parsons, a beautiful looking dark-haired girl, who was about 18 at the time. When Mr Wilcox reminded her during one TV interview that she would die if she continued with her drug taking, her reply was something like, 'I don't care, nobody cares if I live or die.'

Gale hated being locked up, maybe due to the fact that she had been abandoned by her mother as a baby and had spent nearly her whole life going from one institution to another. No one seemed able to manage or cope with her for very long. Gale was also highly intelligent and had an IQ of around 165 or thereabouts.

I was once physically attacked by Gale and a friend of hers and received a lot of scratches as a result because I discovered some illegal drugs hidden inside the waistband on her trousers, and naturally she was not happy. The addicts on the ward would get up to all sorts of tricks to try and smuggle illegal drugs onto the ward to supplement their prescribed doses, and we would do everything in our power to prevent them from doing so. They would often bring in a half bottle of orange laced with gin or some other substance, because some addicts also had alcohol problems. Men and women would also bring in drugs in various orifices in their body, and so did visitors, and we would regularly have to strip search patients, which I and others no doubt found degrading. It must have been terrible for the patients, though at times all we worried about was looking for illicit drugs and perhaps we did not give much consideration to the patients' feelings. Nevertheless, it had to be done for the safety of the ward. Sometimes a matchbox on a string would be lowered from the unit down to the ground floor, and a friend outside who would previously have made a phone call, would be there and put some drugs in the box, which would then be hauled back up again.

Whenever an addict died there was always a sense of loss amongst the staff as well as the patients and it happened many times over the years. Gale Parsons was eventually discharged, basically because it was felt that there was very little more that could be done for her and she had become

223

very disruptive. A few days later Gale had come up to the unit to collect her drugs and she was a pitiful sight. She seemed to have deteriorated since she had left. I answered the door to her and dealt with her. She was soaking wet and shivering with the cold and dressed in very lightweight clothes. Her lovely long black hair was all wet and matted and her straight white teeth were chattering when she spoke in a very subdued way, which was unlike her, as she tended to be brash.

'Can I come in and be re-admitted?' she said to me, but I had to tell her that she would have to be seen at the outpatients clinic at St George's Hospital, which was a couple of miles away first before she could be re-admitted into the D.D.U. This was the procedure for most admissions, so that they could be assessed first. She politely thanked me and walked away with a faint smile on her face. Gale was rarely polite and hated authority more than most. I remember when a Roman Catholic priest had come on the unit on one occasion and he had been going round chatting informally to some of the patients who were generally respectful of men of the cloth, and he asked Gale how she was. 'Why don't you fuck off back to the church and fucking leave me alone. You're not really interested in me, are you?' The priest made a hasty retreat and realised he would not be making a conversion with Gale or saving her soul on that particular day! I felt really embarrassed and shocked, because I had never heard anyone talk like that to a priest before.

A few days later I had come on duty as usual at 7 a.m. and within half an hour I heard another addict shout down the ward at the top of her voice, 'Gale is dead, Gale is dead!' I was very shocked and I assumed that the information was probably wrong and maybe it was a wind-up and perhaps Gale was in hospital with an overdose as usual or something, but no, it was true. Gale was dead at only 19 years of age and it was hard to believe. I had only seen her a few days before and now realised that when she asked for help it was not given and maybe she might still have been alive if she could have been admitted that last fateful day. Or maybe she had had enough of living and just did not care any more. Her general attitude, while we knew her and even on TV, showed that she did not care if she lived or died.

Despite what a lot of the addicts who had been treated in the unit may have thought about us as nurses and screws, we also felt a great sense of loss and failure whenever someone died, because despite all our time and effort invested, we had been unable to change or help that individual, and it was not good for our morale. It made you wonder whether you wanted to continue working with such destructive people, who seemed beyond hope. Most of the addicts with us were generally between 20 and 30 years old and it was rare to see addicts reach the age of 40.

Sometime after Gale's death, Desmond Wilcox made another follow-up documentary on Gale. It was called *Gale is Dead*, and it rightly won many awards. When I watched it at home on TV I cried a lot and I felt a certain amount of personal loss because I think that I was the last nurse from the unit to see her alive. The picture of her bedraggled face standing outside the door of Tooting Bec Drug Unit, saying to me, 'Can I come in and be re-admitted', was a vivid memory that would always stay with me.

I like to think that Gale Parsons' death left me with questions about my own and other nurses' attitudes towards patients in our care, and that was: not to be so judgmental and to try and be much more tolerant of people and accept them as they are and not to let our own feelings get in the way of what we should be doing. I hope that I changed a little for the better as a result of Gale's death, because I have tried to. After I had seen the *Man Alive* programme *Gale is Dead*, I wrote a letter to the *Radio Times*, which they published, to express my feelings at the time, and I include it below exactly as I had written it on 13 September 1975, some years after Gale's death.

I'll never forget Gale

I knew Gale while she was a patient in Tooting Bec Drug Unit for a year and I worked there as a staff nurse. Gale certainly caused me and the other staff a lot of problems.

I suppose the thing that was so frustrating was that none of us could get through to her, though since I've seen the programme so many times, I've personally wondered if I tried hard enough to understand her. I wish I knew the answer. Maybe, of course, it was too late for her at 19 to be helped, for like most drug addicts she seemed bent on destruction.

The last time I saw her alive was two days before she died, and a few days after she was discharged from the Drug Unit, because of her destructive influence on everyone. She had returned to collect some drugs and she was a pathetic sight. She was soaking wet, her long black hair bedraggled and wet, her teeth were chattering with the cold and she was very subdued, which was unusual for Gale. Maybe she'd stopped fighting and hating. She seemed incapable of loving.

I've never known anyone so young so full of hate and mistrust. I know I did not do a lot for Gale, but I feel I've learned a lot from her death and seeing the film. I think I've tried to be more tolerant with people who seem beyond help, as I am still with Psychiatric Aftercare in a Cheshire Home. Gale had changed me more from beyond the grave than she had ever done while alive. Her death made a very strong impact on me.

I'll never forget Gale, because she was different. One felt very aware of that in her presence. She was very proud, independent. Society has a lot to answer for in Gale's death, but we mustn't forget there are thousands of people like Gale still alive, seemingly hopeless cases. I know it's difficult battling against the odds, but it's possible to win through, as a lot of Gale's friends, drug addicts who were with her having treatment at the time of her death, can now testify. A lot of those I remember are dead now, but a lot have made it and have settled down to a job, marriage. One has even gone back to university. Most of these seemed as helpless as Gale. I think it would be great if you could do a follow-up programme about some of the drug addicts who are now living a normal life, if there is such a thing. Maybe there are a lot of young people who could get some hope, knowing there is a way back if they really try.

I don't mean to preach or sound too saintly, but I knew Gale Parsons, had an opportunity to help her along with others, and failed. I hope I don't make the same mistake again. Perhaps I could end with a quote by one of the female psychiatrists who worked with Gale in the Drug Unit at Tooting Bec Hospital:

'She has been rejected and let down in love so many times that she has built a thick wall around herself, for fear of being let down again.'

Ray O'Donoghue, Worcester Park, Surrey.

Just to close the chapter on Gale, a few years after, while I was attending a social studies course, I informed the lecturer that I had worked with Gale and he related a story of when he was showing the *Gale is Dead* film to a load of hardened male prison officers. He said that at the end of the film virtually all these tough men were in tears. He admitted that he had never known it happen before and he was very moved. It was a moving and sad story, but then Gale had that effect on many people. She was unusual.

Two more of our patients died within two weeks of Gale. One was a young girl called Pauline and she was only 19 years old and died of an overdose of barbiturates, which were the cause of many patients' deaths. They abused them regularly and, as a result, often had numerous overdoses before their luck ran out. Pauline was a chubby girl with a nice face and smile. She had spent about four months on the unit and tended to be happy-go-lucky with a good sense of humour, although she could be very aggressive at times. She had left on one occasion during the four months and was readmitted in a very bad state. She admitted that she had no intention of coming off drugs and talked freely about her sexual exploits, about her affairs with male and female patients.

Pauline and two of her friends had been changed from injectable methadone to oral, and they were not very happy as the 'buzz' was not the same. They protested to the doctors, but without success, so the three girls decided on a plan of action, which today might be called girl power, to make the doctors sit up and take notice. They would go on a hunger strike and then when they were dying from starvation the doctors would give in and give them back their injections. That would teach the doctors not to mess around with them.

On the first morning of their hunger strike they went without breakfast, or so it appeared! They were seen eating slices of toast in the toilet. We decided not to say anything, but we reminded them that there was something nice for breakfast! Pauline said in her cheeky way, 'No thank you, I'm not hungry,' licking her lips as she answered. Sometimes Pauline was seen taking a plate of cold potatoes and hiding them in all parts of the dormitory. We found one plateful sitting on the toilet floor, although we said nothing. After a few days the girls stopped their official hunger strike, but after a couple of weeks on oral methadone, the doctors decided to give the girls back their injections, so maybe girl power worked and made the doctors think again.

A couple of days before Pauline was due to leave, she was watching TV with the other patients, when an advert came on advertising some food or other. Pauline suddenly jumped up and burst into song and started singing, 'Food, glorious food' with that huge childish grin on her face. The next day, as she was leaving the unit, she was still singing 'Food, glorious food'.

I remembered that day very well, as I had never seen Pauline looking so smart. She was wearing a little knitted hat, which was just sitting on her

227

head, and she reminded me of a little girl dressed in her best Sunday clothes going off to church. Jokingly, I said, 'I'll see you tonight or tomorrow I suppose, if you are still alive.' Pauline, like most of the addicts, treated overdosing on drugs as a joke, but it was not funny when we heard the next day that Pauline was dead from an overdose of barbiturates, an accident I suppose. We were all very upset, as we grew genuinely fond of the patients, and when one died we felt it quite badly because we had come to know them as friends and had invested a lot of time in their rehabilitation. She was only 19, the same age as her friend Gale Parsons, and sometimes it could be hard to bear witness to such tragedies.

Within a few days another patient, who had been readmitted only a few days earlier, was found dead in his bed on the unit. On admission he had been in a terrible state and was suffering withdrawals very badly. He had been given a fix straight away, a meal and a bath and put to bed. He was also an amphetamine user, and in recent weeks he had also started abusing barbiturates. Most of the addicts would take either speed or barbiturates and rarely mixed them, although some addicts took anything they could get their hands on.

According to the coroner's report, the patient had probably taken some illicit drugs during the two days he had been on the unit, besides what we had already given him, and his body just could not take it. When he had been on the unit before, he had smuggled drugs in on many occasions. It was another wasted life and another failure for us, and it was quite depressing to see so many people die whom we were treating.

Another young friend of Gale Parsons, who was only around 22, had two of her fingers amputated because of injecting drugs into her hand, and other patients lost an arm or a leg, and it was all very depressing. It affected our morale from time to time and it also proved the futility of doing internal searches on patients, because illegal drugs were still coming into the ward despite our best efforts. So from then on, although we remained vigilant, we stopped looking up people's backsides, which was a degrading experience all round, because we felt that if other addicts were willing to take illegal drugs after they had been 'up there', then they were welcome to them. All this death was hard to take, for some of us more than others, and naturally staff left from time to time.

33. Are You Talking to Me?

Getting to know the patients was not easy, and in some cases it took a lot longer than others to establish a rapport and trust. I suppose patients and staff were a bit suspicious of each other in the early days. I remember on one occasion I had just come on duty and saw a new patient who had been admitted that morning and I said, 'Good afternoon,' to him as I passed by.

'What the fucking hell is wrong with you,' the new patient said to me. I was surprised at the comment, and I guessed it was directed at me.

'Are you talking to me?' I said, trying to remain as cool as I could. ('Are you talking to me') was a phrase later made famous by Hollywood tough guy Robert Deniro in one of his movies, *Taxi Driver*, but I had already said it back in 1969.

'Yes, I am fucking talking to you,' he said sarcastically.

Bill, I later discovered was the guy's name and he seemed to have an attitude problem, especially towards me.

'What have I done, I've never seen you before, so why the abuse?'

Bill just gave me a sneering look and said, 'I just don't like your attitude man.'

'That's too bad,' I said, 'You'll just have to get used to it,' and I walked away, hurt at the unjust abuse I had been subjected to. As nurses, we did not always appreciate what it was like for new patients, especially those who came to the unit for treatment. Often they were desperate for a fix and needed drugs badly and were probably feeling physically and mentally in a bad way and were locked up and waiting to be seen by a doctor to be assessed. Bill was very sensitive and guarded and seemed to be suspicious about everyone, although I may have worried about it more than I should have done. Bill and I later became good friends, and when I knew him better I asked him why he had been so rude to me when I first said hello to him.

'I just thought that you were being sarcastic,' Bill later told me. I used to offer Bill ten pence on a number of occasions if he could do so many press-ups without stopping. On the first occasion Bill managed to do 8, but later on he did manage 20. It was a strange sight seeing Bill in the middle of the dormitory doing press-ups with an audience of addicts looking on and encouraging him. Whenever Bill wanted a couple of shillings for cigarettes he used to say to me, 'Two shillings for fifteen press-ups?'

229

'You did fifteen press-ups last time, so you have to do twenty now,' I would tell Bill, and Bill would argue and say, 'I'll do fifteen.'

'No, it's twenty or no money,' I would repeat.

Down on the floor Bill would go and strain every muscle in his much abused and unfit body and do the 20 press-ups. I think that it was the hardest money he had ever earned, but at least he did earn it. Bill quite often did not appreciate my weird sense of Irish humour, which coupled with my Limerick accent must have sounded strange to someone in Bill's position. I remember on one occasion a bottle of 200 sleeping tablets were stolen from the clinic room, though we didn't realise it at the time until a number of the patients were seen staggering around the ward. Bill came up to one nursing staff and handed in a half bottle of the tablets. Though Bill never stole the tablets, he confiscated the remainder and returned them, lest the staff got into trouble as a result of the theft. Bill was sober and straight and never took any of the tablets himself, which said a lot for his character and the improvement that he had made since his admission to the unit. We made sure never to allow a patient into the clinic room after that. We pretended at one time that the place was bugged with microphones and small TV cameras and advised the patients to be careful in future, but I was not sure they believed it.

Most of the addicts on the unit had been rejected by their families and friends and some had not seen their parents for years because of the shame they felt, and so they forgot their sorrows for a while by getting stoned. No one seemed to like addicts except other addicts. Many regarded the unit as their home because, as one patient said on admission, 'Man, it's good to be home again,' which made us feel good. Other patients saw the unit as a doss-house and somewhere to sleep. Others still realised that there was really nowhere else to go, and as hospitals went, some agreed that it was one of the best places in London. Most did not want to be treated anywhere else. Other patients did not like all the different meetings and often felt that there was too much spying on the patients. Most agreed that, on the whole, the unit did a lot of good for them, and without it there would have been many more deaths. Most of the addicts hung around the 'Dilly' (Piccadilly) in those days, because there were a lot of late night chemists, but the police also hung around there, and as far as I can see things seem not to have changed much. The Dilly, back then was also known as 'The Junkies Graveyard'.

Drugs were regularly smuggled into the unit, in various ways, by the patients, and they were usually one or two steps ahead of us. The methods they used could be quite clever and devious. One guy smuggled an

230

ampoule of methadone up his arse, but could not find it again and became very worried. For his own safety, he reported it to the nursing staff, who advised him that there was very little we could do, except that he should let nature take its course! He was not very happy but we all thought it was hilarious, and the patient himself later saw the funny side. We were never quite sure if he ever did retrieve the glass ampoule, because we never got to the bottom of the story!

Some of the women smuggled all sorts of illegal medication into the unit in their vagina, but did not always get away with it because that was another area that would be examined, by female nurses as they came back to the ward. It was all part of the job. Internal examinations were a very unpleasant task that none of us liked to do because it was very degrading all round, both for patients and staff, but it had to be done as it could be dangerous if we allowed patients to treat themselves on the ward and do as they liked. Some patients would be allowed out to the shop to get bits and pieces for the rest of the patients, and of course they would be pressured to try and bring something illegal back. A favourite was to part empty a bottle of lemonade and refill it with gin or whisky, and although we did not always stop this practice, we occasionally became suspicious when the top of the bottle was wet and still full, meaning it probably had been tampered with.

We had more than our share of violence on the unit, not always started by the patients. One nurse deliberately aggravated a patient one day, and as a result, came off the worse, with a black eye. As a result he was moved from the unit, because of other similar incidents. No one missed him. One female patient once threatened me with her two brothers and called me a 'Mother Fucker,' which was better than being assaulted I suppose.

Patients were naturally always trying to get one over on the nurses, just like I did with the Christian Brothers when I was in Glin, and it was something that we were aware of. We felt good when we stopped the patients' efforts to deceive us, though from the patients' point of view it must have been very frustrating and annoying. I often secretly admired the patients and hated being the one to thwart their efforts. Patients' body language often changed when they were up to something, as they would start whispering in groups and stop talking if a nurse appeared on the scene.

We had two female cleaners on the unit, one Italian, and Mrs Murphy, of course from the old country. They were extra eyes for the nurses and would tell us if the patients were acting suspiciously. Maria, the Italian, came up to the office one day shouting, 'Come quick, patient has tablets,' which we interpreted as someone having illegal drugs on them. We dashed to the bathroom, only to find one of the female patients unconscious in a half-filled bath of water. She might have drowned if it had not been for Maria's keen observation.

Mrs Murphy was in her sixties and looked like a typical Irish washer-woman, and was still working in two different jobs to make ends meet. She was always on the go and was a great character, although her personal life had been full of tragedy. She found her husband dead sitting in a chair one day after work and a couple of her children had died in accidents, but you would never think it, talking to her. She was as happy as anyone I have ever met, and I felt fortunate to have known her. She rarely spoke about her feelings.

If ever a patient came for his fix at medicine time and we felt that they were slightly intoxicated due to abusing other drugs, we would not give the medication that was due, for reasons of safety. More often than not the patient would create a fuss or violence would erupt because the patient would usually strongly deny taking anything and would demand his drugs, which we would not give. This often created friction amongst staff themselves as some opinions might be divided, and of course, if you did give into pressure from the patient, you would be held accountable by the staff group the next day at the staff meeting, and you had to have a convincing argument for your actions.

In the first months we were opened we decided to give patients who were stoned an injection of sterile water to avoid a confrontation, and it usually worked, but when an American locum doctor came to work on the unit he decided that it was not right to deceive the patients. He wanted us to be straight and clear and not give any more sterile water injections, and to cope with the patients' anger, and it worked okay.

There was always tension and rivalry between staff who wanted to be top dog and rule the roost, and of course some staff left as a result of the added tension and bickering. Romance and illicit affairs also took place, often while on duty, which caused embarrassment and meant some staff had to be moved. All this unit romance, however, passed me by. I did have a childish liking for practical jokes, and Sandra often pointed out that I was having my second childhood, although I don't think I ever really left my first! I used to buy rubber spiders and snakes, which at one time almost caused the receptionist to have a heart attack! I also bought wigs and false teeth and face masks, and even dressed up as the ward cleaner early in the morning. I also pretended to be deaf so that the patients did not recognize my Limerick accent, and of course, the patients took the piss out of me until one of the girl patients told them, 'Don't laugh, the poor girl is deaf and can't help it,' while I controlled my urge to laugh underneath the wig!

I personally thought that the unit was like one big family. We had some serious arguments and some rivalry and falling in and falling out with each other. Misunderstandings often occurred, because we were all still individuals, and some of us were more stubborn than others, including myself. But we all worked together extremely well.

Another patient who had been discharged was found by the night staff lying groaning on the grass outside the unit in the middle of the night, badly injured. He had apparently tried to climb up the drainpipe to see his girlfriend on the third floor while stoned, and he fell to the grassy ground below. I believe that he had to have his spleen removed.

In December 1971, our second child, a son whom we named Kevin, was born, which in some ways was a fairly perfect family set up. So a lot of good things happened to me and Sandra during my period on the unit, and it definitely was the high point of my life, although I did not know it at the time. Nearly all the staff who worked there agreed that it was one of the happiest working periods in their lives.

While working on the unit I helped to start a hospital magazine called *The Cedars*, and I was the editor for a while, but reading it years later, it was pathetic! I guess all budding writers have to start somewhere, and I also felt like a budding writer. The magazine also got me in very hot water! One day the matron in charge of the hospital asked to see me in her office. She was calmly angry and she asked me how the local newspaper had got hold of a copy of *The Cedars*. She was very cross because an article that I had written had got onto the front page of the local newspaper.

My article was highly critical of how the nursing staff had to queue for ages in a long line in the hospital corridor to collect their wages. I commented that it had reminded me of queuing up for the dole a few years before. I told her that some member of staff must have sent the newspaper a copy of the magazine, but I declined to tell her that the member of staff was me! I eventually quit because I was being controlled too much. I also made a serious attempt to write a book called *Diary of a Nurse*, which I made some half-hearted efforts to get published without success. Part of the book was about the unit and my other experiences as a nurse and my time in care. My writing had not been thought out or edited very well.

I also contracted hepatitis while working on the unit, by getting a used needle accidentally stuck in me. I was off sick for a month. I could hardly walk up the stairs at home, but I somehow managed to find enough energy to conceive our son Kevin! I was advised not to run again for six months, but like most athletes I ignored the doctor's advice and I was running a month later, but only just.

The D.D.U. was the benchmark that I would compare every other job to in the future, but for me no other job would ever be as satisfying or fulfilling again. I grew up and matured a lot in the unit and gained valuable insight, not only into other people's problems, but also into my own. I realised that I often identified too much with patients' problems, which was not healthy, and I became frustrated too easily, and I was always trying to put things right quickly. Having control over people, like locking patients up, always made me feel more uncomfortable than it probably should have.

I had been turned down twice for promotion to a charge nurse at Tooting Bec, and so I made my mind up to leave if I was not successful on the second attempt. I applied to Horton Hospital in Epsom, Surrey and got promotion at my first attempt, but soon wished that I hadn't!

34. New Challenges

I had been very settled at Tooting Bec Hospital and I did not really want to leave, but I felt that I needed to prove my worth, which I did, but at the cost of my happiness. Leaving the D.D.U. was to set up a chain reaction that would cause me and my family a lot of frustration and heartache. I would never again feel as settled in a job, and maybe it was part of my personality and a weakness in my make-up that I always looked back too much and tried to recreate what I had. I always wanted something else and something different, and never really found job fulfilment. My life and Sandra's would have been a lot easier and maybe happier if I had remained at the D.D.U., but it certainly would not have been as rich or as varied as it would eventually become. Maybe fate was playing a bigger part than I was aware of.

There was an incident where my running ability came in handy on one occasion. I had to escort a patient to the shops in the hospital grounds. He decided to make a dash for the front gate, but unfortunately for him, he took a wrong turn and then continued to make another wrong turn, with me in hot pursuit behind him with my long white nurse's coat flapping as I ran. We ran in and out of different corridors, but I was in no hurry to catch him because I knew that he would not outrun me and he was too far away from the main gate anyway to go into the public domain.

We passed the same point on a number of occasions and he seemed to be running out of energy. Everyone in the different departments along the corridors was looking and wondering what was going on, especially as I was laughing to myself because of the situation, which resembled something from a Charlie Chaplin film. The sound of our shoes banging on the stone-covered corridor was also very noisy. If you have ever tried to laugh while running you will realise just how difficult it can be! Eventually the guy stopped and said, 'Fuck it, I'm giving up, you're too good for me,' and we walked calmly back to the unit in a more civilized manner, with no hard feelings and some unexpected sprint training under my belt!

After our second child, Kevin, was born we decided not to have any more.

While I had been working in the drug unit, I had kept notes, with the intention of trying to write a book one day because I felt that the experiences that I had witnessed there might make interesting reading.

One of the female patients Mary (not her real name) knew the London gangster Ronnie Kray who was serving life in prison at the time for murder, along with his brother Reggie. I asked her if Ronnie would mind me using his name, if I ever did write a book, and she said that he wouldn't. I did not want to upset Ronnie Kray as I did not relish being buried in concrete somewhere and I told her so. She gave me his address in prison and so I wrote to him. Ronnie wrote me a very polite letter on prison notepaper and said that he indeed knew Mary very well and he had no objections if I wished to use his name. Mary had said that Ronnie Kray helped her in her battle with drugs. She said that he never gave her any drugs and did not approve of them, and tried to discourage her from taking drugs. He had given her a place to sleep and a lot of support when she had no one else to turn to. Ronnie himself was never involved with drugs.

Mary thought very highly of Ronnie and she showed me several letters that he had written to her while he was in prison. He seemed genuinely fond of her in his letters and said that he hoped she would come off drugs. I found it hard to believe that a man such as Ronnie Kray, with the reputation that he had in the underworld, could write such a simple and touching letter to a drug addict friend. Was this the same man who was now serving a life sentence in prison for murder? I found it hard to understand. I had always believed that criminals should pay for their crimes, but somehow I was suddenly filled with compassion and sorrow, thinking that a fellow human being was doing life in prison. It seemed too harsh despite his crimes.

Ronnie Kray died a few years ago still in prison. I did see Ronnie during a visit to Broadmoor secure psychiatric hospital around 1993. I saw him on the ward but I did not speak to him. I also saw Peter Sutcliffe, the Yorkshire Ripper, who killed around 15 women in the seventies. It felt weird to see someone who had been such an infamous killer.

Horton Hospital, unlike Tooting Bec, was in the Epsom countryside in many acres of land, surrounded by walls, with lots of orchards. It was also very bleak looking as I walked through the gates on my first day at 6.50 a.m. It was a misty, damp morning and the hospital looked like something from a Gothic film, shrouded in the early morning mist. God, it looked like some workhouse from the Charles Dickens era. I paused for a moment, wondering if I should go to work or not, because I was filled with foreboding, and I had no enthusiasm for my new job. I would gladly have walked away if I did not have a family depending on me. I suddenly realised that being responsible for a family was a hard burden to bear and I did not always bear it easily, but I was responsible and I had to go to work, at least to give it a try. I had never easily adapted to changes, but this was a change that I felt from the outset was not right. We had foolishly sold our house in Tooting and were now living in a hospital house so I was stuck and had to get on with it.

I looked around the empty hospital grounds to ask someone where Ward 14 was, but there wasn't a soul in sight to ask. I eventually got to the ward about five minutes late and walked up the long corridor, only to find the charge nurse looking at his watch and watching me walking towards him. 'You're late' the charge nurse said sarcastically. 'Fuck yourself, you wanker,' I said quietly to myself. I was already in a bad mood and didn't want to be there, but I was to work with different charge nurses on different wards for a couple of weeks to gain experience of the hospital as a whole, and it was a fucking hole.

I found the wards much too large, with up to 60 patients on some wards, with beds cramped together. The hospital looked archaic, but the staff attitudes seemed just as old-fashioned, and very few seemed to say what they felt. Attitudes to patients also seemed to be very controlling, and patients seemed to be very submissive. Because I had been working with drug addicts for three years in an open way and was used to them questioning nurses' decisions, I found it hard to see psychiatric patients being treated in what appeared to me a very offhand way. Psychiatric patients, because of the nature of their psychiatric illness often lack self-esteem and rarely challenge nurses whom they feel always know best. They look up to them and respect their decisions and are often afraid to challenge nurses' decisions, in case there are backlashes in some way or other, which has proved to be true as I have observed myself over the years. Patients were often in awe of the nurses who cared for them, and while most nurses respected the patients in their care, there were a lot who did not. One thing I had learned from working in the Drug Unit was to treat patients with respect, because if you didn't, you would be challenged by the patient, whereas psychiatric patients rarely challenged any nursing decisions. The attitude that I observed among some of the older charge nurses at Horton were attitudes that I had sometimes seen in Tooting Bec and in many other places, and it made me feel uneasy and uncomfortable. It reminded me of my time at Glin Industrial School where you dared not challenge one of the Christian Brothers.

Most of the patients at Horton, as was the case in most of the large psychiatric hospitals in those days, were long-stay institutionalised and damaged patients, who seemed on the whole very subservient to nurses. It was a legacy from the past and to some extent it still continues today. In experiments within the last few years it has been shown that even the most powerful people in authority will be subservient when they are in hospital under a nurse's care, so it isn't surprising that patients with low self-esteem, such as is evident with those with mental illness, will feel under the nurses' authority and feel gratitude and often put them on a pedestal.

Being in a new hospital on my first day, and feeling so insecure and unhappy, got me thinking about keeping a diary to record my feelings and my observations. It occurred to me that if I felt like this, a qualified nurse, what must it be like for a person with mental illness coming into a mental hospital for the first time? Perhaps psychiatric patients did not see things as I did, but maybe they did and maybe I was empathising too much with patients' problems, but was that bad? Years later, I realised that my attitude had not been that far wrong, when a counsellor on a course I was on quoted from a book. 'Unless you have walked in someone's shoes you cannot understand how that person feels.' My trouble has always been that I sometimes identified too much with the patients in my care, due no doubt to my own troubled past and my own time in care, and I always seemed to be at odds with those around me.

One of the American locum doctors on the Drug Unit once told me that I liked to identify myself with the addicts. A lot of them had come from a broken home as I had, but I did not understand where my feelings were coming from in 1971. I tried to walk in too many other people's shoes and often took on their pain, which, in psychiatric nursing, was not a healthy thing to do. Yet I had a great awareness of the sometimes 'silent' voices of psychiatric patients who rarely complained and seemed to accept anything that was deemed best for them, by those who cared for them. Yet we who cared for these patients did not always seem to listen or have their best interest at heart. I also seemed to resent authority and continually challenged other people's attitudes and I upset a lot of people early on at Horton Hospital, which did not make my job or life very easy. My attitude also affected my family life. I had got promotion and should have been happy, but I seemed to be lost and unsure and unable to comprehend my new and strange circumstances. I felt depressed and wished that I was still back in the security of Tooting Bec Drug Unit. In fact, after only a couple of days, I tried to cancel the sale of our house in Tooting, so that we could get out of the hospital house, to make it easier for me to resign my job, but it was too late, as we had signed the contract. I now felt truly trapped.

It was especially hard for Sandra, and although at the time I was more concerned about my own predicament and did not give as much thought to her feelings as maybe I should have, I had no choice but to stay where I was and try to tolerate my situation. Sandra was prepared, and indeed expected, to move back with the kids to her parents in Bath if I did pack my job up and had nowhere to live for a while. She was also desperately unhappy and insecure, with two very young children to support, and it was a very difficult period in our lives. I made my mind up to try and knuckle down to the job as best I could until we could get back into a house of our own again. Cheryl was around 3 and Kevin was only 5 months old and thankfully unaware of the situation. Even my interest in running was waning and I did not feel like training much, due to my feelings of depression and high levels of stress. Sandra was great, and rarely complained, and was always supportive and loving.

35. Bedlam

Bedlam* is a word often used to describe a noisy and confused situation, and it's a word often used in reference to mental illness, especially back in the early part of this century, but it's also the most appropriate word to describe the ward that I was about to spend a few days on to get some experience of the different wards in the hospital. It was Ward 5, an acute admission ward, where acutely mentally ill patients came straight from the community. Some, however, were brought in by the police, because they may have been found behaving in some bizarre or dangerous way in the community and were seen as a danger to themselves or to members of the general public. They were admitted to an admission ward, such as Ward 5 for assessment and treatment, and more often than not, against their will on a section.

You might get alcoholics, suicide attempts, drug addicts, and a wide variety of mental illness. Some were very depressed and some suffered manic depression, meaning they would be totally depressed for a number of days and would not talk or eat or wash properly in their depressive state, while in the manic phase they would not stop talking and would hardly sit down for a minute and would often require extra medication to calm them down, less they wear themselves and those around them out! They had mood swings and would have periods when they were fairly normal. In the manic phase they could be very elated and at great risk as they seemed to lose all sense of what was right or wrong. I have seen married women behave in a very sexually promiscuous way, which they would never normally do. They also needed protection from other amorous mentally ill patients who would quite happily take advantage in such a situation. As nurses we had a responsibility to protect these vulnerable women while they were in our care. However, Ward 5 was an all-male ward, with around 45 mostly very ill patients.

After my first day at Horton I decided to keep a diary to give me an added interest in my job and also help me to get through the day. I had been unable to get to sleep that night and was really fed up, and the idea of keeping a diary of day-to-day events inside a mental hospital appealed to

*Bedlam actually refers to St Mary of Bethlehem Hospital in London, one of the world's oldest institutions for caring for people with mental illness.

241

me. I thought that if I could keep a diary and make it into a book, I could show people what it's like to be in a mental hospital in the so-called progressive seventies and maybe help to improve the facilities available. How naive I was! Most of the nurses that I spoke to then agreed that hospital managers were out of touch completely or just not interested in what was going on at ward level at the grass roots. I remember one patient had said to me in all seriousness, 'It's enough to drive you mad!'

As I was escorted to Ward 5 by a Chinese nurse on my first day there, along the never ending dreary corridors I wondered if I would ever find my way around the place. It all seemed so vast, much bigger and more spread out than Tooting Bec. There were a few badly dressed patients hanging around the corridors, some laughing and talking to themselves, while others were looking for dog-ends on the dirty floor. 'God, it must be terrible to be mad,' I thought to myself, and I hoped I would not have to come to a mental hospital, if I ever did get some mental illness, although most of the patients were not here through choice.

I asked my Chinese nurse escort what it was like on Ward 5. 'Oh it's terrible at the moment, we have some very disturbed patients and it's really chaotic,' he said, which did not fill me with any enthusiasm or relieve my already anxious state. I then asked how many patients were on Ward 5. 'We have forty-five, but only thirty-eight beds.'

'Bloody hell, that's an awful lot. In the hospital where I just came from thirty patients on a ward was too many,' I replied with genuine surprise.

'Oh that's not too bad, there are some wards with sixty patients on them,' my Chinese friend said.

As we turned the corner the nurse said, 'This is it.' He then opened a very heavy door with a big heavy key, just like the one I had been issued with a few days earlier. The hallway inside the ward was dull and badly in need of decorating, and I wasn't impressed at all.

I was even less impressed when I saw six single side rooms, each just about big enough to hold a single mattress on the floor and an old tin locker. On each bed was a patient apparently asleep or drugged up. The doors were obviously locked to contain the patients, and all the rooms were dirty and strewn with garments and newspapers on the unpolished wooden floor. Most of the patients were dressed in their day clothes, and as we passed, one of the patients seemed to come alive and started shouting and banging on the door. His speech was slurred and incoherent. I couldn't understand what he said.

'What's wrong with him?' I asked my escort.

'Oh he has been getting into fights with other patients and we sedated him, but the sedation does not seem to have done much good,' and with that he opened the door and started talking to the very tall, bearded, dishevelled man. 'He is a manic-depressive,' the nurse whispered to me. 'And right now he is very manic.'

Roger was the man's name I later discovered, and he was in his forties and looked like an old tramp off the streets. I could not make out his accent because of his slurred speech, but later discovered that he was English. I was even more amazed to find out that he was a doctor and an author of some repute, and in fact one of his books was on the ward and some time later when I looked at the book's back cover there was a long list of Roger's scholastic achievements. He had been to Cambridge University and had held some very high positions in various jobs and had also won a famous American literary prize for something or other, but in the midst of it all he had decided to drop out and live the life of a vagrant, no doubt as a result of his manic-depressive illness, and this was the result. 'God, what a waste and who would ever believe it?' I thought. As the next few days progressed I was to discover just how bad Roger could be, especially in his manic phase.

Most mental illness can be debilitating, but manic depression can be particularly cruel. While there have been many famous personalities (Vincent Van Gogh and Spike Milligan to name two) with this illness, on the whole it is disturbing to witness and to observe someone's behaviour change so much: from complete elation to utter despair over a period of weeks; back and forth with the occasional bout of normality. Being a manic-depressive is indeed a very cruel form of mental illness and has destroyed many people's lives and is difficult to control, as I was to discover years later in my very last job as a psychiatric nurse.

Patients were normally put into isolation, due to their disturbed state, for their own protection and safety, and for the protection of other patients and staff, but the practice had been stopped at Tooting Bec Hospital some years earlier, as a result of a patient dying, due to setting himself on fire while smoking. He had not been searched properly. It was always hazardous, because patients still needed very close supervision, as they had been known to either attempt to hang themselves or cut their wrists or attempt some other self-harm. I did not like it and felt that I had stepped back in time. As time went on, I became more convinced that Horton was a long way behind Tooting Bec in its treatment of the mentally ill. My problem was compounded by the fact that I had not really worked with the mentally ill for over three years, because I had been working with drug addicts, and it all came as a shock.

As we walked through the main dining-room, I was looking all around me, taking in as much as I could. I heard a few sudden moves of chairs and looked around sharply to see who was fighting, but it was a false alarm, and I realised that my nerves were getting the best of me. I was in a strange environment and unsure of myself. Groups of patients were sitting around doing nothing much, and a few more were walking up and down the ward with vague expressions on their faces. There was a snooker table at the end of the ward and a nurse was playing a game with a patient. I was introduced to the charge nurse and we spent an hour in the office talking about the ward. A fattish patient came in and asked me if I was a doctor. 'I'm sorry, I'm only a nurse,' I said.

'Have you seen my glasses?' the patient asked the charge nurse.

'They are in your top pocket,' the nurse told him.

'Oh, yes,' the patient said and put them on his head.

'That's the trouble on this ward, you never get time to sit down and talk to the patients,' said the charge nurse. 'We have far too many patients and too much book work to do, and we don't have time to do any real nursing.' He was extremely annoyed about having more patients than beds, which only worked because some of the patients were either on leave or may have absconded or were just temporarily sleeping out in some other wards. Even the patients who had absconded had to have their beds kept open because they were likely to be returned by the police at any time. I asked Michael, the charge nurse, if he ever complained. 'Oh all the time, but it's no use; no one seems to care. I am leaving soon anyway and what's the point of worrying too much over something that I can't change anyway.'

Just then a huge black man, about six foot four, dressed in pyjamas and wearing a hat with tassels on top which dangled from the end, came and asked Michael, 'Can I have my clothes back?'

'Not yet,' said Michael.

'Why not?' said the black patient, waving an empty beer can in his hand.

'Because the doctor does not want you to have them yet, that's why,' said Michael in a quiet voice.

'Man, you wanna keep my trousers for yourself,' said the patient in his strong West Indian accent and stared at Michael as if about to attack him, but Michael remained seated and calmly asked the patient to leave the office. Michael had to ask the patient a few more times before he eventually left, muttering something under his breath. I later discovered that some of the patients had their clothes confiscated on admission if they

244

were likely to be troublesome or likely to abscond, because that way they would be easier to spot in the community, at least that was the theory anyway.

At tea time, Roger, the manic-depressive scholar, was allowed out of his room, although he was still in a manic mood and very over active, despite all the medication that he'd had, and he seemed determined to upset someone or other and he did. A young guy with a personality disorder and psychopathic tendencies, and a short temper had just returned from a walk in the grounds, and immediately Roger started to aggravate him and direct comments at him. 'Here's the fucking psychopath,' said Roger in his usual loud tone of voice, and with that the young patient immediately grabbed Roger by the throat and attempted to strangle him, but I and some other nurses immediately stepped in to separate them before any damage was done.

'You cunt,' snarled the young guy to Roger and sat down at the table where Roger was also sitting. I knew, as did the other nurses that there was more to come, especially from Roger who had salad cream all down his dirty beard, and his nose was covered in dry blood and he had a plaster over one eye from a previous fight. It seems that Roger had not been getting on with the young guy that he had just taunted for some time, so more trouble was anticipated, and I stood by, just in case. Roger continued to goad the young guy who by now was very angry, with justification, and to make things worse, Roger took some lettuce off the young guy's plate. The young guy said nothing but just stood up and hit out at Roger with the back of his hand and caught Roger unawares on the side of his eye.

Roger gave an almighty scream, which brought the other nurses running, and the charge nurse told Roger to go to his room, and gave him extra medication. I felt very sad to see such an intelligent man as Roger reduced to such squalor and violence, all because of his mental illness. He was not a violent man himself, but just seemed to upset and irritate everyone around him by his manic behaviour. He even irritated us nurses, but at least we were not mentally ill and we went home after our shift was over, whereas the other patients were stuck on the ward 24 hours a day and all had their own problems to cope with.

Roger rarely took his medication without an argument, which often lasted for 15 minutes or more. I thought that perhaps arguing about his medication was one way of getting attention, because nurses were so busy that unless someone created a fuss they were unlikely to get much attention, but it was not the nurses' fault. My nerves were already on edge and I was not looking forward to spending a few more days on this ward. It was, for me, a chaotic place to work, and no doubt for the patients a far from ideal place to recuperate from a mental illness.

One confused old patient went through the door marked exit, which he thought was the toilet and caused a number of the other patients, who were watching him, to laugh. It made me laugh as well. This is the same patient who kept asking the charge nurse if he could leave the ward. He was obviously suffering from some confused state and did not know whether he was coming or going. The charge nurse talked about the difficulties of running Ward 5. He had been here for a year but said that the charge nurses on this ward were moved very often. 'This ward wears out a lot of nurses. No one can stand it for very long,' he said, and then went on to mention one young charge nurse in his twenties who had committed suicide shortly after starting work on this ward. He admitted that it was not the stress and strain of dealing with the different patients that was the problem, but the constant losing battle of trying to create vacancies for a constant flow of new patients being admitted.

It was a losing battle and a very frustrating problem, but as we spoke, another new admission arrived, making it five patients without an actual bed. After a few minutes, the newly-admitted patient complained that he only had two biscuits and a cup of cocoa, but the doctor asked him if he expected a first class meal immediately on arrival in 'this hotel'?

'I'm sorry that I came to this fucking place,' the patient muttered out loud. 'It's worse than the fucking Salvation Army.'

One thing that I found hard to understand was why, on the two wards that I have been on so far, every patient was automatically prescribed the same medication, in some cases before they had even seen the doctor? And nearly every patient was given night medication. One patient told me that he never took night sedation in his life until he came here! Another patient, who was a qualified nurse in a general hospital, was being treated for depression, told me that he felt that it was nursing that had brought on his illness and made him depressed. He had taken two overdoses in an attempt to commit suicide. He said that he was a homosexual and was waiting a divorce and that he had only had sex with his wife twice in the last 18 months. He also told me that his wife wanted a 'sexual athlete', and that he himself was no 'James Bond!' when it came to the bed department and admitted that he preferred boys. One of the nurses had warned me beforehand that George would tell me that he was queer without any qualms and was probably trying to shock me, but he didn't succeed!

George then stroked the cat and said that he believed in reincarnation and that, 'Perhaps the cat is a famous ballet dancer reincarnated.' He told

246

me that he thought that all cats were reincarnated ballet dancers, and who was I to doubt him?

I was very moved and impressed seeing a grown man kneeling by his bed and saying his prayers. It took a lot of courage to do that in front of a lot of other grown men. A female patient came into the ward looking for a taxi number. She was very attractive and was showing a lot of cleavage, which I couldn't help noticing and so had the other nurses. After she was given the number, one of the nurses said that he should have offered her a lift home and implied that he would not mind, 'Giving her one'. The charge nurse jokingly reminded him that it was against the law to fornicate with female patients!

The average length of stay on the ward was meant to be around six weeks, though one patient, who worked in the kitchen, said he had been on this ward for six years! I spent about 30 minutes talking and listening to George, the homosexual, who admitted to feeling very tense and anxious. He seemed very glad to talk to someone and to pour out his troubles and remarked that there wasn't enough staff to just sit and talk to patients. He expressed his annoyance at the lack of tea and sugar on the ward as he smoked incessantly. George was obviously very anxious and said he was worried about the fact that there was only one nurse on night duty, compared to four or five on day duty, and wondered what would happen if there was trouble or violence at night, and how would the one nurse cope in an emergency?

It brought back my own memories when, as a student nurse, I was left in charge of a ward on my own, which was, I felt, a great responsibility, and I often wondered at the safety of it. I was once left in charge, on my own, in a ward of around 30 patients, of which about a dozen were incontinent and most needed changing at least once during the night. Of course I did not always change them, because it was often too difficult on my own, due to the patients being uncooperative and half asleep as a result of being sedated. The lack of tea and sugar might seem a small problem to nurses but it could be a big problem to an anxious patient who was locked up with lots of time on his hands.

'God, I made a terrible mistake coming to this fucking hole,' I kept thinking. I hated the place and found it very depressing, and God only knows how the mentally ill patients on the ward were feeling. The atmosphere on Ward 5 was very depressing, but at least the staff were friendly, which made my stay bearable. I kept thinking about Tooting Bec and how clean it was and how happy I had been. I had badly wanted promotion, and got it, and my pride had been restored, but at a price! Here

247

I was on Ward 5, and I would just have to try and survive from day to day, and hope it would get better. There was really no going back to Tooting Bec, as that would hurt my pride too much. Patience was not one of my virtues, and I often made hasty decisions.

As I was in the office talking to Michael, a patient came in. He had long, dirty, matted hair which was half blond and half black, as if it had been dyed at some time. He had a jet-black beard with piercing big dark eyes. He looked funny, because he was wearing very tight riding breeches, which clung to his legs from the knee down, but very baggy around the waist. He was about 37 and spoke in a very quiet and effeminate voice and was difficult to understand, until he opened his mouth and pointed to a loose tooth. I gathered that he wanted to see a dentist and told him that we would make an appointment, and with that he nodded and walked away. A nurse told me that he was Polish and that, 'He came to England from Poland in 1956 after the uprising. The Russians must have sent all their Polish nutcases to England in 1956. England is the only place that would take them. If he went back to Poland now they would shoot him as a deserter.' Some of the nurses laughed out loud and thought the remark was funny. I gave a nervous smile, but really did not think it was funny.

At 8 p.m. a new admission, whom we had been expecting all afternoon, arrived under police escort. The male patient had been found naked in the middle of a main street in London shouting at the top of his voice that he could see faces all around him. (What's changed?)

He was an alcoholic, but he was not drunk and said that his hallucinations were probably due to his heavy drinking, or probably lack of drink in his case. Some heavy drinkers can suffer from delirium tremens, due to suddenly stopping alcohol, and as a result can suffer from hallucinations and become very confused and see all types of imaginary things. At its worst it is not very nice to observe and it must be terrifying for the person concerned. I have seen one such patient who thought that there were rats climbing all over his bed, and he was in constant terror.

The police handed over some personal possessions belonging to the new patient including part of a deck of playing cards, although they were not normal cards. 'Have you seen these?' said the patient excitedly. One of the nurses reached out and took the cards, and as he looked at them his face brightened up considerably. We all had a look at the pornographic playing cards and the usual sexual remarks were made by one and all. Just then another Polish patient came into the office and asked the charge nurse, 'Am I mad?'

'Of course you're not, you're just a bit depressed,' said the nurse.

'A bit depressed?' I thought to myself. The patient had cut his wrist in a suicide attempt a few weeks ago and was awaiting for an operation to join some of the tendons back together again. That was bad enough, but I almost got sick when later one of the nurses told me that the same patient had attempted to cut his penis off! 'Christ, he must be mad then!' I acknowledged to the nurse.

Depression is a terrible thing to suffer and can be very debilitating for the person concerned, and although I have been depressed myself at times, it has been very mild and of short duration compared to the severe depression that this patient was obviously suffering from. Such patients always needed close supervision as the risk of attempted suicide was very real, which was also an added strain for nurses, because a suicide on your ward was a very serious matter for all concerned.

It was time to go off duty and boy was I glad! I felt physically and mentally drained and I had only been there one day! 'I'll never stick it,' I thought to myself. 'But at least I'm off until tomorrow, and hopefully seeing Sandra and Cheryl and Kevin will give me some strength to carry on.' My family always gave me the strength and the motivation to do things that I would not normally do, but I was still feeling very low and vulnerable, and I was not sure if I could survive very much longer. Ward 5 was a real challenge and I did not feel that I was up to it, although I was only going to have to work there for a few days. Whenever I worked on a locked ward, such as Ward 5, I felt some of the anxieties that the patients felt, because I was locked in with some very disturbed, sick and often violent patients. Acute admission wards are always very stressful areas to work in, because all the patients are new and unpredictable and, until they are assessed properly, it is often difficult to know how to respond to them, at least in the early days of their admission. Some nurses, of course, loved the constant activity and the challenge of such a ward, and it was always the best place to work on if you wanted promotion. It was seen as a high profile ward, where doctors were constantly coming and going and nothing or no one stood still for very long. In my last years of nursing I observed that things still had not changed on such wards and noticed that nurses working on these acute admission wards were still under a terrible amount of stress, and many could not stand the pressure for very long and either left nursing or went off sick regularly. I personally could not work on such a ward regularly but I had great admiration for the staff who did.

On Ward 5 I met the regular charge nurse, named Jim, who was a small, lightly built Irishman and younger than I had expected. He was naturally very friendly and he told me that he had been in charge on this ward for the last seven years! I asked him if he wanted to go to another ward for a change after all these years? 'I do, but they won't move me.'

'That's crazy, surely they have to move you after all that time here,' I said to Jim.

'No, they won't, he said.

Michael, the other nurse piped in, 'The trouble is, no one else likes working this ward so they prefer to leave Jim here.'

The trouble was there were very few good wards to work in, and if Jim did not work on Ward 5, he may have finished up working on one of the many geriatric wards where most of the staff either stagnated or lost interest. At least on Ward 5 he was kept busy all the time, sometimes too busy, but at least it kept him on his toes and motivated. Jim's complaint was that there were too many patients and too few beds.

Out in the large day room, two big African patients were playing bongo drums and chanting in their own lingo at the top of their voices. The only trouble was that they had to use tin cans as substitutes for drums and were making a hell of a racket, but what else can you expect in a mental hospital? Although it was now very quiet on the ward I could still feel the tension.

I heard about one of the top consultants, who used to try all the drugs on himself before prescribing them to patients, though not all at the same time. It seemed a good idea, though I would not fancy it myself. I later met this doctor who was very popular with the patients and staff, because he was certainly different in every way. He was from abroad, maybe Polish, and was a giant of a man with a huge personality to match, and he used to take the patients on long walks in the nearby countryside. He also had an animal sanctuary in the hospital grounds, with ducks, geese and goats, and he encouraged the patients to look after them. At one time someone strangled some of the geese, which was very sad. He was indeed a very humane and unusual doctor.

An elderly alcoholic man wanted to leave and was obviously very anxious. 'I can't stand this atmosphere for another six weeks,' he said to the charge nurse. 'Neither can I,' I thought to myself, 'at least someone else feels like I do.' Jim advised the patient to stay, at least until he saw the doctor. Some patients were informal, or voluntary, which meant that, as a rule, they could leave if they wished, although some informal patients could be detained against their will, if it was felt that they might be a danger to themselves or to others. Patients who were on a section or detained against their will couldn't leave if they wanted to. The patient agreed to stay, but asked to be let out for some fresh air.

Roger's, the manic-depressive, piercing voice could be heard on the patients' telephone, out in the passage way. He was complaining to the police about something or other.

At tea time, all the patients lined up in a long queue and were each handed a cup of cocoa and three biscuits. It seemed very degrading to see a lot of grown men queuing up for food, and it reminded me of a poorhouse. Each patient was only allowed one cup of cocoa, because that was as far as the ward supply stretched on this particular ward. Personally I found it hard to believe that there was such a shortage of food, and I asked the charge nurse why there was not enough food available. He muttered something about it being very hard to get extra supplies.

'Anyway, we don't want to make them too strong.'

I did not appreciate that type of joke and he did not seem that interested one way or the other as regards the patients' shortage of food. No doubt the shortage of beds was his main problem and uppermost in his mind. Often what was very important to a patient was not necessarily important to a nurse, and it often led to frustration and acts of violence and aggression.

As nurses we concentrated too much on administration, rather than on a patient's immediate needs, partly due to the nature of the job, and it was an aspect of nursing that I never liked. One of the most important things that we could give to patients was our time, just to sit and listen, and the longer I remained in nursing, the more I realised how important it was to just listen.

Later, in the 1990s when I did a year's counselling training, I began to realise that I was not as good a listener as I should have been, probably because I also needed someone to listen to me. It was brought home to me while I was doing one-to-one counselling with a patient in my last job before I retired. My mind started to wander during our 15 minute session and I started to look up at the clock, discreetly, I thought, and I was not concentrating properly on listening. The patient suddenly said to me. 'Are you listening, Ray?' The patient knew that I was not listening and picked it up in my body language and I felt embarrassed.

There was no trouble at teatime, but I observed that nurses always seemed to be in a hurry to clear all the tables before the patients had finished eating, which prompted one elderly patient to remark, 'There seems to be a race to see who gets finished first here.' I nodded in agreement with him. Another patient said to me, 'I'm Jewish, but I don't care about my religion. Fuck my religion, I'll be what I want to be. Religion is in the heart. This fucking hospital is fifty years behind the times,' he continued. 'We have mice here running around the floor at night and they must be mad to be here.' It seemed a funny comment, but he seemed quite serious. The rest of the afternoon passed without any incident and I was glad. I slept a lot better that night.

18/1/1971. It was very quiet today, thank God. Most of the patients were escorted to occupational therapy on another ward. One of the nurses told me about the time when he was a nervous student some years ago on night duty. He said that when he was giving out night sedation, one particular patient kept asking him for an extra sleeping tablet. At first he refused, but later on he gave the extra tablet to keep the peace, even though he knew that he was not supposed to without the doctor's permission. I agreed that it still went on quite a lot, even by senior nurses who should have known better. The nurse continued and told me that the same patient eventually wanted even more night sedation than he was entitled to and he gave extra, because by now he did not want to fall out with the patient. However, he began to realise the serious situation that was now developing with this particular patient, and he began to get worried in case the patient might save up the sleeping tablets and take an overdose. The patient in question had previously attempted suicide, so the nurse could not wait to get off the ward. He began to feel trapped because he had put himself in an uncompromising position. Eventually he did get off night duty and only just in time! The particular patient committed suicide a couple of days later with possibly some of the sleeping tablets that he had been saving up. The nurse said that he learned a valuable lesson from the experience.

I remembered at Tooting Bec Hospital it was not unusual to give patients extra medication beyond what the doctor had prescribed, as nurses often felt that enough medication was not being prescribed, and often they were right, but it was a dangerous and irregular thing to do and was not to be recommended.

A young schizophrenic named Norman asked me what day it was. He had just returned from having E.C.T. and he was still a bit confused and disorientated, which is normal after E.C.T. Some patients were quite happy to have it on a voluntary basis, while others seemed absolutely terrified and had to be dragged to have it from the ward, kicking and screaming. I hated it as it produced a violent epileptic-type fit and a number of nurses had to hold the patient firmly, lest bones were broken, which happened from time to time. In the early days of this treatment patients were often awake and it must have been horrendous to have and to witness. While E.C.T. was often effective for schizophrenia and also depression it was often debatable how much good it really did in the long term and may have done some brain damage. Most of the long-term patients who had it year in, year out, were often zombie-like in their behaviour.

Norman talked about his two mothers! His real parents were divorced. I asked him about his real mother and what she was like. 'You mean Mrs Brown?' said Norman.

'Mrs Brown,' I said, 'that's a nice way to talk about your mother.'

'She's not my fucking mother any more,' said Norman, 'she's fucking crackers.'

'Is she in a mental hospital?' I asked Norman.

'Not yet, but it won't be fucking long,' Norman replied with indifference.

Another patient came and asked for something to help him to go to the toilet, but one of the nurses told him that one of the other nurses had left the ward with the medicine keys. 'We'll give you something when he gets back,' he told the patient. A couple of minutes later the same patient asked me the same question and I gave him the same answer, but he just stood there looking vague and did not seem to understand what I'd just said to him. A Canadian patient was wandering about the ward wearing only pyjama bottoms with his huge stomach bulging out over the top. He kept turning lights on and off and talking to himself, something about wanting 'two Bloody Marys and a cup of kauffee,' and occasionally went down on his knees and looked through various keyholes. He was in his fifties and had not been diagnosed yet, so no one was sure what he was suffering from.

Roger, the manic-depressive, had been asleep all day as a result of a lot of sedation early in the morning and it made a great difference to the sanity and peace of the ward. The difference was unbelievable! An elderly Ethiopian man of about 67, who was suspected of having leprosy, was brought to the ward. All his fingers were gone and only stumps remained, but he still seemed quite cheerful. The doctor gave him a general anaesthetic and as it took effect, the old Ethiopian started praying out loud, but only managed to complete a very small part of the Lord's Prayer before he was asleep. I presumed he was asleep, because his eyes remained wide open for the next six hours and it was really weird. He looked dead. The doctor checked the patient's pulse and, yes, he was still alive, but fast asleep. The doctor cut into the old boy's wrist with a scalpel, and after about half an hour he managed to remove a piece of nerve and a piece of skin tissue which were needed to test for leprosy, but the strange thing is that there was no bleeding to the area that was cut. It seemed that the blood supply was very bad to that particular part of the body. I thought that I would faint watching but managed to stay alert and on my feet, despite the unpleasant experience.

At 5 p.m., Roger came to life and his voice could be heard all over the ward. He started banging on his locked door to be let out. As I was near, I opened the door and let him out, but as soon as the door opened, he fell out like a bag of flour. 'Oh fuck it,' he said as I help him to his feet. 'Have you read my book?'

'No,' I said to him.

'Well fuck off then,' he said. 'Unless you have read my book you're not fucking fit to treat me.' Roger had apparently written a book about his illness.

Within a few minutes Roger had upset the whole ward and everyone was complaining about the noise, including staff and patients. I kept thinking about how terrible the ward was and if I was suited to this nursing lark. I was not so sure and felt like a clock that had been wound up too much. I asked Roger why he made so much noise! 'What a stupid question,' I thought to myself.

'Because they will let me out quicker that way. They will be glad to get rid of me.' It seemed a sensible enough answer at the time. A newly admitted patient asked, 'How do you blokes stand it, it's driving me fucking crazy here.'

'I don't know, it's driving me mad too,' I told him.

'At least we're all going mad together.'

'All locked up and in the same boat, nurses and patients, sometimes not knowing who is who, except for our uniforms.' I was trying in vain to empathise with him and be accepted as one of them.

The doctor decided to sedate Roger again for his own safety as well as for the peace of the ward. The amount that it took to sedate him would knock out half a dozen ordinary people or even an elephant! What a blessed relief though it was when Roger was asleep again, because awake he was noisier than all the other patients put together and it was like a miracle to feel the calmness on the ward. He was uncontrollable without heavy sedation and I wondered what it must have been like in the early days of psychiatry, before all the modern tranquillizers, for both patients and staff. One of the nurses had told me that he felt like 'chinning' Roger, and I do not think that anyone would have minded if he had done.

Throughout my stints on this ward, Roger had been assaulted on numerous occasions, but it made no difference, he just took what was

254

given to him and kept on coming back for more, noisier than ever and sometimes worse. 'Everyone's fucking mad in this fucking place, all stupid fucking nutters. It's impossible to have a normal fucking conversation with anyone in this nut house,' Roger shouted at the top of his voice at no one in particular. His constant barrage of noisy abuse was getting on my nerves and sometimes I wished that someone would belt him one, but whenever he was assaulted I felt sorry for him. It was a sad sight to see such an intelligent man behaving in such a way, all because of his manic depression.

The odd-looking Polish patient with the odd name gave me a letter with no stamp on it, with an address to somewhere in Hungary. I presumed that he had no money for a stamp and I asked the nurse what the procedure was for such letters. 'Oh leave it there,' he said, 'and I'll throw it in the dustbin later on.' I was appalled at this attitude and I never dreamed that the nurse would behave in this way. Maybe the patient was very odd but you don't just throw away a patient's letter. I had seen other nurses throw away patients' letters before, though I knew very well that doctors and the hospital authorities did not approve of such actions. I did not make a fuss of the situation as I should have done, but I did not have the confidence or the courage of my own convictions and I decided to put a stamp on the letter and post it on the way home, which I did. With Roger fast asleep, the remainder of the day was quiet.

19/5/1971. It was my day off today and it gave me a chance to unwind, which I needed badly. I was going to an open admission ward tomorrow and surely it couldn't be as bad as Ward 5. I Went to Noak House, which was the name of the admission ward and, God, what a difference! The ward was nicely decorated and clean looking and there were very few patients, and most of them were sitting on the lawn outside sunning themselves. I went in to the nurses' office to meet the staff and there were about eight nurses drinking tea and some were going off duty. Some were just coming on and they barely seemed to notice my presence. I felt like an intruder, and I suppose I was. No one introduced themselves, although one did mention his name, which I did not hear clearly. From the general conversation I gathered that the staff were complaining about having too many patients for too few beds, just like Ward 5. It seemed to be a general problem.

An elderly patient came into the office complaining that he couldn't urinate. One of the nurses made a joke about the patient's problem and told him that after a while he would get like a balloon and we could stick a pin in him and he would burst. The patient did not really appreciate the joke and walked away. One of the nurses said that all the patients were sitting out on the grass. 'The lazy bastards should be working instead of sitting on their arses,' he said, but I could not make out whether he was joking or being serious. His facial expression left me feeling that he meant what he said and I did not like his attitude.

A more relaxed attitude was obvious amongst the nursing staff on this ward, no doubt due to the less difficult patients here, and they were discussing patient aftercare and seemed very enthusiastic, although aftercare generally was practically non-existent. The ward doctor came in, but was practically ignored as hardly any of the nurses took any notice, and they continued to discuss aftercare. I was very impressed with the few doctors that I met because they seemed to be down to earth with staff and patients. I found out that one of the nurses was from my home town, Limerick, but I couldn't quite figure him out. He jumped from topic to topic and did not stay on any one subject long enough.

I walked down the ward to have a look around to see what it was like. There were a group of patients sitting in a corner, some playing cards with a nurse and another reading the paper. There were two effeminate-looking patients sitting alongside each other holding hands One was wearing cut-down jeans to look like hot pants. I walked by and pretended not to notice.

A patient dropped his cigarette end on the floor deliberately and a nurse shouted at him to pick it up, which he did immediately without complaint. I wondered would he do that to a patient in a general hospital. Somehow even nurses treated patients as second-class people, despite all our training to the contrary. We always felt that it was the ignorant public who should know better!

Even the ward cat seemed to be a bit neurotic. He tried to bite me when I stroked him, but maybe he did not like strangers. Still, even cats can't be too careful these days. The previous night on Noak House had been very quiet, but one young alcoholic patient who had only just been admitted the night before for treatment, had already discharged himself against doctors' advice; no doubt he had been dying for a drink. Alcoholics are sometimes like that. One day they are full of good intentions and the next day they are gone, the lure of a drink was just too much to bear. I was finding it difficult to continue keeping a diary and wondered if it was all a waste of time, but I found it satisfying and interesting and decided to continue to do it.

A Greek nurse asked why there were so many mental hospitals in England. 'Because there are so many foreigners, like you and me living here,' I said. A Jewish patient asked me if I wanted to buy his car for £500. I had a look just for curiosity, but the mileage did not seem very genuine, as it only had 4,000 miles on the clock in three years. The patient had admitted that he had put the clock back 10,000 miles. 'More like 30,000,' I reminded him. The Jewish patient asked a nurse to play a game of tennis with him, but the nurse told him, 'You can't play.' The patient offered to bet his car against the nurse, but the nurse just laughed it off.

The same patient with the urine problem came back again and said that he would die if he couldn't go soon. He looked very confused and dribbled saliva down his shirt. The nurse told him to drink more water, but the old patient just stood there with a vague look on his face, as if waiting for reassurance, but he did not get it and the nurse ignored him. George, the homosexual patient, came into the office and asked me what I was writing and I told him that I am just writing notes and he asked me if I would like to see an article that he had written. I followed him to his single room and I read his article but I could not understand what it was about, because it was too deep for me. I asked George why he got married when he knew that he had homosexual tendencies? I wished that I had not asked the question, because although George spent the next 30 minutes talking to me, I never got an answer to my question, though I heard practically his whole life story. He said something about the girl that he had married was related in some way to some millionaire in the soft drinks business.

'Of course,' George said, 'it opened a lot of doors for me being married to her and people clicked their heels when I told them who I was.' I didn't know whether George was telling the truth or not, but I suppose it did not matter, but at least having someone listening is what mattered to George.

Over a cup of tea there was a lot of talk about the Troubles in Northern Ireland, and one of the charge nurses, who came from one of the troubled spots sounded very bitter about the ill-treatment of the Catholics. The same charge nurse mentioned one of the patients who has just been discharged and was living on social security, which amounted to about £5 per week but had to pay for his own medication at an outside chemist which he really couldn't afford. To make matters worse his doctor on the ward had prescribed more drugs. The charge nurse said that the patient wouldn't be able to afford to buy them. The whole situation seemed too ridiculous to me. I always thought that mentally sick people did not have to pay for their medication, but I must have been wrong. I know that drug addicts get their large daily supply of drugs free of charge, so why not the mentally ill?

A new admission arrived, a Biafran who said that he was a boyfriend of

Princess Anne. He was also here a couple of months ago and he asked for special soap to wash with, but we told him that we did not have any special soap. The young student nurse told me that the Biafran came to this country as a boxer but lost all his fights. 'That's not all he lost by the looks of it,' I said. The student then phoned his wife and told her to, 'Keep it hot for me tonight,' and I don't think he meant his dinner! 'I didn't think that you were married,' the Greek nurse said. 'Perhaps he isn't phoning *his* wife,' I said jokingly.

A patient brought in a tray of coffee to the office. He had longish hair, and was wearing thick black glasses and the tightest sky-blue jeans imaginable. He looked comical because he had a 40 inch waistline and was in his forties at least. He made a joke about when he was in the navy, but I wasn't quick enough and didn't get it. 'Queer as a puddin,' said one of the Irish nurses as the patient walked out in his high-heeled boots with a seductive wiggle and his arse almost bursting out of his silk trousers. I laughed, because I thought it was very funny. The patient seemed to be flirting with the nurses just like a girl might do.

'Jasus,' I said to the Irish nurse, 'I never saw nothing like that back in Limerick.' I was beginning to feel at home on this ward, as it had been a very quiet day but I had to go to a different ward the next day and I supposed my anxieties would start all over again. I had to go to the TV room to get a nurse and two of the male patients were holding hands, but no one took any notice except me. No doubt all the other patients and staff were used to it. Although it did not bother me, it did surprise me, and it took some time getting used to, because I thought that such shows of affection between two men only happened in private, but I was learning fast.

The Jewish patient gave me a Jewish paper to read and told me, 'I'm going to a Roman Catholic mass tomorrow.'

'Christ, the Rabbi will kill you if he finds out,' I said.

'Oh fuck the Rabbi,' said the patient and then told the Greek nurse that all Greek Cypriots were cowards, but the Greek ignored the derogatory comments. The Greek nurse then told me that he was not really interested in nursing and intended to save £10,000 in the next five years and return to Cyprus and start his own business there. He seemed to be a good nurse and knew his job and was planning for the future and seemed very intelligent.

Most of the nurses that I had come in contact with lately seemed to be very dissatisfied with nursing and seemed to be doing it because they didn't have much choice, yet many seemed to enjoy what they were doing and liked the actual work, but were hindered by bad conditions and too

258

many frustrations. They all felt, as I did that those in authority were out of touch and did not seem to care anyway.

The Jewish patient told me that a patient on another ward had cut his own throat. I asked why he did it and got a blunt answer. 'Because he wanted attention.' His answer got home to me, as I felt that there was a certain amount of truth in it. Often it was the only way patients felt that they could get attention. Well behaved and quiet patients sometimes got ignored, while the noisy ones would often get an immediate response, rightly or wrongly.

23/5/1971. I went to my new ward today and it was drizzling with rain and very misty at 7 a.m. as I wandered through the orchards, trying to find the ward. It was such a big place with so many wards and I was not yet familiar with where they were. The wards looked grey and ugly, and I agreed with one nurse who told me that, 'All the wards need knocking down and rebuilding again.' Most of these large mental hospitals are over a hundred years old and probably look the same today as they did when they were built. Although the treatment of mental illness has improved and varied a lot over the years, there still seems to be as many mental patients around as ever, as the chronic overcrowding of wards proves.

As I walked up the cold and stony grey stair, I said, 'Good morning' to a patient who was busy cleaning a pile of rugs, but he never answered me. You get used to talking to people in this job and not getting a reply, but it was not nice, and is often difficult to come to terms with. I met the charge nurse who looked like Sherlock Holmes with a bent pipe in his mouth, and as we walked up the dormitory there was about 30 long-stay patients all wide awake and sitting side by side like sheep, seemingly waiting for an order or a command as to what to do next. I wondered why they were all up so early, especially on a Sunday morning, as they would probably be sitting there for the rest of the day.

Most of the long-stay wards were like this, regimented just like the army and run like a barracks with everything done at exactly the same time every day, day in, day out for years, which all contributed to the long-stay patient becoming institutionalised. They were like little children who were never allowed to grow up and never encouraged to challenge those who looked after them. The nurses were like surrogate parents, some good and some not so caring and always reprimanding and controlling. Patients' individuality was suppressed and everyone was treated the same regardless of their potential or intelligence. They were subservient and saw the charge nurse as a figure of great authority, which they were, and

259

they rarely challenged their authority. These long-stay patients had often lost their self-confidence and went with the flow, because it was easier not to rock the boat. That's the way it always was, although it was gradually, and very slowly changing. New nurses like me, were being trained in a different way to stop patients becoming institutionalised and prevent them from sitting around the ward in easy chairs, side by side, waiting to be told what to do and when to move. It had to be changed, but it would not be easy and would take many more years, at least until some of the older nurses had retired.

Of course it makes running such a long-stay ward easy if all the patients are under control and do as they are told. It also takes fewer nurses and therefore less money, but more often than not more medication is used to achieve that control. The new nurse training encouraged nurses to work with patients rather than just supervise them. It was easy, I suppose, to criticise the old style of training and the old attitudes, but in some ways, older nurses were only behaving in the way that they were trained to do, and it was hard to change, as it is for most generations and for most older people in whatever profession they are working in.

The charge nurse reprimanded a patient for still being in bed and it was still only about 7.30 a.m. 'Why are you still in bed, you lazy bastard,' he bellowed at the meek looking patient, who wiped the deep sleep from his tired eyes and shot out of bed, almost falling on the floor as he did so.

'Too much medication last night, charge nurse,' the patient apologised, as he hastily dressed.

'And don't forget to tidy your bloody locker after breakfast, it's a disgrace,' the charge nurse shouted.

'I'll do it now,' said the patient, obviously getting into a state of agitation. I did not know whether to laugh or cry, partly from embarrassment at the situation and partly because of the humiliation of the patient. I wondered if the old charge nurse was trying to impress me by displaying the authority that he had over these very gentle and ill people. Sometimes I wondered if being locked up for so long contributed to all the malaise that so many institutionalised patients displayed.

It seemed that the charge nurse was as institutionalised as the patients; he seemed to be helping to institutionalise. He later told me that he had been on this ward for the last 17 years. 'That's terrible,' I said. 'Doesn't it drive you mad?'

'Oh, you get used to it,' he nodded. 'I bet you make sure the patients get used to it too,' I thought to myself.

'Seventeen years, that's soul destroying for any man,' I said out loud, but he did not acknowledge my comment and kept puffing on his bent pipe. No doubt some of the patients had been on this same ward a least as long as the charge nurse or even longer. I felt what was needed here, if it was not too late, was some new blood with some new ideas.

These regimented type of nurses will tell you that the patients are happy, but I wonder if anyone ever asks them? Most of the patients, like the charge nurse, are not aware of the drastic changes that are taking place in the treatment of the mentally ill. The patients seem to think that they have to get permission to speak. The old charge nurse was doing his job in the only way that he knew how, and he should not have been on the same ward for such a long time. It was no good for him or for the patients, because the ward and its patients constantly needed new ideas and stimulation. I later discovered that there were 60 patients on this ward, which was about 40 too many in my opinion, with only two nurses. I was shocked and it confirmed my views that I had stepped back in time and had indeed made a retrograde step.

A patient in his forties said, 'Good morning' and continued to tell me excitedly that his parents were coming to see him today. There are so many mental patients in all these large mental hospitals who never get any visits, hence the great excitement on the patient's part.

One of the patients brought me a cup of tea while I was making some beds. 'Thank you,' I said, but the patient just walked away without saying anything. I did not drink the tea because it was too strong and hardly had any milk, but also because I know that some patients have a habit of drinking out of the bottle before using the rest of the milk to make the tea. Still, I suppose they probably picked up that bad habit from the nursing staff. I have also seen patients urinate in the teapot, and wonder if they had seen the staff do that as well! One old boy was sitting on the side of his bed and apparently heard voices coming from an open door, although there was no one there and he wanted the student nurse to close it. The student said that he would close it in a minute when he was ready, but the patient wanted it closed immediately and seemed to be getting very agitated about it. The student gave in and closed the door, and the old gentleman smiled, because he couldn't hear the voices now and seemed more relaxed. As nurses, it is impossible to understand just how upset a patient may be, because of their symptoms, and it is only with long years of training, as you get to know patients as individuals, that you get to understand and respond to an individual's needs, but I still had a long way to go, and I was trying to observe and absorb as much as I could.

At 7.30 a.m. the patients sat down at the tables for breakfast, all very quiet and orderly and I couldn't help noticing how the tables were laid. There were six slices of butter on each large plate, apparently one for each patient, and I hated that, because it reminded me of when I was in a reform school in Ireland as an 11-year-old delinquent boy. I was now 30 years old and I was being reminded of my past by these wafer-thin slices of butter being given to grown men, and that's what annoyed me. Seeing grown men being treated like kids, just like I had been nearly 20 years ago. Was it really necessary and was money that short in the health service to have to ration butter like this? I wanted to change it immediately and let the patients have a big dish full of butter so that at least they could help themselves and give them back a little bit of pride and self-esteem. After all, this was a hospital and not a prison, although you would not think so at times.

Everything on the ward seemed in the proper place and so orderly, in fact, too orderly. I helped the student nurse give out some cornflakes and we put them into separate dishes and I poured on the milk and asked the patients who wanted more. Before I had gone halfway with the cornflakes, the student told me that I was using too much milk. 'Have you ever tried eating cornflakes without milk?' I said to the student, but I put less milk in because I knew that it was not the student's fault that there wasn't enough milk to go around. There was no sugar available at all. Patients, I suppose, get used to anything and they rarely complained, which I was not used to. In Tooting Bec Drug Unit there would have been a riot if there was no sugar available. I began to realise how well off we had been at Tooting Bec, as I had rarely seen such scrimping and saving with food since I started nursing six years ago.

Of course we had been spoilt in the Drug Unit, as our budget was much better.

36. Thrown in at the Deep End

The phone rang and I was told to go to Ward 5, as the charge nurse had not turned up for work. I was glad to get off the long-stay ward, though I had hardly been on it for half an hour, but my enthusiasm soon dissipated as I approached the ward, because I could hear the noisy and unmistakeable voice of Roger, the manic-depressive, reverberating up through the corridor outside the ward, and he sounded very manic indeed.

As I stepped into the ward a young schizophrenic patient asked me if I could speak German. 'No,' I replied, 'I can't even speak English properly.'

'You speak a lot of rubbish though, don't you?' he answered back. I just nodded in agreement, because it was too early in the morning to be getting into anything too heavy and, besides, he was entitled to his opinion and who was I to argue?

Except for Roger shouting, the ward seemed fairly quiet. One newly admitted patient was sitting on a chair rocking backwards and forwards. I started talking to a patient called Mike who had Huntington's Chorea, a disease that affects the nervous system and is characterised by the patient having sudden and uncontrollable muscular movements of different parts of the body. It is also hereditary and there is no known cure. The patient gets progressively worse as years go by until in the end he is unable to guide a cup to his mouth. But one of the worst aspects is that in the early stages the patient is aware of the consequences and what the final result will be. Mike was only 35 and had been a successful businessman for about the last four years, but had to give it up because he could not cope any more. He was so bad now that he could not go out of the ward on his own and neither could he climb the stairs. He kept falling off chairs and hurting himself and there was nothing he could do about it because he could not control his movements. There was no treatment available to help him. He described his disease as 'A living death'.

He also told me that he had attempted suicide twice because of the natural depression that was part of the disease, and that he was not scared of death, but only of decay, and here he was decaying before his very eyes.

Mike could talk quite clearly at the time but later on, as the disease progressed, he would be only able to babble like a baby and not be able to communicate verbally any more with his family and friends. God, it was sad and cruel and I felt so helpless. I did not know what to say to give him hope or to cheer him up. He seemed reasonably cheerful, more cheerful than I was despite his terrible affliction. He was a doomed man, and he knew it. 'At least when I get really bad I won't be aware of it,' Mike said. Inwardly I felt like crying because he was such a nice ordinary man.

One other young patient was sitting on a chair in the corner rocking backwards and forwards, laughing and talking to himself, while another newly admitted patient was walking up and down wearing only a dressing-gown, with his head bowed low, and he did not speak. In fact he had not spoken since he was brought here by the police a couple of days ago. He had been found wandering in the streets. Someone said that maybe he was deaf. He was only 20 and looked like a refugee from one of the horror camps from the last war and was emaciated with a terrified look on his face. He had not eaten since his admission and he was obviously very sick and disturbed.

Roger walked beside the new mute admission and shouted in his ear as only Roger could, asking him his name, but the young man just carried on walking, as if he never heard anything. Roger asked me my name and I told him, but in the next couple of minutes he asked me the same thing twice more. He then told me that when he is told something three times he never forgets it! I admired his logic but I began to feel like a parrot having to repeat my name.

One of the top nurse managers paid a fleeting visit, but as I had never seen him before and did not know who he was, I did not pay much attention to him, as he never introduced himself. He wagged his finger at me, and beckoned to me as if to 'Come along'. I hated people who call me with a gesture rather than speaking to me, as I felt it was belittling me, and it got up my nose. I felt that it was rude and bad mannered and it was something that I personally would not do. He then reprimanded me for allowing too many nurses in the office reading newspapers when there was so much work to be done. I reminded him that I had hardly been on the ward for an hour and had barely orientated myself and I did not know the routine and did not think it was a good idea to start throwing my weight about just yet. I was not diplomatic and often spoke my mind rather than pandering, especially to figures of authority.

He was not really listening to me and seemed too full of his own importance and had an arrogant air about him, which irritated me instantly. 'Another fucking army corporal,' I thought to myself, the place seemed full of them and it was getting on my tits. The corporal then complained that Roger was not wearing a shirt under his jacket, but again I was insubordinate and told him that Roger did not want to wear a shirt.

This little shit of a jumped-up corporal nursing officer seemed only to visit a ward to make complaints and was well known for it. He was apparently not liked very much. It did not help staff morale or my morale to have one of your seniors just going around making criticisms, without ever saying something positive, and he was certainly rubbing me up the wrong way. I was not supposed to take charge of any wards for a few more days and I was meant to be on an induction period and not just to be thrown in at the deep end of a disturbed ward like this. Any bit of confidence that I had was slowly ebbing away and I just felt like pissing off home and telling this little dictator to go and fuck himself, but I refrained.

The senior nursing officer then told me to put some socks and slippers on a patient who was walking up and down the ward. I agreed with him on the shoeless and sockless patient, but I later discovered why. There were no socks or slippers available on the ward. I felt very pissed off at being blamed for the lack of resources on the ward, as I had only been here for a short while and was not sure what I should or should not be doing. 'He's a right bastard, and he is always complaining every time that he visits the ward,' said one of the nurses. I agreed with his observations, but was not impressed with the nursing officer's attitude and certainly did not take him too seriously. The staff nurse from Mauritius told me that once that particular nurse got his knife into you, it was your lot and you might as well leave. I knew how he felt and I really felt like telling the miserable nursing officer to 'get fucked', and maybe I would later on. It was very tempting! A lot of the senior nurses who visited the wards were always trying to tell you how to run the ward, but rarely wanted to know if you had a problem or how they could help you. In my fairly inexperienced way, I felt that they were acting like managers, as they always told you things and never listened to your views. They had forgotten their roots on the ward and were becoming dictatorial and were just interested in delegating and it annoyed me intensely. Most of the ward nurses complained about the nursing officers and saw them as being petty-minded and were always trying to catch you doing something that you should not be doing. Maybe that's how they got promotion. 'Little tin gods', is what one nurse called them, a very apt title and I agreed.

There was a phone call from an angry relative complaining about her brother who was a patient on the ward. Apparently he was at home bothering her and 'Running amok', as she said. I told her that her brother was informal and that there was little we could do and to call the police if she was worried about him. She banged the phone down abruptly!

Roger was on the phone and I could hear him using my name to try and get a free phone call. Now I understood why he asked me to repeat my name a few times! I didn't mind and it did not bother me. Henry the Jamaican nurse expressed his dissatisfaction with nursing and said that no one seemed happy with the present conditions and most felt that they would get out of it sooner or later. I was beginning to feel the same way because I am was very fed up and frustrated. It had been a very quiet day so far and I felt that maybe nursing was not the right job for me after all, but I didn't know whether it was because of the new job or what.

My dissatisfaction and frustration might pass and I thought that I might try and write a best seller as it seemed my only way out of nursing, but I was full of self doubt and felt that maybe I was just wasting my time, that maybe what I was writing was just rubbish, but I kept trying to reassure myself that it was going to be a success. It had to be as I felt that there was so much that needed saying about the conditions and life inside mental hospitals for psychiatric patients.

An Irish patient came back from mass, and one of the nurses said, 'I saw Paddy trying to screw one of the female patients in the long grass yesterday.'

'At least he was in a state of grace and maybe he had been praying for a woman to screw, and I hope that his prayers were answered!' I commented. Another nursing officer arrived on the ward complaining about Roger making phone calls to No. 10 Downing Street, and that I should stop him doing it. I did not agree with the nursing officer and had an argument with him about the patient's rights and told him that I did not think that I had the right to stop someone like Roger phoning anyone he wanted to phone. He disagreed strongly with my point of view, which was nothing new for me. It does them good to have someone disagree with them now and again. It's amazing that I was employed to run the ward and within a couple of hours I had two bombastic bastards telling me what to do! It was all beginning to get on my tits and I really wanted to fuck off from this God-forsaken place because they were beginning to affect my morale and make me lose interest completely. What a fucking welcoming committee! I bet they were sorry that they had given me the job, and I was sorry for taking it. Oh, God, give me strength!

A young patient asked me to open the bathroom to have a bath, which I did. I saw him about 30 minutes later and I asked him if he had had his bath and he said, 'No.'

'Why?' I asked him in surprise.

'I was only messing you about,' he said and walked away. The same patient had asked to see one of the doctors one day and the doctor asked him, 'What can I do for you?'

'Any chance of fixing me up with a good blonde?' the patient asked the doctor. The doctor was annoyed and told the patient to 'Piss off, unless you really want something.' The patient laughed and thought it was very funny and walked away laughing out loud. Maybe it broke the monotony of being locked up in this shit hole. The doctor obviously did not have a sense of humour and I thought that his response was over the top, but maybe even the doctor was having his own problems.

Right up to the time I went off duty, Roger never let up, and kept on with a barrage of noisy and abusive language at everyone who would listen. One of the nurses told me that Roger was getting a lot worse now and the drugs that he had been given throughout the day seemed to be having very little effect on him. God it must be terrible for all the other poor patients being locked in with Roger, with no quiet area to escape to. I don't know what it was like for Roger to be like that. I wished that I had asked him, but it must have been a living hell. At least I was going home to a loving peaceful family in a minute, whereas Roger would have his illness for the rest of his life, 24 hours a day with no escape, except maybe the occasional respite with the aid of drugs, and then he would be in a dazed state of mind, unable to think clearly. 'God, mental illness must be a terrible affliction to have,' I thought as I went off duty with great relief and unburdened myself to Sandra, who, as usual, was a great listener and seemed to be able to understand and comfort me whatever my moods, as well as looking after our two young children with the added anxiety of me possibly leaving my job any moment.

I knew that we would have to leave the hospital house as soon as we could, otherwise if I left my job we would have no accommodation either and it all played on my mind very heavily. I was close to buckling under. Looking at Cheryl and Kevin fast asleep with no cares in the world, and knowing that they were solely dependent on me, gave me strength as well as anxiety for their future. I have suffered from nightmares since I can remember and would continue to all my life, no doubt due, I'm sure, to my violent and unsettled home life. Sleep did not come easily that night because I seemed to spend the whole night dreaming of Ward 5 and keeping my diary. I also kept seeing different patients in my dreams and could still hear Roger's piercing voice, but Sandra's warm body eventually helped me to sleep and gave me strength to face another day in Bedlam.

24/5/1971. As soon I arrived on the ward, I heard Roger's voice, shouting as usual and asking if anyone had any hash. But no one, it seemed had any and if they had, they were not saying. Roger showed me a letter he had just received from South Africa, informing him that they could not find any trace or confirmation of the gold that he had deposited there! He had apparently told the South African banking authorities, just for the devil of it, that he had deposited some gold in one of their banks. The bank, on the other hand, were demanding £22 for phone calls that Roger had made, but Roger said that they would have a 'very long wait for their fucking money.' One of the student nurses told Roger to piss off out of the office, but Roger was oblivious to the suggestion and carried on talking non-stop, trying to solve everyone else's problems except his own as usual, and demanded that one of the confused patients be given back his clothes to put on.

Roger suggested to me that I write a book about him, but I told him that there wasn't enough paper in the world to carry out such a project and neither did I have enough years in my life, but I felt that I could easily spend all my time writing about him alone. Roger told me quite openly that he was a homosexual, but I didn't believe him as he just did not seem the type. He also told me that he was going to be the first married pope, and who was I to disagree! He was really high this morning.

Another patient was complaining about a tin of wax disappearing and kept leaving a nude photograph of a woman astride a motorbike on the table and told me that Roger was improving and that, 'He is a nice chap really'. Another young patient who had been diagnosed as a psychopath told me, 'I will go to Broadmoor if the doctor does not see me soon.' I passed the message on to the doctor who was in the office who replied bluntly, 'What do I give a fuck if he goes to Broadmoor or not?' So much for caring doctors. He saw the patient who told him that, 'A black man called my girlfriend a white pussy.' The doctor did not seem too worried about white or black pussies and barely acknowledged the patient. Maybe he had heard it all before and wished, like all of us, that he wasn't there right now. Roger, especially, had that effect on most of the professionals who came in contact with him.

In the middle of the morning someone from the office arrived in a hurry and in an excited state and suddenly there was another bed crisis. Some new patients were due in for admission and we already had too many! 'What a fucking way to run an organisation,' I thought out loud. A few hasty discharges were made but the staff nurse pointed out, 'They'll be back.' He was not happy about getting rid of sick patients to admit other sick patients. The whole system seemed crazy, although he never expressed his feelings to the guy from the office because as he said, 'What's the point? You might as well bash your head against the wall.'

The doctor asked one of the patients whom he was thinking of discharging, 'Do you want to leave or stay here for ever?' The patient did not know what to say, but perhaps he knew what was going to happen anyway. The discharging of patients before they are well enough was really crazy and it seemed to be a lot of extra work for nothing. Maybe it helped to make the discharge figures look good, but most of the patients seemed to be readmitted again within a short period anyway, so what was the point of it all? The hospital was obliged to accept patients for admission, even though it meant discharging someone who was not ready. It was not a planned discharge and very little discussion went into what was best for the patient. As nurses we all felt that it was wrong, but there seemed to be no other way around it, unless some more mental hospitals were built, because beds were needed now and not in 1980, when it might be too late for these patients.

The Canadian patient was looking into the TV set, which was switched off and talking to it. 'Are you there, Frank?' he said quite matter of fact. He seemed very confused, because he said that someone had hypnotised him. I found it very hard not to burst out laughing at the situation, which might be sad, but it was also very funny. No one else seemed to take any notice of what was happening. Maybe I'd get used to it, but I hoped not. It would be terrible to lose my sense of humour in such a bleak and depressing place, surrounded by so much human misery and mental anguish. The charge nurse and the other nurses on duty seemed to cope very well.

An Irishman who hardly ever spoke to anyone, except to himself, sat in a chair in the corner reading prayers from a book out loud, but no one seemed to pay any attention and he did not seem to be bothering anyone, but suddenly there was a loud crash! Mike, the patient with Huntington's Chorea fell backwards quite heavily, by the sound of the bang. Some of us rushed to his aid to assist him. Mike was rubbing the back of his head and his leg and did not seem to have hurt himself too much. I felt very sorry for him as he did this type of thing every day because he was unable to control his movements. The Jewish patient reprimanded Mike for sitting on one of the hard chairs and told him that he should only sit in a low easy armchair, then he wouldn't hurt himself if he fell off. It was nice to see another patient showing such concern and I found it quite moving. Mike seemed to accept falling over without any great fuss or complaint and I admired his attitude. He seemed to accept his condition, at least outwardly, and rarely complained.

Roger was on the phone again. This time he was phoning the BBC, complaining about the bad conditions of the nurses, but the BBC was not too happy about Roger phoning them and so they complained to the hospital authorities, who in turn complained to us, who in turn complained to Roger, who treated it all as a big joke. 'Oh fuck the fucking BBC and fuck the hospital management,' he shouted, which were my sentiments too! He often made me laugh, though I don't think he was aware of it. I found the situation hilarious and wished I had the balls to do what he did. Of course, when you have a mental condition you can virtually get away with murder!

Roger seemed to like upsetting people, just to see just how far he could go. I think he was like a little boy at heart, playing pranks and getting up to all sorts of mischief. Still, I suppose it broke the monotony for him and helped to ease the boredom and tension on the ward, which must have been unbearable for someone of Roger's intelligence. I found it difficult to get annoyed at Roger's antics, and in a way, I had great admiration for him and felt inferior to him, because of all his degrees and book writing. I had great respect for him, despite his obvious mental deterioration.

A sexy looking woman came to the ward to see one of the very disturbed patients. One of the nurses said that she must be very kinky. Apparently she took the patient home for weekends and everyone jumped to the same conclusion, and that is, that the patient did not seem very capable of much sexual activity, but the girl certainly did!

25/5/1971. On arrival on the ward the first thing I noticed was that Roger was as quiet as a mouse. The manic phase of his illness seemed to be over for now and he did not acknowledge me when I said good morning to him. He did not seem to be the same person, and the change in his personality was dramatic and had to be seen to be believed. Roger wandered around the ward not speaking to anyone. It was all so strange, which is how manic depression manifests itself. It must be terrible to have to live with it as a patient or a close relative.

An elderly Irish patient wandered around the ward with no trousers on. It seemed that he got drunk last night and could not remember where he left his clothes. He kept asking each nurse in turn where they were, but no one knew. He apparently slept in two different beds during his drunken state and lost control of his bladder and wet both of the beds. He must have jumped out of one bed into another spare vacant bed and apparently ran out of spare beds after that!

A West Indian patient who came in yesterday because he had cut someone with a knife was still waiting for a psychiatric report and waiting for his case to come to court. He was very smart looking and quietly spoken and it was hard to imagine that he had assaulted someone yesterday with a knife, although we did not yet know the full story. He told me that he is shy and a bad mixer and always stays on his own, and admitted that if someone looks at him the wrong way, that he feels like 'putting one on them', but does not know why. I immediately averted my gaze just in case he misinterpreted my look! I told him that I was just like that myself, a few years ago but that it did not worry me now. Leroy, I discovered, was the patient's name and he seemed to take heart in what I said. He seemed to be interacting very well with some of the other patients and appeared to be very understanding of some of their very odd behaviour. Leroy seemed to have taken to the confused Canadian patient and felt sorry for him and led him by the hand everywhere, which I found quite touching. Leroy's behaviour did not fit with someone who had knifed someone yesterday.

A young schizophrenic patient was walking up and down with his hands behind his back singing one of the Beatles' songs. 'Cliff Richard is outside the ward,' he said, obviously referring to himself. 'Well tell him to fuck off then,' came a reply from someone. It was these light-hearted moments that made the job more bearable for me and I realised that there was so much natural and unintended humour in mental hospitals that someone could easily write a comedy film on the whole situation.

I looked around the ward and thought what a terrible mixture of human behaviour and variety of mental illness there was all together. Criminals, psychopaths, drunks, drug addicts, down and outs and confused states, and I was surprised that there wasn't a lot more trouble, and wondered what would happen if all the patients decided to gang up on the staff at the same time. Forty-five patients to five staff. We really would be in trouble. It's something that most nurses don't think about and was just my insecurity and nervous state that made me think of such bizarre things.

Over a cup of coffee a nurse said that he felt he was just like a jailer, working on a locked ward, and I agreed with him. Most nurses on such wards felt like jailers, as we spent most of our time opening and locking doors. It must have been pretty frightening for newly admitted patients, most being locked up for the very first time in their lives. Most of the nurses' time seemed to be spent admitting and discharging patients and telling patients what to do and how to behave. Little, if no time, was spent sitting and talking, and more importantly, listening to patients, about their fears, anxieties and needs. Very little actual treatment seemed to be given, except giving out routine doses of pills, and I wondered if all these miracle drugs did more harm than good. They seemed to turn patients into well-behaved zombies, which is I suppose better than unmanageable zombies, or is it?

I was asked if I would like to take some of the patients to occupational therapy. I was glad to get out of the ward for a while and glad for the experience. A small group of patients were selected and escorted to another ward where the occupational therapy was in progress. I noticed that none of the patients were asked if they wished to go or not, but as the staff nurse put it, 'The doctor likes them to go.' As far as I could make out, that meant that the patients had to go, whether they liked it or not. A couple of them objected, but they were gently pushed and persuaded to the door. The whole idea of making grown men do something that they did not want to do did not make me feel very good. I wonder if other nurses felt like I did or was it my own insecurities and my childhood years of repression in care, being constantly made to do things against my will that made me so hypersensitive about how others were treated?

On arrival at the occupational therapy ward I noticed a huge sign in red letters which read, 'No Smoking'. Either everyone was blind or they just did not care, because they were all smoking like chimneys including the nurses. That's one of the observations you make in a psychiatric ward, nearly all the patients are constantly smoking and, if not, they are busy trying to get one off someone else. Maybe it helps to reduce the stress, anxiety and the boredom, and at least it's something to do with your hands and mouth!

There were about 60 patients, all wandering about like lost sheep, and it reminded me of a huge overcrowded classroom, but a little more chaotic. A load of chairs were placed in rows all around the ward, and the door was locked to prevent any of them leaving, otherwise I imagine none of them would have stayed for very long. I asked a Chinese nurse who was sitting down, smoking, and very bored looking, what it was like here. 'Bloody terrible,' he said. I had only been here a few minutes and I was already feeling like he was.

An old lady was playing the piano standing up, which reminded me of Jerry Lee Lewis, the American rock 'n' roll star, but she was not moving much and was playing, 'When Irish Eyes are Smiling'. I still managed to recognize the tune despite a lot of wrong notes, due no doubt to my good ear for music as my old school master Brother Cullen used to tell me. The only difference then was that whenever I played a wrong note I was more than likely to get a bunch of knuckles across the back of my head, which quickly helped focus my mind and stopped fantasising about John Wayne riding across the prairie at the Thomond cinema. Oh, God, what carefree days they were in Limerick when I was a boy! I didn't realise how lucky I was then. No responsibilities or worries, and if I did have any, I would always leave them outside the Thomond cinema and forget everything for a couple of hours. Now, here I was, locked in a ward in a mental hospital in England surrounded by some very disturbed and mentally ill people, and not really enjoying it, feeling somewhat out of my depth and longing to just walk away from it all.

The old lady's piano efforts were not being appreciated, because there was a terrible din going on all around me and everyone seemed to be talking out loud at the same time. Added to this was the noise made by the patients wearing heavy thick-soled hospital boots on the bare wooden floor boards. It was really chaotic and there were far too many patients here and I didn't see how it was possible to do anything constructive with so many patients, all with very different problems and needs. After spending a couple of hours, I was convinced that it was impossible. Another student nurse told me that he hated coming here.

A couple of male patients went on to a small platform and shouted, 'Silence', which was largely ignored by everyone. They then proceeded to read from the day's newspapers. Most of the captive audience seemed bored to death and were looking all around them and noisily moving about in their chairs, coughing and asking each other for cigarettes. They seemed to be doing everything except listening to the daily news being read out loud. I personally could not hear what the patients on the platform were saying and neither could I understand very well. One staff nurse described it as being, 'Chronic up here'.

A young nurse with what sounded like a BBC accent (anyone outside of Limerick sounded posh to me) took his turn at reading the newspapers. He obviously had been rehearsing or had taken some elocution lessons. I wondered why the papers were being read publicly to the patients, because I was sure that most of the patients could probably read for themselves anyway! The whole atmosphere was too regimental and I certainly was finding it very boring. There was still another one and a half hours to go and I wondered if the morning would ever pass. Most of the patients spent about five hours a day here, for five days a week and it was no wonder they did not get any better, although it did get them off the ward.

The Canadian patient whom I had brought up said he was feeling sick and wanted to return to the ward, so I helped him down the stairs. On the way down he started to cry. I asked him what was wrong. 'Just memories,' was all he said. I did not pry into his private grief, but felt some of his sadness. I returned again to the occupational therapy ward, where a patient told me that no one could understand what the paper readers were saying and that no one seemed to like it here, but just accepted the regime, because that's what it was, a regime. It's ironic that if you take the last six letters in 'regimental' it spells 'mental'.

The whole atmosphere seemed to be too strict and oppressive and to my mind, not very therapeutic or happy and relaxed as it should be when you're dealing with very ill and vulnerable people. It just did not seem right, but I was a newcomer and was just observing my new surroundings, seeing how things were being done in the progressive seventies, but I was not happy or impressed. I never saw anything like this in Tooting Bec Hospital and wondered why things were so different here, but then again my experience of different hospitals was very limited at this point in my nursing career. It all seemed so ancient and backward, and I was finding it hard to come to terms with.

A number of the patients that I spoke to told me that they liked it here only because of the free tea and biscuits. A young patient told me, 'I'll go out of this place madder than I came in.' He probably would too. Personally I did not have a lot of faith in the treatment of the mentally ill in our large and outdated mental institutions as they stood at this time. It seemed that the powers that be, including the hospital authorities and the government, had their heads buried in the sand. They either didn't want to know or maybe were just unable to do anything about the system. The government, like the public in general, had a similar attitude towards the mentally ill, that is that they preferred to just forget about them and pretend that everything was okay. I felt a great empathy for anyone coming in to a mental hospital in 1971, and not necessarily because they were mentally ill, although that was an awful thing, but because of the lousy facilities that were available to them. A lot of great work was being done in mental hospitals against great odds and constant set-backs. Almost everyone involved with the treatment of the mentally ill were frustrated at having to do things on the cheap all the time, and because of this, a lot of nurses were leaving the profession all the time. The public, in general seemed to have very little interest in mental hospitals until they had to come in to one. Perhaps it was not their fault, as they are not always aware of what was going on.

Horton, like most hospitals, had management committees who were responsible for overseeing that hospitals were run properly, and one of their functions was to visit various wards from time to time to see how things were, or looked. We would always be phoned up in advance by someone in the nursing office when the committee was due to visit, as a sort of warning, basically so that we could tidy the ward in a superficial way just to impress the committee. I hated this nonsense and did what I was told under great protest, as I was fuming inside. These faceless people did not seem to implement many changes and they were not necessarily interested in hearing patients' or nurses' views, so what was the point of it all? They usually went away feeling very smug after they had a large free meal. Most of the management committee were made up of lay professionals and often business people who had very little knowledge of mental illness, and who often came across as arrogant and pompous.

It was some of these silly bastards who had asked me stupid and irrelevant questions back in Tooting Bec Hospital when I was interviewed for a charge nurse job. 'And what do you know about running a hospital magazine, Mr. O'Donoghue, and do you think you are experienced enough?' I remember one fat arrogant bastard had asked me at one interview when I was editor of the hospital magazine. God, that question made me fucking livid! I wanted to tell him that I knew as much about running a magazine as he did about my suitability for promotion to a charge nurse, and that I was not applying to be editor of the *Sunday Times*! My only regret is that I never told him to go fuck himself. It would have been a fantastic feeling, at least for me, although I did write to him to express my dissatisfaction with his interviewing technique. I never did get a reply or promotion, but I did get some satisfaction in telling him what I thought! In later years I read that most people who interview people for jobs are not very good, so at least I was not far out in my judgement and comments.

One ward (F3) that I had worked on at Tooting Bec was nicknamed the 'Monkey House' and for a very good reason. The long-stay patients there were really bad and behaved in a very inhuman and abnormal way and were really retarded. They could not talk properly and mostly grunted. They smeared their own faeces on the wall and were often seen to put their soiled hands in their mouths and urinated everywhere and anywhere. They would eat eggs with the shells still on if you did not watch them and would just guzzle their food and drink down like animals. It was a very sad sight to see, as they must have been normal human beings at some point. They were almost left there in a locked ward with little or no effort made to stimulate them, and indeed it may have been too late for some anyway. No one liked working there as it could be very depressing and soul destroying, as often you did not know what to do, but it did not worry me too much, as I got used to it during my three month stint as a student nurse. What did bother me was the constant filthy state of the ward. It had not been decorated for what looked like 50 years! The walls of the ward were decorated from top to bottom on all sides with all the same white tiles, just like the ones that you see in most public toilets. It may have been used as a TB ward at one time and it was obvious that the unfortunate patients who were kept there were low on the hospital priority list. According to what I heard from most of the other nurses, the hospital management committee never visited the Monkey House. I suppose it was too distressing even for committee members and they probably did not want to get shit on their shoes either! Maybe if they had visited they would have been so shocked that they would have felt compelled to take some action.

Back to the occupational ward. I heard someone shout, 'Tea up'. I had never before seen 60 patients trying to get through a normal door before, all at the same time, until now! It was like a stampede, just for a cup of tea and a biscuit! I would never have believed it if I had not seen it. All grown men. Even when I was at Glin I never did see such a panic and determination to get a free drink. What made it more chaotic was that some patients tried to get more than one cup of tea and an extra biscuit. I overheard one girl complain about the two cups of tea, because both of them had sugar in them.

'You're lucky,' I said, 'Most of the tea you get here is without sugar.' It has never ceased to amaze me the great significance a simple thing like a cup of tea has for psychiatric patients within a psychiatric hospital. I asked her what she thought about the place. 'It's cold and dark,' was all she said. She looked depressed and lost in the crowd. It seemed that some of the most difficult patients from different wards were sent here for rehabilitation. There were too many patients, with some very difficult ones mixed up with some of the less acute.

An Irishman had overheard me asking the patient whether they liked it here or not and said to me. 'I like it here nurse.' Surprised at his comments, I asked him why he liked it here. With both his hands stuck deep in his baggy trouser pocket, and a twinkle in his eye, he told me, ' Because of the food, of course!' 'Ah, a man after my own heart,' I thought.

At 11 a.m. we escorted our group of patients to a large hall for some PT. Although I was officially in charge, no one told me what to do and I did not know what was expected of me. There were about six of us, including the twinkled-eyed Irishman, all playing badminton in a disorganised way

276

and just acting the fool and having fun. I certainly enjoyed it and I was amazed at the Irishman's energy. I now understood why he liked his food! Michael, I found out, was the Irishman's name, and he decided to have a go at the piano, because that's the only way to describe his efforts! At the same time Michael broke into song. 'Me name is McNamara, I'm the leader of the band.' As he sang he made a noise on the piano and just banged the keys for all his worth, playing lots of different notes at the same time. He was no concert pianist, but who the hell cared or who even noticed, because he was certainly entertaining the crowd of patients. Michael, like most Irishmen of the period, was not a great or indeed a natural mover, at least not on the dance floor, so his dancing efforts to his music, were to say the least, a little uncoordinated, as his legs seemed to have a life of their own. Wearing heavy boots only added to his comedy dancing, as he was having great difficulty lifting his feet up and down, and it all added to his comic appearance. But I admired his bravado.

Dave, the young West Indian patient, was laughing his head off at Michael's musical interlude, and so was I. We both obviously appreciated Michael's sense of humour. It's nice to see mentally ill people behaving in a normal way and it's the side that the public does not usually see. As soon as we go back to the ward, Dave, the West Indian, led the confused patient around the ward by the hand and it seemed hard to think that this was the same person who has been behaving in such an aggressive way. The more I saw of Dave the more impressed I was with him. He told me that he wanted to be cured while he was here. I told Dave that if he could go one day without losing his temper on the ward, then it meant that he was improving. He admitted that he wanted to go to another ward because he was afraid that he might hit someone and get himself into more trouble, because he found the atmosphere here very disturbing, but at least the doctor had promised to move him to an open ward as soon as possible. I wondered to myself if Dave's condition was not aggravated by the use of illicit drugs, although I did not know enough about him to make such a judgement, but it was just a feeling, as he seemed quite placid and normal at the time.

The Canadian had lost his jacket, so I looked around to try and find it. I looked in one of the single rooms just in case it was left in there, but as I opened the door I saw a newly admitted patient lying on the bed. I had already been told that he was a readmission and had been here many times before and had a bad record of violent behaviour on the ward towards staff and other patients. He looked up at me and said, 'What do you fucking want?' He looked as wild as any patient that I had ever seen.

'I'm looking for a coat,' I said nervously, as I backed out, just in case he did not like my Limerick accent. He never said any more and just stared at me in a menacing way and carried on smoking. He looked the type that would as soon slit my throat as say hello. I'm sure that he would be trouble sooner or later, though I hoped I'd not be around at the time. He was a schizophrenic with psychopathic tendencies, quite a dangerous combination.

A young patient who had been diagnosed as an aggressive psychopath and who had already assaulted Roger the manic-depressive and many other patients on the ward came up to talk to me, which was a surprise, because although I had been on the ward for almost a week now, he had never spoken to me yet. He started to pour out his troubles about his wife and two kids and said that he had not seen his kids for ten months now. He told me that his wife did not want to know him because of his violence, though he said that he could not help it. The guy's name was Joe. He told me that even when he was in a pub and he saw someone looking in his direction, he automatically thought they were talking about him and so ' I want to punch them', which he had often done. Naturally, his antisocial behaviour had got him into trouble with the law. It must have taken him a great effort to open up to me, a stranger, and admit his weaknesses and I felt flattered. I told Joe that if he did not learn to control his temper, he might finish up in a much worse place than this mental hospital.

Despite his aggressive behaviour and reputation, Joe talked like any other father about his children and he seemed very anxious to continue to talk to me, so I listened, which made me feel good. It was nice to feel that someone like Joe wanted to talk to me. I felt honoured in a vain sort of way. As nurses we often forget what a powerful position we are in and how much patients rely on us and how they often place us, unjustifiably on a pedestal. Just giving our time to stop what we are doing to listen to patients' worries and fears is probably our greatest asset, and it took me years before I realised it.

An elderly Scotsman who worked in the kitchen, doing odd jobs, started talking to me. He asked me how long he had been in the hospital and what he was suffering from, as he couldn't remember why or when he came in here. He told me that his happiest years were when he was working for the Queen, before she was Queen, and that he also spent seven years working for the Duke of Windsor. He admitted that he wept when the Duke left. He asked me about my private life and told me that he adored kids. He struck me as being an old queen, although he looked like a gentleman. 'I love sex,' he said, 'It keeps me looking young.' He didn't believe me when I told him that I was 30 years of age, and said that I looked a lot younger than my age. 'Maybe that sex recipe does really work then!' I joked.

26/5/1971. Another day back in the closed ward again and a newly admitted patient asked me could he go out of the ward for a while and addressed me as 'sir'. I don't like being called sir, by anyone, as it tends to make me feel important and it also reminds me of my time in care in Glin where our teachers, the Christian Brothers, demanded that we address them as 'sir', and I never understood why. Maybe they thought that they were getting respect by being called 'sir'. For me, it never felt like I was showing respect, but more like fear, because I knew what the consequences would be if I did not comply. It's quite likely that the patient who addressed me as 'sir', probably spent a long time in prison, because they say that old habits die hard.

A young Irish patient left for Ireland. The charge nurse told me that he gets deported every other week, but comes back again the following day. I asked the charge nurse what was wrong with the Irishman. 'Oh he's just a layabout,' was the reply. Norman, the young schizophrenic came into the office and declared, 'My daddy is rich. He owns a supermarket.'

'So why do you keep looking for cigarettes?' I asked him, sarcastically.

'Because the bastard won't give me nothing,' Norman said, waving his hands as if in despair. I never found out if what he said was true or not.

There was haddock for breakfast this morning and it smelt vile and obviously had been dead for some time so one of the patients remarked, when he was offered some of this nutritious food, 'I don't want this shit.' He obviously knew his own mind and there was no doubting his sincerity. I wondered if my Irish friend Michael would refuse to eat the haddock, but if he was anything like me, he would never refuse food, even if it was foul-smelling haddock!

I told the charge nurse that one of the patients wanted to see the doctor. 'Oh fuck him, he's as mad as a hatter,' was the nurse's reply. Maybe he was as mad as a hatter but he should still be allowed to see the doctor, after all, he was here because he had problems. This was an attitude that I witnessed often during my early years of nursing. It was a bit like a doctor's secretary denying patients the opportunity of seeing the doctor, without first informing the doctor. I don't know if the patient did get to see the doctor, but no doubt he would have eventually.

A big, fat, simple looking patient came in. He kept sleeping in other patients' beds during the day and was sitting at the table shoving spoonfuls of marmalade into his mouth, which he seemed to do every morning. Perhaps he did not like the haddock either! I guessed that maybe he was hungry, so I gave him some more bread, which he ate heartily. He looked just like Billy Bunter of comic fame.

The Canadian came and asked me about the other patients. 'Are they dangerous?'

'Yes, some of them are,' I said.

'Why are we all kept together then?' he queried. 'They'll kill me, can you handle them?' he said anxiously. He sounded genuinely scared and he had reason to be, as I was myself from time to time. I reassured him and told him that we could handle most situations on the ward and that we would make sure that no one bothered or harmed him. I think that he believed me, but I know I wouldn't have!

I went to the occupational therapy again today, but without any real enthusiasm, because I just found it very boring and I imagined so did many of the patients. They do not seem to be allowed very much freedom of expression and everything seems to be too controlled. The foreign charge nurse, who had been high up in some army or other, told me that he hoped to re-socialise the patients that came here.

'Some hope,' I thought. What he appeared to be trying to do was to indoctrinate them, and his army training and discipline showed. I did not agree with his forceful attitude as I felt it was not the way to treat sick and vulnerable people, but then I was a newcomer and full of new ideas from my student nurse days, and was optimistic that I could improve patients' lives.

As the charge nurse started to read out loud from the newspaper, sitting up on the small stage, shuffling feet could be heard amongst the group, and then Norman, the young patient, started to sing, 'Yesterday', at the top of his voice. He never did get any further with the next line, 'All my troubles seemed so far away', because his troubles were nearer than he thought. He was disrupting and annoying the charge nurse who was reading the paper out loud and who was in total control up to that point with a captive audience. 'Take him back to the ward,' the charge nurse bellowed. Norman looked very pleased at this order and continued singing all the way out of the door. Maybe if I started singing he might have told me to leave, which would have been a very welcome change. The charge nurse seemed to lack any sort of tolerance, and maybe he had been doing this particular job for too long, or maybe it was just his army training, and he was not used to being challenged. It struck me as odd that so little tolerance was shown toward Norman's high spirits. Surely, if the patients were all well behaved, they would not need to come to occupational therapy? But then what did I know?

A student nurse from Trinidad told me that if you're a Roman Catholic in this hospital you'll get on okay. It seemed that those in the top managerial positions were mostly Roman Catholics, and so they didn't want their nursing staff behaving in an immoral way in their private lives. He told me of a nurse who was pressurised to leave because he was fooling around with another woman who was married. Even in the seventies I thought this attitude was outdated and that what people did in their private lives was their own affair.

One young female patient told me that she had got the religious bug and had collapsed at the underground tube station and was brought here and that the police had taken £6 from her handbag while she was unconscious. Whether the allegation was true or not I did not know. I later discovered that she dabbled with illegal drugs and was an art student. I asked her if she would do a portrait of me and she agreed. She told me that I was difficult to do. I said maybe it was because of my hidden beauty, which seemed to remain hidden! I enjoyed posing for her, for how else could I get a pretty girl to look at me for such a long time! She finished the portrait in about half an hour and it was as like me as it could have been. A group of patients were sitting around the table doing simple drawings. One elderly gentleman, who seemed to be concentrating like mad was drawing a picture of a bird, while another girl was drawing a house. Another old man was drawing a picture of a toilet! The Canadian patient asked what would be done with his painting when he had finished it? 'It will be hung up if it's good,' the female art therapist told him.

'And if it's no good they hang you up instead,' I said.

A black male patient offered to marry June, the female portrait drawer, but he was turned down politely. 'No thanks,' she said, 'you're too kinky.'

The patients seemed to be enjoying just drawing and doing their own thing and not being under staff control. A young girl started singing out loud, 'If I were a blackbird I'd whistle and sing.' She did not sing like a blackbird but she was happy. The male art therapist chatted up June and, judging by his body language, he seemed to have more than a therapeutic interest in her, if my observations were right. June wrote her address on a piece of paper and gave it to the therapist, which he slipped carefully into his pocket.

'He'll be okay tonight,' I thought to myself. Life goes on even in a mental hospital and why shouldn't it?

Back on the locked ward a young patient still refused to eat his dinner. A young student nurse from Kenya encouraged the patient to eat. 'Please, have a glass of milk,' but the patient still refused. He was very ill. At the end of the dining-room the oversized Billy Bunter was last to leave the table and continued to gorge himself on the remains of the other patients' left-overs. He seemed to do nothing else but eat, sleep and borrow cigarettes whenever he could and seemed to have the mentality of a child.

27/5/1971. Today was my day off and I felt as though I needed it. Having a day off in this job felt like a week's holiday, but the trouble was that in the evening I became depressed and felt fed up at the thought of going back to work in the morning, and I hated myself for having left Tooting Bec Drug Unit, where going to work every day was a pleasure and where I felt secure and part of a great and friendly team. I tried to hide my worst fears from Sandra, but she knew I was not happy because she knew me too well and no doubt had her own anxieties and fears for our future. I was the only bread-winner, and with two very young children to support, I found the burden hard to bear and wanted to run away, but knew I could never do that because my family was everything to me and I would rather die than desert them. It was at times like this that having my own family gave me strength and hope and someone to care and to work for. Going for a ten mile run most evenings was great for relieving stress.

28/5/1971. I was allocated to an open long-stay ward today and I was in charge. There were two black nurses, one whom I had seen before and I said, 'Good morning,' but he never answered me and I wondered if he did not hear me, though I think he did and it hurt my feelings when someone did not acknowledge my courtesy and good manners. It was understandable from someone who was mentally ill, but I found it hard to tolerate in a colleague. Good manners cost very little and even when I was young and at Glin I was taught good manners and always tried to use them. The black nurse who ignored me did not seem to take too kindly to me, at least that was the impression I got, or maybe I was just being too sensitive. I asked the other student if his friend was always in this mood, but he just laughed and didn't really comment, but even that response told me what I wanted to know. The unfriendly nurse seemed very arrogant and walked about the ward as if he owned the place and shouted at the patients to get dressed, but they did not seem to respond to him. He had the air of a bully about him, like some sort of sergeant major and I did not like his attitude.

The younger student began to shave three patients who were normally shaved every morning by the staff, presumably because they were unable to shave themselves, so I offered to give the student a hand and gave one of the patients a shaving brush to soap his face, which he did perfectly. I then gave him the razor and showed him how to use it, just in case he was not sure. This particular patient had been shaved by the nursing staff for God knows how long and now he was shaving himself perfectly okay. It only took him about five minutes from start to finish and I wondered why he was being shaved. Perhaps he did not shave himself fast enough for those in charge of the ward and it all seemed so ridiculous and unnecessary. No wonder patients became institutionalised and dependent on the system. Too many nurses, it seemed, wanted to turn patients into obedient cabbages and keep them under control. I was taught as a student nurse that we must encourage patients to do as much as they could for themselves as soon as possible, to prevent over dependence on the staff and prevent them falling into the sick role. I was not a very experienced nurse but I could see that treating grown men like children was not right and I was not going to do it myself. It was degrading and humiliating.

There was one female nurse working on the ward 'as an experiment', she said. She was in her fifties and had been on the ward for the last two years and said that she preferred it here rather than working with all females. She pointed out one breakfast table where all the patients were on diets to try and lose weight. It seemed drastic to me to reduce patients' food against their will, and besides, as she later told me, 'They only go out later and buy sweets and chocolates.' It all seemed ridiculous to me, as I knew that I would not want to be forced to diet against my will. 'They need a bit of discipline here,' she continued.

'Oh yeah,' I said sarcastically, though she did not notice my remarks because she kept on talking, which she seemed to like doing.

One elderly patient walked by with the aid of two walking sticks and asked the student to lock the door because he heard voices coming from behind it. Apparently he was like this every morning and the student usually obliged by closing the door. I later went to see which door had been locked and found a piece of toilet paper stuffed in the keyhole, to keep out the voices no doubt. I took out the toilet paper and unlocked the door because it was not supposed to be locked, as it was a fire door. I stuffed the toilet paper back in the keyhole and hoped that the elderly patient did not notice that the door was unlocked because I did not want to upset him too much.

The big black student nurse shouted, 'Tables'.

'Just like the bloody army,' I thought.

The younger student asked the older arrogant student a question, but was ignored. 'Ignorant bastard,' I thought. The younger student seemed a bit frightened of his older and bigger colleague and did not seem to like him very much. I hated anyone with a bossy attitude and it always got my back up and made me very defensive and resentful and caused me personal stress.

A fat patient whose food was being reduced asked me for a slice of bread, so I gave it to him and nearly caused a riot! The female nurse shouted, 'He is supposed to be on a slimming diet.'

'So what,' I said, 'he is still hungry, I'll answer to the doctor if he complains.' She did not seem very happy with what I said, but never said anything to me, though I wish she had, because then I could have explained my actions to her. I did see her talking to the student, but as I approached she stopped talking. I felt that I was probably upsetting the status quo, and interfering and questioning what was going on and I had been on the ward for less than an hour. It was not a good way to make friends and influence people, but I felt I was right and knew that people should be treated like human beings and not like psychiatric patients, but I already was beginning to feel like an outsider and felt that my forthright attitude was beginning to annoy people and would in time cause me a lot of personal stress. But I felt a compunction to say what I thought and I had a strong conviction that I was right. Nothing I saw there ever changed my mind.

A Polish patient in his fifties complained that another patient had knocked his front teeth out last week and said that he did not complain before, because he did not know any of the nurses. He put his hand to his mouth and showed me his remaining loose teeth. I told him that I would make a dentist appointment for him, but I never did, as I was moved to a new ward the following day and forgot all about the patient's loose teeth.

An aeroplane passed overhead as the same Polish patient was talking to me. He pointed up to the sky and expressed his fear of planes. He started shaking with fear all the time he was talking and looked nervous and frightened. He looked like a man who had experienced some horror in some prisoner of war camp during the war. The young student nurse took the Polish patient by the hand to a nearby chair and reassured him, telling him that he did not have to worry and that 'everything would be all right.' Reassuring patients was something that as a nurse we were always told to try and do, and maybe it helped at times, but it may well have been false assurance as it was sometimes difficult to know how much good it did; but if done in a genuine way, it might at least give some temporary relief to the insecure patient just to know that at least someone was taking an interest in them.

I later learned that the Polish patient had been in the Second World War and that a great number of Polish patients had come to Britain after the war and after the Polish uprising of 1956 against the Russian invasion. As a result many of them, not surprisingly, had finished up in many of the mental hospitals. Some could not speak English very well, and being put in an English mental hospital with mental patients and staff who mostly only spoke English must have been very traumatic for them. I also learned much later on that many of these Polish patients did not even suffer from mental illness, as many were not put on the usual medication, and a lot of them were misplaced and sent to the various groups of mental hospitals in the Epsom area from London. When I came to Horton Hospital in 1971, there were a cluster of about five mental hospitals all within a couple of mile radius of each other, and each probably had over one thousand patients, all, of course sent from different parts of London and surrounding areas 'to be kept out of sight and mind'.

After breakfast some patients were taken to do occupational therapy, off the ward, which was run by an Irish nurse called Jim, who seemed to be very well respected and liked by patients and staff. He only had patients in his group that other departments had failed with; in other words the hopeless and institutionalised ones. I decided to go and see for myself what Jim was like. I was introduced to Jim who was in his late fifties, and wore glasses and had a slight stoop and was suffering badly from arthritis in his fingers. Jim's fingers were bent and he seemed to have difficulty in moving them. Observing Jim, I could see why he was liked. He was very kind and had great patience and never hurried or rushed the patients, but just encouraged them with kind words. Jim told me that most of his group were long-stay patients and were unlikely ever to leave the hospital. Some were retarded and were not very intelligent, and he told me about one particular patient who had been sitting around the wards for years doing nothing, but deteriorating more and more. Jim proudly showed me the small boxes that the patient had made out of cigarette cartons, which could now be used as little play bricks for a child. Jim was very proud of the patient's improvement over a period of time.

Jim then showed me another patient who had learned to make little wooden toys, which impressed me. I suggested to Jim that the toys could be sold to the public or to the staff, and he agreed that he had already thought of that and intended to sell the toys, but he did not like selling

285

something that a patient took months to make. He said he was sentimental like that.

The patients seemed happy with Jim and no pressure whatever was put on them. Jim was not a strict man, but he referred to himself as being very liberal. His only complaint was that his particular department had not been decorated for nearly 33 years! He did not seem to be too bothered by it, because as he said, 'You can only do the best you can with what you've got,' and he was doing his best. 'I keep asking to get the place decorated, but they keep passing the buck,' said Jim in his soft, friendly accent. He spoke very highly of the hospital and would not say anything bad about it. He had been here for 20 years and was due to retire in two years' time, but would, I felt be badly missed.

As I was leaving Jim to return to my ward, a group of his patients were going off to play a round of golf in the hospital grounds, but one of the patients, who should have gone, remained behind sitting on a seat. Jim asked the patient why he had not gone, but the patient never answered and kept his head bowed down. Jim took out his tobacco tin and rolled a cigarette and then gave it to the patient. 'Off you go now,' said Jim. The patient never spoke and neither did his face show any emotion, but he stood up and followed the group of patients for his game of golf. I was a very experienced nurse but realised what something simple like a cigarette could mean to a patient. Jim obviously understood and cared about the patients in his care, and I was very impressed and moved. I was sorry to leave and had only intended to stay for ten minutes, but realised that I had been talking to Jim for nearly one and a half hours! I had observed and learned a lot and hoped that I could be a bit like Jim in 20 years' time, if I remained in nursing. Some hope of that!

Back on the ward an elderly patient showed me his single private room. It was homely looking with some family photos on his bedside locker and a few little flowers arranged nicely. 'I like a bit of privacy,' he said. ' It's too noisy in the dormitory at night and it drives me mad.' Some of the better and more settled patients were often given one of the few individual rooms on the ward, and it must have made a great difference to their well-being and peace of mind.

Another patient told me that I looked like Danny Kaye, one of my favourite Hollywood comedians, which he had already mentioned to me before. Some other patient told me that he used to be a waiter, but that he could no longer do it because of his hands. I couldn't see anything wrong with is hands.

The female nurse told me that they had a lot of mice on the ward, and she opened a cupboard door in the kitchen and the smell was terrible! She had put down some poison and presumably the mice had died under the floorboards and could not be got out. She told me that the mice were everywhere and one day a mouse had jumped out of a nurse's white coat when she had left it in the locker!

29/5/1971. I was working in an elderly man's ward today and one of the men asked me to butter his bread and when I asked him why, he said that he had a bad hand and that the regular charge nurse usually did it for him. I encouraged and showed the man how to do it himself, despite his protests about the other nurse always doing it for him. He kept saying, 'I wish the other nurse was here, he would do it for me.' He did eventually manage to butter his own bread, although he did not seem to be very pleased with his own achievements, but I was. The same patient then asked me to cut his bread up in small pieces, because he had no teeth. He told me that he did have dentures once, but nearly choked when he almost swallowed them, so his doctor would not let him have another set, just in case! I witnessed a high incidence of things being done for patients, instead of us showing them how to do it for themselves. I had learned as a student nurse that patients should always be encouraged to do things for themselves, and that it was not necessarily good or kind to always do things for patients, which I was seeing a lot of at Horton. I wondered what type of training, if any, they had been given, but maybe it was just some individual nurses who could not be bothered to show patients how to do things for themselves. Maybe everyone was institutionalised, both nurses and inmates and were behaving robot-like.

As I walked down the corridor, an old lady came up and said, 'Good morning, dear,' to me. I wondered what an elderly lady was doing on a men's ward so early in the morning. She asked me my name and where I came from and she was extremely polite and spoke in a very soft and quiet voice. I later enquired from one of the student nurses what the old lady was doing here so early in the morning, but I was in for a surprise! The student told me that the dear old lady was really a dear old man! I was really shocked and surprised. 'Surely,' I thought, 'The student is joking.' But he wasn't. The old lady was on old man of 69 and was a transvestite who wore women's clothes on the ward. He seemed to be accepted as a woman by the other male patients, most of whom were either too old or too confused to care or to notice the difference anyway. It was the first time that I had ever seen such an occurrence on a male only ward and it seemed strange, but then I was in a mental hospital where all sorts of behaviour was acceptable and in some ways, normal for the environment. No two days on duty were ever the same. Working at Horton, while difficult, had given me great experience and material hopefully for a book one day! I found that no experience in life is wasted.

While at Horton I had been reported by a nurse for writing what they described as 'Inflammatory comments about the hospital', and of course I had to go and see the head nurse and explain why I was writing such 'rubbish'! I explained that I felt that conditions here were not good for patients and some staff's behaviour left a lot to be desired.

I was on my own, but there were about six nursing staff grilling me, including the charge nurse who reported my writing and keeping notes. I had never kept a secret of what I was doing and often left my notes open for others to read, which was a bad mistake. I was rightly informed that while I was writing I was not doing my job properly and there were proper channels to go through if I had any complaints. I argued my case as best I could and I left with my tail between my legs and a warning that my job was at risk if I continued to write about the hospital. I felt very low and wondered if it was all worth the effort, but nevertheless I continued making notes, but in a more secret way despite the dire warnings. I was not easily put off and, while I was shaken badly, I was not stirred up too much!

37. Leaving Horton

I eventually left Horton in 1973 with no real plans, just ideas, and worked at various odd jobs and remained very unsettled and not sure what to do any more, but I applied for a job as Head Warden at a local Cheshire Homes Psychiatric Hostel and got the job, which turned out to be another long battle with the management committee! There were four separate houses with residents (mentally ill) who were seen as fit to live in the community and who were ready to work in various jobs.

One of the problems was that we had close to 40 residents all scattered in the four different houses, though all close to each other, with only one or two staff to cope. It turned out to be a very stressful job, often because of lack of staff and, of course, the committee who were mostly lay people. I fell out with them for all sorts of reasons and problems, some of my own making, and after two years, I applied for a job back at Tooting Bec Hospital Drug Unit, but this time as a charge nurse. I was lucky to get it, partly because I knew most of the staff who were still there since I had left in 1971. It was now 1977.

While it was great being back in my once favourite job, I realised that it was no longer the same, and I had also changed a lot. The once vibrant atmosphere was no longer there and the hospital as a whole seemed to have changed or was it me? The staff seemed a little more cynical and perhaps stale, doing the same jobs, which at that point meant about nine years for those who had continued to work there. In my life I always tended to go back to what I knew, but it was not always the best thing to do. I did have some good and new experiences there, but I was not happy and so I left another secure job in 1979 after only two years without a job to go to. Sandra seemed to cope with my erratic working career and rarely complained. I seemed to have a compulsion to leave jobs and always needed new challenges, or maybe it was just me getting bored easily again. I never left jobs because I was lazy.

From 1979 to 1981 I did odd jobs again, painting, decorating, gardening, and somehow we managed to get by. Most jobs that I had left over the years filled me with regret and foreboding, but I did not seem to be able to alter my behaviour and I was never quite sure what I wanted from life. I felt that perhaps I should return to nursing again because it was what I knew and did best, and the money was always better than doing odd jobs.

38. Sudden Death and Living with Alzheimer's Disease

I often tried to imagine what it must be like to suffer from delusions and hallucinations; to live in a world that was confusing and different; often being shunned because you were different, by people who did not understand. The public have never seemed to come to terms with any form of mental disability, because it is hard to understand. It's often much easier to sympathise with someone with a physical illness. All you can do as a nurse is to try and empathise and try to be as understanding as best you can and go home at the end of a shift and hope that you gave the best care that you could. At the end of the day you could switch off and be glad that neither you nor any of your relatives suffered with any form of mental illness.

My wife Sandra's 76-year-old mother Kathleen, who had been living on her own in Bath, since her husband's sudden death in a road accident five years previously, had been coping very well and, on the face of it, did not seem too affected by his untimely death. Sandra, however, had taken it very badly. Kathleen was managing to keep her house going and was eating well and still cycling to the shops. She was an independent woman and physically very mobile. She was also a woman with whom I had difficulty getting on when I first got married to Sandra, though we had got on much better in later years. It was not necessarily her fault, but I was from a different background, being Irish, and my wife and family were English. She tended to like things her own way and we had a few clashes, but I appreciated her generosity and her hospitality whenever we visited her in Bath. In many ways she had provided a family environment for me, which I had not had since I was about eight years old. Looking back now, I realise just how much our visits to Bath meant to me and what Kathleen had meant to me and what she did for me. She provided a second home and I loved it, but our relationship was always a little strained, which I regretted.

Around 1981, Kathleen's next door neighbour had phoned Sandra to say that she was worried about Kathleen's behaviour. She had recently been leaving her garage door open, often until midnight, and when her neighbour had asked her why, she was told, 'I'm waiting for George to come home.' Leaving the garage door open for George had been going on for some time, unbeknownst to us, and it was worrying, especially as we lived well over a hundred miles away.

We then started to remember back when Kathleen used to phone us and tell us that her son had been there with his family and gone out for a walk and not returned and she had tea ready and wondered where they had gone to? We thought it strange at the time, but did not give it too much consideration, until we decided to visit Kathleen, and she told us many things that did not ring true. It seemed from what we saw and observed, along with my own experience of dementia, that something was not quite right. We arranged for her to be seen by her GP and we were not surprised when he diagnosed the early stages of Alzheimer's disease, although he would have to do more tests.

It was very sad when the diagnosis of Alzheimer's was finally confirmed beyond doubt. Alzheimer's disease is a chronic, progressive and irreversible brain disorder, which interferes with daily living skills and causes personality and behavioural changes and, of course, loss of memory. There is no known cure. I had helped to nurse such patients in many of the mental hospitals that I had worked in, and I realised that it was a cruel disease for all concerned. We suggested that she come to live with us and were surprised when she agreed.

We had been advised by many people that we were taking on a lot, as Kathleen would only get worse and might well affect our own relationship as husband and wife, but neither I nor Sandra wanted to see her mum put into a nursing home, because I had worked in various private homes and, on the whole, I was not impressed by the care that I saw. I also felt that Kathleen had been good to me and I felt that it was the least that I could do.

We were lucky in that Kathleen was not incontinent and was still fairly independent and could go for walks on her own and still had some reasonable memory, but that was to change during the next four years that she lived with us. On one occasion when she went missing I found her walking in the fast lane of a local dual carriageway, the Kingston bypass, but at least she was going with the traffic. It frightened the life out of me. She was completely unaware of the danger and it was worrying.

Despite prompting, Kathleen was unable to remember Sandra's name or what day or time it was, and when we told her, she would say, 'Are you sure?' Then she would ask, 'Is it day or night?' which started to annoy us after a while. She would spend hours counting and recounting the change in her handbag and would write fictitious accounts in her diary of where she had been during the day, such as 'Had a nice day out at the seaside.' 'This is a nice hotel and the landlady is very nice.' It was very sad, but what was even more sad was that she would often say to us, 'You don't understand how I feel.' Despite having Alzheimer's disease, Kathleen was aware that she was not right. Sandra felt it very hard, especially when we found ourselves becoming more intolerant and finding it difficult to cope with her mother's unpredictable behaviour. The situation was beginning to get us down and was also affecting our teenage children, both of whom never really got on with their grandmother. We needed a break, so we decided to try and get her into a day centre for a couple of hours twice a week, but that only seemed to confuse her even more. She also did not get on very well with the other clients in the centre, so we gave up. On returning home she would say, 'I'm going home now,' and would start packing her suitcase and say, 'I must go home and get George's dinner.'

When Sandra explained that her father was dead she would say, 'I hope not.' This comment especially hurt Sandra because she had been very fond of her dad and had been devastated by his sudden death. 'I'd better phone my mummy and daddy,' was another comment Kathleen often made. We also got her into a local nursing home for a weekend to give us a break, but the owner of the home said that she would not have her back again, because Kathleen, due to being very ambulant, was restless and would not sit still in a chair so that she could be observed like the other residents. It was sad to see a member of our own family struggling to put a simple sentence together, and to watch her personality deteriorate, knowing that there was nothing that we could do.

There were some amusing incidents, which, while not really funny made us laugh at the time. Kathleen used to come down for breakfast at around 9 a.m. and would reprimand us for not calling her for school. Another very irritating habit she had was of accusing us of stealing her handbag, which she had usually temporarily misplaced and could not remember where she had put it, which annoyed us after a while. Looking after Kathleen and trying to give her a better quality of life was to have consequences that neither I nor Sandra could have foreseen.

Sandra had been diagnosed as an asthmatic at the age of six months and it had been well under control. She always coped with it very calmly, but it started to flare up, as a result of the stress caused by looking after her mother, and it came to a head one night. Sandra awoke in the middle of the night barely able to breathe and asked me to call her GP, but I called the ambulance instead and then waited for the longest ten minutes of my life.

Before the ambulance arrived, I thought Sandra was going to die on the stairs, because her asthma inhaler was ineffective and she was struggling to breathe. I felt helpless and hopeless. The ambulance arrived and Sandra was administered oxygen and then spent the next five days in intensive care in a very bad state. I wondered if she might die, all because we had decided to look after her mother. Kathleen, of course, was unaware of the drama, as she had been asleep in bed all the while and would not have understood anyway.

The next day, after Sandra's admission to hospital, I decided, without any reservations that her mother would have to go into full-time care, and with the help of her social worker she went into a local authority home in Kingston. Sandra could have died and it was a wake-up call.

One of the observations that Sandra made was that her mother was worse than a child, meaning that a child will learn as it gets older, but her mother was incapable of learning any new skills and, in fact, was losing the ones that she had already learned.

We visited Kathleen regularly in her new home and brought her home for weekends, but even that upset her routine and caused her some confusion. She had forgotten both our names by now, but she looked well and was never incontinent and could always dress herself and remained ambulant. She also seemed just as happy there.

One Sunday when she came to us for the day, she seemed cheerful, but Sandra thought that her lips looked a bit bluer than usual and we eventually returned her to the nursing home. We had a phone call from the home around 2 a.m. that Kathleen had died, due to a heart attack at the age of 81. It was sad, but a relief in many ways, because she was not happy and it was sad to see the deterioration in her personality and the empty look in her eyes.

Sandra felt very guilty that we had not done as much as we might have. I also felt bad that I was not as tolerant as I could have been. Balanced with our guilt was the good feeling that we had at least given her four years living with her family in a normal home, which was the least that we could do, despite the almost dire consequences. Sandra would always feel guilty that she did not do as much for her mother as she could have done, but I did not agree with her. Sandra loved her mother dearly and she could not have done more or been more tolerant. It had been a very difficult and trying four years and it is always easy to have regrets afterwards. One of the positive things that had come from living with Kathleen was that we both saw a different side to her than we had previously known, and I came to like and understand her much more than I had in the previous 30 years. At least my nursing experience had come in useful and her mum's illness had brought us closer if anything.

One of Kathleen's pastimes was to sit in the sun reading the paper, and she often remarked that she was a summer bird. She died at the end of the summer and had flown, we hoped, to happier climes, maybe where the sun always shines.

39. Long Grove Hospital and Capturing History

It was 1981 and I was now 41 and still unsettled and not quite knowing what to do or which direction to go in. I did not know my own mind and I had a constant restlessness that I could not explain or understand. It was as if some unknown force was driving me on and on, to what I was not sure. Most of my former nursing colleagues seemed at least settled and content and often spent all of their working lives in the same hospital in the same position.

I obtained a staff nurse job at Long Grove Mental Hospital in Epsom, Surrey in 1981, which turned out to be a very enlightening experience in more ways than I could have imagined.

It was a good year for me in some ways as I had run in the first London Marathon and completed it in 2 hours 45 minutes 47 seconds, the fastest I had ever run for the distance and at the ripe old age of 41. I was going to be working in the Patients Social Centre, which was a kind of drop-in centre within the hospital for the chronic and very long-stay, institutionalised patients who could not be occupied in any meaningful way either within or outside the hospital. Most had been in the hospital for close to 40 years, virtually all of their adult lives. Many would have been put in there for other reasons other than mental illness.

Some of the long-stay women patients had been put there in a less enlightened period for having illegitimate children or often because they were abandoned as children or had been simple or illiterate. Many could be seen wandering around the huge 80-acre estate looking lost, with heads bent and shoulders stooped, as if trying to be insignificant and unnoticed. They usually dressed in ill-fitting and shapeless hospital clothing, another form of depersonalisation and indignity. They generally had a fag in their mouths and more often than not would be wearing bedroom slippers that were usually too big with the edges bent down, because they never put their feet into them properly. They dragged their feet and seemed bewildered, as if time had passed them by. On a very hot day you could observe patients overdressed, as if it was winter, while others would be dressed very sparsely on a freezing cold day. Behaviour they had learned as children was long forgotten due to their mental illness. They looked as if they had come straight from the Charles Dickens era and that time had stood still.

Their faces were often lined as a result of years of illness, too much medication and incarceration and depression. They generally appeared dishevelled and downtrodden. Most walked with an odd shuffling gait and rolled their fingers, as a direct result of the side-effects of the various tranquillizers that they would have been taking since the fifties. The one thing that most of them had in common was their distinctive appearance. They looked like mental patients and they stood out wherever they were amongst the normal public; often it was because of the horrible clothes that were available to them.

Some walked as couples, holding hands like couples anywhere, others on their own, alone with their thoughts. You would often see a patient just staring into space or looking up into the empty sky and gesticulating as if talking to an imaginary figure, who was very real to him or her. Hallucinating, they called it, seeing something that was only in the mind and only visible to that individual.

Mentally ill patients often did not have the same awareness or standards of those normal people around them, and would behave in a childlike way. Years of illness had robbed them of any dignity, inhibition or self-respect, and they behaved in a way within the hospital grounds that would not be acceptable in a more public place. They would go to the toilet anywhere, and seemed oblivious of other people around them. They were seemingly unaware of what was normal and acceptable. Some personal habits were bad, as indeed are those of many normal people, but in a large mental hospital everything seemed exaggerated and was accepted as normal.

Patients within Long Grove, as in any mental hospital, were not all the same, and many somehow managed to hold on to their dignity and self-respect, despite the system and being institutionalised. Some would dress very smartly. Men would often wear a tie and the women would have nice dresses and wear nice necklaces. The nursing staff tried their best to ensure that patients looked smart before they left the ward in the morning, but some patients just went their own way and did their own thing regardless. Maybe it was a way of holding on to some patient power and not being controlled in every aspect of their lives. Long Grove was not special regarding the way the mentally ill behaved. Similar kinds of behaviour could be seen in any of the large institutions at any time, which was one of the many reasons that there was a concentrated effort to close down all the old mental institutions. Most, if not all, of these institutions were around a hundred years old and the numbers of the mentally ill were declining, as community care, or care in the community, was seen as the way forward.

When I went to Long Grove Hospital in 1981, the in-patient number was down to around 500. At its peak the hospital would have been home to around 2,000 patients from all over London. There was an air of despondency amongst the patients and staff, as most knew that Long Grove was doomed and living on borrowed time. New nurses who came as student nurses left as soon as they qualified and moved to new and more dynamic areas of nursing to pursue their careers.

Patients would become attached to staff and then the staff would move on, leaving the dependent patients to get used to another group of young interns. What the patients thought of all this was difficult to know as no one really asked them or indeed cared too much about their views. In a mental hospital, as in any hospital, things were done to patients, sometimes with their consent and sometimes not.

From an outsider's point of view, working in such an environment must have seemed a depressing way to earn a living. Working amongst so much degradation of the human spirit would not seem the type of job that most ordinary people would want to do, and yet most nurses that I knew were ordinary people who came into nursing for various reasons. Some may have felt that they had a special calling, but many, like myself, came into it as a job of work and were glad of it. You either liked it or you didn't, though some people often brought their own problems and frustrations into the job, and at times took it out on the patients, by their bullying and controlling behaviour.

I remember the first day that I drove into Long Grove grounds and observed an elderly, but very sprightly and athletic looking patient, kicking a football just in front of him. Then he would get to the ball and kick it ahead of him a little further and continued doing that as I slowly approached him from behind. He was wearing a peaked cap, a nice smart-fitting suit and tie, and as I approached him, I slowed down. He stepped to the side of the small private hospital road to let me go by. He took his cap off and waved a soldierly salute to me and gave me a nice smile. He seemed a nice happy man. I later learned that he was Polish and was known as The General. Our paths would cross a lot during the next four years and he would make an enormous impression on me, more so than many of the nurses I had met over the years.

The social centre itself was away from the main hospital wards, and from the outside it looked like an old shed and not very inviting. 'What a fucking dump,' I thought and wondered if I had made another mistake coming back into the nursing profession again. 'At least I can leave next week if I don't like it,' was my next thought.

I very rarely had good impressions of any new job at the start, and I usually had negative thoughts already before I started. Sometimes they went and at other times they got the better of me. I definitely had a restlessness about me that was hard to explain and I usually reacted to my feelings and instincts, but often too quickly.

After I got to know the staff, we opened the doors at 9 a.m. each day for any of those patients who wished to come in. Some patients would already be sitting on the benches outside waiting to come in, and individuals would go to a particular area in the centre and sit on their own. One lady regularly sat on her own playing scrabble and never engaged with staff or patients. As the morning wore on the centre would fill up a little more and become more noisy.

It was interesting to observe patients sitting and conversing together. They looked to be talking about something interesting, so out of curiosity I would sit near and try and hear what was being said. After a few minutes I realised that their conversation made no sense and was pure gobble-degook, but they seemed content as if they had a language and understanding all of their own. I was surprised, although I knew it was a little rude to listen to others' private conversations, but then observation was a very important part of a psychiatric nurse's job. The psychiatrists often had to rely on what nurses told them, because we were with the patients 24 hours, whereas doctors had very limited time to spare for each patient and then it was difficult to make a judgement or a diagnosis on a sometimes brief interview. As the morning wore on, more patients would drop in for either a cup of tea, to meet their friends from other wards, or often just for somewhere different to go. We arranged games and tried to engage some of them in activities. Sometimes a patient would just leave in the middle of a game, unable to concentrate or just not in the mood.

There was a piano in the corner and one day I was surprised to see a lady in her sixties who walked with a bad limp and never spoke. She would mumble, but she was generally incoherent. I never understood anything that she said, although she would gesticulate that she wanted a cup of tea or a drink of water. She was badly dressed with ill-fitting clothes and bedroom slippers and she had badly stained fingers from the many cigarettes that she had smoked over the years. She ambled over to the piano and lifted the lid and just sat there for about five minutes, wringing her hands in an anxious manner and looking around her, as if for approval. She tinkled a few notes as if to warm up and then, to my amazement, she started playing some classical music, which knocked me sideways. I could not believe what I was hearing. If I had closed my eyes I might have guessed that I was in some concert hall listening to some famous pianist. Each time she finished a tune she left a gap and went through the same ritual of wringing her hands and looking around her. No one took any notice, it seemed, except me. Had they heard it all before and was she looking for some applause? I did not know.

She went into the next tune and played for maybe 20 minutes, stood up and calmly closed the lid. She walked awkwardly as if one leg was shorter than the other, out of the social centre, and not a word was said.

'Who was that lady?' I asked Barbara, one of my female nursing colleagues.

'Her name is Lily and she used to be a music teacher. She is a wonderful pianist when she is in the mood,' Barbara told me. It made me realise that my preconceptions of mentally ill people needed to be revised. I had seen Lily and just saw a psychiatric patient with a bad leg and never gave much consideration to what else she might be capable of doing. In future I would see her in a different light. As a psychiatric nurse I should have been more aware that many of the mentally ill patients that I had known were normal people who had just as many talents as other people, but sometimes I lost sight and just saw them as patients rather than people.

I would witness many other wonderful pianists and musicians during my time at the social centre, and sometimes it was difficult not to feel sad at the great waste of talent. Another talented patient who came to the social centre was Rupert, a wonderful portrait artist who did the most lifelike portraits of anyone, patients or staff, who would give him a few shillings or even some cigarettes in return. Sometimes, though, Rupert was so full of self-doubt and anxiety that he was unable to do any drawing and would ask me or someone else for approval or advice about whether a drawing was good or bad and was he doing the right thing. It was very sad to see such a man, barely in his thirties, who at times was unable to function. He committed suicide eventually. As a nurse you were not supposed to get emotionally involved and take things personally, but that was often easier said than done, at least for me.

Around this period I started to get a little more serious about photography and would often bring my camera with me to work. Rupert was one of the first patients that I took a photo of. I just wanted to capture him, holding one of his drawings, because I believed that he was very talented and what he did was so lifelike. He was quite happy for me to take his photo and he would often ask me if his paintings were any good or not.

301

I always told him that they were great, which I really believed. I later learned that he often sold some of his drawings, but within a few days he would try and buy them back again. I have been told by a very reliable source that Rupert had sold a drawing to Mick Jagger, and as usual, a few days later, tried to buy it back again. One art therapist told me that Rupert was amongst the best in the country. I eventually took around 400 photos while working at Long Grove Hospital. If patients objected I respected their wishes. Most seemed to enjoy the attention I gave them and, for many, it might well have been the first time that someone had taken a photo of them.

One man, Fred, who was in his seventies, told me that he had never had his photo taken before. A few days later I showed him the photo, which he just looked at blankly. 'Who's that?' he asked me.

I thought that maybe he was joking. 'Don't you recognize yourself? It's you.'

'That's not me, that's some old man with white hair and wrinkles. That can't be me, that must be someone else,' he insisted. I could not persuade him otherwise and I was shocked and surprised at his response. I had never had such an eerie encounter before and it made me feel a little sad. There I go again, getting involved and feeling too much of other people's pain.

Many of the patients who came to the centre were incredible characters and all so individual. I got to know many of them by sight, though I never even got to know many of their names or even spoke to them. Some just did not communicate or were unable to, but would at times communicate by gestures. Many were Polish. They had come to Long Grove shortly after the last war, often it seemed as refugees and finished up in Long Grove as psychiatric patients, never to return or see their own country or relatives again.

Some did speak a little English and many did not seem to suffer from any mental illness, save maybe from depression, which was understand-able being in a different country, in a mental institution away from everything that they had ever known and loved. Some attempts had been made over the years to repatriate them to Poland, but it rarely worked out, due to lack of cooperation from the Polish authorities.

What most of the Polish patients had in common was that they had always seemed very cheerful and had lovely personalities, and their attitude made an enormous impression on me. They seemed to have held on to their dignity, despite their circumstances. They formed their own social group and could be seen regularly playing card games for money or cigarettes quite intently. They had great character in their faces and I started to take photos of many of them as they played or talked together. One Polish man in particular who was called The General was a great character. He always looked immaculately dressed and always wore a nice suit, smart tie and a peaked cap. He also wore medals on his lapel of various types, some religious and many sporting medals, which he had won when the mental hospitals held their annual sports days. The General was very good at all sports, table tennis, snooker, skittles or whatever he turned his hand to, and he was just over 70 then. I gave him a few of my own sporting medals and a London Marathon medal, which he proudly wore.

The General became one of my favourite photographic subjects. He had a wonderful carved and tanned face, with a lovely friendly smile to match. He enjoyed his photo being taken. I would gesture to him that I would like to take his photo and he would stand up and say, '*Momento*'. He would take his cap off, flatten his wonderful head of fair, which he rarely showed, straighten his tie, and then stand erect with his hands by his side. I was told that he liked to be known and addressed as The General. Although his English was practically non-existent, like most of the Polish patients, I could usually understand what he meant. He could be seen regularly playing football on his own, either down in the sports field or on the hospital private road, kicking the ball ahead of him, and he would cover long distances in this way, almost daily.

What I did not realise at the time when I started taking photos was that the photos, years later, would be of some historic social interest after the hospital closed down. I was capturing a slice of history, which could not be repeated again, especially as the large mental institutions would be gone within the next ten years or so.

40. Long Grove Characters

I got to know many of the regular visitors to the social centre, although not in any great depth. Some would spend every minute of their time there meeting their friends or just getting off the ward. During our monthly Darby and Joan concert, which we put on in the centre for the patients' benefit, we often saw a different side of them.

Ron, who was our MC and Patients Activities Officer was great with the patients and was well liked by them. He would encourage them to come up to the mike and sing a little song and give them either some cigarettes or sweets, which might now seem a little patronising, but the patients looked forward to it. Remember, most of these were people who had been in Long Grove practically all of their adult lives. It was what they knew. They loved the attention that Ron gave them. He made them all feel special, which of course they were.

The Polish General would often come on and do a recitation in Polish and always took his cap off. I often wished I knew what he was saying. Our regular pianist Jack would accompany him on the piano and it sounded quite moving. The General had been in Long Grove since 1945.

Jack had been a bandleader in the forties with his own band and seemed to be able to accompany patients no matter what they sang, even when they changed key several times in the middle of a song – no mean feat even for the best musician!

Maggie was a little Scottish lady with a very sweet and beguiling manner about her that endeared me to her. She spent a lot of time in the centre and would either ask me, 'Got any fags? Give us a fag.' As I did not smoke I could not oblige her, but then she would ask, 'Ge us a cup o tea then will you?' I could hardly refuse a lady with such polite manners. I discovered that she was a very good singer as she usually did a turn at our monthly concerts. She had a nice voice and always sang in tune and often would start before the pianist was ready, so Jack spent the next few seconds trying to catch up with her. She might start with, 'My bonny lies over the ocean, my bonny lies over the sea' and without missing a beat would sing, 'I'm a Yankee Doodle Dandy, I'm a Yankee do or die'. While Jack was just getting into his rhythm, and starting to look perplexed, Maggie would sing, 'I'll be your sweetheart if you will be mine' and then, just as suddenly and in the same key, 'Yankee Doodle went to London just to ride a pony, I am a Yankee do or die'. This changing of songs part way through was very clever and whether it was intentional or not I do not know, but I never figured how she could manage it. She must have had a great ear for music, but poor old Jack did his best and generally managed to keep with her eventually, though sometimes a beat or two behind, which was more entertaining than just singing a straight song.

Big Jesse was an ex-guardsman and was really a gentle giant, but he never engaged in any meaningful conversation, although he had a passion for doing the horses and could be seen leaning on the piano with the daily newspapers trying to pick out winners.

He enjoyed doing a turn and was always as nervous as hell and held the microphone as if his life depended on it. The trouble was that Jesse wore dentures, which were a few sizes too big for him and, during his song, his teeth would work loose and come out a few inches, which did not help his diction or performance. However, he always persevered to the end and you could not help but admire his tenacity.

Old Paddy was another Irish character who would regularly come to the centre and, again, he never made much sense in what he said. He was always recognizable by the number of jackets, shirts and often scarves that he wore, all at the same time, whether it was summer or winter. He was rarely without his battered cap. He also wore two pairs of trousers with the outside one done up by a big piece of string. Generally his boots, which looked a few sizes too big, were either undone or done up with string, but he always seemed happy. He also loved to do a song, but even poor old Jack could not accompany Paddy. He had a song and a style of his own.

As he sang some obscure song, that no one had ever heard of he would suddenly stop and give a wink at the audience and say something like 'What the fuck's going on bejasus' and carry on as if nothing was amiss. Jack would raise his hands in the air in frustration as if to say, 'What's he singing?' Unfortunately Paddy never wanted to leave the stage and had to be helped off before he commenced another ditty. It was difficult not to laugh, though most of the other patients were oblivious to Paddy's musical meanderings as they either coughed or spoke to each other very loudly or tucked into their monthly meal special. Paddy could have sounded like Pavarotti, not that he did, but the other patients would not have noticed or cared; their food was more important and much more satisfying.

Johnny was another small man who liked to try a song, but it is almost beyond comprehension to describe his performance. It was not necessarily bad, but very different and seemed to grab your attention. He wore a peaked cap and had no teeth, which made his appearance that much more

306

funny to look at. Johnny spent most of the time on stage grinning and looking around and winking to no one in particular and attempting to sing. He was inaudible, but tuneful, despite Jack not being able to figure out exactly when the next note was going to come out. 'We'll meet again, da, da, da, dum, dum, sometime' as he stopped and winked and looked around. All the time he seemed to manage a great big grin as he struggled with the song. Ron, the MC, would eventually start clapping to signify the end of the song and to encourage Johnny to leave the stage, but Johnny was not finished yet or ready to leave a captive audience and would start another song.

'You are my sunshine, my only sunshine' and then he would stop dead as if looking for the next few words and notes and look all round again with his usual grin. 'You are my sunshine, dum de dum de dum dum.' By now Jack had given up and gone for a cup of tea, very unprofessional but understandable under the circumstances. It was either that or shoot himself. He was beaten and he knew it. He was a musician, not a magician.

Victor was a man in his twenties who had been very ill, mentally, but it did not stop him from trying the boards and getting up on the stage. 'What are going to sing for us then, Victor?' Ron, the MC, asked.

'Yesterday,' replied Victor as he took off his steamed-up spectacles to wipe his eyes. Ah, I thought, something modern to listen to. 'Yesterday, all my troubles seemed so far away.' It was out of tune but the good intention was there and you had to sit up and listen. 'Yesterday all my troubles seemed so far away, what's the next line?' he asked, looking towards Jack for inspiration, but Jack was not familiar with the Beatles' songs and he in turn looked around to the staff for support which was not forthcoming.

Victor then asked, 'Can I sing another one instead?'

'Carry on,' said Ron.

It was 'Bring me sunshine, in your smile, bring me laughter, all the while,' the old *Morecambe and Wise* signature tune. By now the audience, instigated by myself, started to clap with the beat and this encouraged Victor to sing even louder and even more out of tune, and with a mixture of jumbled up words the song built to a crescendo with Jack getting more into the song and pounding out the keyboards like an older-style Jerry Lee Lewis. Jack was over 70 and had difficulty moving around.

Victor's performance was the turn of the day and it helped bring at least one show to a close and was a fitting climactic finale, which left the audience wanting more. As the audience were leaving the centre, Paddy jumped on the stage again, as he had been hovering nearby, desperate to do another song, and tussled with Ron for the microphone. 'That will do for today. Paddy, we'll see you again next month.' But Paddy was not that easily put off.

'Let me sing one more fucking song, you fucker, you,' said Paddy. By now the microphone system was turned off and Paddy was eventually encouraged to leave the stage for another day and another performance.

Jean was another character who always insisted on nicking all the metal ashtrays from the social centre, but as she said, in her posh voice, when confronted to return them, 'I'm only borrowing them, my dear.' She used to carry about four large bags with her everywhere, which were always bulging with all sorts of personal possessions and items from the centre. Whenever we asked her to return the items to us she would refuse and then we would go through her bags and remove what belonged to the centre. 'Don't you dare, I will have to call the police and put my lawyer on to you. It's disgraceful how you nurses treat a lady,' she would protest. She may have been a lady but she was hard to take too seriously with her nylon stockings down around her ankles, but she did not hold a grudge and the next day she would be back again and we would have to go through the same procedure from time to time. Jean was another lady who I took many photos of. She was generally cheerful but, at times, had a look of black depression about her and would say very little.

Lily was another character who, though not saying an awful lot, would at times say a few words, but always with a fag hanging out of the side of her mouth, which gave her a comic-like expression. Like most of the patients who had very little money, Lily valued her cigarettes and kept them down her see-through nylon stockings as if it was quite normal. Whenever she lit up a new fag, she would undo her nylons and get out a packet, take out one fag and stick them back again for safety. I could not resist a photo of them, as I felt it was a unique photo opportunity.

Sammy was a little Jewish man who got by by buying and selling cigarettes. He would undo old discarded dog-ends and mix them with some new loose tobacco and sell them as new. Very ingenious! Patients got by somehow and there was always someone with some scheme to enhance their couple of pounds per week pocket money.

Patricia was in her forties. She was the social centre's and possibly the hospital's good-time girl. She was quite simple and would often ask, 'Have you got a fag, mister?' Patricia had another way of making ends meet; she would take some of the male patients around the back toilet for a good time! in exchange for a few fags. She could often be heard saying, 'Give me ten fags and you can do it.' The male patients would often beat her down to one or two fags. She was desperate for fags and maybe affection and would rarely refuse a male client. Though it was funny at times to hear the interchange between Patricia and her clients, it was also very sad to see her going out around the back of the male toilet in the pouring rain in her slippers and dishevelled appearance to lie on the wet concrete floor and ask, 'Have you got it in yet?' She was a very sad and pathetic figure and no doubt was someone's relative.

As nurses we were unable, thank goodness, to control many aspects of patients' lives, so the more vulnerable were often taken advantage of by other more sensible patients, and they used each other as people in ordinary walks of life do. In mental hospitals there was also a pecking order, which was beyond nurses' influence, unless it was very blatant, but life went on, regardless for good and for bad.

Johnny was an epileptic who, for most of the time, was quite normal in his behaviour, but was no angel when he had a seizure. One day he was sitting in a group near where I was talking with someone, and everything seemed fine, until he suddenly slumped over and his head just lay on the table. He was unconscious and luckily it was only a very mild *petit mal* seizure and he was not unconscious very deeply.

Barry who had been chatting to Johnny just before at the same table and was a good friend of his, did his best to wake him and kept shaking and calling him. I had had a previous altercation with Johnny when he had come round from such a seizure and I knew that he was often confused and had a tendency to be violent on awakening, so I just observed from a safe distance to make sure that nothing untoward happened or no harm came to Johnny.

Barry was less cautious and continued shaking Johnny. Johnny suddenly came to and shook his head and looked a little dazed and confused. 'Are you all right, Johnny?' Barry asked. With that Johnny stood up and made a grab at Barry's throat, but Barry managed to pull away.

' You fucking bastard, come here, I'm going to kill you this minute,' said Johnny, and he looked as if he meant it. He was not very big, but when a man such as Johnny was mad and confused it was best to take evasive action, which is what Barry did.

I had never seen Barry run before as he was always sleepy looking and falling asleep on benches in the social centre, so it was a great surprise to see him legging it out of the front door with his boots partly done up and sprinting down the corridor with Johnny in hot pursuit, shouting obscenities and stating what he was going to do to Barry when he caught him.

Barry's voice could be heard for a long way outside in the corridor. 'Don't kill me, Johnny, I'm your friend,' but Johnny pursued Barry with even greater vigour.

'Stop, I'm going to wring your bloody neck when I catch you!' Johnny screamed as he chased the innocent Barry. What the eventual outcome was I was not sure, but as Barry had a good start I doubt if Johnny, in his partly confused state of mind, ever did catch him and I hoped that if he did, he would have been calmer and forgotten what it was all about anyway.

As an observer, I could not stop laughing to see the whole situation unfold before my very eyes. It was like something from a Laurel and Hardy film. I only hope that Barry learned from the situation and would not be so helpful next time! I still laugh at the situation whenever I think of it.

I never ceased to be amazed at the talents that some patients displayed. Even Johnny, who could be a tough character, partly because of his epilepsy over the years, which must have contributed to some deterioration in his personalty, displayed a very tender side to his persona. He regularly sang at our monthly concerts and his favourite tune was a hymn called 'Abide With Me'. He not only sang it in tune, but was word perfect and sang with great feeling.

Fred was a 90-year-old man of great character who was wheelchair-bound and had to rely on a nurse to bring him along to the monthly concert. Ron always made a great fuss of him and always kept him last to close the show. His favourite was 'Memories', which he sang with great feeling and emotion. He knew every word and, with Jack on the piano, it made for good listening. Fred often brought a tear to my eye because it was very moving. He also had the sweetest smile despite his circumstances.

Bill was another singer who had one eye, but besides singing at our monthly concert, he also kept his good eye on the ladies and was always in the company of one. He was an old charmer and his lack of an eye did not prevent him enjoying himself. Bill's favourite song was 'Danny Boy', another tear-jerker, especially the way Bill sang it. He was usually terribly out of tune and never knew more than a few words, but his performance certainly entertained me.

As the numbers in Long Grove were declining there was a great reluctance on behalf of the hospital authorities to improve the facilities, especially in the social centre. The decor was beginning to show signs of neglect and it was looking dilapidated. There was talk of closing it down, which we argued against, and it was reprieved temporarily, but the writing

310

was on the wall and there was talk that all the large mental hospitals should be closed down. Sometimes we would arrange a snooker competition for the patients and arrange dates with patients in advance. More than once we had to cancel the games, as I or my colleagues were needed on the wards due to staff shortages or sickness. As a consequence, the social centre was often just closed down at a moment's notice without any explanation, and many of the regulars had to either remain on their wards or just wander the grounds. The centre had meant a lot to those patients who went there and decisions were made purely for financial reasons, but then that was not new. I wrote a letter to the local paper, which was published, and it annoyed the managers so much that they gave me an official warning in writing, but I did not care by then, as I had intended to leave.

It was all unsettling and gave me itchy feet to perhaps move on again or even leave nursing again. It was a long and well-established pattern of behaviour. Whenever I felt unhappy, insecure or unsettled, I ran away from the situation without giving too much thought to what I might do next. I was now 46 and still not sure of what I wanted to do with my life. The social centre was a very easy job and not taxing enough, as I was working below what I was capable of, but it had been very interesting and quite rewarding in many ways. I had made some new friends amongst both patients and staff, and I had also taken some unusual photos of the many patients and staff there, which I could always reflect on later.

Shortly before I left there was a reunion arranged by the hospital authorities to take place between a Polish lady living in Poland and her brother who had been in Long Grove since just after the last war, so I decided to be around to take some photos of the special occasion. She was very tearful during their first meeting, but her brother never spoke due to his illness, and it was difficult to know whether he recognized her as his sister or not. My photo of their reunion was in a local Epsom paper. They never met again, because he was in his eighties then.

Another reunion was arranged between a Polish lady in Poland to meet her dad who had been there since the last war. He did not recognize her as his daughter. It must have been heart-rending for the daughter. The Polish patients certainly suffered a lot, not only with their inability to speak English, but being so far away from families and friends with no means of ever returning to their homeland.

One of the saddest stories must be the Polish man who refused to leave Long Grove after all the wards were closed down for the last time around 1992, and all the patients were gone. He continued to wander the hospital grounds alone and without food or drink and nowhere to sleep for days. The hospital authorities did their best to encourage the patient to leave but still he refused. After all, Long Grove had been his home virtually all his life and he was expected to comply, with no choice in the matter. Polish people are very proud people and he was stubborn and would not leave. There was a sad and undignified ending to the situation. The authorities naturally felt that the patient was at risk to himself, so it was arranged that he would be forcibly removed to another hospital, and so it was that a large group of nurses came to escort him away. Force was not needed in the end and the man went into the bus voluntarily and eventually settled down somewhere else.

Although I had left by then, the closure of Long Grove had been a very sad and messy affair, with patients and some staff having very little say as to what was right or wrong, or indeed what was the best for the patients, who had been uprooted from the only home they had known for most of their lives. The professionals had won again and had known best, or had they?

Over the years Long Grove had many different inmates. Some short-stay and some spent their lives there. Ronnie Kray, one of the famous gangster twins had spent some time there in the late sixties due to his mental illness. His brother Reggie visited him and on one occasion they swapped places and Ron left instead of Reggie unbeknownst to the nursing staff who could not tell the difference. Ron had been on a section, which meant that he could not leave voluntarily, hence the swap. In those days, if a sectioned patient escaped and stayed away for a month, the section would be seen as null and void, and Ron stayed away for over a month, which meant he was no longer a detained patient, but I believe that he did return at some point, having won his argument that if he could stay away long enough he could not have been that ill. Many psychiatric patients challenged the authorities and won their freedom and had their sections removed. The rule of staying away a month for escaped section patients no longer applies, for safety reasons no doubt.

I later saw the Polish General in 2005 where he is now living near Bournemouth, and he seemed to have changed little during the last 20 years. He is around 97 and may well make it to 100. Though I spoke to him, I doubt if he remembered me. However, he still had one of my running medals pinned to his lapel.

I spent the next four years unsettled and working at DIY as a self-employed person, not making much money and not really happy. No matter how many times I left nursing I always yearned to go back, but I

312

desperately wanted to be my own boss and independent. Although I had loved my job as a psychiatric nurse, I also hated the politics and the wheeling and dealing, and as I saw it, the often ill-treatment of psychiatric patients. Nursing seemed to be changing too quickly and never, it seemed, for the better. Nursing staff were fed up with the constant changes and reorganisation, and it seemed they were the last people to be consulted, as managers always thought that they knew best. I was also aware that sometimes I became too emotionally involved in my job and took on too much of other people's pain and problems. I was still trying to change the world and quickly, but I was running out of time.

41. Behind Closed Doors, Again

Although I was determined never to return to nursing, I found myself being drawn back again, partly because my wife Sandra had told me it was what I was good at it. I did not totally agree, but I realised that she was right and the money from nursing was a lot better than it was doing odd jobs, so in 1990, at the age of 50, with some trepidation, I applied for a job in a small local psychiatric unit, and was given a job as a staff nurse working on a locked ward for ten male and female patients who had various and very difficult problems. I hated the idea of working behind closed doors; it reminded me too much of my childhood, and I also hated locking other people up, even if it was necessary for their safety and that of the public. Doing things to people and sometimes forcing them to have treatment they did not want, had always been difficult for me to understand and to cope with. It was a part of psychiatric nursing that was always alien to me. Even though I had worked on a closed drug dependency unit at Tooting Bec, I never felt comfortable with the situation. There was also a lot more tension and stress working behind locked doors, as patients were generally more disturbed and it could rub off on you. A locked ward was in some ways like prison, without the bars, and sometimes there was less freedom and choice for the mentally ill patients. Often they seemed to have fewer rights and facilities than a prisoner had. I identified too much with the patients I was helping to treat and it just went against the grain to work in such an environment, but I did not have very much choice, as jobs for a person of my age and unsettled record were hard to come by. So I had to swallow my pride and take what was available.

The unit was for difficult and offender patients, meaning that many behaved in a sexually inappropriate manner (just like I used to as a teenager!), and many did not respond to the regular treatments that were available. It was a very small unit and much too cramped, with two patients often having to share the same small bedroom. These patients were not always compatible due to lack of beds, although we did our best to put those patients together who were as compatible as could be under the unusual circumstances. The rooms were small and pokey, with very little room for personal possessions. Privacy was non-existent, although it was an advancement to what it was like in places like Tooting Bec, Horton

315

and Long Grove hospitals where the patients generally slept in large dormitories in groups of around 20 or more.

Although the patients were behind closed doors, so were we as nurses, the difference being we had a key to come and go, but nevertheless it made me uncomfortable and I often argued as to why the door could not be unlocked, but to no avail, despite having regular meetings to discuss the matter. One patient during my stay there said something very heart-rending.

'You only work here for the money and get six weeks' holiday a year and you can go home at the end of each shift. We're here twenty four hours a day, seven days a week for years without a break.' He was so right and I had never given it much thought before then.

The ward was very claustrophobic and the very narrow corridor made the whole place look too cramped for ten very ill patients, not counting the three or four nurses and cleaner that worked there. I was immediately filled with self-doubt and wondered why I chose to come back into nursing, and my heart sank. Could I stick it for a week at least? Only time would tell.

I was soon to learn of the type of patients that were there. At least two were manic-depressives, who could be extremely difficult and demanding, whether their moods were high or low, and would try the patience of a saint, not to mention a mere psychiatric nurse. There were a few patients in their twenties, one with severe behavioural problems who seemed to hate his mother and was angry at everyone it seemed, amongst his many other problems, and one patient who could be very sexually inappropriate. Some also had the added problem of abusing alcohol and drugs. At least one young man was suffering from Asperger's Syndrome. One was extremely paranoid and would burst into very loud bouts of verbal profanities, often non-stop throughout the day and night, which could be heard around the whole hospital. His behaviour was enough to drive the sanest of people mad.

Some of the patients were potentially dangerous, either to themselves or others, which was why most of them were detained on different sections of the Mental Health Act, which prevented them leaving, even if they wished to. The ward often took patients who were at the end of the line, and a few were there who had come from one of the larger mental hospitals, which were also closing down, so there was a very mixed bunch, too mixed and volatile for such a small ward. I hated the atmosphere and the confinement.

On my first morning there, while discussing the previous night's activities and orientating myself, I heard an almighty roar. 'Who stole my fucking shirt and my CDs. I want them back now or someone's going to die.' I nervously made for the corridor to see what the disturbance was. 'Oh, don't worry, it's only Tim, he's always making a fuss about something or other,' the young female Filipino nursing assistant reassured me. Nevertheless I went to see for myself.

'Are you all right?' I asked the patient.

'Who the fuck are you and no I'm not all right, unless you can find my stolen property,' Tim said in a loud voice. I was soon to learn that Tim made a drama out of everything and nothing in particular. Even asking for a cup of tea sounded abrasive and threatening.

'Can I have a fucking cup of tea before I die of thirst, if you fucking nurses haven't drank the whole fucking lot, you horrible bastards. None of you are any fucking good and I'm writing to the hospital management to complain if I don't get one immediately,' Tim would shout at the top of his voice. Rightly or wrongly his attitude only helped to make the nurses antagonistic and we often ignored him despite his threats. He would return to his room and bang his bedroom door, shouting words that even I had to look up in the dictionary.

There was never a dull moment I was soon to learn; some drama was always unfolding, even if it was because there weren't enough biscuits. I suppose even simple things become magnified when you are locked up for 24 hours a day with nine other disturbed people and your every move is observed and reported on, with little or no real privacy, just like being in a fish bowl. We virtually told the patients when to get up and when to go to bed, although they did not always comply. We gave them medication whether they wanted it or not and we controlled virtually every aspect of their lives.

Tim was very deluded I learned, and seemed to be tortured by voices in his head, and all the different types of medication he had been given made no difference. He was often like this for hours on end and I certainly found it unnerving and hard to take. I could not imagine what it must have been like for the patients confined with him, with no chance of escape. Nowhere in the small ward was immune to his loud and abusive tongue. No one was safe. As far as Tim was concerned, all nurses were queers, bent and corrupt and trying to kill and poison him, and there was no reassuring him otherwise. The whole medical team had been frustrated at Tim's lack of response to all types of treatment, to the time, effort and medication lavished on him, but then that was why he was on this ward.

Often during a ward meeting, while we were discussing some important

317

issue, Tim would be walking up and down outside the room in the narrow corridor shouting at the top of his voice, 'Why are you bastards trying to poison and kill me. I want to get out of this fucking place before I fucking well die. Bastards, bastards and you're all a load of wankers. Doctors? You're all a lot of phoneys.' This tirade of abuse would regularly carry on for half an hour while we all tried to carry on with our meeting, pretending not to hear. Tim was very disruptive and eventually the consultant would ask one of us to have a word with Tim. Tim would keep quiet for a few minutes but then he would start again. 'This place is driving me fucking nuts, it's killing me in here. I can't even get a cup of fucking tea. Everyone here is fucking mad, you're all fucking mad. All you do is give out fucking tablets for this and fucking tablets for that. No wonder patients never get better.' I had great difficulty in not laughing out loud, so I would put my hand in front of my mouth in an infantile way, hoping that no one would notice my unprofessional behaviour, but what could I do? Tim, although in his late thirties, was displaying infantile behaviour, which I found funny, although there were times when I could have easily strangled him to death.

Drugs made no difference to improve or modify his behaviour, and often he would rant and rave for hours on end, with no respite for staff or patients who seemed to tolerate his noisy behaviour much better than we nurses did. He also seemed to have no redeeming or likeable qualities and seemed to do his best to be as obnoxious as possible, at least that was what it seemed like. He tested my patience to the outer limits. Even though I had as much experience as most psychiatric nurses, I had been away from the job for four years and any time I started a new job I always found it a little unsettling until I got to know the patients well and built up a rapport with them. It was then easier to know how to respond to their different ways and behaviour. Even patients with the same mental illness are different from each other. Some you got on better with and some you liked more than others.

About 8 a.m. when breakfast was served I heard a female nurse shout, 'You can't come to breakfast like that, put your clothes on.' John, the young autistic patient, was walking down the corridor in a very short nightshirt with nothing else on, revealing his wedding tackle for all to see, and he did not seem to worry too much about it. That was the thing about this autistic patient, his behaviour could be totally inappropriate and unpredictable and he seemed to lack common sense in many areas. I had seen many situations in my years of nursing, but I had been here for only about an hour and already I was getting a flavour of what life was going to be like. 'This is truly a madhouse,' I thought, 'and what am I doing here?'

'Is he always like this?' I asked the Fillipino nurse Lila. She smiled and seemed unconcerned.

'Oh, he's a lot more difficult than this sometimes.'

What I later learned about John was that despite his many behavioural problems and tantrums, he could be very humorous, even though his dad did not think so on his visits to the ward. John knew how to wind his dad up, who was on the whole a fairly serious character. John would give a Nazi salute and say, '*Achtung, Achtung*', and smile with a huge grin at the same time. John's dad would get furious and tell him off. As nurses we found John's behaviour amusing, considering his many problems and it was better to see him happy than throwing tantrums and chairs around, as well as assaulting the odd nurse. 'That's not very nice, if you were in the last war, you wouldn't be making that silly salute,' his dad would say, getting all worked up; but it only encouraged John even more. '*Achtung, Achtung*, we haf vays of making you talk you know, ve vill send you to ze concentration camps in ze morning,' John said, giving the Nazi salute, and at the same time he put his left finger on his lip to imitate Hitler's moustache. He then added the Nazi goose step for more effect. Although it was inappropriate behaviour it always made me laugh because it was nice to see John being normal in some ways, which was rare to see. He did not always follow the normal rule of social interaction, he just did not know how to, and our job was to try and show him how to behave with other people. Some hope!

Sometimes he would just walk up to one of the pretty female nurses and say quite casually, 'I want to have sex with you now.' And the nurse would say, 'That's not very appropriate behaviour.' 'Why not, it's okay,' John would say very matter of fact. 'You have to know someone very well before you can say things like that,' the shy young English nurse Mary told him. This did not deter John. 'But I do know you, you're my key nurse and what's wrong with having sex with you?' John would ask in all innocence. Mary always blushed whenever she was in an embarrassing situation and said, 'Well we can have a talk sometime later about it when I have more time.' 'Fucking bitch, I bet you let your boyfriend have sex with you,' John would say, storming back to his bedroom and banging the corridor wall on the way back.

He was someone I came to understand and like when I got to know him well. Like many of our clients on the ward, he was very insecure and unhappy and had very little quality in his life. His interests were very

319

simple and basic, like music and reading about trains and of course, sex. He was also a great *Doctor Who* fan and he also contributed a lot to the ward, by his humour and his unpredictable and irrational behaviour.

I drove a van with about six patients and staff to Brighton on an outing one day, and in the middle of the motorway John decided that he did not want to go after all and was becoming more and more agitated as we approached Brighton. I decided that we would carry on and not spoil the other patients' day out and eventually calmed John down. In Brighton the other patients went off for a couple of hours and we arranged to meet back where I and another nurse waited with John, because he was still in a very excited state of mind and body.

A few minutes after the other patients had gone, John became very worked up and had one of his panic attacks and decided that he was going home on his own, which we could not let him do, due to his unsettled state of mind. We gave him some extra medication, which did not improve the situation, and he made a move to leave. We struggled on Brighton beach to restrain John from leaving. All the time John was shouting, 'Help, they're trying to kill me, help, help.' Amused members of the public looked on while licking their ice cream cornets, wondering what was going on. I was totally embarrassed and waiting for the Brighton police to arrive at any moment to investigate the disturbance on an otherwise peaceful summer's day. After a mammoth struggle we were all tired and John eventually calmed down. We pacified him with some crisps and Coca-Cola, which he was virtually addicted to. It had been a new and embarrassing situation, but we tried to remain calm and professional and only just saved the day, thanks mainly to our strong and fit male Filipino nurse, who had to use some strong arm tactics to prevent the situation getting worse. I decided never to volunteer to go on such a trip again.

One of the things about being a psychiatric nurse was that every day was different and you rarely got bored. It was always challenging and a great place to observe all types of human behaviour, which you would never otherwise see, and it kept you on your toes.

Giving out the medication at regular times throughout the day was a time that often caused some conflict or disagreement. Patients would either not come for their medication or sometimes they would refuse to take it. If the patient was informal, as nurses, we could not insist that they took it, so we would gently encourage them and point out the benefits, even if we did not always believe it ourselves.

Usually it worked. Some patients just hated taking their medication and they would pretend to swallow it and keep it under their tongue while they drank some water, but after a while we would get wise to such tactics and offer more water with the tablets. Another thing we did was to talk for a while to the patient who was trying desperately to conceal his medication under his tongue. It was difficult for him or her to talk with a number of tablets under the tongue. Often we would just look into the patient's mouth or follow him back to his room to see if the tablet was spat out into the hand basin. It was often a battle of wills and I could well understand why some patients did not like being forced to take medication three or four times a day with little choice in the matter, but we had to give prescribed medication, one way or another. Patients who were sectioned would also, at times, refuse to take their medication and we would do our best to encourage them or leave it for a while to see if they might change their mind. But if they still refused, as nurses, we had to make sure that prescribed medication was taken some way or another, otherwise the doctors would want to know the reason.

Sectioned patients had, in some ways, less choice in their treatment and had to accept what the medical team felt was best, although there was the opportunity to see a mental health tribunal from time to time to appeal against their detention. Sometimes they were successful, but mostly they were not. Whenever such a detained patient refused his or her medication we eventually had to threaten them with an injection if they did not agree to take their oral medication. Sometimes the threat worked and they would agree to take their medicine, which we all preferred. Forcing an injection on anybody was a part of the job that I detested, as did many nurses, but there were many times when it had to be done. It was a very degrading experience to have to subdue a patient and bring them to the floor with four or five nursing staff holding them down. It must have been very unpleasant and terrifying for the patient.

There was always the possibility that either the patient or a nurse might get injured, as did happen from time to time during the struggle that often occurred. It was not a good way to earn a patient's trust either and to have a good relationship with them, although patients soon forgot such episodes and, on the whole, did not seem to hold any grudges. Very occasionally a particularly violent patient would threaten to get a particular nurse outside, but it was rarely a problem. Patients on the whole trusted the nurses that took care of them. I was beginning to realise that this ward was like no other that I had worked on since I became a nurse in 1965. The variety and challenging behaviour of the patients was very testing for all concerned. We had many different psychologists during my stay there who, along with doctors and other members of the medical team, were unable to sort out the often very complex behaviour of some of the patients and we had more psychologists come and go than virtually any other type of staff. It was as if the challenge were too great and frustrating at times. An awful lot of work went on from many different types of professionals with little to show at the end. Some of our patients seemed resistant to everything we did with them and for them. It could be extremely frustrating and usually it was we, the nurses, who were blamed for lack of progress. We were told that we were not trying hard enough and not doing enough to encourage patients to participate in activities, but the fact was that we had very damaged patients, who were proving very difficult to treat. And often the facilities were woefully inadequate, but we did our best. I liked my job and got on well with the patients and staff, but as usual for me, it was the managers I was often in conflict with.

42. Characters and Situations

We had such a variety of characters and situations that would challenge my own and everyone else's skills to the very limit, yet there was some progress, although it was painfully slow. How could you turn around someone like Charlie, who had been in a large mental institution since the age of 16 and had now come to us at the age of 50, due to one of the large institutions closing down. It would not be easy. He was often described as one of the last dregs of the large institutions, who was hard to place anywhere else. He was also a manic-depressive, who had suffered severe mood swings all his life and he was very institutionalised and had bad behavioural problems. Not very surprising!

When he came to our ward, he came with his long-term girlfriend Theresa. They had known each other for over 30 years and were inseparable. They were reassured and promised before they left the large institution that they would never be separated, a promise that would be broken in time. Charlie was assigned to me, as his key worker, which was the start of a lifelong friendship with him and his girlfriend Theresa. They were like husband and wife and she adored him and he her. No matter what he did or how badly he behaved or whatever verbal abuse he gave her, it made no difference to the affection and devotion that she showed him. She was always the one and only person who was always accepting and understanding towards him, no matter what we, the medical team, and professionals, thought about him. She remained loyal despite his terrible mood swings, and she would always make allowances for him. Her love and affection were unconditional.

'He can't help it, poor thing, it's not his fault,' she would often say. 'Don't you nurses and doctors know he is a manic-depressive, you should be more understanding, shouldn't you?' She was right, of course, we were not always as understanding as we should have been.

Despite suffering from mental illness virtually all of her adult life and being incarcerated for over 30 years in mental institutions, she was very intelligent and articulate and voiced her opinions on her own and Charlie's behalf and she was not easily fobbed off with convenient answers. She also suffered from very steadfast delusions that were unshakeable and were totally convincing, unless you knew her well. She once told social workers and doctors how she rode a horse in the famous Grand National race and when reminded that women were not allowed to ride in the race, quick as flash she said, 'Well I was dressed as a man and no one recognized that I was a woman.' She believed what she was saying and no argument could convince her otherwise. She was very happy with her delusions because, to her, they were real, and she had lived them, though at times they could create problems for the nurses on the ward. While not necessarily disagreeing with her we also did not openly agree with her.

She would often make a complaint that she had been either raped or beaten up by the night nurses the night before, and she would telephone the police and make an official complaint, which the police naturally had to investigate as we ourselves had to, and of course, it was all fantasy. She would also make allegations that Charlie had been beaten up by the nurses, which again we had to investigate officially, although such allegations were nearly always false.

I came on duty one morning and Charlie, who had been up most of the night due to his mania, showed me some bad bruising on both of his upper arms, which he said had been done by the night nurse pushing him. The bruising did indeed look like finger marks on both sides of each arm. Charlie did not want to make a complaint, but I advised him that I would have to make a note of the bruising anyway and investigate how the bruising had come about. A night nurse was named, who denied it, and it was difficult to take the matter any further, especially as Charlie did not want to pursue the matter. Personally I believed that Charlie had been treated roughly during the night. Sometimes even the doctors, managers and other nurses colluded with what seemed like an abuse of patients' rights, as often that particular patient was difficult anyway. Charlie did need more persuasion at times to toe the line, which often meant using some physical force.

No doubt Charlie was a difficult patient as a result of his mood swings. When he was low and very depressed, he would not eat or talk, wash or come out of his room for about two weeks. He would neglect his personal appearance and worst of all, his sense of humour, which was always lively, would desert him completely. It was a sad sight to see Charlie so depressed and dysfunctional, unable to be a part of anything and not caring whether he lived or died. During this period, his mood control medication would be drastically reduced.

Charlie would very gradually come out of his very black and depressed mood and have maybe a week or ten days of being as normal as anyone else, then, very slowly, his mood would gradually become manic, until he was so bad that he was unable to stand still or sleep or indeed stop talking

24 hours a day. He would overeat, give all his possessions away, including his money and cigarettes, and the next day Theresa would replace many of the items Charlie had given away or had stolen while in his manic mood. Charlie constantly broke the many music centres that Theresa had bought from her own money, and she would always replace them as soon as she could, and she never complained. Her patience was boundless. Charlie would be incontinent and need help with dressing and washing and would, at times, tend to be a little aggressive and always very noisy. His medication would have to be gradually increased again, often with little or no effect. The effect on patients and staff was a lot more stress, but the other patients were there 24 hours a day, so the effect on them must have been horrendous, though they rarely complained and seemed to cope with Charlie's moods better than we did.

Patients generally had more tolerance than we nurses. Charlie's manic mood would last for around two weeks and then he would steadily sink into a black mood. This pattern of behaviour went on all of Charlie's life and Theresa was always there for him and always understanding. Sometimes we would find her in his bedroom, trying to change his clothes on her own, before we knew about it. Their relationship was one of really true love, which endured years of institutionalisation, medication and finally separation, as each of their needs in the end were different. Theresa eventually moved into the community where she is coping very well as did Charlie a few years later, but in a different place. Their ideal would be to live in the same place together, but that seems unlikely to happen, as Charlie can be a fire risk due to his carelessness with his smoking. Theresa has remained devoted to Charlie and has spent most of her money on him and never complained. Her loyalty and love needs to be seen to be believed; it is truly amazing. It is one of the most enduring love stories that I have ever witnessed in or outside a mental hospital.

Because Charlie was a manic-depressive with his various and disturbing moods to match, he was like two different people at times, and so Theresa often referred to there being two Charlies. One she said was her husband, while the other one was her boyfriend, but at other times she was not sure which was which, but she loved both of them anyway. Maybe it was her way of coping with Charlie's two very different personalities, but whatever his mood was, she always coped and remained cheerful. Charlie was very trying on everybody, but we also had another lady called June, also a manic-depressive, who was, on the whole, a much more severe case, whose mood swings went on for much longer periods than Charlie's. Medication did not touch her, except to occasionally knock her out, almost to an unconscious state, where her breathing would almost stop and become very laboured. There were times when we called the doctor, as we felt she was dying, only to see her suddenly come round. She gave us many a fright.

Although June was in her sixties and a frail looking woman she could be very aggressive when in her manic phase and she would often terrify even the biggest of the male patients who were never quite sure exactly what she was going to do next. She would sling china plates and cups while having a cup of tea or attack another patient without warning, and more than once grabbed a patient by the balls, which she thought was great fun! She had to be put on special observation with a nurse by her side for virtually 24 hours a day, often for weeks on end, which annoyed her intensely. When she and Charlie were having mood swings at the same time, and Tim was shouting verbal abuse at no one in particular, the ward was bedlam and there were often other patient problems to cope with at the same time. It was obvious that staffing levels would have to be increased for everyone's safety.

Arguments and misunderstandings between patients often occurred. Just like a large dysfunctional family, only a lot worse. Staff, too, had many disagreements between themselves. One incident occurred that left an unpleasant taste in my mouth. One of the most disturbed and potentially dangerous male patients lashed out at a male colleague and hit him on the side of the jaw quite hard. The patient was quickly overpowered by the other three nurses and was being held securely, when it was alleged by a number of the staff holding the patient and other observers, that the nurse who had been assaulted punched the patient very hard while he was being restrained, as if in retaliation and in anger, something that you do not do as a nurse. It could be viewed as a common assault and could mean that such a nurse could be struck off the nursing register and lose their job and possibly be prosecuted, if the assault was proven.

The patient was no doubt potentially violent, but he did not deserve to be abused in this manner, which was in contradiction to what we were taught as nurses. You only retaliate in defence if it's necessary. I was not on duty at the time, but I was informed, as were those in authority who later investigated the incident, that the nurse did in fact assault the patient while he was being held. The nurse in question was a trained nurse and should have known better, but he denied hitting the patient and claimed that he lashed out in defence. The managers believed him and chose not to believe the untrained Filipino nurses who had witnessed the incident.

In the NHS there are many cover-ups as we are often reluctant to see our colleagues, who may otherwise be good nurses, struck off because of some indiscretion, and they are often given the benefit of the doubt. I felt sorry for the patient, despite his past violent history, but he did not deserve to be treated like a thug, by a nurse who lost his cool. I also wondered how the Filipino nurses felt at not being believed. One told me that they did not believe him because he was only a nursing assistant. While this may have been partly true, it was quite common to cover up for bad nurses or bad doctors, just as it is at times for bad policemen and many others in large organisations for the good name of that particular organisation. I know who I believed, as it was later revealed to me by another non-Filipino nurse who had been there at the time of the incident that the patient was indeed assaulted. The nurse felt a little guilty at not speaking out, but felt a certain loyalty towards the nurse in question and did not wish to see him lose his job and possibly his career.

I thought that I had experienced everything there was to experience in psychiatry, but I was wrong and I was on a new and severe learning curve, which made me realise that there was always something new to learn, no matter how old I was. Lewis was another patient in his early twenties who was allocated to me during my first few months there, and although only small in stature, and weighing less than 9 stone, he presented a huge problem with his behavioural problems, which tested all our skills and patience to the limit. He seemed to be angry at everyone and there was at least one incident every day involving him. He often had to be forcibly restrained and given extra medication, especially during my first couple of years there. One of his many problems in the early days was that he would not eat. He had a lot of guilty feelings surrounding food, as well as clothes, religion and getting treatment in hospital. He felt that he did not deserve to be treated in hospital and felt bad because he was not paying anything towards his treatment, no matter what I or anyone else told him. Even clothes that were given to him would be given away or folded up neatly in his room and never worn.

He also had an obsession with washing and would spend many hours during the day washing and re-washing his face and hands. Many of his personal belongings in his room would be laid out in neat and orderly rows and even spare boxes of matches and cigarettes would all be stacked in neat rows, even though they were often empty. He was being brought to the table and was not allowed to leave until he ate something. I felt he was being coerced too much. Every day at every meal there was a big scene, so I decided that I was going to try a different approach and sit with him and eat what he was eating and often he would get up and not eat and I would be left on my own eating food that was in fact meant for patients, which was generally not approved of by the management. I got around this by getting the doctors to agree to my plan in writing, so as to cover myself in case of any complaints. I also told Lewis that if he did not want to eat it was up to him. While not very successful, he did relax a bit more and it avoided a big scene at every mealtime.

His mother, who was a very sweet and hard-working lady, came regularly to see Lewis. He would verbally abuse her at the top of his voice at almost every visit, which she took very passively, without ever getting annoyed. It was heartbreaking to listen to, but she would come back the next day and never complain. She also did a full-time job to help support the family, which was not easy as other members in the family also suffered from some milder forms of mental illness. She was an unusual woman who seemed to have a lot of inner strength to cope like she did.

As I had completed a course on the use of counselling skills, I would try and see Lewis at least once a week on his own for about 15 minutes of undisturbed quality time just to listen to what he had to say. He was a very tortured individual, and during one of our sessions he said to me, 'I have a crying heart, my heart is aching and I don't know what to do.' It got to me when he said that and I did not have an answer for him, but I did tell him it was good to express his feelings. For someone who was normally not very articulate, his words were very descriptive and meaningful. He found sitting and talking difficult as indeed I did. My skills as a listener were not great, but at least we were both in the same boat and learning together.

One time I found him in the bedroom standing on his bed with a leather belt knotted around the curtain rail around his bed, and when I asked him what he was doing he coolly replied, 'I am trying to commit suicide.' I was shocked and, of course, removed the belt and spent some time asking him why he wanted to commit suicide, but he was very vague and started laughing. As the person in charge, I reported the incident to the doctor, and Lewis was placed on continuous observation as a suicide risk. We had to take his gesture seriously, even if he was just joking. We could never be sure what a patient might do and it was our worst nightmare trying to prevent self-harm.

Some time later, on another ward, a female patient who was a high suicide risk, had been allowed into the toilet on her own, and a few minutes later she was found hanging, but she was discovered by the nurse in time. Unfortunately she suffered brain damage and was like a vegetable afterwards. Of course, it was the nurses' fault for not being more vigilant, but the girl's parents sued the hospital for around a million pounds. These were some of the kinds of stresses and strains that you were under on a closed ward as patients were more disturbed and therefore needed more supervision.

Lewis did amaze me one day with his break-dancing, which took me by complete surprise. He danced around on the floor on his head and his performance was a real revelation.

John, the autistic patient, decided to join in with Lewis one day, which brought some light-hearted relief to what, at times, was a depressing atmosphere. John was very large, and at 17 stone he was almost twice the size of Lewis, very fat and not very agile, so to see him trying to break-dance and spin on his head made for good entertainment and he entertained many of the patients and staff for a few minutes. He was also allocated to me as his key worker for our weekly counselling sessions, which both John and I found long, because he was unable to express his feelings very well, so we would both sit opposite each other looking uncomfortable. Once he saw me looking up at the clock at intervals during the session and he asked me directly why I kept looking at the time. I told him that as we had 15 minutes, it was important to keep to it, but I was lying. I was bored and finding it difficult to cope with the silence. 'What would you like out of life?' I asked him. 'I just want your care, that's all.' Sometimes patients would say such simple and apt things that really made me think a lot about why I was here and what I was doing, and it made me look at my own behaviour and motives.

Working with such difficult clients, like most jobs, had its ups and downs, like the day the hospital chief executive came to visit our ward, surrounded by many of the hospital management, all trying to look happy and pleased to create an effect. Charlie, my manic-depressive friend, was talking to me in the day room as this big noise walked towards us. Charlie left me without saying anything and walked toward the official group with a smile on his face and no shoes on. I fretted at what he might say, as I knew he could be very inhibited at times and without batting an eyelid, Charlie asked the chief executive, 'Are you a poof?' Secretly I almost wet myself trying not to laugh and not betray my position of being in charge of the ward. The executive maintained his dignity and kept on walking as if he had not heard Charlie, but Charlie followed and was not to be ignored. 'All you lot are queer, aren't you?' At that a manager who knew Charlie from the old hospitals eased Charlie to the side and had a word in his ear. Yes, mental illness can sometime give poetic freedom to say exactly what you are thinking.

During one of his regular visits, the Church of England vicar was in the kitchen while I helped serve food through the hatch, when Charlie popped his head through and said to the vicar, 'Have you heard about the queer vicar?' The vicar smiled and said 'No, Charlie, I have not and you're going to tell me no doubt.' I was dreading what Charlie was about to say.

'Well,' Charlie said, 'The vicar says Amen and the queer vicar says Ah, Men.' I thought this a hilarious joke, and even the vicar saw the funny side. These were the little moments that I personally appreciated, bursting through someone's pomposity and only someone like Charlie could have the nerve to do it and get away with it. Even during our once a week ward meeting with doctors, nurses, social workers, psychologists and patients, Charlie would not stop clowning and would continue to make jokes, especially if he was in his manic mood. The consultant psychiatrist was not amused, but there was no stopping Charlie and he could not take anything seriously. It surprised me that I was not given the sack for encouraging him, which I did secretly. It was an open meeting after all and it was time for all present to speak as they felt.

During his depressive moods, Charlie could be very nasty and irritable and, on more than one occasion, he assaulted male and female nurses and would just lash out if anyone was trying to be too forceful with him. He once got hold of my finger, as a joke, and if I had not pulled away he would have broken it. Even when he was very high, he could be a bit too playful and cause damage to someone who was trying to help him. He would often throw punches or throw a chair at someone who was helping him.

Charlie's big passion was music, mostly fifties and sixties rock 'n' roll, and country and western, with some modern stuff thrown in, and he was extremely knowledgeable. One of his ambitions was to own a record shop; it often looked as if he had enough records and tapes to start his own shop. He had his own room, due to his many moods, and all his records would be spread all over the bed, and he would just pick one out at a time. Charlie also liked to play his music very loud, as did most of the other patients, many of whom also had a passion for music during their incarceration on the ward.

There were very few organised activities that the patients were interested in, and most patients just wanted to be left alone and do their own thing. For the most part they were too doped up with either antidepressants, tranquillizers or sedatives, to either cheer them up or reduce their levels of aggression or activity.

Some days, you could hear Bob Marley music blasting out from one West Indian's room, while Charlie would be blaring out rock 'n' roll, while some younger patients would be playing the modern stuff. Everyone, it seemed, was trying to out do each other as to how loud they could play their music. It added to the state of bedlam in what was a very small area, with thin walls between rooms, and the music would waft down the narrow corridor on the ward, often to the annoyance of any visiting doctors and people in the nearby offices.

After about six months on the ward I applied for the vacant charge nurse job and I was surprised to get it and to be back where I felt I should have been. It gave me new responsibilities and motivation, but it also upset some of my colleagues who had been there longer than I was. At age 51 I did not expect promotion again, but it boosted my confidence, although Sandra always convinced me that I was good enough to be promoted. She was right again as usual.

As in most of my psychiatric jobs, staff were always more trouble than the patients, and trying to keep them happy and contented was far more of a problem than dealing with patients who had severe psychiatric problems and behaviour. We had a multiracial staff made up of Irish, English, Filipino, African, Asian with a Spaniard thrown in for good measure.

The least demanding and the most hard working were the Filipinos who were the largest group, and they were mostly untrained nursing assistants. I liked working with them and they seemed to enjoy their work and were, to my mind, the happiest group of nurses that I ever worked with. Although their English was on the whole pretty good, there were some occasions when they got their words mixed up.

There was the time when we had a big patient and staff meeting, and Charlie was in one of his usual manic moods and kept getting up and down from his chair and disrupting the meeting, so we asked one of the Filipino male nurses to try and control Charlie by sitting next to him. Every time Charlie stood up, Henry, the nurse, would tell him, 'Shit down, Charlie, you making too much noise, be a good man now and shit down.' I had great difficulty in trying to keep my composure and not to laugh. The charge nurse had to set an example of good behaviour and I was sadly lacking in this department. Henry never did manage to say 'sit' in all the years I worked with him, but then I always had difficulty in pronouncing my 'THs' and I often put them in where they should not have been, so I was no great linguist myself. Even the consultant psychiatrist told me not to slur my words and to slow down, as he could not understand me, which was great, especially coming from an Asian who could not pronounce his 'Ws' or 'Vs'. When John, one of our male patients, was being interviewed by the same psychiatrist in a large group of staff, it had been discussed that

331

he was seen masturbating in a public area outside the ward the same afternoon and there had been complaints from various quarters.

'Why were you masturbating in public?' he asked the patient. The patient looked confused and looked to me as if for guidance, but I was too embarrassed to say anything and just looked at the floor. I also was afraid that I might burst out laughing any minute. 'Why were you masturbating?' he asked again. 'Why was I what?' John asked, obviously not realising what the word meant or maybe it was the doctor's accent that was confusing him. 'What were you doing in the garden this morning when Joe, the nurse, told you not to do that?' the psychiatrist asked again, getting a little impatient. John's face broke into a large smile as if he had suddenly seen the light. 'Oh, wanking, you mean, doctor,' as if he was discussing the time of day or washing his teeth. 'Oh, yeah, I was wanking all right,' he replied, now beginning to laugh a little louder, which quickly spread to the staff.

The psychiatrist was now looking confused because he did not understand what the work wanking meant. 'What do you mean you were wanking?' he asked, looking around for guidance. 'I think he means masturbating, doctor, one of the nurses whispered. Trying to keep his composure and maybe feeling a little bit put out that he had not learned this word during his medical training, he then asked John, who by now was in a very good mood. 'Why were you wanking in the garden this morning?'

'What do you mean, "why was I wanking in the garden this morning?" Because I like it, that's why.'

'You don't want to be known as a wanker, do you?' the doctor continued, not fully realising the implications of what he was saying.

'I'm not a wanker, doctor,' John said indignantly. There were sly sniggers all around, especially from us male nurses. It was one of the great moments in psychiatry as far as I was concerned and it was nice to see a patient who was not very bright turn the tables on an eminent psychiatrist. It had been a conversation that a top writer could not have invented.

I always tried to sit beside any doctors at meetings in case I got a fit of laughing, at least that way I could avoid staring eyes. There were no more questions after that, because the doctor felt that he was getting nowhere and, as John left the room, we all had a good laugh over our cup of coffee, despite the obvious bad behavioural problems that John had displayed earlier that day. It would not be the last time that John would behave in this way because he found it difficult to realise what was acceptable and what was not in a public place. John, in his childlike innocence, was unperturbed about the whole episode. But with regular counselling sessions, some behaviour training, and much hard work by the whole medical team over a number of years, John's sexual exploits would be less embarrassing and less frequent, at least in public.

John was an avid *Doctor Who* fan and was extremely knowledgeable about the actors in it. He was like a 22-year-old child in a man's body and he could be very demanding and want things done on the spot, no matter what you were doing. When I first knew him I did not know how to deal with his demands and I often got cross with him, which upset him even more, causing him to misbehave even more than usual, by either slinging a chair around or banging windows.

After a while, if I was on the phone when he wanted something immediately, I learned by being calm and treating him with some patience and respect, he was very different, and it often avoided more problems for everyone. I would just say, 'I'll be with you in a second, John, and we can have a cup of tea together,' and he would accept that and stay calm. It was simple, but it worked most of the time.

Some staff often behaved in a sexually provocative way, despite all our efforts to set an example for the patients. One very attractive female nurse would often lift up her skirt to reveal her black suspenders and matching underwear and tease a particular patient and say, 'What do you think of that, Tim?' Another day she dressed in some new underwear and nothing else while she was on duty in the office, and called in another female nurse to ask what she thought of her new gear. Even the other female nurse was flabbergasted when she saw what the nurse was wearing and told her to change back to her normal clothes, before one of the nurse managers came round and saw her. Life could be difficult on closed wards and sometimes we all did things to break the monotony and help release the stress and pressure. Most of the pressure that I personally felt was from managers and other nurses. The patients I could cope with easier and they seemed to be more understanding, despite their mental illness!

Another older male nurse, almost near retiring age, opened a container, which was used to collect and store urine samples overnight. Out of curiosity he sniffed the contents inside and, within seconds, had collapsed and was rushed to hospital, where he was found to have had a heart attack, brought on by the ammonia in the container! He did recover from his curiosity, although he did retire early due to medical reasons.

One of my male nursing colleagues, Seb, like myself, had a good sense of humour and liked a laugh and joke while on duty. When we worked together we were always doing impersonations of various people. His best

333

was Jimmy Saville, which brought some light-hearted relief to what was at times a very depressing atmosphere to work in. There were times when something very serious was being discussed and I would just look across at him and see a glint in his eye and we both would start laughing for no obvious reason. Not very professional and it often annoyed the more serious nurses who lacked humour.

We had various types of people working on the ward, including an art therapist and occupational therapist, although very few of them stayed for very long for all sorts of reasons. A music therapist came for a couple of weeks, but eventually gave up out of sheer frustration. She would try and organise music therapy with various instruments and she would try and get the patients to follow her music in an orderly manner, but our patients were having none of it and would just bang away at a drum or blow a whistle in a disorderly way and havoc would prevail. Maybe it was their way of getting some control over their lives, and they often would just get up and walk out without saying a word. This was very disconcerting and disappointing for the therapist who was not used to such rejection, but as nurses, we were more used to it because we had worked there for some years.

Another therapist tried some relaxation techniques to get the patients to relax while lying on the carpet listening to some soft music, but that didn't work either. The only one who fell asleep was an elderly male nurse, yes, the same one who had sniffed the container! Within minutes of the music being played he could be heard snoring.

No doubt our patients were definitely very difficult, and our ward was often seen as a dumping ground for those patients who were not responding to the normal medication and treatment. Many of the other nurses on the other wards did not want to work there, because it was not exciting and progress was very slow, so slow in fact that progress was often measured in years. Most of us who did work there enjoyed it and we helped create what I think was a good atmosphere for patients and staff. During the time that I worked there I also had an opportunity to photograph many of the patients whom I got to know very well, and that often helped to break barriers down.

Our job not only involved working with the patients but also with their family members, and some could be more difficult than the patients themselves. Tim was in his twenties and could, at times, be very difficult and stubborn, and most of the medication was ineffective. He also would not wash regularly or change his clothes as often as he should have done, but we could only encourage him so far and offer some incentives, which usually did not work anyway.

His sisters, in particular, could be very loud and abusive when visiting Tim on the ward, and would ask, 'Why hasn't Tim shaved or washed today and how come he has not even fucking shaved for a few days?' This abuse would often go on for a few minutes, much to our dismay and annoyance, but we just listened and politely told them that we could not force him to do something if he did not want to. Secretly, we wanted to tell them to fuck off but, as nurses, we had to be polite to relatives no matter how wrong or abusive they were.

Tim's sexually inappropriate behaviour was getting bad, especially to the more attractive female nurses and being locked up for longer periods made no difference to him. He would touch a nurse's hair or backside or rub her arm and all sorts of threats made no difference.

We decided, on the instructions of the psychiatrist, to call the police the next time there was an incident and that is what we did. The local police came, a man and woman, and had a chat to Tim in a side room. To let him know that they took his offences seriously, they handcuffed him and told him that the next time he would be taken away in handcuffs to the police station. They left the cuffs on for a few minutes and then decided to take them off, but had realised they did not have a key! So they had to go back to the police station and get the key while Tim waited in cuffs, totally unconcerned. The incident made a difference only for a few days, before he was back to his antics again. Strangely enough, he never bothered the older female nurses!

Some parents were very grateful that their relatives were in a secure environment, because they knew that, at the very least, they were safe and getting treatment. One West Indian family would regularly bring home-made Jamaican cake for the staff and, of course, at Christmas time many visitors would leave presents. Some relatives would come daily, while others came less frequently and, of course, some patients never had any visitors at all, because they had no living relatives.

William was an overweight patient who looked very like Billy Bunter. He wore thick dark glasses and had chubby cheeks and a big smile with a big temper to match. He was very unpredictable and, at times, would be very charming and tell me or some other nurses, 'I think all you nurses are wonderful and the very best, and you should all be given a raise. I am going to write to the prime minister John Major and tell him what I think of you all. And as for you, Mary, you take the biscuit for being my absolute favourite nurse of all time.'

He was an insincere bullshitter, but we just accepted what he said as if it were true. He was loud and noisy and could be very disruptive and once threw all the dinner plates on the floor during dinner time, because he was not given a cup of tea instantly. He certainly knew how to get attention and was often throwing tantrums, and he was in his forties! Even William's humour would desert him at times, when he was depressed, and he would go about the ward not talking to anyone. We became used to patients' mood swings and behaviour and let them be until their mood improved.

One Asian patient in his early thirties, who rarely mixed with the other patients and spent most of his time in his own room, was one of the most disturbed, and all his massive daily medication did was to help stabilise him. He rarely became disturbed, but when he did, both patients and staff were on their guard, because he was perceived to be potentially very dangerous, but not dangerous enough to send anywhere else because he had not done anything really bad, although he eventually did get sent to a more secure unit somewhere else.

He had been locked up for a number of years and it was seen as inadvisable to let him out of the hospital even with two escorts, for fear that he might abscond, and do something awful. He had a sad life, but at least he had many members of his family who visited him regularly. He was very deluded and would pace up and down the corridor when not in his room, often smiling and talking to himself. He would sit in his room for hours and not come out and he rarely sat with the other patients for meals.

When he was very agitated he would pace up and down the narrow corridor very quickly with his arms folded, often knocking into other patients and not speaking, with his jaw clenched. He would not respond when you spoke to him, which was another warning sign. As prevention was better than cure, extra medication would be offered to him to forestall any possible outburst, and generally he would accept or sometimes he would say, 'No thanks, I'm all right,' and usually he was. He could often be seen sitting in the garden area just looking up into the sky with his mouth open wide and not speaking, as if in a trance, alone with his thoughts.

Some staff did not always behave in a kindly way towards patients. There was an instance on a ward near mine, which was for even more disturbed patients than ours. Many of the patients who were there either came directly from the community, and may have been brought there by the police because they had been disturbed in a public place, or been a danger to themselves or others. Some others would come from another ward because they could not cope with a particular patient. Sometimes a patient may have been violent or sometimes a suicidal risk and needed closer supervision until they became more settled again.

336

One female patient had been sent there because she had become very depressed, due to the loss of her baby shortly after childbirth and was at some risk to herself. She sat down to watch television around 10.30 p.m. and, before long, a member of the night staff came and switched the TV off without asking the patient, and told her to go to bed, because it was too late to watch TV. The patient argued that she did not want to go to bed because she could not sleep, but the male nurse insisted anyway.

The patient duly obliged and then asked if she could have a hot drink before she went to bed to help her to sleep, which was refused, because she was told it was too late to have a drink. The patient, already very depressed, went to bed but could not sleep and went back out to the TV room around midnight, only to find the same nurse who had banned her from watching TV, watching TV himself, and drinking hot drinks. She rightly reported him to the managers the next day. That male nurse was eventually struck off the nurse register for other unbecoming behaviour. This was the same nurse that Charlie had made allegations about when he said that he had been manhandled at night. It is behaviour like this, which to my knowledge was very rare, that tends to give some parts of the nursing profession a bad name.

All nurses are not angels and some are very nasty with a sadistic streak and you wonder why they ever became nurses. Some can't cope with the pressure and lose patience, and take it out on the patients, but from my own experiences most nurses have a good and caring attitude.

I have seen many nurses very devoted to the job and take patients into their own homes for a meal and bring in their own clothes and give them to some needy patient. Managers very often collude with nurses who get away with too many instances of bad behaviour. Those patients who are less well or less intelligent or unable to verbalise or to make a proper complaint often are not listened to enough and their complaints are often just shoved aside, but the female depressed patient who made a formal complaint was more articulate and also had the confidence to pursue her complaint to the end. As a result she obtained more satisfaction. It is just possible that if the nurse who had been struck off had been disciplined earlier, he may have been able to change his behaviour and the outcome might have been different for everyone concerned. Those patients who spoke up for their rights, like some staff did, were always described as being difficult and troublesome.

When I worked at Long Grove I was told by a colleague about an incident that he had witnessed on one of the wards. It was while a very quiet Asian man called Aslam was being made to have a bath and was being somewhat manhandled by a nurse. Aslam objected to having a bath at this particular time and tried to make his point that he was happy to have one later on in the day, when he felt like it, which was reasonable. The nurse, however, was having none of it, and he was not about to have his authority questioned by a mere patient and a foreigner at that! As he was getting nowhere with the patient, he called two other male nurses for assistance to force the patient into the bath. I had often met Aslam in the social centre but I did not know him very well and he was very quiet and timid and rarely spoke, and when he did, it was a quiet whisper. He seemed like a man who had very little self-esteem and just came and went like a puff of smoke.

In the bathroom the nurses continued to pester Aslam and goad him, despite his quiet protestations. They mocked and basically took the piss out of him, but quick as a flash the quiet and timid Asian turned on his tormentors and knocked three nurse out cold on the bathroom floor. What the staff had not realised was that Aslam had been a boxing champion before he became mentally ill and, obviously, despite his mental illness, had not lost his boxing skills. I laughed when my colleague told me about this incident, but I was only disappointed that I had not witnessed it!

Working behind closed doors is more stressful by the very nature of the type of difficult clients that you are dealing with, because that is why they are locked up. At times I just wanted to open the doors and see how the patients would get on. The whole medical team would discuss whether the ward should remain locked or not at least every Monday morning at our major ward rounds, so at least the topic was aired, but we never got to opening it during my time there, and often it was because of one patient in particular who was perceived as being too dangerous to let him come and go as he chose. The particular patient had been on the ward for almost six years, and the ward was totally unsuitable for someone like him, who would have had better facilities if he had been in prison. The trouble was that there was no suitable place for him, because he was not dangerous enough to be sent to Broadmoor and there were very few other suitable locked environments to contain him, although he was eventually moved to a more secure and more suitable ward in south London.

The atmosphere on a permanent closed ward is edgy, strained and tense amongst patients and staff. Staff have to be constantly vigilant as to the often sudden and rapid change in a patient's mood and the effect it can have on those on the ward. Those patients who are allowed out into the community on their own, have to ask to be let out, and places like the kitchen area are out of bounds and have to be locked and only opened under close supervision. Patients could not make a cup of tea on their own and had to ask a nurse to unlock the door, and they often got on each other's nerves due to the lack of space. Often two patients could not walk in the corridor side by side without virtually bumping into each other, which all added to the tension, for the staff and patients. Luckily most of the patients got on well together, despite their very different types of illness and behavioural problems. I hated locking people up and having control over their lives, although I realised it was sometimes necessary.

Personally, I found it embarrassing for patients to keep asking me for a cup of tea, because I felt it degrading for them, and I often voiced my feelings about how I felt. The new consultant psychiatrist gave me a very nice compliment when he told me that if he was a patient who had to be locked up, he would prefer to be locked up by someone like me, who did not like locking patients up, so at least I had one fan, and he was top man!

I realised that my own feelings and emotions were often too strong, and that I took the job too personally, and as a result it caused me more stress than it should have done, but I could not put my life's experiences to one side, although I did try. I was a very sensitive person and took patient's problems on board a little too much. I was on duty one evening when there was a call from the police outside of London, asking about one of our patients who had absconded a couple of days earlier. Tim, the noisy and paranoid patient, had scaled the high wire fence in our secure garden while a nurse had been distracted and had absconded before it was realised that he had gone. Tim had assaulted a male member of the public while they were both in a public toilet. Tim did not like the way the man had looked at him and he struck him with a hand axe on the head. Luckily for the stranger, he was not seriously hurt. After this incident, Tim was moved to a much more secure unit in London, to the relief of all of the nurses and other patients on our ward, who were glad of some peace and quiet at long last.

Another patient had attempted to rob a local bank with another colleague, but it was not very well executed, in fact it never took place at all. One guy had stayed outside the bank, on the lookout, so to speak, while the brains behind the idea went into the bank to rob it.

In the meantime, the police had been called as a result of the guy waiting outside the bank behaving suspiciously. Ben was sitting outside the bank door on the public footpath with his legs crossed, rolling his own fags, while people going into the bank had to either step around or over him. Ben often used to sit or lay on the ward floor watching TV or just lying around in the most peculiar positions, so for him it was part of his routine, but maybe on this occasion he forgot what he was there for. I could not invent such situations! When the police came with their sirens blaring, Ben just carried on rolling his fags and made no attempt to run away. The police asked him what he was doing there and Ben, cool and innocently replied, 'We're trying to rob the bank, my mate's inside.' Needless to say both Ben and his friend were arrested, which was how Ben eventually finished up on my ward, following a court appearance. He described it all in such a matter of fact way when I eventually got to know him that it was obvious he was not an accomplished bank robber at all. He admitted that he only went along to keep his friend company and for something to do! Ben was the most laid back person I met during my years of nursing and, although he had been on a section, he was harmless and very incompetent, and apparently not very bright. He eventually moved into the community and now lives in a psychiatric hostel.

43. End of the Line

I found that psychiatric nursing was changing very rapidly and sometimes not always for the better. Many changes were being made, which often alienated the staff. My own position was changing and I found that, like other people in the health service, we were being asked to do more, with little or no consultation or support, and no extra money. I also discovered that I had some heart problems, and within a year I had to resign my job on medical health grounds, bringing my nursing career to an abrupt end.

My last stint in nursing was in many ways more demanding and difficult than I had ever known in any other job, partly because we had some very difficult and varied clients to deal with and not always the right resources to treat them as they deserved. The clients took longer to cure or to stabilise, which caused a lot of frustration, not only to nurses, but to doctors and management who seemed to feel that it was the nurses' fault that patients were not getting well enough and quickly. As nurses, we were the ones who carried out the prescribed treatment and very often felt isolated and unsupported, which was damaging morale. Of course the good nurses moved on, leaving the patients to try and get used to new personalities, which broke the continuity in care, although that has always happened.

I had learned so much as a psychiatric nurse about myself and about people's behaviour in general. The experiences that I had could never be had anywhere else in any other type of job. My life was far richer because of the various characters that I had met, amongst the staff and the mentally ill whose lives I hoped I may have helped make a little more bearable, but I'm not so sure. I have never regretted being a psychiatric nurse, although it was only a chance meeting that brought me on the long journey through the maze of psychiatric nursing to where I am today.

I never considered myself a typical or even a good nurse, but I genuinely liked it, and most of the people that I have met have made a lasting impression on me. Some I wished I had never met, but it's all part of a working life as a psychiatric nurse, and I wouldn't have missed it for anything.

44. Conclusion

In a lot of ways I have been very lucky in my life and in some ways maybe I have achieved a lot more than I could have realistically hoped for, coming from a less than ideal background and not having had a very good start to life. I was very lucky to meet Sandra in 1963, and marry her in March 1965, which was the best thing that ever happened to me in my life. She was the only woman I ever loved, the second being my mother, but ironically I would have never met Sandra if my mother had not died when she did. I only wish my mother could have met her, but it was not meant to be. I would probably have continued to live in Brighton as I had no interest in coming to London and only moved to London due to my mother's death and the work situation. And it was pure coincidence that I got a job in Tooting Bec Hospital as a porter and met Sandra. I only got a job in Tooting Bec Hospital due to my interest in running, which again goes back to Glin and Brother Gill, who fostered in me a real interest in sport, which has played a significant part in my life.

Having both our children Cheryl and Kevin ranks as the other highlight of my life, and they mean more to me than anything in life. I have felt totally inadequate as a father, but did the best I could in the only way I knew how.

Being married to the same woman for 39 years is an achievement and something that I am very proud of. I was prepared for a lifetime as a labourer when I came to England in 1956 but found myself sidetracked due to being sacked and being offered a lifeline by Tom Richards, a charge nurse at Tooting Bec Hospital who was looking for someone to run for the hospital team. Tom was a real class runner, an international long-distance runner who finished second in the 1948 Olympic Marathon at Wembley, the highest position ever achieved by a British man since. Tom was good to me and encouraged me to enrol on the three year course as a psychiatric student nurse, and most of what I have in my life is indirectly due to him giving me a helping hand during the bad winter of 1963 when I was unemployed and desperate for a job.

Obtaining my RMN nursing qualification at the first attempt in 1968 was a great bonus and a surprise. I have also met some famous runners over the years and shook hands with the great Steve Ovett, British, 1980 Olympic 800 metres gold medallist, and the great Emil Zatopek, Olympic triple gold medallist.

343

I have developed as a self-taught photographer and a hundred of my photos depicting life in a mental hospital were bought by Surrey History Museum for their archives, which I had taken when I worked in Long Grove Hospital in the eighties. I have had a number of exhibitions with these same photographs and I now regularly have many of my athletic photos published in magazines and local newspapers. I have never felt that I have achieved that much and have always felt very frustrated and have a continuous desire to prove myself, though compared to my parents I have achieved an awful lot and have had a much more fulfilling life. I still have some terrible nightmares on a regular basis. Sandra once told me, 'You must have a tortured mind.'

Unfortunately Sandie died of cancer on 27 January 2004 and left me with a broken heart and a deep depression that I am unable to shake off. Two weeks after Sandie's death I had a quadruple bypass, which lasted nine hours, although physically I feel fine. My feelings and attitudes toward God have changed. I never asked Him for anything for myself, but when I did ask Him to spare Sandie, He was strangely silent. I have not been to church for three years now, although Sandie and I went regularly every Sunday. I have cried every day for the last three years because of what happened to her and every day is a struggle to find a reason to keep on living. Most days, thoughts of suicide cross my mind. Sandie always made me feel alive and important, but most of all loved, but now all I feel is emptiness and sorrow and just take life from day to day now. My whole attitude to life has altered and I realise that we have very little real control over our lives in the long term and it can change so quickly.

I have many regrets about different aspects of my life with Sandra. She never liked expensive jewellery, fancy clothes, fancy cars, a fancy house or fancy anything, but what gave her great delight more than anything was that whenever we went for a walk, I slipped my hand into hers, often just to see her expression. She would immediately squeeze it and give me a beaming smile, which always made me feel good. She loved that simple act. It was as if I was reassuring her that I still loved her. I wish that I had done it more often. Sandra was the greatest thing in my life and my greatest love. Her passing is the greatest tragedy that I have ever endured in my life. I can never again imagine holding another woman's hand or kissing someone, like I did with Sandra. I could stare into Sandra's eyes and keep eye contact for long periods because I loved her. I have never done that with anyone else.

My personality and make-up was very flawed in many ways, but to me Sandra was as near to perfection as any human being could ever be. She would make a decision about something and be happy with it, whereas I was always full of self-doubt and constantly changed my mind about things and was never sure of my own worth. She was my hero and inspiration. I now fear the future without her by my side. I often feel invisible as if I am no longer here because I no longer feel that I matter to anyone except perhaps to my children.

We always trusted each other in every way and from the beginning of our married life in 1965 we even had a shared joint bank account and our houses were always in our joint names. But since her tragedy I have found it emotionally very difficult to have to alter them to my name only. We worked together as a couple for everything that we had and I hate the thought of now being the sole owner of our house. It somehow does not seem right and I hate it. It is so final.

All through our life together we regularly sent each other birthday cards, most of which I have kept. I recently looked at the last card that Sandie gave me in June 2003 where she apologised for being ill and spoiling my birthday and promised that she would make up for it when she was better. It made me feel very sad, but that was what she was like, always thinking about me and my feelings rather than her own. She was indeed a beautiful and special person and, best of all, my wife. I know that I will never meet her like again.

Whenever I went to bed before Sandra I always used to put toothpaste on her brush at the same time. I miss doing that now. I loved having her by my side and especially in bed. It was always reassuring to wake up at night and to reach out and touch her, especially if I had some bad nightmare. She said that we were joined at the hip, which I took as a complete compliment. I feel as if I am part of a jigsaw puzzle that has been broken up and can never be put together again. Sandra and I have a million memories and experiences that are special only to us. In our front room is one of my favourite photos of Sandra, which I took in Yugoslavia about 20 years ago, and I always look at it and kiss her before I leave the house, and when I return. Her eyes seem to follow me with her lovely smile as if reassuring me that she is okay and not to worry too much. It does reassure me, but still I feel sad and I wonder why she was taken away and I feel as though she was stolen from me and from our children.

I find the stillness and emptiness of our house now very hard to bear. It is a lifeless house with no soul. Sandie was always so happy and rarely complained about anything. I rarely play music any more, because so many tunes make me think of her and she is not there to share it with me. She was also a great optimist about nature, the environment and people.

345

The garden is now overgrown and neglected. Sandra was the knowledgeable gardener and loved spending time cultivating it. She took great pride in it and I learned a lot from her. The apples still hang on the trees now and the fallers lie there for the birds to feed on. A month or so after Sandie's passing I came down for breakfast and saw a robin in the porch trying to get out. The door to the porch was open and it must have flown in and could not find its way out again, so I tried to encourage it to go out, but instead it flew into the hallway and into the kitchen and landed on our sink and stood there watching me. My video camera was in the kitchen, so I thought it would be nice to video it, because such an occurrence never happened before. I filmed it for a few seconds and then it flew around the kitchen and I eventually caught it to release it.

As I walked towards the front door, the robin broke free and flew up the stairs and stood on the very top step, which I filmed again. I eventually caught it again and directed it to the front door, which I still have on video. It seemed a very strange thing to happen and no doubt it was a coincidence! But was it? When Sandie was first diagnosed with her illness, whenever I cut the lawn I often cried because of what the future was going to bring. I did not want Sandie to see me, but I remembered a robin landing near me, looking for food, and I spoke to it and wondered if maybe Sandie might come back to me as a robin, another of my stupid dreams, or did it happen? Some clear nights when I gaze up at the stars, I wonder if Sandra might be looking down and guiding me. I like to think that she is. I have to keep on hoping and dreaming! Every day I long to touch and see her again, and the feeling and longing is awful and cannot be imagined because what happened to her is my worst nightmare. The only difference is that it is real and I will never wake up from it.

She gave me the greatest happiness in my life, but sadly the greatest unhappiness in the end, but not through her own fault. I have started writing letters to her again each evening because it helps me to think of her and to explain to her how I miss her and how much she meant to me. She is the only one that I can express my real feelings to and I know that she will understand. I do not want to burden my children about how bad I feel, but they probably know anyway.

Sandra always made a great fuss of me on my birthdays because she knew that I never had any as a child, and I miss that so much. She loved to kiss my cheekbone just below my eye where I never had to shave, and she always told me how soft and smooth it was. Just a fond memory now, and I miss a million and one things about her.

The only way that I can get through Christmas or holidays now is just to pretend that it is an ordinary day, because every day is ordinary now. I find it hard to appreciate a sunny day or nature any more or to be happy without my great love by my side, but I have to go on or else!

Most nights when I go to bed I still cry for her and most mornings there are still 'Tears on My Pillow'.